THE LIMITS OF OKINAWA

ASIA-PACIFIC: CULTURE, POLITICS, AND SOCIETY
Editors: Rey Chow, Michael Dutton,
H. D. Harootunian, and Rosalind C. Morris

The Limits of Okinawa

*Japanese Capitalism, Living Labor, and
Theorizations of Community*

WENDY MATSUMURA

DUKE UNIVERSITY PRESS
Durham and London
2015

© 2015 Duke University Press
All rights reserved
Typeset in Whitman by Westchester
Publishing Services

Library of Congress Cataloging-in-Publication Data
Matsumura, Wendy, 1977–
The limits of Okinawa : Japanese capitalism, living labor,
and theorizations of community / Wendy Matsumura.
pages cm —
(Asia-Pacific:culture,politics,andsociety)
Includes bibliographical references and index.
ISBN 978-0-8223-5788-9 (hardcover)
ISBN 978-0-8223-5801-5 (pbk.)
ISBN 978-0-8223-7604-0 (e-book)

1. Okinawa-ken (Japan)—Economic conditions.
I. Title. II. Series: Asia-Pacific.
HC463.04M387 2015
330.952'2903—dc23 2014037967

Cover art: Yukinori Yanagi, *Banzai Corner*, 1991. Plastic toys
(approximately 380 pieces) and mirror, 90 × 240 × 240 cm. ©
Yukinori Yanagi.

FOR MY PARENTS,
EIKO AND RICHARD MATSUMURA

CONTENTS

≡

ILLUSTRATIONS ix

ACKNOWLEDGMENTS xi

INTRODUCTION 1

CHAPTER ONE
The Birth of Okinawa Prefecture
and the Creation of Difference 27

CHAPTER TWO
The Miyako Island Peasantry Movement
as an Event 49

CHAPTER THREE
Reforming Old Customs,
Transforming Women's Work 79

CHAPTER FOUR
The Impossibility of Plantation
Sugar in Okinawa 115

CHAPTER FIVE
Uneven Development and the
Rejection of Economic Nationalism
in "Sago Palm Hell" Okinawa 146

CONCLUSION
Living Labor and the Limits
of Okinawan Community 182

NOTES 189   BIBLIOGRAPHY 247   INDEX 265

ILLUSTRATIONS

1.1. Entrance gate, Shuri, when Perry arrived. 39
2.1. Miyako Island, Japanese Empire, 62
2.2. Seventh Kyushu-Okinawa 8 Prefectures Mutual Promotion Alliance (1888), 63
2.3. Map of Japan and Loo Choo, 76
3.1. The production of sweet potato starch, 83
3.2. Surveys during the land reorganization, 90
3.3. Tatoo marks on the hands of a Loo Chooan women, 102
3.4. Naha cloth market, 105
3.5. Female weaver, 106
4.1. Nishihara sugar factory, 123
4.2. Kadena sugar factory, 123
4.3. Yonabaru station and employees, 125
4.4. Loading of brown sugar barrels, 126
4.5. Takamine Village sugar factory, 129
4.6. Sugar cane market, 133
4.7. Sugar Mill in Loo Chooan Village, 135
5.1. Yanbaru boat, 162
5.2. A home in Yanbaru, 164
5.3. Yaeyama's bonito factory, 170
5.4. The main road in Nago, 179

ACKNOWLEDGMENTS

Louise Young has been a critical, yet compassionate, mentor without whom this project could not have been completed. Her support and encouragement as I studied under her guidance at New York University enabled me to take lines of flight that I would not have been allowed to make under a less trusting advisor. Harry Harootunian's enthusiastic and critical engagement with social theory as well as historical texts continues to be a constant source of inspiration and challenge to me. His support for this work has been an invaluable source of encouragement. I would also like to thank my dissertation readers at New York University, Rebecca Karl, Joanna Waley-Cohen, and Tom Looser, for taking the time to provide me with critical feedback, which has continued to inform this manuscript during its long revision process. Katsuhiko Endo provided valuable advice and focus for this project during its formative period.

    The bulk of the research for this manuscript was supported by the Fulbright Foundation, which allowed me to spend 2002–4 at Waseda University. My experience in Japan was greatly enriched by the kindness of Okamoto Kōichi, Umemori Naoyuki, Gabe Masao, and all of the scholars and students at Waseda's Institute for Ryukyuan and Okinawan Studies. Their intellectual generosity and friendship helped me get through the long days of document gathering and translations. The graduate students that I encountered at Waseda, most notably Takemasa Ando, provided great conversation and camaraderie during this time. I am also grateful to the scholars at the Hōsei University Okinawa Kenkyūjo for inviting me into their study groups and sharing many stories of Okinawa's earlier scholars with me. I would be glad to make a contribution that equaled just a fraction of what they have accomplished to enrich the field of Okinawan studies.

    My colleagues and students in the History and Asian Studies Departments at Furman University have provided me with numerous opportunities to share my work on Okinawa both inside and outside the classroom. I would especially like to thank Erik Ching and Lane Harris for reading large portions of the manuscript and providing valuable feedback. The institutional support that Furman has provided over the years has enabled me to travel to Okinawa to conduct supplementary research as the project has developed. In addition to the Dean's Office, the Humanities Development Fund and the Research and Professional Growth Fund have provided valuable resources that have aided in the completion of this project.

Over the years, I have been given the opportunity to present my work to diverse audiences at the University of Wisconsin, Madison, the International Symposium on Okinawa Studies, the Association for Asian Studies Conference, and the Historical Materialism Conference. The critical feedback that I have received at these venues has transformed this project into one that is more squarely situated in Marxist theory. Along the way, my new friends in the Okinawa studies field, Chris Nelson, Tze Loo, and Uechi Satoko, have provided important intellectual stimulation and opportunities for discussion that enabled me to sharpen my focus on the theoretical and political underpinnings of this work. I would like to thank the anonymous readers for Duke University Press and Ken Wissoker, its editorial director, whose critical feedback and suggestions have pushed me to engage more explicitly with fields outside of the narrow boundaries of Okinawan studies.

I am also grateful for the opportunity that Nagahara Yutaka and Adachi Mariko gave me to present my work at Ochanomizu University in the fall of 2013. This was a challenging experience that reinforced my conviction of the need to engage the broader field of critical political economy when writing about Okinawa. A year at Dōshisha University's Graduate School of Global Studies, funded by the Fulbright Foundation, allowed me to put the finishing touches on the manuscript. During that time, Tomiyama Ichirō generously offered me friendship, a space to present my work, an opportunity to study with other scholars and students, and encouragement to carry on with the project. A Japanese Studies Travel Grant from the Association for Asian Studies Northeast Asia Council also provided generous support for this project by allowing me to travel to Okinawa for supplementary research one summer. The librarians and archivists at the University of the Ryūkyūs Library, University of Hawaii Hamilton Library, Okinawa Prefectural Archives, Naha City Museum of History, and National Diet Library, especially Tomita Chinatsu, Tokiko Bazzell, and Kaz Nakamoto, helped me locate essential sources and provided much-needed help obtaining copyright permissions.

I would like to express my thanks to my mother and father, who were silent and gentle witnesses as I struggled to complete this project. Their encouragement provided me with the energy and strength to continue even when the end seemed very far away. Finally, I would like to thank Paul and Karl, who have provided me with love and laughter every day.

INTRODUCTION

Okinawa's Three Dispositions as Three Moments of Primitive Accumulation

Marxist theoretician, activist, and documentary filmmaker Kawada Yō wrote in the early 1970s that Okinawa's impending reversion to Japanese rule following two decades under American occupation was neither a joyous moment of liberation nor a time of profound despair over the region's continued subjugation by external powers. Kawada predicted that reversion would simply inaugurate a new phase of the region's expropriation by capital. As many in Okinawa and Japan celebrated or bemoaned the impending transfer of political power as part of a longer trajectory of national unification, he placed the political changes that disrupted his present within a cycle of conflict that began centuries earlier: the current moment was nothing more than the third disposition that the region had experienced in three and a half centuries.[1] Invoking a repetitive rather than linear history, Kawada argued that each disposition inaugurated a struggle among local power holders, invaders from outside the region, and small producers that gave no signs of abating.[2] He warned his readers that the biggest gift that 1972 would bring to the people of Okinawa was a new round of enclosures, whose negative consequences would far outweigh any positive aspects of liberation from formal occupation.[3]

Kawada's measured stance toward reversion stemmed from his approach to Okinawa's dispositions—the first in 1609, the second in 1879, and the third in his present—as distinct moments in capital's so-called primitive accumulation process.[4] He approached each shift in Okinawa's political status as coinciding with and inaugurating a radical reconfiguration of the region's material and social relations within a broader conjuncture of transformations in capital's organic composition. For example, the first disposition began when the feudal lord of the Satsuma domain, Shimazu Iehisa, invaded what was then the Ryūkyū kingdom and started a reorganization of agrarian village economies in a way that expanded the economic and political authority of wealthy peasants.[5] The resulting differentiation in the villages forced many self-sufficient cultivators to become serfs who worked the property of a new cadre of large landowners.[6] Similarly, Kawada read the second disposition of 1879 as an event that transformed small peasantry (shōnō) who did remain in the kingdom's villages as self-sufficient producers into creators of surplus value to fuel Japan's nascent capitalist development.[7] This was yet another round of dispossession that destroyed the communal resources and practices that those small cultivators needed to sustain their household economies. He predicted that the transfer of rule to the Japanese state in 1972 would be accompanied by another major reconfiguration of property relations in Okinawa that would result in parasitic landlordism becoming a significant part of its landscape for the first time in its history.[8] As Kawada's designation of three distinct moments of the transfer of political authority as key events in the history of capitalist development in Okinawa shows, he understood the political and economic spheres as inextricably linked in the region's transformation into a distinct social space.

Kawada knew where power resided, but he also knew that Okinawa's workers and cultivators had struggled against their dispossession at every turn and would continue to fight tooth and nail against their expulsion after reversion. One of his main goals as a documentary filmmaker was to give voice to small producers and record their struggles. He knew that the discourse of national reunification, whether celebratory or despairing, would overwhelm and expunge these actors from the grand theater of Okinawa's modern history if left unchallenged. The stories that intrigued him pit the extreme power of capital backed by the state against the persistent, intense struggles of small producers against their expropriation and enclosure. He was committed to documenting the numerous confrontations between producers as bearers of living labor and capitalists aiming to increase the proportion of dead labor in the production process as a struggle over the valorization of surplus value.[9] What distinguished Kawada from other Marxists writing about Okinawa in the moment of reversion was that he understood these contests to be immanent to the development of Okinawan society and productive in the construction of revolutionary subjectivities. These struggles were central, rather than mere footnotes to more dramatic processes of unification or colonization.[10]

This study takes Kawada's view of violent confrontations between producers, capitalists, and political power holders as immanent to processes of disposition as its entry point. It focuses on the period between 1879 and the reconfiguration of global capitalism in the early 1930s, decades in which the Japanese nation-state qua empire consolidated and expanded. Specifically, it clarifies the relations of power among the Japanese state, Okinawan leaders, and small producers within the prefecture as it became a frontier of the Japanese empire and traces the way that a merely coincidental and historically traceable peripheralization in the economic sphere quickly became evidence of collective difference in a cultural, racial, or ethnic sense.[11]

The Japanese nation-state incorporated Okinawa during the late nineteenth century differently from territories that had previously existed in the Tokugawa regime as feudal domains. Nine years after the Meiji Restoration, the disposition of Ryūkyū was enacted in a manner that left the former kingdom without the necessary foundations for capitalist relations of production. As in the northern territory of Hokkaido, the Meiji state restaged old systems, relations, and hierarchies to fulfill the needs of the nation-state, itself in the early stages of formation.[12] It masked its own strategic maintenance of the forms and practices of the kingdom with a benevolent-sounding term, the Preservation of Old Customs Policy (Kyūkan Onzon Seisaku; hereafter, Preservation Policy), and claimed that inclusion of Okinawa in this manner would benefit the local people as a whole. At the same time, it granted concessions to a select few inhabitants of the prefecture whose cooperation was necessary for a smooth takeover of control.

Such measures reveal the lack of uniformity in state policies in the early years of consolidation and signal a need to reexamine the degree to which Meiji leaders pursued a uniform project of nation building during the years immediately after the Restoration. The idea that national consolidation was pursued through policies of differentiation is unusual in theories of nation-state formation. However, it is entirely consistent with Marxist theories of imperialism that argue that late developers like Japan and Germany, which began capitalist development in the so-called imperialist stage, did not have to completely dismantle previous societies to achieve modernization. Theorists ranging from Uno Kōzō to Antonio Negri have argued that in such cases "extraction can occur while production continues to function through non-capitalist relations."[13] In Okinawa, the state decided to maintain the former kingdom's core economic and administrative systems even as it insisted that the people of Okinawa were Japanese subjects; this set the stage for the transformation of the region into a cultural, economic, and political periphery of the nation-state whose difference from the empire's formal colonies was not entirely clear to observers or policy makers from mainland Japan.

The ambiguous position Okinawa seemed to occupy as both inside and outside of the national community intrigued scholars of various stripes and disciplines. Linguists, economists, archaeologists, legal scholars, and many others flocked to the region to study its customs, systems, language, and people decades before the so-called Okinawa fever famously brought Yanagita Kunio and Orikuchi Shinobu to the islands in the 1920s.[14] The violence of 1879, the struggles of small producers in response, and the discursive battles that local intellectuals and politicians waged in order to appropriate or quell these struggles ensured that even though Okinawa was a prefecture rather than a colony of the Japanese empire, visitors approached the region like a culturally distinct space that they need to introduce, explicate, or extol to their readers in mainland Japan. Okinawa's exoticization was well under way by the end of the Meiji period.[15]

One of Japan's early Marxists and an economics professor at Kyoto University, Kawakami Hajime arrived in the islands in the spring of 1911. It was less than a decade after the state had established private property in Okinawa, and the islands were in the midst of the final round of land redistribution (*jiwari*)—a practice that the state preserved in the prefecture as part of the Preservation Policy.[16] Kawakami's university had sent him to examine the impact of this redistribution on the social composition of agrarian villages.[17] Early in his visit, he gave a speech called "A New Era Is Approaching" ("Shinjidai Kitaru") to a group of Okinawa's educators and politicians, in which he extolled the lack of nationalism he observed in the prefecture while the rest of the country was drunk with imperialist sentiment.[18] His audience, most of whom were working hard to inculcate this very spirit into their pupils, was incensed by Kawakami's enthusiastic declaration that Okinawans were deficient in their devotion to the Japanese empire. There was a further uproar when the local newspaper published a transcript of his speech. Kawakami quietly left the prefecture without completing his scheduled two-week itinerary of travel and investigation.[19]

Despite the negative reception and the brevity of his visit, Kawakami was intrigued with what he encountered in the islands. He published an article titled "Individualistic Families of Ryūkyū's Itoman" ("Ryūkyū Itoman no Kojinshugiteki Kazoku") in the *Kyoto Law Review* (*Kyoto Hōgakkai Zasshi*). In the article, he completely left out the original intent of his visit, excitedly discussing instead the "extreme individualism" that he discovered in Itoman, a fishing community located at the southern tip of Okinawa's main island.[20] Noting his desire to return to the prefecture for further studies of this community, Kawakami went on to describe the distinctive family economy that he discovered in the sleepy village.

In retrospect, what piqued Kawakami's curiosity in Itoman may have been the very thing that got him in trouble with the leaders of Okinawa's political and educational establishment. Itoman's resident fishing families observed a strict division of labor between men who went off to fish in groups of two or three on small canoe-type vessels and women who raced to the market in Naha—over seven miles away—on foot to sell the day's catch in its freshest condition. On their long trek home, their pockets full of the rewards of their hard work at the market, the women collectively decided the price at which they would retroactively purchase that day's haul from the fishermen. Once arriving home, each woman settled her accounts accordingly with her suppliers—her husband, brother, or both. They effectively controlled their own income and that of the men in the community as Itoman's petty merchant capitalists. What intrigued Kawakami was that this gendered division of labor seemed to have produced a very distinct type of household economy. He observed that residents of Itoman valued their individual assets and preferred making loans to giving cash gifts, even to their closest family members. Women had more opportunities to accumulate savings, for example, but these did not accrue to the household. Rather, it was common for husbands to borrow funds from their wives if they wanted to build a new boat or make significant repairs to their current one. Kawakami quoted a local saying—"we do not even give money away to our own brothers"—to emphasize the degree to which this was true.[21]

Kawakami celebrated the practices of these fishing families as expressions of "extreme individualism," evidence of progress that had yet to arrive in the prefecture's largest city, Naha, or even mainland Japan's agrarian communities. Their individualism was the primary reason for Itoman's prosperity (he noted that people there ate meals of rice and meat three times a day, while most Okinawans battled constant hunger as they subsisted on meager diets of sweet potato and tofu). In contrast to the patriarchal large family system, which he said bred stagnation and promoted dependency, the individualism of the Itoman families' economy promoted exploration and movement beyond a single locale. Although state actors in the first decade of the twentieth century also encouraged the movement of people from their hometowns as part of a broader strategy of territorial expansion, cultivation of new markets, and expulsion of agrarian crisis outside the nation-state, Kawakami celebrated mobility for a completely different reason. He saw in the spirit of exploration that developed from this "extreme individualism," a powerful antidote to the state's efforts to inculcate nationalist sentiments that were intimately linked to a belief in an organic community bound together by shared kinship relations or territorial boundaries.[22]

Kawakami would have found much to confirm his theory that the logical outcome of the social relations he observed in Itoman was outward movement if he had spent more than one day in the village. In the years before his visit, a significant number of fishing families had already left their hometown in search of new seas to fish. Beginning in the Meiji period, some went to Yaeyama, an archipelago of thirty-two islands under the jurisdiction of Okinawa Prefecture but much closer to Taiwan. Between the 1880s and the start of the First Sino-Japanese War in 1894, 108 families (159 people) had moved from Itoman to Ishigaki, the second-largest island in the Yaeyama archipelago.[23] These families were instrumental in forming the island's first fishery association in 1911, the year Kawakami arrived in Okinawa.[24]

If Kawakami had extended his study to these fishing communities on Ishigaki, he would have been struck by the wide range of people with whom these transplanted people shared their lives: former noble families from Shuri who arrived in Yaeyama soon after Okinawa's annexation to take advantage of state funds for groups interested in embarking on reclamation projects; mainland industrialists who impatiently waited for their investments in mining and sugar to bear fruit; local women who had gone to Taiwan when it was annexed by Japan in 1895 as maids, prostitutes, entertainers, and small merchants but who returned to Ishigaki after being ridiculed as "Japanese aborigines" for their tattoos; young men from impoverished agrarian villages on Okinawa island who had ventured southward seeking jobs as agricultural laborers and coal miners; eager small merchants from the mainland positioning themselves to take advantage of new trade routes that had opened up with the colonization of Taiwan and Korea; a small number of young educators who had wandered into the outer islands to teach at one of several new elementary and middle schools; budding poets like Iba Nantetsu, Ishigaki Yōkichi, and Yamanokuchi Baku, who searched for words to express the changes that the expansion of the Japanese empire had brought to their hometowns; and, of course, local men and women of various stripes who looked on with a mixture of curiosity and worry as they detected the subtle transformations in the most intimate of their everyday relations with crops, animals, land, neighbors, and families.[25] This diverse mix of people on Ishigaki—a condition that led to the naming of the island chain of which it was a central part, the Republic of Yaeyama (*Yaeyama Gasshūkoku*)—would have provided Kawakami with further confirmation that Okinawa was a region that was too much in flux to respond uniformly or positively to state efforts to inculcate a nationalist spirit.[26]

The shallowness of the Okinawan peoples' identification with the nation elated Kawakami but confounded those who associated the impoverishment of the prefecture with their failure to inculcate a strong sense of nationalism in the islands. Their disappointment was the reverse of Kawakami's overly optimistic evaluation of mobility. Both views reflected a failure to understand that state policies toward Okinawa since annexation had created the very conditions that they either lamented or extolled. Fishing families' decisions to move to the Yaeyama archipelago in search of new markets and small cultivators' abandonment of their fields in search of alternative methods of survival were two sides of the same coin.[27] These and other paths that people took after the second disposition were responses to the dispossession that accompanied Okinawa's incorporation into Japanese capitalist society as a single administrative unit. The language of disposition effaced this process of dispossession and masked Okinawa's violent incorporation into a particular type of smooth space for the operation of capital—a national space—as opposed to a colonial space occupied by regions like Taiwan and Korea. By Kawakami's time, 1879 was just a distant memory that had been rewritten as a moment of (peaceful) national unification. Okinawa's difference was explained away as the result of the cultural deficiencies of the local population and their inability to handle the requirements of the new age, rather than the outcome of specific policies of dispossession enacted by the early Meiji state in order to facilitate capital accumulation.[28] This narrative led Kawakami, a materialist, to seek culturalist explanations for Okinawans' lack of nationalism.

By the 1930s, Okinawa Prefecture had been part of Japanese capitalist society for over half a century, but local intellectuals and observers from the mainland alike continued to believe, like Kawakami, that the region occupied a distinct time-space from the rest of Japan. The Okinawan people were seen as comprising a natural community, which to some, meant that they were marked with an original sin (they were not truly Japanese) that the state could alleviate to some extent through assimilationist policies but could never completely erase.[29] A variety of discursive and nondiscursive practices produced and reproduced this belief in Okinawa's original sin, which concealed the constant struggles between living and dead labor that took place each day.[30]

Japanese Masks, Unruly Labor, and Okinawan Community

Okinawa's own leaders played the preeminent role in translating the uneven capitalist development of the prefecture into a story of the Okinawan community's cultural difference from the rest of Japan.[31] As they critiqued state policies that promoted Okinawa's development in a manner that seemed overly focused on providing competitive advantages and profits to mainland capital at the expense of the well-being of the local people, they articulated a discourse called *Okinawa-shugi* that was predicated on their belief in an organic Okinawan community whose members were also part of the Japanese nation-state.[32] In their capacity as local experts and technicians, they critiqued their prefecture's growing dependency on mainland markets and capital and called on their fellow Okinawans to organize alternative methods of production, consumption, financing, and selling in order to strengthen local autonomy (*chihō jichi*).

The difficulties that these intellectual, political, and economic leaders of the prefecture faced as they tried to build new associations based on the discourse of Okinawa-shugi pose an interesting dilemma. A close examination of their writings reveals that they had to contend not only with mainland capital's expropriative tactics but also—and just as significantly—with serious challenges to their legitimacy from within the community they claimed to represent and vowed to protect. Indeed, multiple axes of confrontation determined the articulation of community in the region. The dynamics among local leaders; representatives of the Japanese state and capital; and the prefecture's small producers, who made up the vast majority of Okinawa's population, must be untangled in order to gain a clear picture of the shifting terrains of antagonism that accompanied the region's second disposition in 1879.

These complicated and shifting dynamics are not unlike the conditions that anticolonial intellectuals like José Carlos Mariátegui and Frantz Fanon explored in Peru and Algeria, where hierarchies and class relations within a colonized people were crucially important to understanding how new social categories and relations between colonizer and colonized formed and transformed.[33] This book clarifies the relations of power that operated in the prefecture as it was transformed into a sliding frontier of the Japanese empire and focuses on the aggressive attempts of local intellectuals and leaders to win a contest that had serious economic and political repercussions. Like Fanon's anticolonial bourgeois intellectuals, Okinawa's self-appointed leaders wore many different masks. At times they were anticolonial activists, invoking their right to make their own political and economic decisions in spite of a state that rejected the notion that Okinawans were prepared to handle this responsibility. At other times, they were social reformers who called on their people to shed their barbaric ways and even "sneeze as the Japanese do," so that mainland observers would recognize them as full-fledged members of the national community.[34] They were also capitalists who fully believed in their right to capture the surplus value produced in their region by their people for personal profit. Okinawa's self-appointed leaders, like local elites in colonized regions throughout the world in the age of imperialism, aspired to become and at the same time resisted that which dominated them.

As early as the 1890s, local leaders linked Okinawa's fate to the Japanese nation-state—simultaneously their savior, oppressor, and ideal—and unwittingly constructed a logic in which Okinawa could never attain full equality with Japan. This, of course, did not stop them from trying. Equipped with the language of modernity that they acquired at the most prestigious institutions of higher learning in Japan, they identified the people as the biggest impediment to Okinawa's liberation from colonized conditions. Their mothers, brothers, aunts, and cousins who insisted on clinging to their feudal practices, customs, and knowledge emerged as the main obstacles to prosperity, enlightenment, and acceptance. Local leaders constantly clashed with these barbaric people, whose customs, behaviors, and ways of life and work obstructed their visions of equality. They donned the mask of anticolonial nationalists to insist that these people transform themselves immediately into modern subjects to gain equality with the rest of the nation.

This abstract cause, which only barely concealed local leaders' other mask as members of the petty bourgeoisie who aimed to become the primary exploiters of Okinawan labor power, lost out to the material realities of life in the prefecture. For, as Kawakami recognized during his short time in the prefecture in 1911, Okinawa's cultivators, fishermen, merchants, and weavers were far from the feudal remnants that local leaders made them out to be. Many of Okinawa's small producers transformed their practices or moved from their hometowns in response to the pressures that accompanied the penetration of Japanese capital into the prefecture and were unencumbered by the feelings of inferiority that plagued local leaders. They were concerned with protecting their ability to reproduce their household economies and refused to accept the practices and conditions that diminished their ability to do so. They were not willing to be abstracted by their spokesmen as free labor "in the process of capitalist valorization and the production of surplus value" for capital, even if the capitalist wore an Okinawan mask.³⁵ Small producers often rejected their conversion into modern workers by bypassing modern financial organs that local bourgeoisie established in favor of community-based lending associations, purchasing frivolous commodities and paying large sums to female oracles instead of submitting their taxes in full, working in their small sugar huts rather than becoming cultivators for mechanized sugar factories, and so on. Far from being irrational, conservative, or ultimately fruitless responses to inevitable proletarianization, these behaviors were meaningful from the perspective of anticapitalist struggle because they were conscious acts that challenged capital's ability to appropriate surplus value. Frustrated Okinawan leaders at times cautiously aligned themselves with Japanese capital in order to jump-start the process of converting these stubborn men and women into an industrial or agricultural proletariat. Their primary goal, however, was to mobilize the abstract Okinawan community to advance their project of building an autonomous economic space. This vision put members of the local bourgeoisie in a difficult position—caught between their desires for full political equality and complete economic autonomy vis-à-vis the Japanese nation-state.

Instead of labeling Okinawa's leading intellectuals and politicians as either pure collaborators or resisters, this study draws attention to the multiple masks that Okinawa's intellectuals and politicians wore. It argues that the Okinawan community gained its fullness from the clashes that took place between local leaders, who believed themselves to be the most authentic spokesmen for a region that was in constant danger of being demoted to a colony, and Okinawa's small producers, who rejected many of their leaders' modernizing policies.³⁶ Small producers, like the nineteenth-century French worker-poets that Jacques Rancière celebrates in *The Nights of Labor*, preferred to speak for themselves and carry out their own visions rather than sacrifice their days and nights to protect an abstract Okinawa.³⁷ Their refusals posed significant challenges to both the stability of the category of Okinawa and the establishment of capitalist relations of production in the prefecture.

The Problem of Okinawan Victimization: A Historiography

Despite the existence of multiple actors that shaped Okinawa's modern history, the dominant tendency in narratives about modern Okinawan history has been to prioritize the telling of a single story whose ending is determined from the start. The milestones that scholars have commonly used to mark Okinawa's never-ending condition of subjugation to external forces confirm this tendency. Its occupation by the United States, during which the most fertile lands were expropriated for the construction of military bases; the violence perpetrated against women that accompanied the culture of those bases; political discrimination that continued long after the end of formal occupation in 1972; continuing high unemployment rates and impoverishment; and even representations of Okinawa as an island of peace and naiveté are common entry points into the study of Okinawa that confirm a foregone conclusion. The question "Why Okinawa?" informs such studies, as if a more equitable distribution of such acts of violence among other Japanese would lead to a more favorable outcome.[38]

The recording of Okinawa's differential treatment by the Japanese state was an important task particularly in the years immediately after World War II, as local scholars responded to what appeared to be a double betrayal. As if the sacrifice of Okinawa Prefecture as a fortress against Allied attacks on Japan proper during the latter stages of the war were not bad enough, Emperor Hirohito had authorized a second betrayal of Okinawa that culminated in Prime Minister Yoshida Shigeru's negotiation of the Ryūkyū and Ogasawara islands' continued occupation by the United States following mainland Japan's liberation.[39] In light of these historical developments, scholars committed to the study of modern Okinawa viewed the recording of the economic and political sufferings that the people had endured since 1879 as an urgent task whose performance was necessary for ending the cycle of betrayal. As the intellectual historian Yakabi Osamu traced, histories written by Okinawa's scholars in the 1950s and 1960s primarily explored the question of how the region was incorporated into the Japanese emperor system economically, politically, and culturally since the Meiji period.[40] Implicit in these investigations was the question of why, despite loyal service to the state, Okinawans had been sacrificed like pawns in exchange for the safety of a more important chess piece at the end of the war.

Methodologically, these works began implicitly or explicitly with the recognition that the Ryūkyū kingdom's incorporation into the Meiji state had been incomplete, in much the same way that Japanese Marxists emphasized the failure of the Meiji Restoration to bring about a true revolution as a way of explaining the rise of Japanese fascism. Just as Japanese capitalism was assumed to possess a unique character that had deviated in tragic ways from the English model, Okinawa's development in the modern era was measured against the trajectory of modernization in mainland Japan, and introspection was deemed necessary for understanding the true nature of this distortion.⁴¹ The formulation of the problem began with the assumption that Okinawa as a single region had deviated from the path of modernity from the moment of its annexation, and local scholars working during the occupation period debated the question of who should be held accountable for their society's inability to enter the time-space of modernity.⁴²

A challenge to this approach came from people's history (*minshūshi*) scholars in the 1960s and 1970s. Authors in this field did not assume a fundamental difference between Okinawa and Japan or believe that complete assimilation was necessary for the resolution of the so-called national question; rather, they focused on the way that ordinary people resisted the exploitative practices of the Japanese state in their communities.⁴³ Hiyane Teruo, Ōsato Kōei, Aniya Masaaki, and Yoshihara Kōichirō celebrated the energy and courage of commoners who demanded political or economic reforms; as Japanese subjects, they had the right to make such demands on the state.⁴⁴ Their works also depicted mainland capital and local politicians as seeking to extract the surplus labor of peasants, workers, and activists and to expropriate their communal lands and rights. The rise of this approach made the establishment of oppositional binaries impossible, just as the rise of social history and historical materialism in Anglo-American scholarship forced scholars to revise or abandon the core-periphery framework of dependency theory that had provided a critical edge to analyses of the relationship between advanced capitalist countries and their peripheries.⁴⁵

These historians lauded the courageous efforts of the Okinawan people in the face of overwhelming power imbalances, but their celebratory remarks were limited by their shared belief that resistance had not been successful or powerful enough to completely rid the region of the state's despotism. They could not help but write historicist narratives in which the state suppressed or co-opted potentially transformative movements or events and in which commoners' efforts to resist exploitation constantly stopped just short of primitive or elementary forms of resistance.⁴⁶ These scholars were still awaiting a final moment of liberation from the American occupation, so it is understandable that they could present stories of struggle before the war only as examples of courageous attempts by the people to fulfill their desires for equality and autonomy that were crushed by the overwhelming power of states and global capital.⁴⁷ In many ways, these stories merely offered sparks of hope, fragments of a much larger picture that was still awaiting its triumphant completion.

More recent works on Okinawa have built on this perspective, employing both comparative and despatialized approaches that sought to explore a hitherto neglected theme in modern Okinawa's history: the high volume of migration from the prefecture to mainland Japan's industrial centers, colonial possessions, and beyond. As we have seen, people such as fishermen, colonial bureaucrats, maids, farmers, merchants, singers, workers, and actors traveled across the vast spaces of Japan's expanding empire in the early decades of the twentieth century. By critically examining these inflows and outflows of Okinawan workers in light of the broader transformations of Japanese and global capitalism, scholars like Tomiyama Ichirō and Sugihara Tamae linked political economic analysis with a study of the material conditions of production and the transformation of subjectivities. They explored how people accepted or resisted their economically disadvantageous conditions or transformed themselves and their communities as they left the boundaries of their hometowns and sometimes returned.

In *Kindai Nihon Shakai to Okinawajin* (*Modern Japanese Society and the Okinawan People*), Tomiyama examined the discursive and material practices through which Okinawan workers were installed in a discriminatory labor market that functioned to discipline Japanese workers at the height of labor unrest in industrial centers in mainland Japan. Okinawan workers served as examples of bad workers and, hence, bad Japanese. Anticipating a broader shift in colonial studies that emphasized the mutually constitutive relationship between colony and metropole, Tomiyama clarified the structural relationship between the creation of a discriminatory labor market in the mainland and the so-called agrarian question in Okinawa's villages.[48] He argued that the transformation of the agrarian population into an industrial reserve army for capital, not stagnant conditions in agriculture, constituted the agrarian question of Okinawa that required further dissection. Contra Kurima Yasuo, an agricultural economist of the Kōza faction who argued that Okinawa's agrarian villages did not develop capitalist relations, Tomiyama and the agricultural economist Mukai Kiyoshi asserted that the countryside experienced significant class differentiation and developed landlord-tenant relations characteristic of capitalist society.[49] Tomiyama's work therefore brought together an understanding like that of E. P. Thompson that saw proletarianization as a process and the Marxist theory of Uno Kōzō that approached the agrarian question after World War I as a global, rather than a national, problem.[50]

Like Tomiyama, Sugihara brought a new perspective to Okinawan studies—in her case, through an analysis of family-style agriculture and its transformation in Kenya and Okinawa.[51] Her comparative study took its cues from the French economic anthropologist and Africanist Claude Meillassoux, who in 1975 critiqued dependency theory for neglecting the internal workings of the domestic economy.[52] The dependency perspective argued that in preserving, using, or destroying small-scale agricultural households, the capitalist system stripped away the peasantry's capacity for autonomous development. In contrast, Sugihara granted the peasantry agency. She argued that farming families reorganized themselves and adjusted to changing conditions as they became enmeshed in the global capitalist system; illuminating their actions is crucial to understanding the process of development. Dependency theory told stories that confirmed Okinawa's subjugation, and people's history anticipated a revolutionary outcome in the future. In contrast, her analysis emphasized the daily struggles of peasants to make the productive and reproductive decisions that confronted them every day.

This study draws from both Tomiyama's and Sugiyama's approaches, integrating political economic analysis with studies of subjectivity.[53] Such an attempt counters the approaches outlined at the beginning of this section that were ultimately limited by the assumption of Okinawa's victimization at the hands of the Japanese state and capital. Leaving aside the objectification and homogenization of Japan that historicist approaches depend on, the problem with them is that the outcome is determined from the start. The only conclusion that can be reached from a history that begins with an understanding of Okinawa's past and present as one of subordination is to prove how this unfortunate result came about, and doing so unwittingly validates the discourse that state actors and capitalists used to enact policies that discriminated against the people of the region.[54] Although the political significance of earlier approaches that operated in the dark and cramped spaces of capitalist exploitation, Japanese discrimination and American imperialism must be acknowledged, a different reading of Okinawa's modern history is not only possible but imperative, if we are to mount any significant critique of the cynicism that comes from the "social subjection to capital."[55]

The Antagonism of Living Labor and the Possibilities of a Nonapocalyptic History

The turbulent waves of organized and spontaneous struggle; natural and manmade disasters; economic crisis and resolution that Okinawa and the rest of the world have recently experienced provide us with new cramped spaces within which to maneuver. The last round of globalization brought devastation to vast segments of the population and the commons but has also elicited new challenges from activists, theoreticians, and ordinary people who have rejected both neoliberal and neo-Marxist discourses insisting that calls for revolution were outdated and ineffectual because of the flexibility and overwhelming power of global capital.[56] The groundswell of anticapitalist and prodemocratic struggles around the world—including the Arab Spring, the Occupy movement, the rejection of austerity measures in the Euro zone, and antinuclear movements—reenergized skeptics and necessitated a recalibration of thought in order to keep pace with the energies and desires of the participants in these struggles.[57] The present study takes its inspiration from these struggles and the theoretical interventions that accompanied them. It is driven by a desire to seize hold of the current conjuncture that is always in danger of becoming subsumed into a narrative of ultimate defeat.[58] The historical task and challenge is to suspend each moment of collective action—the anger, elation, confusion, and camaraderie that characterize it—in full color through an antihistoricist style of storytelling that can counter narratives of failed struggle with those of ordinary people who came together in their differences, united in their desire to destroy the forces that threatened to mutilate their lives. Only by suspending these moments of collective action in service of a counterdiscourse of anticapitalist struggle can we work against the privatization of desire and belief that deems struggle ineffectual after all.

Such a project requires the rejection of methodologies that organize the multiplicity of struggles and subjectivities into a single story of resistance that constantly confronts the overwhelming power of the Japanese state or capital. In contrast, this work employs an approach to the writing of modern Okinawa's history offered by Gilles Deleuze and Elias Sanbar: "Against apocalyptic history, there is another sense of history that is only made with the possible, the multiplicity of the possible, the profusion of possibles at each moment."[59] This requires a slight reworking of Marx's famous assertion in *The 18th Brumaire of Louis Bonaparte* that "men make their own history . . . under circumstances directly encountered, given and transmitted from the past."[60] In contrast to Marx's method in *Brumaire*, which separates the agents of history who operate in the present from the conditions that they inherit from the past, a nonapocalyptic history values the "contingency of the encounter," a concept enabled by a specific reading of Marx that depends on "a particular thought of causality in which every effect of the capitalist mode of production must also and at the same time be a cause."[61] This particular Marxist understanding of transformation does not prioritize revolution per se but understands various revolutionary moments as causes and consequences of social transformation. The utterances, organizational attempts, literary works, expressions of desire, and small movements that implicitly or explicitly challenged existing notions of propriety, assumptions of hierarchy, norms of ownership and usage of the means of production, conventions surrounding the pursuit of individual and collective desires, and restrictions against speech and performance—the *socius* rather than the mode of production narrowly conceived—constitute the stuff of Okinawa's modern history rather than its collateral damage. As small producers, Okinawans took matters into their own hands and acted to reject and destroy the material relations that were the cause of their suffering, articulating visions of society that had nothing to do with the local leaders' concept of an abstract Okinawan community. Understanding the significance of their actions requires a theoretical perspective that pushes against the economism and functionalism that has long been associated with classical and Western Marxism. In short, it requires a nonteleological understanding of capitalist development.[62]

The autonomist tradition of Italian Marxism represented by theorists like Mario Tronti and Antonio Negri was a major addition to the Marxist canon.[63] Deep schisms had emerged in this school of thought by the early 1980s, but it remained a powerful project because of its insistence that a careful reading of Marx's *Grundrisse* and *Capital* revealed the serious threat that working-class struggles, no matter how big or small, posed to capital's valorization process.[64] These theorists' insistence on the centrality of working-class struggle to the process of capitalist reproduction and on the identification of capital's strategies—for example, factory rules, contracts, and social pressures on the state—to seize control of the behaviors and subjectivities of workers outside the factory gates highlighted both the power and vulnerability of capital vis-à-vis labor power, the only commodity it could not produce on its own.[65] The theorists focused on capital's necessary reliance on increased cooperation from the workers as the organic composition of capital advanced. Although this revealed capital's successful and more real subsumption of labor, they argued, the contours of conflict and antagonism also necessarily intensified because workers' internalization of the logic of capital meant that their desires in society multiplied and became impossible for capital to fulfill.[66]

The autonomists' theoretical contribution is that "the capitalist mode of production cannot be critically grasped except as a production of subjectivity."[67] They highlighted Marx's concept of living labor as both condition and limit of capital's valorization process. In so doing they took as their central text the *Grundrisse*, which exposed the antagonisms inherent in the process of converting people's work into dead labor that could be plugged into machines, rather than *Capital*, which explicated capital's successful conversion of people's work into undifferentiated human labor power. They also linked the concept of living labor to the concept of necessary labor, which Marx elaborated in his chapter on absolute and relative surplus value.[68] Increasing the portion of the production cycle designated as necessary labor time was understood precisely as a struggle between living labor—that part of labor associated with the needs and desires of workers and producers—and dead labor, the uncreative and unproductive part of the organic composition of capital as the working class emerged as a self-conscious category. No matter how successful capital's indoctrination process is, living labor—or the "constituent side of surplus labor"—conducts struggles over wages as part of a broader struggle to "communicate and constitute new social relations."[69] Thus, it is exceedingly difficult for capital to control. Resources that are beyond the normal boundaries of either the state or capital are required to harness these desires.[70] Recognizing the need for force to maintain the delicate balance between living and dead labor enables us to understand capitalist society as one in which a latent condition of violence—described by some as a "perennial civil war"—underlies all relations between capitalist and noncapitalist actors.[71] Working-class subjectivities that emerge through the constant struggles to increase the proportion of necessary labor time are immanent to capitalism's reproduction process. Despite its inherently antagonistic relation to living labor, capital requires the production of subjectivities that have revolutionary effects on the way people relate to each other, their own bodies, and the world and is constantly forced to transform itself through its antagonistic confrontations with workers who have desires and needs of their own.[72] It is this relationship that Kawada wanted to highlight through his writings and film-making activities in occupied Okinawa.

Conflicts, or moments of antagonism that arise as dead labor and living labor clash in the process of capitalist development constitute modern Okinawa's history.[73] Far from being futile acts of failed resistance, producers' refusals to transform themselves into dead labor formed the conditions and limits of capital as it extended its reach to the prefecture.[74] Furthermore, the strategic alliances that were forged and identities that were adopted through collective struggle operated as countersubjectivities to capitalist, nationalist, and Okinawan subjectivities. Such an understanding enables us to combine our examination of multiple, conflicting, and shifting subjectivities with a political economic analysis that can draw the study of modern Okinawa away from the apocalyptic narratives that remain dominant today.

This approach reminds those who are discouraged by the revolutionary moment that never comes that "practice does not come after the emplacement of the terms and their relations, but actively participates in the drawing of the lines."[75] The anticapitalist struggles waged by Okinawa's small peasantry since the 1879 disposition and the countersubjectivities that emerged in the process take center stage in our account.

The Revolutionary Possibilities of Noncapitalist Sectors

Although the autonomist perspective provides us with an alternative to apocalyptic narratives of modern Okinawan history, it assumes that capital is continuously moving to higher organic compositions through working-class struggles—that is, autonomists did not escape the stagism that has been another dominant tendency of Marxism after Marx.[76] Problems with this approach have been noted by scholars centered around the journal *The Commoner* and the new enclosures project. For example, George Caffentzis, Silvia Federici, Massimiliano Tomba, and Mariarosa Dalla Costa have argued since the early 1990s that the autonomists' focus on working-class struggle leaves the struggles carried out by people who were not part of the most advanced sectors of capitalism or did not reside in parts of the world that were really subsumed by capital outside the scope of revolutionary struggle.[77] That is, autonomist theory does not enable scholars of the non-West, so-called late-developing countries, colonies, or other regions like agrarian villages that did not experience a clear-cut transformation in the technical process of production to view struggles that emerged from those societies as serious challenges to global capitalism. Instead, the people who resided in regions that were only incompletely subsumed into the capitalist mode of production have to wait for the revolutionary struggle to materialize through either their region's transformation into industrial society or salvation from the vanguard who reside elsewhere.[78] Due to these theoretical shortcomings, ascribing revolutionary meaning to Okinawa's prewar struggles that were waged primarily by small cultivators and producers requires us to go beyond the autonomists' boundaries of worker-capital confrontation into a murkier site, particularly for the Marxist revolutionary tradition. It requires us to look beyond classical Marxist definitions of the small peasantry as a transitional form that did not yet possess the proper revolutionary credentials.

Though autonomists virtually neglected peasants as agents of revolutionary change under capitalism, a thin line connects Marx and later writers who regarded small-scale cultivators as potential agents of enduring social transformation. Marx, through his encounters with Russian progressives in the late 1870s and early 1880s; Mariátegui, observing Peruvian society in the mid-1920s; and Mao Zedong, as he formulated revolutionary strategies in the 1930s, all broadened their focus beyond a narrowly defined proletariat as the true drivers of revolution and brought the agrarian population front and center as transformative agents in capitalist society.

Marx's encounter with the work of Russian populists like Nikolay Gavrilovich Chernyshevsky, who wrote about the Russian commune during the period of the great reforms in the 1860s, provided him with material for a comprehensive exploration of how the peasantry might serve as a revolutionary force without first becoming capitalist producers who only had their labor power to sell.[79] He began to see revolutionary possibility in the agrarian villages that had not fully undergone capitalist transformation while being incorporated into a capitalist state. Populists' writings, political activism, and direct provocations led Marx to clarify his views about the universality of capitalist development and, by extension, the protagonists of revolution.[80] Vera Zasulich of the Black Repartition (Cherny Peredel) group sent him a letter in February 1881, asking him for his thoughts about what role the Russian rural commune might play in revolutionary action. His draft letters to her reveal that he, more than his comrade Engels or his successors Kautsky or Lenin, saw the peasantry as a potentially revolutionary force.[81] In these drafts, Marx left open the possibility that "the rural commune may appropriate all its positive achievements without undergoing its (terrible) frightening vicissitudes" precisely because it existed alongside capitalist production but had not yet become subjugated by a foreign power.[82] As Haruki Wada and Teodor Shanin have argued, Marx seemed to agree that the agricultural commune as it existed in some parts of Russia could produce the destabilizing forces necessary to fuel revolutionary activity against the tsarist state.[83] He tempered these views by cautioning Zasulich that this was a temporary opening, but these letters indicate that Marx did not assume that there was just a single road to revolution by a single protagonist, as classical Marxism subsequently insisted.

In his mid-1920s writings on the so-called Indian problem in Peru, Mariátegui also considered the revolutionary possibility of peasants who resided in agrarian villages that had not fully undergone capitalist transformation while being incorporated into a capitalist state.[84] Like the Russian populists, Mariátegui and his allies who founded the journal *Amauta* saw this as the most pressing issue for Peruvian progressive intellectuals. Although he did not exhibit the type of romanticism that some Russian populists felt about the commune and the figure of the peasant, Mariátegui shared the conviction that if the triad of the *garmonalismo*, latifundium, and large capital could be broken, indigenous farmers who comprised four-fifths of Peru's population could be released from their conditions of servitude.[85] Once that was accomplished, the Indian community and its elements of practical socialism could form the basis of a new Peruvian society. Like Marx in his draft responses to Zasulich's letter, Mariátegui contemplated the possibilities of using existing communal practices and relations to form the foundations of a future noncapitalist society.

More than Marx, the Russian progressives, or Mariátegui, Mao believed that the peasantry was not only a transient social element that would inevitably disappear with the development of capitalism. Mao lived, fought, and worked with revolutionary peasants and saw that they had a distinct culture, sense of solidarity, and economic potential that others had been less willing to celebrate.[86] Spontaneous organizational activity by peasants in the mid-1920s convinced Mao that they possessed the revolutionary consciousness that was necessary to accomplish the threefold task of overthrowing landlordism, opposing capitalism, and defeating imperialist forces.[87] In turn, the Chinese Communist Party's victory in 1949 inspired peasant-led anticolonial struggles throughout the world—which challenged scholars who had long relegated the peasantry to the background of development to reconsider their own characterizations of agrarian communities as veritable black holes of thought and activity.

Peasant studies and colonial studies were two interdisciplinary fields that developed in this context.[88] In its early years, the former was a radical field that organized itself in the 1960s with the goal of situating peasants firmly in the story of modernity as active agents of struggle. It established its first institutional voice in the Peasants Seminar and the *Journal of Peasant Studies* in the early 1970s and consisted of a diverse group of scholars with various intellectual orientations—who, despite their differences, sought to bring the study of peasantry to center stage in academia.[89] Though its participants were committed to a Marxist framework, they challenged orthodox Marxism that relegated peasants to the time of premodernity and their actions to the realm of the prepolitical. Scholars in the field also critiqued the dominant approach in anthropology that saw the peasant as an eternal cultural Other.[90] Through their collective efforts, they showed the peasantry to be capable of cohesive political action and highlighted the need to expand the definition of the political beyond state action.[91]

Furthermore, peasant studies scholars introduced a new problem for Marxist studies through their critical reading of the work of A. V. Chayanov, a 1920s Russian populist. Chayanov formulated a specific theory of the peasant mode of production and argued that peasant societies had a logic of their own that was separate from the logic of capital, even after they had become formally subsumed by capital.[92] The reception of Chayanov's theory was mixed, but the translation of his work into English and the creation of peasant studies journals, study groups, and workshops focused on the peasant question as a question of modernity provided an intellectual community for scholars who wanted to understand peasant political action on their own terms.[93] This field produced many seminal works in the social sciences, including James Scott's *The Moral Economy of the Peasant*. The positive reception of this work fortified links between radical peasant studies, new work in economic and political anthropology, and New Left Marxism.[94] Scott's work also revealed the overlapping concerns of the peasant studies field with Marxist theories of class formation and new anthropological approaches that were concerned with tracking "pathways of power."[95]

Scott and Sidney Mintz, whose ethnographic works focused on peasants' responses to colonial capital's attempts to install plantation labor in their communities, played major roles in the development of the field of colonial studies. Taking their studies as starting points, Dale Tomich and Michael Taussig analyzed the ways in which peasant communities manipulated colonial capital's attempts to draw them into plantation labor. These acts of subversion frustrated plantation owners' ability to accumulate capital.[96] This approach, which converged with contemporary anticolonial struggles, rewrote colonial history as one of constant tension, violence, and struggles over the valorization of the colonial subject's surplus labor.[97] These and other works that took a historical materialist approach to colonial studies combined cultural studies' critique of economic reductionism with the experience of peasants drawn into proletarian labor in plantations to make clear the political significance of seemingly irrational responses by peasants to new forms of exploitation.[98]

Recent Marxist Challenges to Classical Marxism's Teleology

Thus a small number of prewar Marxists and a larger circle of postwar social scientists attempted to grant peasants and agrarian villages status as actors and sites through which meaningful anticapitalist struggles could be waged. They implicitly challenged the historical stagism and economism of classical Marxism while avoiding the romanticism and nostalgia for an unchanging precapitalist space within the modern nation that plagued many scholars who took a populist or agrarianist stance.[99] Despite their vast differences, these theorists argued that the dominant version of Marxism was unable to escape the idealization of capitalist development in England. They aligned themselves with Marx, who insisted during the latter part of his life that the discussion of primitive accumulation that he unfolded in *Capital* should not be understood as a universal process.[100] In his late works on Russia, Marx concluded that there was no single developmental path that any single country could follow to revolution and insisted that development on a national scale would take place through a complex convergence of global and local struggles, accumulation, wars, and alliances.

The latest incarnation of these challenges to traditional Marxism's stagism and Eurocentrism has come from theorists and activists gathered around *The Commoner*. Theorists affiliated with this journal retained the autonomists' commitment to illuminating the struggles against capitalism's reproductive process as part of capitalism's accumulation process but critiqued their clear designation of the working class as the vanguard of revolutionary struggle. Their deep engagement with feminist theory pushed its members to highlight the importance of nonwaged work and the antagonism of nonwaged workers to capitalist reproduction.[101] Engagement with postcolonial studies also led scholars like Caffentzis and Federici to focus on illuminating how capitalist accumulation could occur without dismantling old structures or relations (gender and class) and how at times it reinforced existing hierarchies of power.[102] They located within the *Grundrisse* the existence of transitional forms and the coexistence of earlier modes of production in capitalist societies to show that the time-space of capital was not one-dimensional, nor did it produce homogeneity as it enclosed larger swaths of the planet. By rejecting the transition from formal to real subsumption as capital's proper evolutionary path and by highlighting the importance of nonwaged work to the process of capital accumulation, their approach allows us to consider the struggles by peasants, workers, and women as meaningful moments of constitutive action that limited capital's ability to extract surplus value from their labor. Tomba explains that this inherent unevenness makes primitive accumulation not simply an originary moment in the birth of capitalism but a permanent feature of capitalist society: "Primitive accumulation and large-scale industry do not represent the beginning and the end of an historical process; both are traversed by state violence that, even today, regulates them as co-present elements in the contemporaneity of diverse forms of accumulation. According to these considerations we must speak of *permanence of primitive accumulation . . . 'accumulation' is the continuous driving-power of capitalism.*"[103]

This theoretical intervention allows us to reconsider dominant assumptions of historical stagism and epochal transformation that have been prerequisites to historical materialist analysis. It also reminds us that multiple temporalities; noncapitalist modes of production; and so-called feudal thought, sentiment, and customs persist in countries regarded as having been successfully incorporated into the capitalist order since the late nineteenth century. What Ernst Bloch called "living and newly revived nonsynchronisms" in the context of Germany in the 1930s gain theoretical sharpness with an understanding of capitalism that no longer presupposes a clean break from one mode of production to another in a single national context.[104] This study highlights the moments of anticapitalist struggle that emerged from within these nonsynchronisms in modern Okinawa.

The Becoming and Limits of Okinawan Community

With the exception of this introduction and the first chapter, each chapter of this book has a similar structure. Each first presents the long view of history, or the electrical charges that accumulated in the air in a particular region of Okinawa that set the stage for a struggle. The next section narrates the eruption of a confrontation between dead and living labor, understood as peasants' and cultivators' decision to separate from their old community and to construct a new one. In contrast to labor histories of Okinawa and Japan that conflate the moments of separation, creation, and absorption into a broader story about the development of a particular movement, this project treats each as a distinct moment to illuminate the attempts that various Okinawan political and cultural leaders made each time to resolve the crisis. I clarify the desires and demands of my protagonists through an examination of their songs and other cultural productions. Each chapter then examines how Okinawa's intellectuals and politicians responded to resolve the conflict between small producers, local leaders, and capital. Typically, local leaders reformulated particular demands and problems into a more general Okinawan problem and attempted to reorganize production in a manner that alleviated some of the economic pressures but that did little to respond to broader demands made by producers and cultivators to win greater control over their own lives. Each chapter concludes by examining what escaped re-territorialization even as Okinawa's leaders quelled particular struggles through force or compromise. These excesses that persisted, often times as collective memories of struggle or continued refusals to fully accept the forms of community that left Okinawa's producers and cultivators in their place as dead labor, amount to a powerful alternative history of struggle in the region.

Specifically, the first chapter traces Okinawa Prefecture's inclusion in the Japanese nation-state qua empire beginning in the 1870s in a manner that established it as a periphery—simultaneously inside and outside the Japanese nation-state—in political, economic, and cultural terms via the Preservation Policy of 1879. Through this policy, the Meiji government transformed traditional overlords into its functionaries and put them in charge of maintaining its authority in their old communities, expecting the people of Okinawa to fulfill their traditional responsibilities to them. Incorporating the former Ryūkyū kingdom elites into the bureaucratic structure of the Meiji state exacerbated existing social tensions and prepared the ground for new conflicts that subsequent chapters will illuminate and trace.

The second chapter investigates the Miyako Island Peasantry Movement (Miyakojima Jintōzei Haishi Seigan Undō), which unfolded between 1893 and 1895 and forced the Japanese state to revise its Preservation Policy. I read the movement as an act of refusal that exposed how the discourse and policy of preserving old customs and structures rationalized the endocolonization that the Japanese state required in its peripheries during the initial stages of its own formation. Capitalist relations were established in Okinawa partly because of the Japanese capitalist state's demands but just as importantly because of Miyako peasants' demands for a fundamental transformation of old systems. Though Okinawa's policy makers used the conflict as an opportunity to conduct the reforms that they had already been planning in the prefecture as a whole, we should not dismiss the significance of this refusal, which was born out of the determination of a small group of cultivators to destroy the existing society that threatened their well-being and to articulate an alternative.

The third chapter examines the tensions that emerged between the first generation of Okinawa's intellectuals and female weavers soon after the Miyako Island Peasantry Movement. It focuses on the conflicts between local advocates of the Movement to Reform Old Customs (Fūzoku Kairyō Undō), a project designed to transform the hearts and minds of the Okinawan people in preparation for the establishment of capitalist relations of production in the prefecture, and Okinawa's female producers and merchants. Ōta Chōfu, a prominent local intellectual, and others urged the

Okinawan people to Japanize their habits and customs based on the belief that assimilatory policies were necessary for Okinawans' acceptance in Japan and for the successful establishment of capitalist relations in the prefecture. Intellectuals and entrepreneurs established quality-control mechanisms and marketing strategies to strengthen local industry and appealed to an Okinawan nationalism to encourage greater participation in their program. To their chagrin, they found that weaving women, who were also the main dyers and peddlers of cloth were not at all interested in conforming to Japanese or modern industrial standards. Ōta was particularly concerned that these women were focusing on their immediate and petty profits at the expense of the development of the industry as a whole. He and other local intellectuals couched the conflict between local advocates of reforming old customs and these women as a problem of the backwardness of Okinawan culture, but it was actually a fight over who had the right to control and manage the prefecture's human and material resources.

The fourth chapter examines the difficulty that large-scale mainland sugar capital, which entered the prefecture in 1910, had in keeping its factories operating at full capacity. The problem was that central Okinawa's sugar producers chose to manufacture their own lower-grade sugar using small-scale, labor-intensive, and communal methods instead of submitting the cane that they grew as raw material to newly established modern factories. After clarifying the state and large sugar's response to nonselling alliances that the peasants formed, this chapter will link those responses to a move away from assimilatory strategies that local intellectuals had advocated during much of the Meiji period. This chapter will focus on Ōta and Iha Fuyū's newfound focus on instilling pride in the Okinawan people through the promotion of history, arts, and culture as the only way to counter the state's proposal to transform Okinawa into a colony under Taiwan's jurisdiction.

The final chapter investigates two major instances of political mobilization that unfolded in the summer of 1931 in northern Okinawa, the Ōgimi Village Reform Movement (Ōgimi Sonsei Kakushin Undō) and the Arashiyama Incident (Arashiyama Jiken). It situates these movements within the internal tensions that were heightened by the collapse of Okinawa's economy following the recession after World War I and the establishment of Marxist organizations in the 1920s, which undermined the type of Okinawan solidarity that prominent local intellectuals like Ōta and Oyadomari Kōei thought necessary for the attainment of economic recovery and political equality vis-à-vis mainland Japan. Both struggles allow us to see that local residents and their supporters responded to their economic hardships and the monopolization of political decision-making power by local elites in ways that could not have been anticipated by Okinawa's leading intellectuals, who advocated both economic nationalism and spiritual unity based on their belief in the existence of an organic community of Okinawans.

This study concludes with a reading of "Horobiyuku Ryūkyū Onna no Shoki" ("Memoirs of a Declining Ryūkyūan Woman"), published in 1932 by the Okinawan writer Kushi Fusako. This short story, which appeared in a major women's literary journal, was a bold attempt to tear down the existing boundaries of Okinawa—something that the participants of the Miyako Island Peasantry Movement, the weaving women who refused to sacrifice their own profits for the good of the prefecture's industry, the peasants of central Okinawa who engaged in nonselling alliances, and the participants in the Ōgimi Village Reform Movement and the Arashiyama Incident all did implicitly—by pointing out the hypocrisy of those who invoked the Okinawan community to establish their dominance over other Okinawans. Kushi's story highlighted an important problem that all people critical of the peripheralization of the Okinawan community had to grapple with: how to reaffirm the existence of Okinawa and Okinawans while believing it necessary to transcend their status as Okinawans in order to have some sort of value in Japanese society. The story showed that as long as the category of Okinawa depended on reference to Japan or an essentialized understanding of community, meaningful connections and alliances between Okinawans and other exploited populations within the empire could not be forged. Although Okinawa's self-professed leaders could not imagine a notion of community that was not wedded to the Japanese nation, through their rejection of the abstract category of Okinawa offered by these members of the local bourgeoisie, small producers, weaving women, sugar producers, and other groups in the prefecture formulated radically different notions of belonging, working, and playing that did not seek to rescue, strengthen, or construct the Okinawan community. The visions of the small producers and others, which emerged out of their collective anticapitalist struggles, reflected their refusal to allow others speak in their name. Finally, these visions revealed the impossibility of those in power locally to take control of the reproduction of Okinawa as capitalist society and as such, constituted the limit of the Okinawan community.

CHAPTER ONE

≡

THE BIRTH OF OKINAWA PREFECTURE AND THE CREATION OF DIFFERENCE

The Historical Significance of Ryūkyū's Second Disposition

March 27, 1879, marked the birth of Okinawa Prefecture and the death of the short-lived Ryūkyū domain, which came into being on September 14, 1872, after replacing the Ryūkyū kingdom. The kingdom, whose establishment in 1429 required the subjugation of rival kingdoms and territories, experienced rapid change and growth as it maintained control of its subjects while building profitable relationships within and without its political boundaries. Broader geopolitical transformations in Asia had profound repercussions on the fortunes of the kingdom, which since its unification had forged active trade and tributary relationships that facilitated the movement of goods between East and Southeast Asia.[1] As the Tokugawa regime faced serious challenges to its legitimacy from within and without, Ryūkyū's nobles and officials clung to a political arrangement called dual subordination to Japan and China in an attempt to maintain the kingdom's autonomy in a world that they knew was rapidly changing.[2] Contrary to the desires of its leaders, the kingdom was converted into Okinawa, a full-fledged prefecture of the Japanese nation-state, in a process that the postwar thinker Kawada Yō called the second disposition.

In its disposition, the Meiji regime settled upon a policy of incorporating Okinawa into the polity as a prefecture, rather than a colony. However, from the beginning, it treated the former kingdom differently from other prefectures.[3] While insisting that the people of Okinawa were Japanese subjects, the policy that it instituted to facilitate the transition from kingdom to prefecture—called the Preservation of Old Customs Policy (Kyūkan Onzon Seisaku; hereafter, Preservation Policy) was formulated on the assumption of cultural difference. Ostensibly designed to alleviate the tensions and conflicts anticipated by the kingdom's traumatic absorption into Japan, the policy transformed Okinawa into a distinct cultural sphere and a ground for Japanese capital's primitive accumulation process. It provided the material conditions for Okinawa's conversion into a periphery of the Japanese capitalist state, which in turn provided the foundations for a discourse of Okinawan community that local intellectuals and politicians mobilized in order to resist the discriminatory conditions imposed on the region. This chapter traces the process through which the Preservation Policy was arrived at by examining the conditions that early Meiji leaders encountered in the Ryūkyūs.

The Ryūkyū Kingdom under Satsuma Rule

The settlement that the Japanese nation-state qua empire reached with kingdom leaders during the second disposition cannot be understood without understanding what Kawada called the first disposition of 1609. This first moment of subjugation coincided with an earlier moment of unification, this time, of feudal states by the Tokugawa regime. As a result of the kingdom's subordination to the head of a powerful southwestern domain, Shimazu Iehisa, who arrived in the islands with a 3,000-man force aboard a hundred vessels, it was officially incorporated into the Tokugawa polity as the Satsuma domain's subsidiary state. Iehisa's force raided Shuri castle and captured a hundred hostages, including King Shō Nei and the highest political officials of the kingdom, the Council of Three (Sanshikan).[4] The domain justified this annexation as an unavoidable result of the kingdom's repeated refusals to send troops and provisions in support of Toyotomi Hideyoshi's invasion of Korea ten years earlier, but it was in fact a calculated move that had the twofold objective of raising the stature of the domain in the eyes of the Tokugawa government and increasing the wealth of Satsuma's merchants by using the kingdom's strategic location to increase the volume of indirect trade with China.[5]

After 1609 the Satsuma domain promulgated a series of laws in the kingdom that solidified the semicolonial relationship between the two governments. First, it attempted to increase its tax revenues by appropriating the Ryūkyū peasants' products as tribute, transferring part of the kingdom's subjugated territories to itself, and taking over the power to decide what products could be submitted as tribute and how assessments would be determined.[6] The islands north of Okinawa Island that had been under the direct control of the kingdom including Amami Ōshima were placed under the domain's jurisdiction. As a result, it took over collection of their tribute payments, which amounted to one-third of the kingdom's total tax revenues.[7] The domain only dispatched officials and merchants to the kingdom and never stationed troops, but the specter of military force was ever present and the ability of the people to take up arms was restricted by a demilitarization campaign that began in 1699.[8] The stringency of enforcement and degree of exploitation fluctuated according to the domain's economic and political needs.

Despite this officially sanctioned semicolonial relationship, the Satsuma domain insisted on maintaining a façade of Ryūkyūan independence through a series of cultural policies that it enacted in the kingdom, beginning with a 1613 order that prohibited the Japanization of Ryūkyū's customs and habits. Keeping up the appearance of independence was crucial to fulfilling the domain's main objective of profiting from Ryūkyū's flourishing trade, which was enabled by its existing tributary relations with the Ming. The domain promoted the kingdom's appearance as a separate and autonomous state outside of the Tokugawa state system, while controlling its trade and other diplomatic relations behind the scenes.[9]

Ryūkyū's trade with China had always been an important part of the tributary relationship between the two states, which had its roots in the late fourteenth century, even before the kingdom was unified.[10] Through the early modern era, the kingdom customarily sent a tribute mission to China every other year, with 100–200 people on two tribute ships; it also sent 100 or so people on a single ship in the off years.[11] As studies of these missions reveal, this arrangement provided the Ryūkyūan king with political legitimacy and was an important opportunity for merchants to trade with their Chinese counterparts from their base of operations in Fuzhou. During these missions, they procured silk textiles, porcelain and metal goods, medicine, and other items that they sold at much higher prices to Japan, Korea, and Southeast Asian countries.[12] Controlling the kingdom's trade policies became especially important for Satsuma's officials after the Tokugawa regime severely restricted its own ability to trade with foreign states.[13]

Maintaining Ryūkyū's appearance as an independent kingdom was vital to ensuring the continuation of these commercially profitable tributary relations with China. The infamous practice of *edo nobori*—a procession that made Ryūkyūans into a spectacle as they marched, sang, and danced in the streets of Edo (modern Tokyo) on their way to pay their respects to the shogun—was part of the domain's effort to reaffirm the kingdom's difference from Japan proper.[14] This parade of Ryūkyūans dressed in ceremonial garb was designed to make it clear to officials of other domains, the Tokugawa shogunate, Chinese authorities, and Ryūkyū's leaders that the kingdom merely paid tribute to the Shimazu family and was not part of the domain itself.

In addition to controlling Ryūkyū's external relations, the domain established monopolistic control over the kingdom's key commodities like brown sugar, turmeric, and woven cloth. Brown sugar became particularly important after 1646, when the kingdom first used it to pay part of the tribute that it owed the domain. After that, the domain required that the kingdom submit a significant portion of its tax and tribute payments in brown sugar, which fetched a high price on the Osaka market.[15] This transformed social relations in agrarian villages and made it difficult for small peasantry (shōnō) to maintain self-sufficiency especially after the kingdom government began padding its own coffers through the same policy. Compounding the problem was the kingdom's start of the *kaiagetō* system, the official purchase of brown sugar at below-market prices, which obstructed the ability of the peasantry to buy and sell sugar on their own.[16] Through the backbreaking labor of Ryūkyū's peasants and as a result of the kingdom's control over the production and sale of brown sugar, Satsuma merchants were able to make huge profits in Osaka by selling the commodity, whose value rapidly increased in the 1700s as demand for it rose.[17]

The growing economic pressures that the kingdom's agrarian villages had to shoulder after 1609 required significant adjustments to existing social and political relations. King Shō Nei's decision to create a new type of local official—the *jikata yakunin*, who were selected from among the farmers of a particular village to help with the details of administration, including the implementation of agricultural policy and the collection of taxes and tribute—was one such adjustment, which inaugurated a new chapter in both kingdom-village relations and social relations in the countryside.[18] These officials initially occupied an ambiguous position as both servants of the state and members of their communities, but as the kingdom came to rely on them more, they became increasingly loyal to the center.

The elevation of the position of these local officials in the agrarian villages was facilitated by the kingdom's policies that on the one hand, confirmed their status as members of the local community who were entitled to receive a portion of village farmlands through a system of periodic redistribution (jiwari) alongside their fellow farmers.[19] On the other hand, the kingdom government reaffirmed their privileged status as bureaucrats by exempting them from most taxes and tributes, paying them small salaries that included distributions of official lands called *oekachi*, and granting them the right to collect labor and other taxes from their fellow villagers for personal use.[20] Through this doubly advantageous position, many local officials became usurers who lent money to their neighbors who were struggling to make ends meet under heavy tax burdens that absorbed two-thirds of the crops that they produced each year.[21]

Even though the system of periodic redistribution of farmlands to villagers covered approximately 70 percent of all arable land in the kingdom, another 20 percent was granted to various officials of the kingdom. Local officials were entitled to receive both normal distributions of village farmlands and official lands reserved for bureaucrats who served the central government. After 1669 they were qualified to receive yet another portion of official lands that were uncultivated but designated for reclamation projects called *shiakechi*. This was an outcome of King Shō Shōken's decision to bring more land under cultivation to help pay the kingdom's debts to the Satsuma domain.[22] As a result, a new category of large landowners called *ueeki* who held titles to reclamation lands emerged. It goes without saying that official recognition of these large tracts of land as the property of individuals profoundly transformed the socio-economic foundations of early modern Ryūkyū's society and accelerated the process of differentiation in the countryside.[23] The kingdom pursued reclamation together with the promotion of agricultural education, rationalization of management, and strict supervision of cultivators.[24] Local officials who were direct producers themselves and thus most familiar with village social relations and agricultural techniques were deemed best equipped to carry out the important task of the kingdomwide project to increase agricultural yields. Since the kingdom relied on village power holders to donate money and grain to its coffers in times of financial crisis, it was happy to enact policies that reinforced these important donors' standing within their communities.[25]

The harsh repercussions of this differentiation became visible almost instantly, as the practice of selling oneself to escape tax payments (*miuri*) increased and farmers were transformed into serfs whose sole task was to cultivate the vast tracts of land granted to these new large landowners. Studies by Namihira Isao and others reveal that just a decade after the official distribution of these lands, they had already begun recruiting cultivators to aid in the production of rice, sugar cane, indigo, and other commodities on newly acquired lands. Although these landowners and their families continued to serve as direct producers, they had to bring a variety of people onto their lands—not just cultivators, but other types of workers to help with the manufacture and sale of agricultural goods produced on their property.[26] In most cases these people were tied to their landowner through some form of debt—a condition traceable to the emergence of local officials as usurers in the first hand of the century, which preexisted the formal recognition of the reclamation project in 1669. As a result of the heavy debts that farmers accrued, they often had to pawn the farmlands that they had received during the periodic redistributions of land, which left them no other recourse but to sell themselves to those who were willing to take over their tax obligations in return for total control of their bodies.[27] These indebted farmers-turned-serfs had no other choice but to work the lands of local luminaries because the kingdom's policies prohibited them from moving outside their home villages.[28]

The differentiation of agrarian society produced crisis conditions that forced the kingdom to waive payments on unfulfilled tax obligations in 1820. According to figures from 1825, 3,358 people starved to death that year.[29] The kingdom issued a list of rules and regulations of conduct for local officials in 1831 and ordered the dispatch of agricultural specialists into particularly impoverished villages to alleviate people's suffering, which elevated social tensions to dangerous levels.[30] Ironically, the position of local officials qua large landowners, whose drive to accumulate more wealth brought about the disintegration of many farming families was strengthened following this crisis as the kingdom came to depend even more on their donations to balance its own accounts.[31]

As this examination of the changes to the kingdom's agrarian villages following the first disposition shows, local officials who were installed in the countryside to serve as intermediaries between local communities and the central government came to wield significant political influence due to the financial benefits of their posts. Local officials benefited from their unique position as both within and above their village communities. The kingdom's practice of selling official titles to wealthy farmers in exchange for monetary contributions reveals the power that local elites had amassed by the early nineteenth century.[32] Given these conditions, Iha Fuyū's characterization of the process of the kingdom's disposition between 1872 and 1879 as a "type of liberation from slavery" may have meant more than a liberation from the psychological enslavement of the Ryūkyūan people that accompanied subordination to the Satsuma domain; it could have also meant the cultivators' freedom from the shackles of large landowners who bound them to their fields, aided by the agricultural policies of an ailing kingdom.[33] As we will see below, the Preservation Policy accomplished the first type of liberation, but not the second.

The Ryūkyū Kingdom in the Meiji Restoration

The internal problems outlined above put strains on the semicolonial relationship between the kingdom and the Satsuma domain, but it was the European states' encroachments in East Asia, particularly starting in the late 1840s, that brought this relationship near its breaking point. The Tokugawa state's signing of the Treaty of Peace and Amity with the United States in March 1854, which opened the three ports of Nagasaki, Shimoda, and Hakodate to American whaling ships, signaled to Shimazu Nariakira, the twenty-eighth feudal lord of the Satsuma domain, that the opening of foreign trade was inevitable.[34] In an attempt to gain control of the process, Nariakira negotiated the 1854 Compact of Friendship and Commerce between the Ryūkyū kingdom and the United States and a similar treaty between the kingdom and France in 1855. He hoped to prove his domain's ability to control the kingdom that he regarded as an indispensable buffer and unlimited treasure trove through which he could realize his own vision of rich nation, strong army (*fukoku kyōhei*).

The greatest threat to Nariakira's vision of protecting Satsuma's wealth by maintaining control over Ryūkyū kingdom's export trade was the Western powers' own designs on the kingdom. The British, French, Dutch, and U.S. governments had begun expressing their desire to gain a foothold in the kingdom in the early decades of the nineteenth century and showed little concern for preexisting claims. Commodore Matthew Perry, who is credited with opening Japan to diplomatic relations with the United States, wrote in a letter dated December 14, 1852, that although Ryūkyū was a dependency of Satsuma, its status had intentionally been left ambiguous. He proposed to his superiors that they should take advantage of this condition and occupy the kingdom under the guise of freeing the Ryūkyūan people from the oppressive policies of the Satsuma domain.[35]

Sensing that his domain's control over the kingdom was slipping away, Nariakira dispatched Ichiki Shirō, an official of the domain, in October 1857 to relay a new set of demands to the kingdom's leaders and to reaffirm their relationship to the domain. These demands consisted of seven articles that were tied to his plan to use the kingdom's apparently independent status to ward off foreign occupation. Included in the articles were demands for the kingdom to open its ports to foreign trade; purchase military vessels, pistols, and a steamship from the Western powers; send exchange students to the West to learn foreign languages, medical skills, and science; smuggle students from Kagoshima disguised as Ryūkyūans into training programs in gunnery, shipbuilding, sailing, and governance; and expand the territory of the kingdom to include Taiwan and to establish control over its sugar industry.[36] The kingdom's leaders were particularly disturbed by the demand that students from Satsuma be allowed to disguise themselves as Ryūkyūans to obtain knowledge from the West.[37]

Nariakira's sudden passing in July 1858, just moments before treaty negotiations between the kingdom and France were finalized, brought about major changes in the relationship between the domain, the Tokugawa state, and the kingdom.[38] His death and the shogunate's reluctant signing of commercial treaties with Western countries later that month drastically lowered the kingdom's strategic importance to Satsuma. The opening of the ports of Yokohama, Edo, Kobe, Nagasaki, and Niigata to foreign trade with the 1858 Treaty of Amity and Commerce shifted the domain's attention from Naha to Yokohama. The free fall in the value of Chinese goods due to the effects of the Taiping Rebellion and the Second Opium War prompted Shimazu Tadayoshi, Nariakira's successor, to turn the domain's attention from tributary trade with China and to trading brown sugar, woven cloth, and other specialty goods from Ryūkyū and Amami Ōshima with Western countries and other domains through the newly opened port of Yokohama.[39]

The Meiji Restoration took place amid these shifts in Ryūkyū's relationship with the Satsuma domain. The Restoration, which began with Tokugawa Yoshinobu's abdication as shogun in November 1867 was less an indication of the strength of the imperial court or the Restoration government and more of the efforts to equalize the daimyo houses before the court.[40] The relatively weak hegemony of the nascent Meiji state was reflected in its policies toward the Ryūkyū kingdom as it took over jurisdictional authority from the Satsuma domain. The Meiji oligarchs' early approach toward the kingdom was not unlike their relatively hands-off policy toward Korea during this time.[41] They were more concerned with trouble in the north, where the Russian government was sending immigrants and troops to Karafuto and penetrating Japanese fishing and residential areas, than with the subjugated islands that lay to the west and southwest of the borders of the Tokugawa polity.[42] Hokkaido became both the northern territorial buffer against the Russian invasion of Japan and the imaginary destination to which dislocations of the Meiji Restoration could be sent and where they would be contained.[43]

It was only after the major outline of its policy for the northern territories was completed that the Restoration government shifted its focus southward. A clarification of its policies toward the kingdom was deemed urgent once it became clear that Western powers were plotting to increase their presence in the region.[44] Preparation for the kingdom's incorporation into the new nation-state began in late 1871, with its temporary placement under the management of Kagoshima Prefecture.[45] Still, beyond the consensus that the kingdom would be a test of the Meiji state's ability to play by the new rules of international law, little agreement existed among the leaders about what policies should be enacted in the kingdom once the regime established direct control over the islands.[46] The main point of contention was whether the state should incorporate the kingdom into the polity in the same way as the mainland domains or whether it should have a different status. The exchanges between Deputy Finance Minister Inoue Kaoru and the Ministry of the Left (Sain) illuminate the parameters of this debate and will be considered next.

In response to the question of how the kingdom should be treated, the Ministry of the Left produced a report consisting of nine articles that began by laying out the historical relationship between Ryūkyū and Japan. The first article stated: "It is clear that in the past, the Ryūkyū state was under the dual subordination of ourselves and China."[47] The sixth article recommended that the methods used in mainland Japan to abolish domains and establish prefectures should not be used in Ryūkyū because "the Ryūkyū state and the Ryūkyū people are not the same as the people in the inside, and should not be treated as such."[48]

This stance is indicative of Ministry of the Left's desire to maintain the distinctions between inside and outside that had been in place during the Tokugawa period. This followed the understanding implicitly held by the nativist loyalists during the period of Restoration who called for barbarians to be expelled. To them, the imperial realm corresponded to the boundaries of the Tokugawa polity, or all of the lands and people that the feudal lords who served the government ruled over as servants of the imperial court. There was a clear demarcation of boundaries between the realm and territories that lay outside of it, such as Ryūkyū or Korea—which had been inside the Tokugawa tributary system but distinguished from the imperial realm. This pre-history made it impossible, they declared, to argue that the kingdom be subsumed into the new Meiji state in the same way that the domains were reorganized.[49]

The Ministry of the Left further asserted that the resolution of Ryūkyū's status was not really urgent because the kingdom did not pose a threat to Japan even if it remained outside of the normal state structure: "Everyone knows that Ryūkyū is weak in military might and that it is not a direct territory of Japan.... [T]he Ryūkyū king should remain in his place."[50] Above all, the Ministry of the Left took the position that although the so-called dual subordination that governed Ryūkyū was not ideal, the state did not need to assume the risks that would accompany the implementation of drastic changes: "Even if we considered the dual subordination status of the country of Ryūkyū to be unjust, subordinating it only to our country will most likely lead to war with China. This type of conflict will not be profitable."[51] Rather than worrying about formalities, the report recommended that the state be confident that China's influence over the kingdom was merely symbolic. Granting China this "honor in name only" would not diminish the real control that Japan held.[52]

Deputy Finance Minister Inoue Kaoru responded to the Ministry of the Left's position by noting that the Ryūkyū kingdom's relationship with the former Satsuma domain had been established by force when Shimazu Iehisa subjugated Ryūkyū and made King Shō Nei his prisoner. Until that time, the kingdom had been a tributary state of China alone.[53] Following its subjugation, he explained, the kingdom became devoted to Japan, and its language, customs, and bureaucratic system came to resemble those of the feudal domains even though it continued to send tribute missions to China. Inoue took a more reformist stance than the Ministry of the Left, arguing that the state should not be so quick to discard the relationship that the shogunate and Satsuma domain had cultivated for many years with the kingdom. He urged the government to incorporate the region into the nation-state but warned that "it would be unnatural to do this through force and by violating the lands."[54] He recommended that the king, Shō Tai, be invited to pay his respects to the young emperor and be given the opportunity to apologize for his continued reluctance to have his kingdom enter the new polity. Once the king voluntarily returned the domainal lands and population registers to the emperor, the state could incorporate the kingdom as part of Japan proper.[55] Despite their contrasting recommendations, both parties began by recognizing that the kingdom was under a system of dual subordination to Japan and China. Though inconvenient, this complicated political relationship meant that a specific kind of maneuvering had to take place prior to its conversion from kingdom to a territory of the Meiji state.

Meiji oligarchs accepted Inoue's recommendations and summoned the king to Tokyo to pay official respects to the emperor.[56]

King Shō Tai refused this invitation and sent his uncle, Ginowan Oyakata, and several other high-ranking officials to Tokyo in his place.[57] Despite assurances that things would remain relatively unchanged, the young king was not unaware of the transitional nature of the age in which he lived, and he braced himself for the impending changes by clarifying the kingdom's position on the matter of allegiance. He and his advisors insisted on remaining under the control of Kagoshima Prefecture, which amounted to a refusal to be placed under the direct management of the new government.[58] They also requested that the Meiji government return control of the five islands of Amami-Ōshima, Okinoerabu, Tokunoshima, Kikaijima, and Yoron that the Satsuma domain had taken from the kingdom following the 1609 invasion.[59] They used the Meiji government's own language of the return of feudal registers to request the return of their former subjugated territories and vehemently refused total absorption into the Meiji state.[60] Ginowan Oyakata and his entourage arrived in Tokyo in September 1872 prepared to articulate these positions. Much to their dismay, they were greeted with an imperial decree that abolished the Ryūkyū kingdom and replaced it with the Ryūkyū domain.[61] The absent King Shō Tai was granted the status of peer in the Japanese polity and received a new but anachronistic title of feudal lord of Ryūkyū domain.[62] With this public declaration, the Satsuma domain's 300-year semicolonial rule ended, and Ryūkyū was publicly declared to be part of the territory of Japan, albeit a political unit that had recently been abolished in the rest of the country.[63] The decree also stated that the kingdom should sever its tributary relationship with China and demanded that it stop conducting diplomacy as though it were an independent state.[64]

That November, the Meiji government formally notified foreign states that it would be taking over all diplomatic negotiations related to the former kingdom. Two years later, it made a show of its control over the region by dispatching a 3,000-man punitive expedition to Taiwan, led by Saigō Tsugumichi, a lieutenant general of the Japanese Imperial Army. This expedition—which had the three objectives of providing an outlet for former samurai who were frustrated by their loss of status following the Restoration; punishing Taiwanese aborigines for massacring shipwrecked Ryūkyūan fishermen decades earlier; and forcing the Chinese government to concede that Ryūkyūans were legitimate subjects of the Japanese state—ended with the signing of the Treaty of Settlement between the Meiji and Chinese governments on October 31,

1874. From the perspective of the Japanese leaders, the settlement indicated Chinese recognition of the people of Ryūkyū as Japanese subjects and of the former kingdom as part of Japanese territory.[65] Though the Chinese government continued to assert that Japan had never been justified in sending troops to Taiwan to avenge the death of shipwrecked Ryūkyūan seafarers massacred by Taiwanese aborigines, the Meiji state took the signing of the treaty as its admission of Japan's right to defend Ryūkyūans against foreign encroachments of their body or soil and of its renunciation of claims over Taiwan.[66] The Chinese government was acutely aware that the settlement, if unchallenged, could set a dangerous precedent in granting the Meiji state the right to protect, defend, and avenge its subjects beyond its national boundaries, and thus continued to call for a renegotiation of the Ryūkyū issue after the treaty was concluded.[67]

They had help from the former kingdom's rulers, who continued to deny Japan exclusive control over their lands after the Taiwan expedition and sent envoys carrying tribute to Fuzhou to pay respects to the Qing court and conduct trade with Chinese merchants while the terms of the treaty were being negotiated.[68] In November 1874, not long after the conclusion of the Treaty of Settlement, the Ryūkyū domain audaciously sent another tribute mission to China.[69] These public acts of disobedience convinced Meiji leaders that more forceful measures were necessary.

Home Ministry official Matsuda Michiyuki arrived in Ryūkyū on July 10, 1875, to convince the defiant leaders to accept their fate as Japanese subjects. He proceeded to Shuri castle (figure 1.1), the center of government and the former king's residence, where he read a decree that outlined the Meiji government's orders to the domain:

1. The dispatch of envoys to China to send tribute and congratulations should be stopped.
2. When a regime change takes place, the new ruler may not receive gifts from China as they did in the past.
3. The Meiji name [method of dating] should be honored throughout the domain and all of the holidays throughout the year should be recognized.
4. Three representatives should be dispatched to Tokyo to learn about criminal laws that will soon take effect.
5. The reform of the domainal administration shall be undertaken.
6. Ten or so representatives from the kingdom should come to Tokyo for scholarly training.

Fig. 1.1 This is the gate that U.S. Commodore Matthew Perry and Matsuda Michiyuki of the Meiji Home Ministry saw when they arrived at Shuri castle. Entrance gate, Shuri, when Perry arrived, E. R. Bull's photographic plates, no. 75, Taisho era, Bull Collection, University of the Ryūkyūs.

7. The Ryūkyū House[70] in Fuzhou will be abolished.
8. The nobility must come to Tokyo express their gratitude.
9. A standing army division will be dispatched to Ryūkyū.[71]

The new demands that Matsuda brought to Ryūkyū's leaders reflected the Meiji leaders' determination to conduct more extensive reforms in the domain aimed at transforming the consciousness and rhythms of life of the residents of Ryūkyū in a manner consistent with Meiji Japan's own far-reaching changes following the 1868 Restoration.

Ryūkyū's leaders were not in complete agreement about whether to accept Matsuda's orders but eventually decided to allow the presence of the troops and to send scholars to Tokyo to study Japanese criminal laws. However, they firmly rejected the state's demand to sever tributary relations with China. Based on the example of the disposal of the mainland domains, they concluded that if they complied with this demand they would lose any remaining freedom to rule their territory. Their insistence on maintaining political ties with China was the result of a pragmatic assessment of what life would be like without China's protection: "If our connection to China ceases for even one moment, we will naturally lose our right to freedom, invite interference, be tied down and will eternally lose the ability to maintain the state."[72] They reiterated: "Our relationship with China is like father and son, or like master and servant. This is an extremely important relationship and ties with other countries pale in comparison."[73] As their insistence on dual subordination indicates, Ryūkyū's ruling elite believed that their tributary relationship with China protected their ability to govern their own territory.

At the same time, they downplayed the significance of their 260-year subordination to the Satsuma domain and emphasized the autonomy that they enjoyed within the tributary system centered on China. Due to this shift and the Meiji government's own interests in deflecting attention away from Satsuma's semicolonial rule over the kingdom, the image of an independent Ryūkyū kingdom crystallized in the late 1870s. Protecting that independence at all costs, preferably with Chinese military assistance, became the sole mission of the former kingdom's leaders. This mission collided head-on with the Meiji state's geopolitical interests in the region. The leaders' refusal to accept Meiji leaders' demands to suspend all official contact with China led Home Minister Itō Hirobumi to advocate a speedy transition from domain to prefecture.[74]

Still, preexisting differences in language, customs, and habits that the Satsuma domain had gone to great lengths to preserve beginning in the seventeenth century made it impossible to dismantle the kingdom's infrastructure in one fell swoop. Matsuda had experienced the difficulties of this task during his negotiations with the kingdom's leaders and submitted a report in 1878 that became the blueprint for the domain's conversion into Okinawa Prefecture.[75] Matsuda's report revised the historical narrative about relations between Ryūkyū, China, and Japan to emphasize the anachronistic nature of existing relations. This enabled him to make a new argument for reform: instead of arguing that Ryūkyū was more similar to Japan than China, he emphasized the feudal character of the kingdom's structure and cast doubt on the king-turned-feudal lord's ability to rule in the modern era. He underplayed the importance of dual subordination and highlighted the king's central role in the governance of the islands:

> From long ago, it [the kingdom] has been inside of our territory. From the middle ages it has been under the jurisdiction of the Satsuma feudal lord and more recently has been directly ruled by the government [Meiji]. Still, all administrative affairs with the exception of trials, con-

trol over the army, currency and dating have been entrusted to the feudal lord. The indigenous people know that there is a feudal lord but do not know about the emperor. . . . Thus, they revere the feudal lord to an immeasurable extent and would give their lives and their wealth for him.[76]

In Matsuda's rendering of Ryūkyū's history, China disappeared, the king was nothing more than a feudal lord, and Japan's rule over the region was portrayed as something that had existed before the Shimazu invasion. The people of Ryūkyū were miserable and ignorant creatures who were unaware of the oppressive conditions under which they lived. He explained that their barbarism was a result of the kingdom's feudalistic system and implied that the Meiji government's establishment of Okinawa Prefecture would rescue the people by bringing them enlightenment and civilization. The king's dethronement and annexation of the domain were both seen in this narrative as part of the Meiji government's project of modernizing the region rather than as a colonial strategy backed by military force.

Matsuda wanted to emphasize that while the state's primary task was bringing civilization to the region, feudal rule could not immediately be swept aside because preexisting differences in language, customs, and habits made a complete takeover impossible under current conditions: "The indigenous people are not educated, very few of them can read or write, they wear frayed clothing, walk barefoot, live in huts and sleep and sit on earth floors—they are quite barbaric. Their language is a dialect that is a mixture of Japan's old speech, their own dialect and Chinese. The Japanese cannot understand this (their officials do speak Japanese) . . . they tend to be old fashioned, stubborn, and resistant to new ways."[77] He also warned that rapid change would have a negative impact on the nobility: "They will probably not want to engage in their duties, will forget to even eat and will be confused and disturbed. They may go insane and will vigorously refuse the disposition process."[78] Matsuda recommended that the state grant the nobles concessions to win their much-needed cooperation. His analysis determined the basic contours of the Preservation Policy: "We should not expect a rapid enactment of the beautiful policies and rather, should work to not tear down the former customs of the people in realms of land system, customs and commerce. We must not repeat the same mistakes as those who conducted the mainland domain's disposition, which did not occur calmly. With regards to stipends, shrines and temples, forestry and in taxation, commerce, police, education and religion we should reform only those things that are good for the people and those things that will satisfy their desires."[79] With this proposal in hand, Matsuda left Tokyo on March 12, 1879. He arrived in Naha thirteen days later, bringing with him 160 policemen and a 400-man detachment of troops from Kumamoto Prefecture to oversee his occupation of Shuri castle. Two days after his arrival, Matsuda read the decree that abolished the domain and established the prefecture to fifty Ryūkyū nobles who gathered at the Home Ministry's branch office. He explained that because their leader Shō Tai had failed to comply with the Meiji government's orders in 1875 and 1876 to sever relations with China, the state had no choice but to dispose of the domain. He concluded the ceremony of disposition by urging all officials not to be confused by the changes and to cooperate in the task of transferring administrative duties to officials dispatched from Tokyo.[80]

Ryūkyūan Resistance to the Establishment of Okinawa Prefecture

Despite Matsuda's assurances to the contrary, officials of the Ryūkyū domain recognized that its disposal was effectively a militarily backed transfer of authority from Ryūkyū officials to Meiji bureaucrats. According to Kishaba Chōken, the official recorder of the domain's affairs at the time, kingdom officials were extremely upset about the decree and rejected Matsuda's rationale and issued the following statement: "Our domain was originally a country and had sovereign rights. We are different in this way from the former domains of the mainland. The establishment of Okinawa Prefecture means that our sovereignty has been destroyed. No matter what is granted materially to the people and no matter what kind of compassion is shown, we will not be assuaged. It is as though we have been thrust into death."[81]

As the historian Nishizato Kikō has shown, this statement expressed a unified stance by the Ryūkyū nobles, who had been divided but came together to oppose Matsuda's order. Fifty-three high-ranking nobles, also prominent officials of the kingdom government from all parts of the island signed the statement, including some from the minority faction that favored accepting subordination to Japan.[82] What these nobles found unacceptable was not the abolition of the domain and the establishment of Okinawa Prefecture per se, but Matsuda's demand that all administrative leadership be transferred to mainland officials. This was a true annexation—something that the Ryūkyū nobility was not willing to let happen without a fight.

This desire to resist annexation explains why the nobles immediately abandoned their earlier assertions of dual subordination after Matsuda gave the order to vacate Shuri castle and why they called Matsuda and his forces foreign invaders. Led by King Shō Tai, they organized an islandwide noncooperation movement to protest the takeover of their domain. Called the blood oath movement, it began in March, immediately after Matsuda's decree, and ended in October 1879. Kishaba recorded the organized boycott of the new administrative structure: "Every day, the former officials who met in the castle rejected Matsuda's orders and debated how they could remain loyal. Local officials convened at schools and picked four people from each village to engage in national studies (kokugaku). They reported their interactions with Matsuda. They decided not submit to Japan's orders and resolved to await military assistance from China. The nobles, excited, said that those who honored the order and Japan would have their heads cut off."[83] The noncooperation movement required all officials who served the kingdom to sign a blood oath and promised that "anyone who submits to orders and receives some kind of compensation from the Japanese (Yamatojin) will be executed. Not only officials, but villagers who work for or assist the Japanese will be executed. Receiving goods like rice and money from the Japanese or leaking information about local administration will be punished by execution. This punishment may extend to relatives of the perpetrator."[84]

In addition to the oath, Shuri officials relied heavily on their regional and village counterparts to enforce the policy of noncompliance among the people. Complete cooperation was necessary in order to maintain Shō Tai's leadership and the legitimacy of the Ryūkyū state against what they labeled a foreign invasion.[85] From the moment that Matsuda entered Shuri castle with his troops, Japan became the enemy, and the system of dual subordination that the Ryūkyū ruling elite advocated in 1872 completely lost its appeal.

Matsuda tried to reestablish order before he left Naha on June 3, 1879 by urging uncooperative nobles who were determined to wait for military assistance from China to recognize what was taking place around them. He implored them to be more pragmatic in their actions and not be blinded by hubris:

> If you do not come to your senses and do not stop trying to revive the old ways soon, you will not be able to run the prefecture and all of the jobs will go to people from the mainland. Not one local person will be able to get a job in the new government. You will be selling yourself short to the society and you will become indistinguishable from the rest of the

people. You will become like the indigenous people of America and like the Ainu of Hokkaido. . . . When all of the jobs become monopolized by the people from the mainland . . . you will lose your authority and you will lose your profits.[86]

Although his speech captured the fears of the former ruling elite, it was not effective as a threat, and former officials continued to reject the new political organization long after he departed.[87] It was only after the police rounded up over a hundred people who outwardly violated the Meiji government's order in August 1879 and their subsequent detention, questioning, and torture that calm was temporarily restored in the new prefecture.[88]

This reprieve for the Meiji state came after it secured an agreement from a faction of the nobility who were loyal to Shō Tai—a group called the White Party (Shiro-tō)—to cooperate after days of arrests and torture.[89] The government expressed its gratitude to the former king for using his political sway to quell the resistance by granting him a generous stipend: a 200,000-yen bond with a 10 percent interest rate.[90] In order to make sure that he stuck to his end of the bargain, the Meiji state recommended that Shō Tai remain under house arrest in his mansion in Tokyo, also given him by the state. This distance from the prefecture had to be maintained so they could keep track of his communications with other former leaders and, most important, with the Chinese government. From this moment on, the Meiji state and the former ruling family formed an uneasy alliance that was supported by generous material gifts and the threat of violence. As we will see, this alliance was accompanied by the sacrifice of the well-being of the former kingdom's cultivators and small producers. In this sense, the liberation of the kingdom from the shackles of the Satsuma domain did not include the peasantry's liberation from the grips of usury capital in their villages and in fact, furthered their exploitation.

The Significance of the Preservation Policy

The precarious foundation on which the Meiji state established its control over Okinawa Prefecture involved both flexible policies that granted economic concessions to the former kingdom's nobles and strong-armed tactics that deterred traitorous activity.[91] Just as was the case in the former domains of mainland Japan, the Meiji government's strategy for establishing rule immediately after the annexation of the Ryūkyū kingdom in March 1879 was not to completely dismantle the existing power structure but to incorporate former rulers into the new political system, giving them significant economic advantages but no policy-making power.[92] This strategy, which stemmed from Meiji leaders' sensitivity to the tenuous nature of their exclusive claims over the Ryūkyūs required that initial incorporation of the former kingdom into the territorial and political boundaries of Japan be accompanied by assurances of cultural preservation. The disposal of the Ryūkyū kingdom and the establishment of Okinawa Prefecture had to be expressed as simply an administrative or formal change without any disturbance to the collective unity of the territory, if Japanese claims to the islands were to be justified to the Chinese government and Western powers. The policy equivalent to this commitment came in the form of the Preservation Policy, which Matsuda read to the defeated Ryūkyūan nobility at the empty Shuri castle on April 12, 1879.[93] The state's explanation that the role of the Preservation Policy was simply to protect the Okinawan community ensured that whatever material transformations took place in the prefecture, its difference could be explained away as a result of the collective backwardness of the long-standing customs and culture of its people rather than the outcome of a struggle between preexisting socioeconomic structures and the nascent capitalist state.[94]

Under the Preservation Policy, even as the former kingdom became a prefecture, the people of Okinawa were expected to continue to fulfill their responsibilities to their traditional overlords—whom the Meiji government transformed into its functionaries charged with enacting state policy in the villages.[95] The way that the state ruled Okinawa in the early Meiji period was analogous to the model of indirect rule that Mahmood Mamdani described in *Citizen and Subject*. Just as "customary law" was selectively installed alongside "received law" in indirectly ruled colonial Africa during the late nineteenth century, the Preservation Policy in Okinawa proscribed the selective maintenance of older methods of tax collection and older standards of political and civil conduct alongside the institution of modern laws that gave customary practices an entirely new significance.[96] Such an arrangement meant that Okinawa's cultivators remained direct producers who received distributions of farmland and paid taxes to local officials in labor, kind, and currency but became even more dependent on usury capital because their integration into the Japanese commodity economy increased their vulnerability to external market fluctuations.[97] This appeared to observers as merely a continuation of conditions of indebtedness that were rampant in the kingdom era. In reality, the Preservation Policy created entirely new conditions since the prefecture was expected to service the needs of a rapidly developing Japanese capitalist system. The selection of former Ryūkyū kingdom officials to enact the Preservation Policy and serve as local bureaucrats allowed them to maintain and even increase the economic power that they had built up, since the state chose not to reform the system of local administration that had provided many privileges to local officials during the early modern period.

Let us not misunderstand the Meiji state's concessions to the Ryūkyū kingdom's traditional elites as simply a capitulation to this group of unruly actors, who sealed their agreement to resist Japanese rule in blood in the summer of 1879 and threatened to seek military aid from China if their demands were not met. The policies enacted in Okinawa Prefecture were extremely profitable for Japanese capital. This is unmistakably clear when we examine the Meiji state's policy toward one of the former kingdom's major industries, sugar.[98] As we have already seen, the kingdom began the system of kaiagetō in the mid-seventeenth century, which allowed it to buy up large amounts of sugar from the villages at a fixed price that was always significantly lower than the market price at which the sugar was subsequently sold to mainland buyers. In order to ensure that the supply of this valuable commodity would always be available, the kingdom had established an elaborate bureaucracy in which local officials were appointed and held responsible for strictly supervising the entire process of cultivation, manufacture, and collection in each village.[99] Regulations such as a ban on the free sale of sugar until the entire village had fulfilled its tax obligations to the kingdom had kept producers from bypassing this system.

After establishing Okinawa Prefecture, the Meiji government took over the kingdom's role as the monopoly seller of sugar by preserving the system of the payment of taxes in sugar and the kaiagetō requirement.[100] The government profited as mainland consumers' increased demand for sugar after 1868 led to higher prices on the market.[101] Maintaining this policy through the early Meiji period put pressure on small peasants to increase the proportion of brown sugar they produced vis-à-vis staples like sweet potatoes and pushed them to improve their methods without having the ability to decide when and how much to sell. As a result, they became increasingly dependent on a system of sugar advances called *satō maedai*, according to which sugar brokers (*nakagainin*) from both Kagoshima and Okinawa issued loans prior to harvest at a high interest rate and collected on them during the manufacture period. In the case of Okinawa's small farming households, the majority of these loans were used to simply make ends meet.

Conditions of indebtedness in Okinawa's agrarian villages at the time of the 1879 disposition were so serious that the prefectural authorities requested and were granted loans for relief in 1880.[102] Still, for the state, providing temporary relief to Okinawa's brown sugar producers was a small price to pay, considering the importance that this industry held for the country's capitalist development. As Kinjō Isao has analyzed in his works on Okinawa's sugar industry, the development of the cotton and sugar industries were crucial for the country's well-being, as these two industries together accounted for half of the total value of imports in 1880.[103] The state's continuation of the former kingdom's method of taxation and collection in the period immediately after annexation reflected its desire to control this lucrative industry and gain monopolistic profits until more comprehensive reforms could be enacted.

The significance of this monopolistic expropriation of Okinawa-produced sugar by the Meiji state cannot be overstated, considering that in the rest of Japan, attempts were under way to build a different type of social relation between producers and their products through the discourse of liberalism and the institution of the land tax reform that formally established private property in 1873. The political accompaniment to this was the formation of a law-based state, secured to a limited extent by the promulgation of the constitution and the establishment of the National Diet. The rhetoric of freedom based on the principle of equality of subjects under the emperor did not even have to be promised to Okinawans, as all policy differences were passed off as necessary measures in light of the region's belated entry into the nation-state, the continued resistance to incorporation by the former kingdom's ruling elite, and the low degree of formal education of the commoners. The language of the Preservation Policy explained the maintenance of the precapitalist mode of production in Okinawa as a result of the people's preference for outmoded relations rather than an outcome of the Meiji state's strategic efforts to convert the region into a particular ground for capitalist accumulation.

Conclusion: Okinawa's Transformation into a Single Economic and Political Unit

This chapter traced the transformation of relations among the Ryūkyū kingdom, Satsuma domain, and the Tokugawa shogunate and their post–Meiji Restoration counterparts in order to show the contingent nature of the state's policies toward the region. That said, the state's policies toward the prefecture were by no means passive. Contrary to many descriptions of the period immediately following the abolition of the domain and establishment of the prefecture as a time of nonaction, the region's society and economy were greatly transformed by these early policies.[104] The single economic and political unit, Okinawa Prefecture, which was born during this period began to appear as a fundamentally distinct community from other prefectures that were governed at least in theory according to a single national rule. The predominance of rice cultivation in the mainland prefectures' farming households further differentiated those prefectures from Okinawa, which became intensely focused on the cultivation and manufacture of brown sugar.

The consequences of this policy, particularly as it affected social and economic relations in the prefecture's agrarian villages, will be discussed in the next chapter through a consideration of a peasant struggle that erupted on Miyako Island on the eve of the First Sino-Japanese War. We will see the difficulties created by the operation of customary law once the sovereign who had once been considered the legitimate recipient of tribute could no longer claim to be the rightful ruler of the realm, despite his official backing by the Meiji state.

CHAPTER TWO

=

THE MIYAKO ISLAND PEASANTRY
MOVEMENT AS AN EVENT

The Creation of Unevenness in the Early Meiji Period

The previous chapter examined the process through which the Meiji government settled on the Preservation of Old Customs Policy to guide its policy-making decisions in post-disposition Okinawa. This policy was significant economically, as it gave the capitalist state a place in which so-called primitive accumulation could occur. Although the state enacted a system of private property with the Land Tax Reform (Chiso Kaiseihō) of 1873 in the Japanese mainland, until 1903 it maintained in Okinawa the system of land tenure that had prevailed in the kingdom era.[1] The Preservation Policy also kept tax collection policies, land systems, and the forced submissions of brown sugar in place. Still, not everything remained the same. Restrictions were loosened on cane cultivation and generous subsidies were provided for large-scale reclamation projects designed to facilitate the expansion of sugar production beginning in the late 1880s. Through these twin policies of preservation and reform, the state transformed Okinawa into a domestic site of sugar extraction.

Looking at Okinawa's peculiar position, we can discern that the establishment of Japan as a nation-state did not rely only on the centralization and standardization of policies to create a homogeneous space-time. Nation building also involved the construction of various types of peripheries in order to effect capitalist development: regions expressly prohibited from establishing capitalist social relations, like Okinawa; communities granted the legal prerequisites for capitalist relations but structurally limited from their realization, like mainland agrarian villages; formal colonies that served as zones for the extraction of raw materials and therefore saw significant capital investment, like Taiwan with its sugar industry; states that were forced to sign unequal treaties, like China; and so on.[2] Jairus Banaji's definition of formal subsumption as an expression of a technical process of production in capitalism is an appropriate way to describe how the Japanese capitalist state extracted surplus value from producers without completely dismantling old relations of production. Banaji explains that the "*formal* subordination of labour to capital presupposes a process of labour that is 'technologically' continuous with earlier modes of labour" and therefore may "develop *outside* the framework of a specifically capitalist mode of production," while the self-expansion of value is the common denominator of productive activities under capitalism.[3] For Marx, Banaji notes, this process was the "*general* form of every capitalist process of production in so far as it implied (1) the extortion of surplus-labour in the form of surplus-value, and (2) the intervention of capital as the 'immediate owner' of the production-process."[4]

Still, the strategic delay of certain economic and political reforms in Okinawa meant that the illusion of backwardness came to matter for many Okinawans and provided the language through which antagonisms were shaped and articulated in the period under consideration and beyond.[5] The existence of what Jason Read has called a "complex articulation of multiple modes of production—one dominant, the others dominated" in early Meiji Okinawa disrupted not only the legitimacy of old rulers but also the entire moral economy that governed peasant-elite relations.[6] These conditions provided small producers with a new method and language of struggle precisely because of their inclusion into this new *dispositif*.[7] Just as the openness of America provided new hope for impoverished white settlers, as "the bulk of the soil is still public property, and every settler on it can therefore turn part of it into his private property and his individual means of production," the possibilities inherent in Okinawa after its annexation by Japan gave cultivators an opening—a hope that if they could just rid their society of the customary law that limited their mobility, they might be able to end their generations of suffering.[8]

Several hundred small cultivators, several midsize landlords, and a few entrepreneurs residing in Miyako, an island more than two hundred miles southwest of the main island of Okinawa and under the jurisdiction of the prefecture, began a collective struggle in the spring of 1893 after identifying precisely the kind of opening Marx described. Participants recognized that old powerholders no longer held the same political position that they had previously and demanded that the state remove what it had kept intact—what Deleuze and Guattari call "archaisms with a current function"—through the Preservation Policy.[9] This struggle, which erupted fourteen years after the Meiji state conducted its second disposition of Ryūkyū kingdom, came to be known as the Miyako Island Peasantry Movement (Miyakojima Jintōzei Haishi Seigan Undō). This chapter analyzes this movement as an example of the exercise of constituent power, whose significance Antonio Negri defines as "at the same time resistance to oppression and construction of community."[10]

The Miyako cultivators' refusal of the entire sociopolitical system, in which they were expected to toil each day in the sweltering sun or locked in a dark room under strict surveillance, was a violent interruption of the existing order of things. The system that divided the island's population into commoners and nobility and designated the former as toilers who existed primarily for the enrichment of the latter had a tenuous existence to begin with, and its position became even more vulnerable following King Shō Tai's dethronement. In spite of valiant efforts by local officials to protect their positions after the kingdom's dissolution, Miyako's cultivators began to formally register their demands for change as early as the late 1880s. Here, we will consider two often conflated moments in the struggle: the refusal of small peasantry (shōnō) of the existing order and their articulation of a new collective vision. As an event, the Miyako Island Peasantry Movement was the crystallization of its participants' decision to "construct new forms of life, new articulations and novel trajectories."[11]

Their decision was intimately linked to the crumbling of the despotic machine headed by the royal family and exposed the superficiality of the Meiji state's rationale for preserving the privileged positions of the Ryūkyū kingdom's nobility as serving the best interests of the Okinawan people.[12] The Miyako peasantry's refusal to accept the Japanese state's attempts to maintain already existing "relations of production in their totality"[13] exposed the role that the discourse and policy of preserving old customs and traditions played in rationalizing the endocolonization that the Meiji state required in its peripheries during the initial stages of its own formation.[14] The Preservation Policy was the Meiji state's attempt to keep the body of a creature that it had beheaded intact so long as it remained profitable to do so. The Miyako peasantry's rejection of this arrangement stemmed from their awareness of the profoundly transformed conditions in which they lived and was not unlike the discourse and actions—traced by Harry

Harootunian—of the Restorationists of the bakumatsu period who sought not only to destroy the old but also to construct a new space for maneuver.[15] They attempted to tear apart older relations between ruler and ruled, noble and commoner, and tax collector and cultivator and replace them with relations that could lead to the demonopolization of political and economic privilege. As a moment of articulation of this new social space, the Miyako Island Peasantry Movement signaled the constitution of a new subjectivity, unnamed but united through its participants' common struggle against the delegitimized old order and its representatives.[16] Finally, the demands that Miyako's small producers voiced beginning in the fall of 1893 were inextricably linked to new contradictions that manifested themselves on the island as the Meiji government attempted to resolve the challenges that it faced by creating new peripheries.[17]

Scholars have been ambivalent in their evaluation of the Miyako Island Peasantry Movement because the small peasantry involved in it called for the dismantling of the precapitalist mode of production maintained by the Meiji state exclusively in Okinawa—a move that could easily be read as a demand for their transformation into wage laborers through full incorporation into the capitalist system. While some scholars applaud the movement as a grassroots call for an end to the system of collecting poll taxes (*jintōzei*) that required free cultivators to pay a disproportionate amount of taxes and exempted hereditary officials from paying anything at all, others express regret that these cultivators appear to have desired their assimilation into the Japanese nation as tenant farmers and wage laborers. That is, while courageous, Miyako's peasantry unwittingly became collaborators in their own colonization and accelerated the conditions of their exploitation by Japanese capital by destroying with their own hands the precapitalist social relations that curbed their proletarianization.[18]

If we focus not on the consequences of this movement for the extension of the capitalist mode of production and imperial subjectivity to Okinawa but on the revolutionary nature of small peasantry as a constituent power in action, we can complicate existing analyses that absorb the movement into a teleological narrative of Okinawan modernization. Such historicist accounts unwittingly diminish the deterritorializing force of each event by considering them from the perspective of a univocal Okinawan struggle, assimilation, or victimization vis-à-vis Japan; they mistakenly ascribe to small producers a desire to transform themselves into capitalist subjects instead of carefully analyzing their demands as they were articulated.

This chapter aims to bring to center stage the Miyako peasantry's refusal of the status quo and argues that the movement's significance lies in the challenges that it posed to Japanese capital's so-called primitive accumulation process. Although this perspective relies heavily on autonomia's theory of the immanence of working-class struggle to processes of capital accumulation, it also aims to expand the subject of antagonism beyond a really subsumed industrial worker to include agricultural producers whose technical process of production was not capitalist, but who were nonetheless drawn in as suppliers of human and material resources to capitalist society.[19] The Miyako peasantry's refusal to accept their status as taxpayers to, and supporters of, a parasitic nobility challenged a capitalist system that reproduced itself by maintaining the status, functions, and privileges of this customary elite. The collective subjectivity that emerged through the process of struggle guaranteed the constant presence of conflict even after this particular struggle came to an ambiguous political conclusion in the mid-1890s.[20]

Okinawa's Agrarian Villages under the Preservation Policy

As we saw in the previous chapter, the Preservation Policy that kept old systems intact, combined with Okinawa's new role as supplier of sugar to the nation, placed tremendous strain on the prefecture's agrarian villages. Cultivators became more integrated into the market economy but were prohibited from selling their products because of the continuation of the kingdom-era requirement that taxes be submitted communally. They also suffered from a village administration system that kept large numbers of former nobles unproductive and permitted them to use their official positions to extract resources above and beyond tax payments from cultivators.[21] Small peasantry who bore the brunt of these burdens grew impatient for change by the mid-1880s.[22]

In response to the impoverishment of the agrarian villages, Uesugi Mochinori, the most reformist of the early state-appointed governors (*kenrei*) in Okinawa, advocated a wholesale reorganization of the bureaucracy. He targeted the local officials (*jikata yakunin*) who had played key roles in directly governing the agrarian villages during the early modern period and explained that their large numbers, incompetence, and laziness were the main reasons Okinawa's cultivators could not escape their impoverished conditions. He highlighted the role that local officials played as village usurers who made indebtedness an endemic and incurable condition.[23] Despite the perks that they enjoyed, local officials wanted more: "They do not feel well compensated so they collect even more from the people by arbitrarily imposing cruel and heavy burdens on them."[24] Uesugi lamented the existing situation: "Using the preserved system, they take and take until the people have nothing left to give."[25] This relationship hurt the prefecture's overall productivity because cultivators knew that their products would be collected as taxes or turned into the personal property of local officials. Cultivators had no incentive to work hard or make improvements on their lands.[26] Overhauling the bloated bureaucracy, Uesugi argued, was the only way to improve conditions in the prefecture and open a path for the development of industry and education. The main objective of his report was to convince the state that economic burdens were shouldered unfairly by the peasantry under the Preservation Policy and should be redistributed more evenly among all residents of the prefecture.

Despite Uesugi's passionate plea for a reform of the local system of administration, the Home Ministry insisted that the people of Okinawa were not ready for such a drastic change. In his response, Home Minister Yamada Akiyoshi reiterated the importance of the Preservation Policy: "The people of the prefecture were under the despotic rule of the king for several hundred years and have become accustomed to his policies. Their situation is very different compared to that of the people from other prefectures.... The people do not like new things and revere the old. They still have fears and suspicions and a huge change such as the reform of the administrative system will make them more fearful of the new."[27]

Even though the central government responded coolly to Uesugi's report, it was concerned enough about the instability that extreme impoverishment could bring that it dispatched Ozaki Saburō, its representative to the Lower House of the National Diet, to Okinawa for a visit in July 1882. In the report that he submitted soon after returning to Tokyo in November, Ozaki argued that even more perks should be granted to the king and the pro-Japanese segment of the former nobility: "There is a special system in place for the nobility and it should remain intact. The nobility will be able to continue to reap the blessings of the former system and the government will be able to avoid many problems."[28] Perhaps the clearest indication of where the government stood on reforms was its replacement of Uesugi with Iwamura Michitoshi, an accountant who had had experience in prefectural administration as the governor of the Hokkaido Development Agency (Kaitakushi) in April 1883. In the eight short months that he was in office in

Okinawa, Iwamura reversed most of the changes that Uesugi had implemented and reinforced the policy of preserving old customs.

Iwamura's main task during his tenure as governor of Okinawa was to reassure the former nobles and local power holders that, despite Uesugi's attempts to reduce their hold over local affairs, the Meiji government was committed to protecting their interests. Iwamura extended the deadline of 1885 that the first governor of the prefecture, Nabeshima Naoyoshi, had set for hereditary stipends to be converted from cash to bond payments and devised a system of gradually phasing stipends out by lowering the amount paid to each generation. Iwamura also recommended that the Home and Finance Ministries grant a stipend to nobles who did not yet have one, since they had lost many of their privileges after the kingdom's disposition. Home Minister Yamagata Aritomo and Finance Minister Matsukata Masayoshi agreed that "even though the nobility no longer officially have rights to the territory of the villages they have lost their profits and should be pitied."[29] They accepted all of Iwamura's recommendations saying: "As the governor has expressed, the unstipended nobility already received a monetary payment for their scattered lands but this was only a one-time gift . . . we should enact a cash stipend system for them so that they will also be able to receive payments for some time."[30]

The state's reaffirmation of its support of the former ruling elite can be linked directly to its geopolitical anxieties and reveals its continued difficulties in gaining total control of Okinawa. The state's growing tension with China over control of Korea was exacerbated by the activities of a group of the kingdom's former nobles called *dasshinnin*, who continued to reject the legitimacy of the Japanese government's annexation of their home.[31] In the years immediately following Matsuda Michiyuki's forceful takeover of Shuri castle, these disgruntled nobles had fled in droves to the Ryūkyū House in Fuzhou to plead with the Chinese government to oppose the Meiji government's takeover of the former kingdom. Many of them returned to Okinawa and spread rumors of the Chinese military's imminent arrival to restore the kingdom. A report describes the dangerous implications of this activity: "The prefecture's people believe that if China accepts these petitions, things will return to the old days. They believe that China is the strongest country on earth and believe that it, rather than Japan should rule over the prefecture."[32] The stability of the prefecture became of even greater concern following the Imo Mutiny of July 1882, in which Korean soldiers who killed their Japanese military advisor, Horimoto Reizō, set fire to the Japanese legation and forced the Japanese minister in residence out of Seoul.³³ Following a show of strength by the Chinese military in response to this action, middle-ranking members of the pro-Chinese, anti-Japanese faction of the former Ryūkyū kingdom's ruling elite defected to China in greater numbers.³⁴ When they arrived in Fuzhou, they made repeated appeals to the Chinese army to mount a military invasion of the prefecture.³⁵ Chinese troops never did set foot on Okinawan soil, but this flight of large numbers of influential members of the former kingdom forced the state to strengthen its relations with the pro-Japanese faction of the nobility and simultaneously beef up its policing of traitorous activities.³⁶ In these tumultuous times, Uesugi's concerns about the impoverishment of small cultivators in the countryside took a back seat to keeping local officials committed to maintaining peace in their communities.

The Sakishima Islands as Japan's Southern Fortress

It was in the midst of these serious concerns about the stability of the nation's southern borders that the two Sakishima island chains of Yaeyama and Miyako caught Home Minister Yamagata's attention.³⁷ Miyako's stability was especially vital, as it was a stopover point for anti-Japanese activists fleeing to China. Furthermore, it had been the site of the violent Sanshii Incident, which erupted immediately after Matsuda Michiyuki's storming of Shuri castle in 1879. In the Sanshii Incident, a former official of the kingdom named Shimoji Niya had been lynched by participants in the aforementioned blood oath movement for accepting a job as a translator in the new government.³⁸ The state had responded to this violence and other cases of resistance to Japanese rule by increasing the amount of surveillance in the prefecture, but the tension between the various factions of the former nobility, the peasantry, and resident merchants from mainland Japan never completely dissipated. In Miyako's case, because of its position as a point of transit between the main island of Okinawa and the Ryūkyū House in Fuzhou, the state was concerned that any small spark could quickly ignite a much larger geopolitical fire.

Thus, it vigilantly reaffirmed its Preservation Policy in Miyako. After 1879 local nobles and officials had retained their hereditary positions of power as the smallest units of state control in the prefecture and had served as bureaucrats working for the newly established island office in Hirara.³⁹ They also worked as supervisors, clerks, and tax collectors in all forty-one of Miyako's villages rather than as oyakata directly serving the kingdom government. In order to gain their cooperation, the state granted them concessions and rejected reform proposals that governors submitted, even when it was confronted with evidence that the Preservation Policy was obstructing the island's industrial development. As a result, like the rest of the prefecture, Miyako remained governed by a precapitalist mode of production in which "productive activity is subordinated to the reproduction of a particular form of life, and particular structures of subjectivity," even as it was incorporated into Japanese capitalist society.[40]

Due to the special land and tax systems of the kingdom era in Miyako its inhabitants lived under conditions slightly different from people on the main island of Okinawa. The main difference between Miyako's socioeconomic system and that of the main island during the early modern period was the absence on Miyako of the jiwari system and the taxation system based on yields that accompanied it.[41] In place of the land system that governed Okinawa Island, the system on Miyako guaranteed land rights based on ownership rather than use. Because land was considered the owner's personal property, landholders were allowed to make transactions involving lands that they did not cultivate themselves and were allowed to reclaim additional lands if they wanted to increase the scale of their productive activities. The amount of taxes that Miyako was assessed was based on surveys that were conducted on the island between 1611 and 1659. These surveys and investigations of yields clarified total annual production and allowed village lands to be classified according to their productivity and type. Once the tax assessment for the island had been finalized in 1659, it remained unchanged until the entire system was overhauled in 1903.[42]

Millet and woven cloth were the main method of tax payment in early modern Miyako.[43] Villages were divided into three broad categories, and lands in them used to grow millet and hemp were subdivided by grade. Taxpaying villagers were placed in one of six additional categories based on gender and age.[44] Annual tax obligations, levied as a poll tax (jintōzei) based on gender, age, and quality of lands cultivated were regressive, were not determined by land value, and did not fluctuate according to yield. Local village officials wielded a tremendous amount of power in this system because they were in charge of making annual assessments of households and adjusting them as family compositions and village tax responsibilities changed. They, their wives, their first and second sons, and the sick and the disabled were exempt from paying this tax; officials were also given discounts on supplementary taxes that they did pay in part.[45]

The poll tax obligations, supported by the broader socioeconomic system that exempted hereditary officials from payment and did not account for fluctuations in yield, made Miyako's small cultivators extremely vulnerable to external factors like natural disasters, population decline, and illness.[46] They also enabled local officials to take advantage of these vulnerabilities as usurers or large landowners who constantly required additional hands to work their fields. The privilege granted to local officials of collecting additional taxes in kind or in labor at their discretion restricted the ability of Miyako's small farming households to freely use their own surplus labor. This, as well as the lack of systematic mechanisms to ensure equitable redistribution of land, resulted in significant levels of differentiation by the end of the early modern period.[47] Two large landowning families, the Nakasones and Shirakawas, built huge manors in the Hirara region on the west coast of Miyako island during the early modern period and relied on a combination of tenants and serfs for agricultural production. These families compiled illustrious records of service to the kingdom's ruling families and for generations managed to parlay their local political influence into official posts. This gave them the resources necessary to accumulate large properties. By the end of the kingdom period, they collectively monopolized over half of all official posts on the island, 40 percent of paddy lands, 21 percent of fields, and 30 percent of mountain and forest land in the Nagama Ward of Hirara.[48]

These families also benefited from their right to have serfs and household servants called *naagu* on their lands to engage in cultivation and menial labor.[49] According to customary law in the kingdom era, highest-ranking officials were allowed eight naagu, and the lowest village officials were permitted at least one each.[50] Each serf was required to provide labor and a set quantity of millet and grains to his or her owner.[51] In return, owners were required to pay their serfs' taxes and public expenses. According to Shimajiri Katsutarō, the income that the highest officials who held eight naagu gained annually was 12 *koku*.[52] The removal of these men and women from the poll-tax roll increased the tax payments of other local residents. In addition to obtaining a set number of naagu as part of their salaries, many local officials purchased additional naagu to cultivate the lands that they were able to accumulate by virtue of their standing in the community. This system accelerated the degree of differentiation in Miyako's agrarian villages, which forced many new cultivators to indenture themselves to prominent households to escape the severe punishment that accompanied the nonpayment of taxes.[53]

The *yadobiki onna* was another privilege that local officials enjoyed during the kingdom era. This system granted officials who had business in other villages the right to stay at a well-to-do family's home and have them cover all expenses of the officials' stay in exchange for an exemption of the tax on woven cloth. The responsibility for providing these accommodations in a given year was decided by village residents through a rotating system. In addition to being burdened with the accommodation expenses for a year, the designated household was required to submit four barrels of millet to the village in exchange for its exemption from the tax.[54] Officials who benefited from the system considered the hospitality that they received from the household as part of their compensation and did not hesitate to make requests above and beyond what was required for a comfortable stay.[55]

As a result of the preservation of these types of kingdom-era concessions to local officials, tax-paying, self-sufficient cultivators were obliged to donate the majority of their produce and time to state representatives even after Shō Tai was dethroned. They continued to cultivate millet and grains under heavy official surveillance and societal pressure resulting from their embeddedness in the five-household division (*goningumi*) system.[56] Their daily toil began at dawn, at which time they had to arrive at a checkpoint and sign their names on a wooden tag before departing to their fields. Lashings for tardiness and absences were commonplace. During the period of tax submissions, members of the five households were expected to take responsibility for their fellow members if any of them were unable to fulfill their tax obligations.[57]

The monitoring of millet cultivation that Miyako's cultivators endured was mild in comparison to the conditions under which weaving women toiled to fulfill their cloth tax obligations, which composed over 65 percent of the total taxes levied in Miyako. Local officials were particularly vigilant about their surveillance of cloth production because it was Miyako's high-value contribution to the kingdom's tribute payment to the Satsuma domain. Each part of the production process, beginning with the cultivation of hemp and indigo and continuing with the thread spinning process and dyeing, was closely monitored. Weaving took place in small huts that were constructed in every village to enable officials to monitor quality. Women were selected each year to engage in the all-important task of transforming thread into the patterned dark blue woven cloth that was highly prized in Japan.[58] In contrast to the beautiful textiles that they produced, the women worked in abysmal conditions, locked in poorly ventilated, cramped, dark huts and hounded by local officials who used their position to take advantage of them. The numerous folk songs (*ayagū*) lamenting the trials of weaving remain as records of the conditions that Miyako's female weavers endured.

The anger of fathers who could not prevent officials from violating daughters' chastity and the relief that weavers felt when their textiles passed the rigorous official inspections were expressed in song; the music still bears witness to the bodily and psychological violence that these women braced themselves for when they were selected for the prestigious post of a village weaver for the year.[59]

Thus, although household tax obligations were determined by family composition, the production of both millet and woven cloth was necessarily communal, as single households no matter how large could not complete all of the tasks required to produce a tax item without working in concert with their neighbors. In the case of millet, individual households engaged in cultivation and harvesting, but the tasks of grinding, barrel making, and transport required cooperation with producers beyond the family unit. The communal nature of production was even more conspicuous in the case of cloth production, which involved at least ten different tasks, including the cultivation of hemp, the production of raw thread, the cultivation of indigo for the dye, the actual dyeing process, the threading of the loom, weaving, processing, washing, wrapping, and transport. Even though weavers were carefully selected from each village to weave intensively at the village hut, the existence of all these other tasks meant that it was impossible to fulfill individual quotas without the assistance of others. Local officials were ultimately responsible for making sure that these complicated processes of production were completed by the time that submissions were due. The pressures that they placed on the village community to ensure that its annual contributions were fully met provoked numerous struggles against taxation levels during the early modern period.[60] As we will see in the next section, the antagonisms between local officials and cultivators that stemmed from the tax-collecting power granted to local officials from the kingdom era were compounded by new challenges that threatened the livelihood of Miyako's residents beginning in the mid-1880s.

The China Threat, Declining Sugar Prices, and New Antagonisms

If the political advantages of maintaining the archaisms of the kingdom era led the Meiji state to provide significant concessions to the former nobles even at the expense of industrial development in the decade following annexation, economic and geopolitical considerations forced it to contemplate reform in Okinawa during the late 1880s. After its own deflationary policies in the 1880s lowered sugar prices on the Osaka market, for example, the state began reconsidering the preserved taxation system that allowed it to collect surplus sugar at low prices.[61] Between 1883 and 1891, the market price of sugar averaged 3 yen 10 sen per *picul*, while the price that the state offered the peasants was 4 yen.[62] A policy that was meant to secure cheap sugar cane for the state inadvertently became a protectionist policy as a result of domestic market fluctuations.

In addition to the Preservation Policy's growing unprofitability, the transformation of the government's overall policy toward Okinawa was intimately linked to shifting geopolitical concerns. Negotiations with China over splitting the former kingdom between the two states were officially terminated in February 1883.[63] Once these talks broke down, the focus of both Japan and China shifted to strengthening their respective degrees of influence in the Korean peninsula.[64] Japanese leaders believed that war with China over Korea was inevitable and concentrated on building up the military in preparation for this imminent conflict. By 1886 a quarter of all government expenditures went to military spending, in preparation for this confrontation.[65] In conjunction with this militarization, the Mitsui Trading Company (Mitsui Bussan) began looking for suitable coal-mining areas off the coast of the main island of Okinawa and eventually identified a prime location on Iriomote Island, part of the Yaeyama group and just under 100 miles southwest of the Miyako Islands.[66] From the moment of this discovery, the Sakishima islands of Miyako (figure 2.1) and Yaeyama also became important strategic bases because they housed ports near China that could be used for refueling, restocking, and repairing warships. The existence of valuable raw materials brought large flows of mainland capital, surveyors, mapmakers, and government officials to the southern boundaries of the empire.

These developments in the military, strategic, and economic realms forced the state to expand its target of concern from local officials to all residents of the islands. Impending international conflict required that islanders quickly internalize their identity as subjects of the Japanese nation-state. An early political measure that reflected these concerns was a request in November 1884 by Nishimura Sutezō, Okinawa's fourth governor, to Finance Minister Matsukata and Home Minister Yamagata for funds to place an island office, official, and doctor on each of the Sakishima Islands.[67] In his request, Nishimura implicitly grappled with the question of how the islands, including their populations, could be transformed into bastions of strength that could withstand external forces that threatened the borders of the nation-state. He also requested funds to increase the police presence

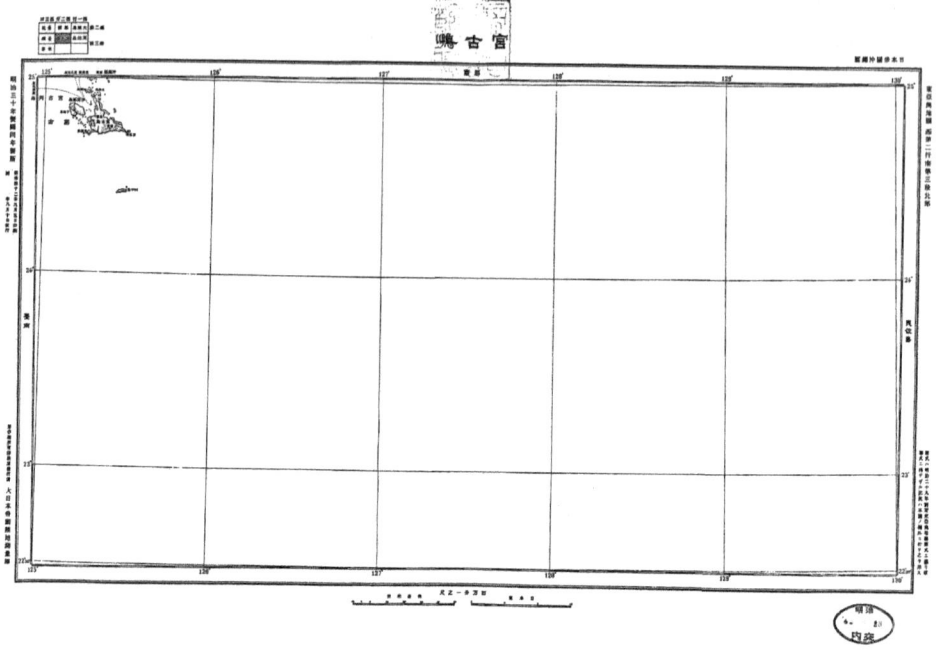

Fig. 2.1 This map was created in 1909 based on an 1896 survey by the Japanese army. The positioning of Miyako in the top lefthand corner of the map and the vast ocean that covers the rest indicates the islands' strategic value in the empire-building process. Miyako Island, Japanese Empire, Okinawa Prefecture, National Diet Library, reference number YG837–76.

on the islands and to dispatch officials from the prefectural administration to investigate conditions on the ground. Yamagata approved both of Nishimura's proposals, noting: "Many things must be considered, especially since the islands are not far from Taiwan."[68] The fact that additional funds were approved at a time of fiscal retrenchment and the slashing of government funds for local expenses on the mainland reveals the strategic importance of the Sakishima Islands in this transformed geopolitical context. The impending war with China also solidified the Japanese state's desire to keep these islands exclusively for itself, though it had been willing to part with them just a few years earlier in exchange for more favorable treaty terms.[69] Foreign Minister Inoue Kaoru confirmed the new importance of the Sakishima Islands to Consul Enomoto Takeaki in a letter dated May 16, 1885: "Time of treaty revision with China which was one of the conditions of the (Ryūkyū) settlement has already long expired; moreover as Europian

Fig. 2.2 This illustration was made in commemoration of a meeting of representatives from eight prefectures, including Okinawa, in order to promote industry and to introduce each region's main industries. Sugar was a main focus of this meeting. Seventh Kyushu-Okinawa 8 Prefectures Mutual Promotion Alliance (1888), National Diet Library, reference number YG913–2329.

[sic] colonial policy is beginning very strong and aggressive in the direction of Asia. We do not wish to surrender the islands, which are of very great geographical importance and also one of them produces coal."[70]

The project of strengthening pro-Japanese sentiment on the Sakishima Islands began with the implementation of economic reforms. A series of reclamation projects that focused on the development of the sugar industry became the main pillars of this strategy (figure 2.2). In a move that echoed the early Meiji promotion of reclamation projects in Hokkaido for former samurai, starting in the mid-1880s, prefectural authorities launched projects that granted loans and subsidies to groups from inside and outside of Okinawa that were interested in clearing and developing uncultivated lands on the Sakishima Islands to construct sugar manufacturing factories.[71] Many elements of the Preservation Policy impeded the realization of these new goals.

The precursor to the start of reclamation projects in the Sakishima Islands was a 3,800-yen loan that the central government made to the people of the Miyako and Yaeyama Islands in 1886 to cultivate sugar cane.[72] This loan was immediately followed by approval for the Yaeyama reclamation project, which was headed by members of the former royal family and which

THE MIYAKO ISLAND PEASANTRY MOVEMENT

brought former nobles and commoners from the main island of Okinawa to manufacture sugar. The prefectural administration granted these families 5,000 *tsubo* of previously uncultivated land in nine villages in return for promises that after three years they would begin paying the state a small fee in kind as rent.[73] They were expected to settle in the villages and use the labor of local cultivators to complete the hard work of transforming fallow lands into productive cane fields.[74] Deeming the sparsely populated, fertile lands of Sakishima to be perfectly suited to the development of a modern sugar industry, the prefecture dispatched technicians and agricultural specialists to these islands starting in the mid-1880s to support these projects.[75] Along with its encouragement of reclamation projects, the government officially lifted the kingdom era's planting restrictions in December 1888. Sugar cane was cultivated for the first time on Miyako Island in that year.[76]

This transformed position of Okinawa and the Sakishima Islands in the expanding Japanese empire brought forth new antagonisms in Miyako in the late 1880s. The electrical charges on the island built up in the years preceding the Miyako Island Peasantry Movement as local officials continued to enrich themselves, while the peasants continued to suffer under the weight of the poll taxes and unofficial obligations to local officials. Life in Miyako under the Preservation Policy became increasingly intolerable as the newly reformist prefectural government enthusiastically mandated modernizing policies that required ever-expanding contributions from taxpayers to help build schools, improve roads, and establish a police system.[77] Miyako's tax-paying residents, who by 1893 were being assessed just under two yen per person per year when millet payments were converted into cash equivalents, shouldered the additional costs of establishing the institutions of modern society.[78] These changes made the existing system of village administration intolerable for many of Miyako's cultivators.[79] Their financial strain can clearly be seen in the years leading up to the Miyako Island Peasantry Movement, as defaults on loans totaled 3,389 koku of millet between the years 1880 and 1891 for an average of 308 koku per year, then skyrocketed to 1,645 koku in 1892 alone, and were 778 koku in 1893.[80] Entrepreneurs who came to the Sakishima Islands—advertised as places of limitless opportunity—from Okinawa and beyond played a major part in exacerbating the burdens of local cultivators but would also be their main allies in the effort to abolish the Preservation Policy.[81]

Gusukuma Seian, a bureaucrat in the prefectural administration and a sugar industry technician, was dispatched to the island from Naha in 1884 in order to teach the peasantry how to produce sugar using modern techniques.

His arrival stoked the fire whose heat small cultivators were already feeling. Gusukuma traveled to different villages and instructed peasants on proper ways to plant sugar cane and presided over the construction of a model factory that would manufacture white sugar.[82] Despite his tireless promotion of cane cultivation, Gusukuma found that the total amount of sugar cane that the peasants brought to the factories to manufacture was much smaller than he anticipated. He discovered that cultivators were discarding the sugar cane after they harvested it because they saw no advantage to bringing it in for manufacture, though they had spent months growing it. They knew that local officials would take the profits that they made from manufacturing sugar away as payment for the use of communally owned tools and viewed Gusukuma's instructions as only increasing their already unbearable burdens.[83] Recognizing that the industry he was so committed to nurturing in Miyako was adding to the suffering of those he had come to help, Gusukuma resigned from his post but remained on the island to cultivate cane on his own lands.[84] It was after he began to manufacture sugar in the Shimoji District of Kadekari Village that he came into contact with Kawamitsu Kamekichi, a midsize landowner from the area who came to play a major organizational role in the movement.[85]

Gusukuma also found an enthusiastic ally for his efforts to alleviate the burdens of small producers in a young entrepreneur from Niigata Prefecture, Nakamura Jussaku. He arrived in Miyako for the first time on November 1892 for a decidedly unrevolutionary objective—to explore the possibility of developing a freshwater pearl fishing business on the island.[86] Like many mainland visitors to Okinawa, Nakamura was excited by the economic prospects that existed in this still unexplored corner of Japan, and he believed that these islands—still relatively free of large capitalists against whom he could not dream of competing—held the key to his fortune.[87] Nakamura met Gusukuma aboard a ship traveling from Naha to Miyako. The two men became fast friends and met frequently to discuss the prospects for the development of industry on Miyako. Gusukuma introduced Nakamura to Yoshimura Kidahiro, the head of the island office and highest-ranking Meiji bureaucrat on Miyako, who had long been opposed to the privileges that local officials continued to enjoy.[88] Their continued presence in Miyako's society was the cause, Yoshimura lamented, of the failure of previous attempts at industrial development.

This conversation with Yoshimura prompted Nakamura to invite Gusukuma to travel with him to Naha in December 1892 to submit a petition to the eighth governor of the prefecture, Narahara Shigeru, calling for a reform of these outdated systems.⁸⁹ The two friends found a sympathetic ear in the governor, who had just been appointed to his post in July. Unlike his predecessor, Maruoka, who took a pragmatic approach to reforming the Preservation Policy, Narahara was a fierce proponent of modernization.⁹⁰ After considering Nakamura and Gusukuma's pleas, he ordered Yoshimura to conduct thorough investigations and submit a detailed report about the conditions on the island.

In a report that he sent to Sasamori Gisuke—a politician and explorer discussed below—in July 1893, Yoshimura blamed the "despotic and cruel old maladies" for the people's suffering. In particular, he identified the poll tax as the main impediment to the growth of industry and education in the region. Yoshimura recommended the immediate abolition of this system of taxation and its replacement with a fairer method based on land yield.⁹¹ He made the case that abolishing the old method of tax collection and outmoded systems of privilege for local officials could transform Miyako into a modern sugar-producing region. Without these changes, he warned, "the civilian industries will not develop, education will not improve and the economy will continue to worsen each year."⁹²

After reading Yoshimura's report, Governor Narahara issued an order on March 18, 1893, that abolished the naagu, yadobiki onna, and okagemai systems of privilege; reformed the system of hereditary succession in official posts; and formed budget deliberation councils that included representatives of the peasantry to prevent corruption in the villages.⁹³ It is important to note here that Narahara's orders were revolutionary for Miyako but were in line with the direction that the Meiji government had intended for Okinawa as a whole since the late 1880s.⁹⁴ Narahara's own interest in enacting reforms on Miyako was linked to his desire to push forth his pet project, large-scale reclamations on the island for the development of the sugar industry.⁹⁵

Local officials responded with outrage and complete refusal to comply. Ichiki Kitokurō, who was dispatched by the Home Ministry to investigate conditions on the island two years later, reported on the chaos that ensued following Narahara's orders: "When the office head relayed the governor's order of this partial reform of old customs through an internal order, the noble officials were extremely angered and held many meetings. They went to the island office and submitted a mass resignation. Some of them cut down the trees in the forests and threatened the policemen and schoolchildren to stop them from going to work and school. This kind of disharmonious activity was rampant and people were also instructed not to sell any eggs or vegetables to visitors from the mainland."⁹⁶ They brought the island's administration to a screeching halt, and Narahara had no choice but to back down and rescind his order for reform. It was still not possible to govern the island without the cooperation of local officials. Yoshimura resigned from his post in protest and was replaced by an official sympathetic to the interests of the former nobles.[97]

Miyako Peasantry's Responses to Governor Narahara's Course Reversal

The wholesale rejection of Narahara's orders by local officials, their destruction of communal property, and the forced resignation of Yoshimura intensified the tensions that had been festering on Miyako for generations. Yet another apparent victory for the traditional elite, this time even in the face of the prefectural administration's calls for change, electrified the island. Residents of Bora, Fukuzato, and Aragusuku in Uruka Village on the eastern side of the island immediately banded together to petition for Yoshimura's reappointment.[98] Sasamori recorded the tensions that he encountered on the island during his two visits to Miyako in early July and late August 1893 in his tour diary, *Nantō Tanken (Exploration of the Southern Islands)*.[99] He recalled seeing hundreds of officials and commoners gather at the main office in Uruka for meetings and debates about how to respond to the recent turn of events.[100] He also presented a useful background for the current round of disputes by listing a few of the earlier orders that Yoshimura had signed and implemented. One proclamation, dated September 3, 1892, stated his intention to abolish physical punishments such as lashings and implement a system of fines in rice instead. It also stated the intentions of the island office to confiscate the *ashiguruma*, a punishment device similar to the cangue that was used to punish defaulters.[101] Another one of Yoshimura's proclamations, dated August 17, 1892, stated that to avoid a complete stoppage of work by the peasantry, a better system of reporting local officials who did not submit the millet that they collected as taxes would be implemented. This was in response to the villagers' formation of an alliance to refuse the payment of taxes the previous year because they thought that assessments were unfairly high.[102] The inspector who served as Sasamori's guide during his second trip to the island in late August lamented that they continued to have difficulties collecting taxes because villagers kept returning the wooden tags that the island office sent them that indicated the tax they owed for the year.[103]

In analyzing the unfolding of the Miyako Island Peasantry Movement, it is vital to distinguish among the interests of its most visible leaders,

Nakamura and Gusukuma—who, like Yoshimura, sympathized with the suffering of Miyako's peasantry but had broader goals of industrial development; local village representatives like Taira Mōshi, Nishizato Gama, and Kawamitsu, whose motivations were much more complex and who shared the leaders' desires for modernization; and the majority of the movement's participants, whose interests are much more difficult to decipher because of the paucity of written sources. It is especially important to avoid conflating the material interests of the leaders of the movement from inside and outside of Miyako with the multiple desires of the island's small peasantry—the majority who held less than one chōbu of land and bore the heavy labor, millet, and cloth obligations to the state—that led them to remove themselves from the community in a way that rendered its continued existence impossible. The cultivators made a risky decision to sign their names to petitions, make donations, and participate in secret meetings against village society as it was controlled by local officials; we might read these actions as outward manifestations of their desire to "destroy whatever mutilates life," to use Deleuze's words.[104] The hopes they placed on the abolition of the old system should not be seen as a result of their naive belief that the abolition of the old system would lead directly to a better life. Instead, they are best understood as a reflection of the cultivators' desire to be freed from the ties in their neighborhoods that continued to restrict their ability to make decisions about how they would reproduce their own lives. Their decision to separate themselves from the community was less a reflection of their acceptance of incorporation into a new regime of exploitation but a realization that the old one could not offer them what was required to sustain their lives. It mattered little to them that both old and new regimes were controlled by the Meiji state. What they knew for certain was that the old hegemons had been replaced and that there was little justification for power holders of the kingdom era to remain in power, especially since they could no longer claim to provide valuable protections and services in return for all that they demanded.[105]

As we have already seen, conditions in Miyako between the end of 1892 and the spring of 1893 contained the seeds of unresolvable tension. After seeing Governor Narahara forced to back down from his reform policies and witnessing angry local officials ravage the communal lands that the entire community depended on for firewood, Miyako's small cultivators decided to submit a petition directly to the National Diet. The demands that they articulated in this petition explain why they decided to reject the Miyako community as the Meiji state preserved it.[106]

This petition, planned for submission to the December 1893 session of the National Diet, was signed by "commoner-peasants" Nishizato Gama and Taira Mōshi, representatives of the peasantry from Fukuzato and Bora Villages who were thirty-eight and thirty-five years old at the time. By addressing the National Diet, Miyako's peasants inserted their demands into a discursive sphere from which they had hitherto been excluded.[107] The petition vividly described the existence of two castes on the island, and how the gap between them had widened following the dissolution of the kingdom:

> There is a huge gap between the nobility and the commoners. On this island, the officials among the nobility leisurely dance and sing about. On the other hand, the people who have to pay the salaries of these officials work all the time without any time to even eat or sleep. They cultivate [the land] in order to pay taxes. They eat sweet potato and narrowly escape starvation. They do not know the taste of millet and the majority of them do not get to eat soybean paste . . . at times, one family shares a single kimono throughout the year . . . some islanders could not endure the heavy burden of taxation and fled to Yaeyama to hide deep in the forests.[108]

To close the gulf that separated commoner from nobility and Miyako residents from their mainland counterparts, petitioners demanded three reforms: the reduction of taxes, the abolition of the poll tax and the enactment of a land tax in its stead, and the abolition of tax payments in kind in favor of payments in cash.[109] These changes had already been requested several years earlier but had not been accepted by the prefectural administration.[110]

The section of the petition that called for the reduction of taxes placed as much importance on the unofficial, customary expenses that Miyako's residents were required to shoulder as on the high rate of official taxation.[111] That is, in addition to the approximately two yen per person that Miyako's cultivators paid in taxes and expenses each year, they also had to bear quite a bit more in unofficial payments. For example, islanders were obligated to personally deliver items ranging from firewood to fish to the houses of local officials on request. In addition, officials routinely used emergency funds, also regularly collected from taxpayers, for personal rather than communal emergencies.[112] By including these burdens in their petition, Miyako's peasants made it clear that they were demanding their liberation from years of living under the thumb of self-serving officials, who used communal funds to line their own pockets and demanded they be given products on a whim with no concern for the rhythms of life or financial conditions of those they governed. The profound disconnect between the officials—who, in the words of the petition, danced and sang without a care in the world—and the peasants who toiled in the fields and dark weaving rooms just to keep up with their payments produced a deep resentment that could not be settled through simple economic relief measures.

The determination of Miyako's small peasantry to separate from this community of indignity and to construct a new one was further expressed in the actions they took to make sure that their representatives Taira, Nishizato, Gusukuma, and Nakamura got to Tokyo to submit the petition. Their actions indicate the difficulty of untangling the moment of destruction from the moment of construction and remind us to take seriously Althusser's concept of immanent causality, that "all effects are equally and at the same time causes."[113] It was through the act of separation or refusal that Miyako's peasants discovered and articulated a politics and a discourse of the new. In many ways, they constructed a common will through their decision to cast their lot with Gusukuma, Nakamura, and the modern Japanese state in its ideal form; their selection of representatives from each of the three villages to travel to Tokyo; their attempts to draft their own demands; and the measures they took, including taking barrels of millet from their village granaries in order to procure funds to enable their representatives to make it to Tokyo.[114] This forging of a strategic alliance was precisely an act of constituent power rising up against the specific method of primitive accumulation that the Japanese state had required the majority of the island's residents to endure since 1879. Miyako's small producers had decided to make public their rejection of the existing relations of power. The struggle that resulted from this action and the collective common that they organized created crisis conditions for Japanese capitalism that the state had to resolve if Miyako was to continue functioning as a differentiated ground of primitive accumulation and strategic stronghold against competing imperialist powers.[115]

Peasantry representatives also held meetings in each village and continued to draft their own petitions for submission to the upcoming Diet session. They collected small donations of two to three sen from peasant households and secured agreements from them to suspend payment on the part of the tax payments that they deemed unreasonable. The fact that thirty-five of the forty-one villages consented to this financial arrangement should not be taken lightly and can be read as the villagers' collective rejection of the entire social structure that enabled excessive and arbitrary taxation by traditional power holders and demanded that cultivators simply produce and stay out of the realm of politics.[116]

The organizers' success in gaining the agreement of peasant households to default on at least part of their tax payments—not as a consequence of their inability to pay but as an act of refusal—should not be underestimated. In Miyako, the traditional power holders' grip on society was strong enough to shock the Meiji government into reversing its policies, and nonpayment had regularly resulted in the abandonment of home and flight to other islands for fear of incurring the customary punishments of flogging and ostracization. In this case, cultivators' refusal to provide the resources necessary for the functioning of the island's administration and for the reproduction of its mode of production created a condition of profound crisis. Even more significant than the material crisis that ensued from the peasants' refusal to pay their taxes was the crisis that resulted from their collective recognition that they were the main producers of surplus in their communities. This recognition—that the people who were considered their rulers could only remain as such by collecting and appropriating what they produced—was revolutionary when it linked up to small producers' decision to mobilize for change.

The Construction of a New Community in Miyako

The Miyako peasantry's joy—a most dangerous emotion from the point of view of those in power—on discovering their collective desire and ability to destroy the conditions that were responsible for the mutilation of their lives is revealed most clearly in the song that they sang for their comrades when they departed for Tokyo to submit the petition to the National Diet. Gathering in the middle of October 1893 at the port of Harimizu, on the northwestern side of the island, the peasants held back local officials who had gathered to block their departure and sent their representatives off to Naha with a performance of a work titled "Jintōzei Haishi no Kuichā" ("Song for the Abolition of the Poll Tax").[117]

In contrast to other forms of artistic expression such as the ayagū, Miyako's *kuichā* is explicitly a communal form of expression: the hands make the beat, the feet stomp, and the participants dance together in a circle. It is a powerful and dynamic performance, with rhythmical calls interspersed throughout the song. There are many different varieties, some calling for rain and others for good harvest, and still others performed by village youth simply for entertainment. Despite their differences in content, what is key about this form is that it is a communal act, mainly performed by the peasantry and designed to be heard by others.[118] Several hundred supporters who gathered at Harimizu to see their representatives off sang, danced, and conducted demonstrations all the way to the horse track located on the outskirts of Hirara Village.[119]

"Jintōzei Haishi no Kuichā" consisted of four verses. The first reconfirmed the leadership role of Taira, from Bora Village. It introduced him and the others who had taken on the mission of lightening the suffering of Miyako's peasants by getting rid of the poll tax system. The second verse expressed the hopes that once this system was abolished, Miyako's economy would prosper and the white sands of Harimizu, where they stood to bid farewell to their representatives, would turn into millet and rice. They would be freed of a life of eating a soup made out of potatoes and potato leaves boiled in a drop of soy sauce every day and would be able to consume the millet that they cultivated whenever they desired. This verse also expressed their hopes of being freed from a life of having one kimono made out of banana-fiber cloth in the summer and an *awase*—a kimono with a second lining sewed into the main one for warmth—in the winter months.[120] The third verse introduced another source of their suffering that has largely been neglected in studies of the movement—the cloth tax. It expressed the hope that the women of Miyako's villages would be liberated by the abolition of the tax system from the hard and tedious work of weaving cloth to fulfill a significant quota of woven cloth as part of the tax obligations in kind. The women who were responsible for this part of the contribution would then be freed from the dark and cramped prison-like rooms in which they wove thread into patterns that resembled the waves that hit the shores of Ōgimi Island—the first of Miyako's islands that could be seen by travelers from Okinawa's capital, Naha—without once having laid eyes on its beauty. Once freed from the cloth tax obligations, these young women would no longer be subject to sexual advances from officials who took advantage of the dark shadows that were cast in the bamboo-covered rooms to impose their will onto them.[121] The final verse also exemplified the peasantry's desire not just to alleviate their tax burdens but to break free of the system that restricted their range of possibilities. It expressed the hope that they would prosper after the abolition of the poll tax system because they would then be allowed to convert some of their paddies and fields—now impossible because of their tax and tribute obligations and because of state-imposed restrictions on land use—into pastureland to raise horses and cattle.[122] Their broader desire for freedom of movement and the freedom of deciding how they wanted to spend their time is revealed in this song and made them, not the officials of the islands, the subjects who were allowed to sing and dance. As such, this was a highly subversive performance whose visceral effects were deeply etched into the memories of the men and women who saw their representatives off at Harimizu port. It immediately transformed all participants from objects of representation into actors in the struggle.

Once Taira, Nishizato, Gusukuma, and Nakamura reached Naha, they still had to figure out how to fund their long trip to Tokyo. Even after selling their paddies and cattle and borrowing more money, they still did not have enough to pay for their travel and accommodations in the nation's capital. The grain warehouse guards of two villages, Uruka Kin and Ikemura Yama, proposed that they convert the millet stored in the warehouses into cash to finance the rest of their trip. Yamashita Shigekazu reports that sixty-eight people gathered at the doors of the warehouses to carry out this risky plan. They entered the warehouses that safeguarded the villagers' millet submissions in barrels stacked to the ceiling and took out barrel after barrel.[123] After just a few days, the money for the trip had been raised and the four men were able to get on a ship to Tokyo. They arrived on November 3, 1893, just one month before to the fifth National Diet sessions scheduled for December.[124] As for the guards back in Miyako, they were taken to the police station and questioned, but they were freed after insisting that they had only removed the grain from the warehouse because they were hungry.

The peasants' song and the lengths they went to in order to ensure their representatives' safe passage to Tokyo clearly shows that despite the formal petition's reliance on quantitative measures to show the peasants' collective suffering, the movement was much more than the sum of its material demands. It was a call for their liberation from the structural conditions that kept them tied to their lands, kept them from having any say in what type of work they engaged in, and gave local officials complete control over the way that communal resources were allocated. The movement constituted a complete rejection of the way that peasants' daily lives were regulated by the power structure that the Meiji state maintained on the island and was simultaneously a demand that peasants too be allowed to prosper from the surplus that they produced as a community.

Reterritorializing Miyako's Event as an Okinawan Problem

As Read reminds us, a serious consideration of Althusser's notion of immanent causality alerts us to the fact that the dissolution of an old mode of production simultaneously entails the production of a new one. A key part of the process of construction of the new is the inscription of intelligibility or unity onto the disparate and multivalent acts that dissolved the old in order to transform it into a prehistory of the present. Read notes the significance of the breakdown of old relations by saying that "they retroactively become the conditions of the capitalist mode of production."[125] It goes without saying that the antagonisms between actors that is central to the process of dissolving the old mode of production and producing a new one risk being forgotten as they become neatly dissolved into the homogeneous empty time of the past.[126]

A similar process of dissolution was guaranteed to take place in the case of the Miyako Island Peasantry Movement, which sought a formal resolution in the halls of the National Diet. It may have succeeded only because Diet members saw the peasants' petitions as calls for modernization and accelerated inclusion into the capitalist mode of production—not as a serious refusal of the state's policies. Indeed, the petitions do raise the question of the difference between Okinawa and the mainland. For example, the first petition demonstrated the unreasonable suffering of Miyako's peasantry by comparing tax requirements on the island with those in mainland prefectures: "We are the people of Okinawa prefecture and even today, we are levied a poll tax and have to submit our taxes in kind. The average tax rate is over two yen per person, and unlike the mainland we are in the depths of impoverishment."[127] The petition explained that commoners remained extremely poor because officials were allowed through their customary power to levy arbitrary taxes on the peasantry while they were exempt from tax payments and received relatively large salaries. The result for the peasants was that "their clothes, food, and living quarters are of very poor quality, and their conditions were no different from the beggars in the mainland."[128] The petition implored the Meiji government to reform these miserable conditions because the lives that the people were forced to lead were unfitting of their status as imperial subjects of Japan.

This appeal to fairness, progress, and the elimination of the nobility's feudal rights was attractive to the mainland newspapers, which widely covered the petition movement after the peasants' representatives arrived in Tokyo.[129] The sympathetic coverage of Miyako's plight in the major national newspapers forced the government to dispatch officials to conduct onsite investigations; it also won the peasantry staunch allies in both the Lower House and House of Peers who advocated their cause in subsequent Diet sessions. Again, the significance of the petition was that its language forced mainland actors to consider the island's difference not as a given but as an issue that had to be addressed as a problem of the national body, because the representatives unambiguously identified themselves as the people (*jinmin*) of Miyako Island, Okinawa Prefecture, Japan. Ironically, this strategy assured the reintegration of the movement into the process of the Meiji state's extension of the capitalist mode of production to further reaches and in greater intensity throughout the archipelago, with its attendant narrative of Okinawan feudality and backwardness.

The temporary convergence of the interests of supportive members of the National Diet and of the movement was a powerful driver of change, but it also risked translating the variegated desires of Miyako's peasantry that were performed so powerfully at Harimizu into a sterile and rational demand for the transformation of a backward system that was suffocating them economically. This intersection of interests was also the point at which the particular demands of the peasants of Miyako's thirty-five villages were rearticulated into calls to transform all of Okinawa into a new type of ground for capital accumulation. Furthermore, the deliberations that took place in the Diet beginning in May 1894 marked an attempt to conceal the violence of primitive accumulation that was inflicted on Miyako and Okinawa since the Ryūkyū kingdom's annexation in 1872 and turned the suffering and impoverishment in those regions into a moral cause that required paternalistic intervention.

For Soga Sukenori of the House of Peers, one of the Diet's most enthusiastic supporters of the petition, the demands from Miyako provided a convenient way to segue into discussing the problems that he saw in the Meiji government's policies for the whole of Okinawa Prefecture. At the eighth National Diet sessions, held in January 1895, he submitted his "Okinawa Kensei Kaikaku Kengian" ("Proposal to Reform Okinawa's Prefectural System"). This can be considered a supplement to the Miyako petitions, which he fully supported, and placed the Miyako movement in the broader context of prefectural reform. After explaining the strategic importance of the islands for fortifying the defense of the Japanese empire, Soga described the pitiable conditions that existed not just in Miyako but throughout the prefecture: "I do not think that the forty million people [of Japan] are aware that these kinds of people, who are not able to eat grains, but have to subsist on seaweed, exist in a corner of Japan. This is like the conditions of Kikaijima in the *Tale of Heike*. That such conditions exist in the era of Meiji is deplorable. Industry does not develop, land is not cultivated, and propriety and decorum do not exist. The ignorant masses thus remain.... This is no different from the rule under the old Ryūkyū kingdom era."[130] He implored his fellow politicians to wake up to the serious consequences of keeping the

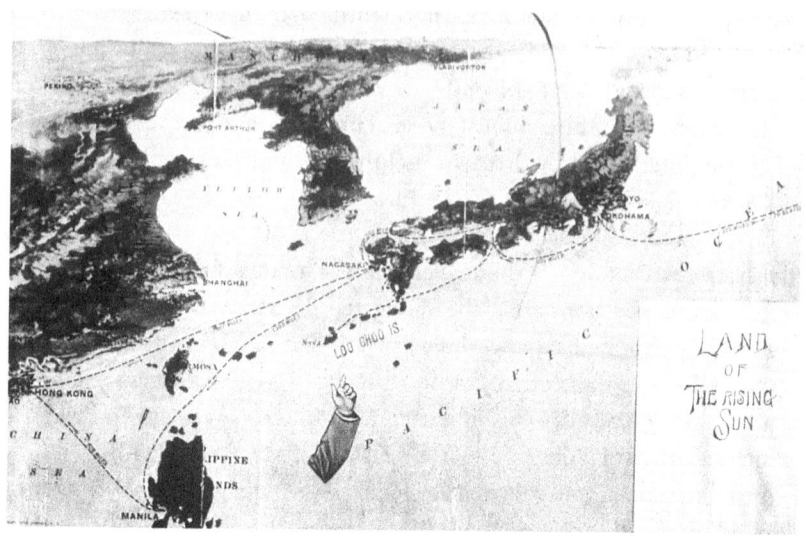

Fig. 2.3 This Taisho-era map clearly designates Okinawa as part of the "Land of the Rising Sun." Map of Japan and Loo Choo, E. R. Bull's photographic plates, no. 63, Taisho era, Bull Collection, University of the Ryūkyūs.

people of Okinawa in such conditions: "You must open your eyes right now and look across the Pacific. You will see Europe. They eye the small islands and will fight and divide them up. It is not a good policy to keep these important islands, which have been under our jurisdiction for ages, the way they are . . . they will soon become necessary for mounting expeditions and fortifying defenses"[131] (see figure 2.3).

In the National Diet, the figure of the impoverished peasant of Miyako Island became a symbol of the cruelty of the Ryūkyū kingdom's ruling elite toward the people of Okinawa as a whole. Rather than exposing the enormous strains borne specifically by Miyako's cultivators, debates in the Diet allowed Governor Narahara to emerge as a hero who would rescue all of Okinawa's people from the cruel and barbaric rule of former kingdom elites. In the process, the Miyako Island petitioners' specific objectives were obscured. The movement's tidy resolution provided a way for the state to conduct reforms that it desired in the name of fulfilling the Okinawan people's calls for modernization and reconfirming its position as a conferrer of blessings equally on all people of the Japanese nation-state. Any discrepancies that remained between Okinawa and other prefectures could be explained away as the result of the Okinawans' unpreparedness for reforms.

Conclusion: Forest Fires and What Escapes Reterritorialization

Seen from the point of view of capital, the Miyako peasants' call for the transformation of their society in a manner productive for capital and their eventual transformation into workers with only their labor power to sell was a convenient convergence of interests. However, instead of dismissing their demands for change as an act that ended up accelerating their self-exploitation, I have argued in favor of distinguishing between different encounters that only in hindsight appear to be part of a singular process.[132] Seen in this light, their demands were significant because they expanded the category of Okinawa beyond the non-nobility strata. The National Diet's acceptance and approval of these petitions granted legitimacy to the commoners' action of invoking the Okinawan people's collective interests. Furthermore, though it is tempting to downplay the historical significance of the movement because it did not yield immediate results in the island and seemed consistent with the Meiji state's reformist line, the petitions of Miyako's activists brought to light the violence that the former ruling elite inflicted on Okinawa's commoners and the contradictions of the Meiji state's economic policies. The state, as we have seen, had no incentive to reveal or rectify these injustices and was content to exacerbate them as long it was able to fill its own coffers.

Even more than simply expanding the category of Okinawa in the eyes of state actors, the Miyako Island Peasantry Movement was a call to dissolve existing social relations and reflected a desire to construct new ones. These twin calls for destruction and creation must be seen as separate from the process of the constitution of a new mode of production in Okinawa. Instead of seeing the Miyako small peasantry's calls for policies as consistent with the interests of Japanese capitalism, it is necessary to understand their decision to separate themselves from the old community as being born out of conditions of crisis—both material and subjective—that simultaneously became a moment of creative construction. The determination by a small group of cultivators to destroy the existing society that threatened their ability to express their own desires must be recognized as immanent to the process of capitalist development in Japan.

We see the legacies of this attempt to articulate and propose an alternative to systems and relations that mutilated their lives in the Miyako peasants' battles against the disposal of their communal lands (*somayama*) in the first decade of the twentieth century. Just as cultivators fought in the 1880s against local officials who used communal expenses for personal profit and took back the grains that they had submitted as taxes to fund their representatives' travels, small producers fought during the land reorganization process to make sure that these earlier efforts did not end in vain. Most of their activities during the first decade of the twentieth century centered on submitting formal petitions and requests to the prefectural administration to keep Miyako's communal lands in the hands of residents instead of officials. However, producers also engaged in more extreme measures, including setting fire to a large swath of these communally held mountain and forestlands in protest of a state-authorized project to clear the forests to build a new village office.[133] Numerous disputes that erupted following the official resolution of the Miyako Island Peasantry Movement in 1895 reveal the hold that the memory of the struggle had on Miyako's small peasantry long after the leaders of movement like Nakamura, Gusukuma, Taira, and Nishizato moved on to more lucrative ventures on the island and beyond.[134]

CHAPTER THREE

≡

REFORMING OLD CUSTOMS,
TRANSFORMING WOMEN'S WORK

Okinawa's Place in the Expanding Empire

The Meiji state's victory in the First Sino-Japanese War brought major changes to its policies in Okinawa. Although before the war its strategy had focused on achieving a smooth transfer of administration from kingdom to prefecture by maintaining the customary privileges and powers of the former ruling stratum, after 1895 the goals of militarization and the expansion of empire necessitated a shift to a new goal: bringing Okinawa to structural and administrative parity with mainland Japan as quickly as possible.[1] The eruption of peasant struggles against preserved policies on Miyako made it difficult for the state to rationalize maintaining the system that had more or less governed the prefecture since the 1879 disposition. Once the state won Taiwan from China, it had little interest in maintaining the costly semicolonial system of preservations in Okinawa.[2]

The importance of Okinawa's sugar industry to the Japanese economy immediately diminished with the annexation of Taiwan, whose exports were three times larger than Okinawa's total output in 1895.[3] The combination of this strong foundation of sugar production and the colonial conditions that allowed the use of coercion in Taiwan made it a place where Japan's sugar capitalists could without reserve and with massive state backing build their ideal sugar factories on a scale that by the 1890s they knew could not be attained in Okinawa.[4] With their new utopia firmly in hand, the state immediately commenced surveying the land and erecting the infrastructure necessary for turning Taiwan into Japan's sugar factory. The state's establishment of the Taiwan Seitō Kabushikigaisha (Taiwan Sugar Manufacture Company) in 1900 with one million yen in capital embodied its new commitment.[5]

With control of Taiwan's sugar industry seemingly guaranteed, the state's focus in Okinawa shifted to the establishment of modern property relations.[6] Over two decades after land tax reforms in mainland Japan, the land reorganization project (*tochi seiri jigyō*), an Okinawan equivalent, began in 1899.[7] Following the completion of the project in 1903, Okinawa's agrarian villages, once the sites of household labor–based agriculture and handicrafts, came to serve primarily as repositories of commodified labor power available for free valorization by capital, just like their mainland counterparts. They contained an industrial reserve army, "a mass of human material always already ready for exploitation by capital in the interests of capital's own changing valorization requirements."[8] The comprehensive reforms provided the structural basis for the dissolution of the traditional village economy by creating a formally free peasantry liberated from old tax obligations and communal responsibilities. As potential wage laborers, small peasantry (*shōnō*) awaited their insertion into Japanese capitalism's growing machine- and factory-based industrial economy.[9] Thus, land reorganization granted Okinawa's inhabitants the formal prerequisites for their transformation into subjects of the Japanese nation-state who could participate fully and equally in Japanese capitalist society as owners of nothing but their own labor power.[10]

Although these reforms satisfied entrepreneurs like Nakamura Jussaku, whose reward for leading the Miyako Island Peasantry Movement was a founding position in the island's fishing industry, they alarmed others who saw that the state's policies were aimed at minimizing its financial obligations to the prefecture and transferring these burdens onto the shoulders of the people of the region.[11] Indeed, the reforms, an integral part of Okinawa's incorporation into the national system of administration, turned inhabitants into participants in the activity of paying off the national debt, what Marx called "the only part of the so-called national wealth that actually enters into the collective possession of a modern nation."[12] By including Okinawa in Japanese capitalist society, the state was able to impose tax rates on Okinawans that were not simply equal to those it levied to subjects of mainland prefectures but proportionally higher than national standards. Some local intellectuals' desire for equality led them to urge the people to accept their economic difficulties and work even harder to prove to the state that they deserved the same political rights as mainland Japanese.[13] The clash over exactly how much the people of Okinawa should have to bear in exchange for acceptance as full-fledged subjects of the Japanese nation-state forms a major axis of confrontation explored in this chapter.

Local leaders who took opposing sides in the contentious debate over the pursuit of full integration into Japanese society and the pursuit of self-sufficiency also clashed with small producers who refused to buy into the project of Okinawa's modernization at all. Among the numerous confrontations over the changes in village social relations, the fiercest were those between local intellectuals who believed that a fundamental transformation of gender relations was necessary for the modernization of Okinawa's economy and society and ordinary women who refused to transform themselves into reproductive machines or wage laborers in the service of capital accumulation. These disputes exposed the limits of early attempts by Okinawa's first generation of intellectuals to mobilize the imaginary community of Okinawa to enact the transformations that they believed were necessary to protect the prefecture from being demoted to a formal colony of the expanding Japanese empire.

The First Generation of Intellectuals Return to Okinawa

Intellectuals who felt it was their duty to mold the people of Okinawa into proper Japanese subjects during this transitional moment for the prefecture came of age during the 1890s. Born in the 1850s and 1860s, they were the first generation of students to identify themselves as Okinawan. Many of them spent a large part of their formative years outside of the prefecture at Tokyo's most prestigious national and private universities. Their arrival in the nation's capital in the early 1880s coincided with the height of Freedom and Popular Rights Movement.[14] In contrast to the former ruling stratum, these young people wholeheartedly believed that the people of Okinawa would be best served by allegiance to Japan, though they disagreed about the ideal political form for the region.[15]

At university, the students organized study groups and political organizations and contemplated the future of Okinawa. In 1890 a group of students in Tokyo formed the Okinawa Youth Association (Okinawa Seinenkai) and began publishing a journal called *Okinawa Seinen Zasshi* (*Okinawa Youth*).[16] This publication accepted submissions from many of Okinawa's future political and intellectual leaders.[17] These discursive arenas predated the 1893 founding of Okinawa's first newspaper, the *Ryūkyū Shimpō*, and were informed by the most progressive intellectual currents in the country.

Most students returned to the prefecture after completing their studies and became low-ranking bureaucrats in the prefectural administration or teachers in one of dozens of schools that were hastily built during the Meiji period. As members of a select group, these mainland-educated youth working in the state bureaucracy maintained the connections and friendships that they had forged during their university days. One young man who emerged as a leader in this fraternity was Jahana Noboru, the son of a commoner from Kochinda Village who returned to Okinawa in late 1891 after graduating from the Tokyo Nōrin Gakkō (Tokyo Agriculture and Dendrology College) that year.[18] He became a salaried employee of the prefecture as an expert in agricultural affairs and played an instrumental role in Governor Narahara Shigeru's administration. As one of the leaders of Okinawa's first comprehensive project for the reclamation of uncultivated mountains and forests (somayama) that were communally owned by the prefecture's villages, Jahana found himself at the center of the action during the planning phase of the land reorganization project.[19]

Jahana was supportive of reforms designed to facilitate Okinawa's industrial development, but he quickly became concerned about the degree to which the prefecture's economy was becoming dependent on the sugar industry.[20] Although he applauded the vast increases in sugarcane cultivation after planting restrictions were lifted in late 1888, he worried that the price of sweet potato—the peasantry's staple food (figure 3.1)—would continue to rise as more area was devoted to cane. He learned during his visits to the countryside that poor farmers whose main source of food was sweet potato were forced to convert most of their land into sugarcane fields to obtain cash to pay their new taxes; with no energy or land left to grow this staple, people were on the brink of starvation.[21] The prefecture's plan to increase the total area over which cane was cultivated by converting communal lands into cane fields was designed to alleviate these pressures by providing impoverished cultivators with increased opportunities for cash income.[22]

Jahana's concerns for the livelihood of the peasantry as well as for the plight of the former nobles who lost their stipends compelled him to initially support Governor Narahara's reclamation project. This project, regarded as the earliest phase of the general reorganization of Okinawa's land system, was an expansion of the reclamation projects that we discussed in the previous chapter. The projects of the 1880s had focused on opening up the previously uncultivated lands of the Sakishima Islands for settlement by the former nobles who had lost their stipends and by impoverished farmers. Narahara's reclamation projects were aimed more broadly at opening

Fig. 3.1 Sweet potato continued to provide an important source of food for Okinawa's peasants even as they were encouraged to switch to cash crops like sugar. The starch was used in place of flour for daily consumption. The production of sweet potato starch, The University of Hawaii at Manoa Library Sakamaki/Hawley Collection, from *Bōkyo Okinawa*, vol. 5, 93.

up uncultivated communally owned mountains and forests in all regions of the prefecture and establishing large-scale modern sugar factories. The first of these began in 1893, as the rumblings of discontent in Miyako reached Jahana's office in Naha. Jahana, who was in charge of the prefecture's reclamation projects at the time, approved the granting of 1,500 chōbu of land to the Yaeyama reclamation association, a group of members of the former royal family and powerful merchants and politicians from the mainland.[23] The stated objective of the project was to loan previously uncultivated lands on a long-term basis to individuals and groups who were committed to developing them. Despite Jahana's precautionary measures, entrepreneurs and politicians from mainland Japan who were interested in making a quick profit streamed into Okinawa and snatched up large swaths of uncultivated land at extremely low rents.[24] The gross abuses that surrounded these reclamation projects, particularly on the part of relatives of politicians who occupied leadership positions in the prefecture, shaped Jahana's negative opinion of subsequent state-led development projects.

Like other young Okinawans who bought into the state's modernization project, Jahana was profoundly affected by the experience of being in the prefecture during the First Sino-Japanese War. Japan's war against China revived latent rivalries between factions of former ruling families and brought tensions between mainland Japanese and local people to the surface. Resident merchants who had established roots in Okinawa spontaneously formed civilian volunteer troops to protect themselves from a local population they viewed with suspicion and from the approaching Chinese fleet. They armed themselves and put themselves under the command of both the prefectural administration and the regiment stationed in the region as fighting escalated. Not to be outdone, members of the pro-Chinese faction of the former kingdom's elite (the Ganko faction) came out of hiding and made the rounds of the temples and shrines in their ceremonial garb, praying for China's victory over Japan.[25] They held secret meetings in Kumemura, the Chinese stronghold in Okinawa, and gathered weapons with which they could assist the Chinese army.[26]

Japan's victory over China in 1895 sealed Okinawa's fate as part of the empire and demoralized the Ganko faction, whose members had harbored hopes that the opposite outcome would resuscitate their kingdom. Although the outcome of the war resolved the question of political jurisdiction, the materialization of the conflict in the prefecture—where resident merchants, students, and the pro-Chinese faction aimed their guns and fists at each other—convinced even the most pro-Japanese segments of the local population that it was necessary to increase the number of Okinawans in positions of authority. Young local leaders like Jahana and Ōta Chōfu found themselves caught between their loyalties to their communities and their belief in the Japanese modernization project.[27] They were opposed to the Ganko faction's attempts to reinstate the old state form with military assistance from China, but were equally uncomfortable about the economic and political power of mainland bureaucrats and merchants who looked down on the people of Okinawa and saw all of them as potential traitors.[28]

Tensions between Okinawa's newly educated stratum and mainland actors continued to worsen after the war as educational leaders dispatched by the Ministry of Education revealed their prejudices. One of these educators from the mainland and principal of the Okinawa First Normal School in Shuri, Kodama Kihachi, made numerous proclamations that Okinawans should not be held to the same educational standards as Japanese students and fired two popular teachers in mid-October 1895 because he considered them too sympathetic to the students. Third-year students organized a strike in response, and most students eventually withdrew in solidarity.[29] The Icchū strike, as it is remembered, left an indelible imprint on the minds of many Okinawan intellectuals—including Iha Fuyū, who came to be known as the father of Okinawan studies.[30] The firing of the teachers was its immediate cause, but a deep discontent among students concerning the discriminatory attitude of the principal was responsible for its continuation into the spring of 1896. Kodama's unilateral decision to remove English-language studies from the curriculum—a requirement under the national curriculum for students who wanted to attend university—was interpreted by students as both an insult to their intelligence and an attempt to eliminate opportunities for their advancement in society.[31] The students' demands for the reinstatement of the curriculum were eventually met, but the experience of blatant discrimination and colonial treatment was ingrained in the memory of many members of Okinawa's future elite.[32] The shared experience of discrimination in the most modern of institutions established in Okinawa led local actors along one of two divergent paths, both centered on the attainment of *jichi* (local autonomy).

Competing Visions of Local Autonomy

Three years after the conclusion of the strike, the young intellectual Ōta led a short-lived movement (the Kōdōkai movement) with the last king of the kingdom, Shō Tai, and his fourth son, Shō Jun, that articulated a vision of local autonomy that lingered even after its defeat.[33] The three men worked with some interesting bedfellows, including the Kaika (pro-Japanese) faction of the former ruling stratum, a segment of the younger generation of intellectuals, and a large group of former low-ranking nobles who had lost their stipends. They drew up a petition to the Meiji state demanding the establishment of a special system that would place Okinawa under Shō Tai's rule.[34] It argued that reinstating the former king was the only way to guarantee a smooth transition from kingdom to prefecture. As the reinstated head of the prefecture, Shō would be granted all the political and administrative powers held by the current governor, Narahara. In an article published in the *Yomiuri Shimbun* in July 1897, Ōta defended this petition, which over 70,000 people signed, saying that only Shō Tai "stands outside of all of this tension and conflict and holds complete and unrestricted authority that can bring the entire island together."[35] The Kōdōkai movement used a logic similar to that of the proponents of the Meiji Restoration, who argued that the transfer of authority to the emperor—who was above factional disputes—was the only way to restore unity across the realm. Ōta argued that "if the special system is enacted and if the Shō family is at the helm, 400,000 people will give a deep cry of gratitude to the grace of the emperor and will display a spirit of service to the realm."[36]

Beyond the primary goal of unification, the movement articulated the problems with current economic and political arrangements in Okinawa. It criticized merchants from Kagoshima and Osaka who took advantage of the people and used their links to the prefectural and state governments to establish a virtual monopoly over commercial activity. Ōta argued that the nostalgia that people felt for the former king could be traced to these unforgivable crimes committed by temporary residents from the mainland. In the most emotional passage of the article, he described the outsiders who came to the prefecture just to make a quick buck: "The mainlanders, in particular, the people from Kagoshima infest and infiltrate the indigenous people of the prefecture." He continued, "The only relationship that will guarantee an end to the gutting of the indigenous people is the one that binds the Shō family to the people. To sever the feelings of mutual affection artificially will not work. The mainlanders first saw the indigenous people of the prefecture as Ryūkyūans and looked upon them as if they were all diseased barbarians."[37]

The wording of this emotional passage reveals the way that Ōta understood the divisions that existed in Okinawa. He downplayed internal differences by using the broad descriptors "Ryūkyūans" and "the people of the prefecture" in place of more specific characterizations of the groups he wished to protect—petty merchants, low-ranking officials in the prefectural administration, students, and teachers who were born and raised in Okinawa. His turn of phrase concealed an important characteristic of the leaders of the Kōdōkai movement: that they were local men of commerce and industry who recognized, more than any other group, what they stood to lose if the existing conditions continued unabated. In particular, those conditions favored mainland merchants who had access to vast resources—including transportation networks, markets, and capital—due to their relationships with mainland banks and politicians. As Ōta phrased it, "the quickness or lateness of Okinawa people in their assimilation with the mainland is where the dividing line between fortune and misfortune is drawn."[38] They feared that Okinawa would remain a place where taxes and natural resources were plundered by mainlanders who gave back nothing to the prefecture. Even after the Kōdōkai movement failed to gain traction, Ōta and other local intellectuals deployed the language of local autonomy in their efforts to formulate class-specific strategies of resistance against the expropriative and monopolistic activity of the mainland merchants and corrupt politicians.[39]

Despite their impassioned pleas to the state to allow Shō Tai to take the helm in Okinawa, the proposal to grant the former king a transcendent position akin to that of the Japanese emperor failed to gain traction. Following the central government's rejection of their petition, Ōta, Shō Jun, and the core members of the Kōdōkai movement redirected their energies to the *Ryūkyū Shimpō*, the newspaper that they established in 1893 with Governor Narahara's permission. The articles in this organ of the pro-Japanese faction of the former nobility stratum reveal that despite their earlier attempts to replace the governor with Shō Tai, their relationship with the prefectural administration was by no means antagonistic. The grand celebration held in August 1898 to celebrate Narahara's triumphant return from Tokyo after securing approval to place a land reorganization project office in Okinawa illustrates this mutually beneficial relationship linked by a common interest in capitalist development.

At this celebration, attended by a thousand or so luminaries, Shō Jun expressed admiration and gratitude to the governor, describing Narahara's successful negotiations with the central government as fulfilling the "long-held desires of the people of the prefecture."[40] In his speech, Shō explained why the enactment of the land reorganization project was so important for the people of Okinawa. He stated that this project, which would place a system of private property in the prefecture by determining ownership rights and distributing land titles to individuals, was necessary in order to correct the current injustice, where not all people enjoyed the right to pay taxes.[41] He was referring specifically to the fact that commoners were responsible for paying national, prefectural, and local taxes, while officials were largely exempt from tax payments. His sudden concern for parity was linked to the defeat of the Kōdōkai movement and his realization that the prefecture was eventually going to be incorporated into the national political system. Under such conditions, having the right to pay taxes was crucial to protecting their already tenuous hold over local politics. Being exempt from paying taxes—once a sign of their privilege—was now an impediment to their political aspirations. Shō Jun celebrated Narahara's land reorganization project, which would determine individual families' tax obligations, as "a merciful act of achieving people's equality that is necessary for raising the status of the people of the prefecture."[42] It goes without saying that taking this stance necessitated amnesia about their own complicity in delaying the enactment of reforms in Okinawa, not to mention the substantial material advantages they had gained from the Preservation of Old Customs Policy.

Jahana, Ōta's former classmate at the prestigious Gakushūin University in Tokyo, had very different concerns. While Ōta's version of local autonomy focused on securing Okinawan elites' control over policies that governed the region, Jahana's was focused on extending people's rights to the prefecture. The difference between them might be compared to the wide gulf that separated state sovereignty (kokken) and people's rights (minken) theorists who clashed in mainland Japan in the 1880s. As Tōyama Shigeki explained, state sovereignty theorists prioritized state's rights and sovereignty vis-à-vis other states with little concern for the people, and people's rights theorists prioritized the rights of the people in relation to their state as an integral part of nation formation.[43] Because Narahara's proposed reforms seemed to lay the foundations for local autonomy, Ōta and the *Shimpō* faction enthusiastically supported the man they had sought to remove from office just months earlier. Jahana's position leaned toward that of the activists in the Freedom and Popular Rights Movement. He had major problems with Narahara's tenure as governor but accepted the prefecture's full integration into the Japanese nation-state because he understood this as a necessary step toward getting rid of the despotism of both local and mainland leaders who were only interested in developing an extractive relationship with the people.

Several months after the grand welcome home that Narahara received from Shō Jun and his allies, Jahana, who had worked in the prefectural administration under the governor since 1892, resigned from his post and headed to Tokyo to mount a campaign to get his former boss transferred out of the prefecture.[44] Once there, he and his comrades Shintani Seijin and Tōyama Kyuzō founded the Okinawa Kurabu (Okinawa Club).[45] Its manifesto expressed its main concerns: "Today, a system of local autonomy has been put in place and the land tax reform is beginning in our prefecture. Appearances are not what they were in the past. At this time, the people of the prefecture must use all of their strength to push for improvement and development in numerous directions in order to bring about happiness and prosperity in the prefecture."[46] The policies that the Kurabu's members supported suggest that the people of the prefecture whom they were most concerned with had a completely different position in Okinawan society than the people that Ota's *Ryūkyū Shimpō* faction was desperate to protect.

In addition to forming the Kurabu, in January 1899 Jahana and his comrades made the rounds among prominent politicians Itagaki Taisuke,

Ōkuma Shigenobu, Hoshi Tōru, Takagi Seinen, Tani Takeki, Soga Sukenori, Nabeshima Naoyoshi, and Kushimoto Marataka with two objectives in mind: to expose Governor Narahara's unethical actions in the prefecture and to have the election law (*senkyohō*) that would allow residents of Okinawa to participate in national and local elections enacted immediately.[47] These two goals were closely intertwined. In contrast to the glowing reviews that the *Shimpō* faction gave Narahara, the Kurabu's members despised and mistrusted the governor for his shameless use of his political position to personally benefit from the prefecture's projects.[48] The Kurabu founded its own paper, the *Okinawa Jiron*, in which the organization's members exposed his self-serving activities and articulated their own visions for political change in Okinawa.[49]

Central to realizing their version of local autonomy was a fair resolution of the issue of communal mountain and forest lands. They explained their position to both houses of the thirteenth National Diet in the form of a request to revise the land reorganization plan that prefectural authorities had submitted. Specifically, they objected to article 18 of the plan, which read: "Communal mountains and forests, riverbeds, embankments and other lands that are not considered civilian-owned will all become officially owned . . . with regard to the protection and management of the communal mountains and forests, those things other than what is decided by imperial rescript will be conducted according to previous customs."[50] Kurabu members objected to this article because they feared that its ambiguous wording would enable the transfer of vast amounts of communal lands from the hands of Okinawa's cultivators into the hands of large mainland corporations and local capitalists. Though they did not have the right to directly participate in the committee sessions, they collaborated with sympathetic Diet members to shape the contours of the debate when it went before the House of Peers in February 1899.

They found a sympathetic ear in the second governor of Okinawa, Nabeshima, who had been forced out of his post in 1881 after being labeled too sympathetic to the plight of the commoners. Now a member of the House of Peers, he used information that Jahana entrusted to him prior to the opening of the Diet sessions to argue against the government's efforts to turn communal mountain and forest lands into state-owned property.[51] In a speech before the Diet, Nabeshima requested that the land reorganization project follow the spirit of the 1873 land tax reforms that decided the ownership of communal lands by usage; he argued that titles to farmlands should be granted to those who had cultivated them in the past. This

Fig. 3.2 Prefectural authorities conducted surveys of land quality throughout Okinawa Island in the second half of the 1890s to grant land titles and determine taxes based on yield. Surveys during the land reorganization, Naha City Museum of History photo no. 02008391.

stance would provide tenant farmers an opportunity to gain ownership of the fields that they had cultivated for generations.[52]

Nabeshima countered the prefectural authorities' insistence that determining ownership of these lands was impossible because written records pertaining to usage did not exist (figure 3.2).[53] Although he agreed that "in Okinawa's villages, there are no documents that clearly specify what is communal, what is civilian owned and what is officially owned," he emphasized: "But the people know what is theirs."[54] In the case of the mountain and forest lands, village members who held decision-making rights received distributions of farmlands, paid taxes, and shared the right to freely use their village's mountains and forest resources to build a residence or gather firewood.[55] At the same time, they were responsible for maintaining and managing those lands according to a system that divided work equally between them. Nabeshima implored his fellow Diet members to uphold the spirit of the land reforms undertaken on the mainland and asked them to prevent the state from taking away these resources, which people relied on for their livelihood.[56] Despite his efforts, the state's interpretation of article 18 eventually prevailed, and half of Okinawa's land was enclosed by the state.[57]

Even after Nabeshima's defeat in the Diet, the Kurabu continued to oppose the conversion of the communal mountains and forests into state-owned lands through the *Okinawa Jiron*. They also began working more closely with local communities that were embroiled in real struggles against authorities over these lands. One of Jahana's first tasks in this regard took him to Miyako. He learned from two peasantry representatives who traveled from Uruka Village to pay him a visit in Naha that the conclusion of the Miyako Island Peasantry Movement had not brought stability or prosperity to the island.[58] In fact, the land reorganization project had heightened tensions by raising new questions about the way that lands, including those newly reclaimed by resident merchants and other recent settlers, would be doled out.[59] Jahana traveled to the village to speak directly with the cultivators and to investigate the conditions of Uruka's communally managed lands. Once there, he realized that the conversion from communal to state management would not only strip the small peasantry of their ability to freely use the resources of their mountains and forests but would also deny them the ability to collectively decide how the revenue from large deforestation campaigns would be used. He published an article about his visit to Uruka on August 17, 1900, in which he clarified both the economic and political stakes involved in the disposal of communal lands. He remarked that local residents would "no longer be able to cut down one tree. The poor will have to cultivate these lands but will not profit at all from them."[60]

As the main drafter of Okinawa's regulations that governed the reclamation of communally owned lands in the early 1890s, Jahana was all too aware of Governor Narahara's willingness to decimate Okinawa's forests once the conversion to state ownership was completed. During a visit he made to Taiwan in October 1896, he granted an interview to the *Taiwan Shimpō* paper that only confirmed Jahana's fears. In the interview, Narahara expressed his desire for Okinawa and Taiwan to build close economic relations in the near future and revealed his plan to export lumber from Okinawa to the new colony, which could use these raw materials to construct tea boxes and railroad tracks.[61] He emphasized that the cheap and convenient supply of Okinawan lumber would benefit the Taiwanese, who would not have to deplete their own natural resources. Soon after this visit, Narahara commenced the prefecture's third major project to open and develop communal mountains and forests.[62]

One step that Jahana and the Kurabu took to counter Narahara's attempt to transform Okinawa's communal lands into state property was to advocate for the swift enactment of the election law in the prefecture. To this end,

Nakamura Yaroku, a forestry expert and Diet member from Nagano Prefecture, sponsored a petition called "Shūgiin Giin Senkyohō Kaisei no Ken" ("Reform of the Election Laws for Lower House Members"), which called for the enactment of the election law so that the people of Okinawa could immediately participate in national elections.[63] In response, the Lower House formed a special committee to investigate the possibility of revising the election laws to grant Okinawa immediate representation in the Diet.[64] Jahana's mouthpiece in the special committee was Takagi, who faced off against the government representative to the committee, Ichiki Kitokurō in several of the Diet sessions.[65] The heated debate in the special committee between Ichiki and committee members sympathetic to Jahana's position was a repetition of a battle that had already been fought between the *Ryūkyū Shimpō* and the *Okinawa Jiron* factions in the prefecture.[66]

Ichiki, who represented the government's view in this debate, stated that electoral rights could be granted to the people of Okinawa only after the completion of the land reorganization project.[67] He explained that voting rights could not be granted yet because under the existing system, only a small number of people would meet the eligibility requirements for participating in the political process.[68] Since eligibility was determined by the amount of direct national taxes an individual paid to the government, most Okinawans would not qualify because private property was recognized only in a few areas. Furthermore, villages in the prefecture paid taxes collectively, so it was not possible to accurately determine how much each person paid to the state.[69]

Takagi unleashed a scathing critique of this rationale at the third meeting of the special committee, on February 18, 1899. He argued that Ichiki's explanation before the Diet was merely an excuse, and that the real reason the government did not want to enact the election law in Okinawa was because no one in Naha and Shuri—the main residential areas of the former nobility—paid taxes: "Since these nobles are still receiving stipends, of course they do not pay the land tax or own any land."[70] In contrast, commoners who bore most of the expenses of their villages had distinct plots of land that they worked and resided on. It would be possible to determine individual families' tax obligations even without the completion of the land reorganization project if the government was committed to its speedy implementation.[71] The only reason the government did not want the election law to be enacted was because small cultivators would gain participation in the national government, while members of the former ruling stratum would not.

Their divergent positions on the election law clearly show that the Kurabu and the *Shimpō* factions had completely different goals for the prefecture. Jahana and the Kurabu wanted to increase the people's degree of self-government to protect them from all groups that wanted to exploit the resources of the prefecture. In contrast, Ōta and the *Shimpō* were primarily focused on maintaining their own leadership position in Okinawa. These former rulers of the Ryūkyū kingdom feared that rapidly changing global conditions would make their role in Okinawa obsolete, and they did everything in their power to carve out a secure place for themselves. Seeing the new group of young, non-noble, mainland-educated leaders exemplified in the Kurabu faction as the largest threat to their aspirations, they circled their wagons in an effort to protect their position of power. They insisted that they, not Jahana or other upstarts of the Kurabu, were the rightful leaders of Okinawa.

Jahana's retreat from the prefecture's political and intellectual scene signaled the victory of Ōta and the *Shimpō* faction in the fight to articulate and represent Okinawan interests.[72] More significantly, it revealed that the state sovereignty version of local autonomy triumphed over the version that called for the extension of rights and equality to the Okinawan people. The state's support of the Ōta faction in the Diet confirmed and legitimated the position of the former kingdom's old guard as the rightful protectors of Okinawan sovereignty, even as it stripped them of their official posts and stipends. As we will see next, while Ōta's version of modernization triumphed over Jahana's, he faced another difficult challenge—this time, from the very people whose interests he claimed to represent.

Village Reforms and Economic Nationalism

Ōta's version of local autonomy, which argued that placing Okinawa's elite in the center of the prefecture's political and economic scene was the only way to counter its current semicolonized state, also required that they take a leading role in transforming social relations in the countryside. The Movement to Reform Old Customs (Fūzoku Kairyō Undō) that Ōta led since the late 1890s was the mechanism to actualize these changes. Ōta's first step in this regard was urging local men of authority to take leadership roles in implementing these much-needed reforms. He and his allies in the *Shimpō* faction appealed to the paternalism of these men in an effort to mobilize them in the project to restore discipline and decorum in Okinawa's agrarian villages. These efforts were considered necessary accompaniments to the impending reorganization of land, taxation, and administrative systems.

Local elites responded enthusiastically to the Movement to Reform Old Customs because they feared that the impending comprehensive land and tax reforms would turn them into remnants of the past if they failed to prove their worth within the new system. Reforms of the prefecture's administrative systems had begun in 1896 with the reorganization of the county and ward systems, which were followed by the reorganization of the structure of village administration throughout the main island of Okinawa and Sakishima.[73] In concrete terms, these laws fired a significant number of local officials and required those who were lucky enough to keep their jobs to submit their taxes in full and were based on a report submitted by Home Minister Nomura Yasushi to Finance Minister Matsukata Masayoshi in 1895, which estimated that the restructuring would cut 15,000 posts and 121,000 yen in wages per year.[74] In a desperate attempt to salvage their jobs, local elites frantically organized study groups in their communities to research the administrative changes taking place, discuss possible responses, and formulate strategies to deflect the growing discontent among commoners with their feudalistic style of rule.[75]

Local leaders and intellectuals associated with the *Shimpō* faction were also motivated by concerns about the post-disposition weakening of social sanctions that had previously held village communities together. While they wholeheartedly supported the land reorganization project and industrial development, they also recognized that vast transformations in social relations could derail their ability to realize local autonomy. They observed that ever since Preservation-era regulations in villages limiting people's mobility, choice of occupation, and commercial activity had been abolished, villagers had become much harder to police and control. Ōta examined how the removal of these sanctions affected life in both city and country in an article in the *Shimpō*. The present, he argued, was an extremely vulnerable time: "After the fall of old sanctions, new ones have not yet come up in its place. Society is dark because of it. Various systems have fallen and new systems that should take their place have not yet begun to show their effects. There are hardly any laws and regulations in place and Okinawa is without morals or proper social relations."[76] He likened the resulting spread of "bad" customs, particularly in the cities, to an infection that resulted from a weakening of the immune system of the collective body of the Okinawan community. Ōta called on local leaders to pay close attention to the activities of the youth, who were most susceptible to infection during these vulnerable times.[77] Without vigilant monitoring, the entire community could be decimated.

Signs of deterioration were evident. Young men and women ventured outward from their villages—something that customary regulations had expressly forbidden in the past—to Okinawa's growing cities in search of jobs and entertainment as soon as the laws that prohibited them from traveling outside their villages were abolished. An article in the *Shimpō* of October 28, 1899, vividly described the seedy, dark corners that had recently emerged in Nago, a city in the northern part of Okinawa Island, and their negative impact on social relations: "Peoples' customs are changing and they are becoming more extravagant. Nago is growing into the second capital of the prefecture. Institutions into which money can be squandered are emerging there."[78] The author of the piece disapprovingly singled out restaurants as a major cause of the degradation of morals in Nago: "The sign says food but the biggest draw is the women. This is a well-known secret."[79]

Okinawa's leaders were especially concerned about the repercussions these developments would have on the economic health of the countryside. As Ōta explained, young people, tempted by stories of life and work in the cities, had began to shun agriculture, which required long hours of arduous labor that tied them to their farms year after year. The problem was that if one villager lost the motivation to cultivate and daydreamed about moving to the city, this sentiment would quickly spread and communities would lose their collective desire to work.[80] It was only a matter of time before entire villages would be forced to declare bankruptcy. In this transitional moment, reports of sons of rich farmers and merchants frolicking around town hand in hand with prostitutes and spending hundreds of yen at the drop of a hat were just as serious problems as bodily infection through the spread of sexually transmitted diseases.[81]

Based on this diagnosis of the dangers that Okinawa faced as the prefecture entered the age of modernity, Ōta and the *Shimpō* faction implored men of influence in the countryside to take back control of their communities, this time as representatives of a new Okinawa. They urged local elites to clarify the new rules of the game to the people who continued to look to them for direction. Ōta hoped that enlisting local elite to implement these much-needed reforms of old customs could energize them and make them committed to rebuilding the prefecture's agrarian villages. If local elite could take the reins and successfully install codes of conduct and customs appropriate to the new age, staving off financial collapse in the process, there was still a glimmer of possibility that local autonomy might salvaged.[82]

Upon closer examination, for Ōta and the *Shimpō* faction, maintaining local autonomy was synonymous with directing the way that capitalist development would take place in Okinawa. To them, a transition to capitalism was a given, but successful transition required a radical transformation of social relations. Ōta described Okinawa's existing conditions with some concern: "Today, there is no clear division between capital owner and worker. Today's worker may be tomorrow's capital owner and vice versa." He then clarified the types of reforms that were necessary in the prefecture's agrarian villages to realize capitalist relations: "Only when the small farmers of the countryside begin to move freely in pursuit of profit and the division between capital owner and worker is clarified, can large machinery in both agriculture and industry be used."[83] He anticipated Okinawan society after the land tax reforms as one in which small peasantry would be gradually expelled from their lands and transformed into tenants or agricultural and industrial wage laborers that provided the necessary labor power for capitalist industry.

Still, Ōta took seriously his position as an aspiring Okinawan bourgeoisie. Unlike entrepreneurs from mainland Japan, Ōta performed a dual role as both petty bourgeoisie who hoped to convert the peasantry into members of a society "in which capital is able to ensure the capture of surplus labor power on its own" and as a protector of Okinawa's small producers against mainland capital.[84] His primary goal of establishing "the economic law specific to the commodity economy . . . as the general social relationship" in Okinawa clashed with his belief that local actors should take the lead in reorganizing the prefecture's agrarian villages as its rightful managers and owners.[85]

This dual role that Ōta and other local leaders identified during this transitional moment in modern Okinawa's history crystallized in the formulation of an economic nationalism that was founded on the belief that some forms of exploitation were more benevolent and therefore, more desirable than others—that of Okinawans by other Okinawans.[86] The reform of social relations in the villages that Ōta advocated was a prerequisite to the ultimate goal of creating an autonomous sphere over which local bourgeoisie could become "the ones doing the using." The rise of this type of economic nationalism was accompanied by the emergence of a belief in an organic Okinawan community whose membership was inextricably linked to the territorial boundaries of the new prefecture.

Reforming Women's Morality and Rationalizing Village Relations

Ōta's economic nationalism led him to call for a wide range of reforms in appearance, everyday behavior, play, and customary practices. All of these required that existing gender norms be dismantled. Mainland observers had long observed that social relations in Okinawa were inversions of the proper order: "The men just lounge around at home while the women engage in commerce outside. The men pretend to be gentlemanly with a long kimono sashes and parasols while women wear short sashes and go barefoot into the sun . . . the men are very gentle and the women are slightly rugged."[87] Correcting these inverted roles and transforming the temperament of men and women was considered absolutely necessary for Okinawans to realize modern social relations.[88]

The transformation of gender norms was a prerequisite for the establishment of a new sexual division of labor that subjugated women's labor and reproductive functions to the reproduction of capitalist society.[89] A main target of the Movement to Reform Old Customs was the perceived loose morals of the young men and women of the agrarian villages. Although most observers conceded that women were extremely hard workers, they were disgusted by the enthusiasm with which these women engaged in after-hours activities. The policing of pleasure was one of the main priorities of the movement from the start. Local intellectuals took Ichiki's warnings in his 1894 report, which discussed the prevalence of practices of *mōasobi* (young men and women meeting at night in the empty fields to sing and dance together) and *yagamaya* (young men singing songs while the women engaged in handicraft activities indoors) in the villages that he surveyed as responsible for the spread of syphilis in Okinawa, to heart.[90]

Reports in the local papers reinforced the bad reputation that mōasobi and yagamaya gained among local reformers. In Nakagami and Shimajiri regions of the main island of Okinawa, restricting these practices became an urgent matter after reports surfaced that a young man had contracted syphilis after paying a visit to a prostitute and had infected the entire village. The *Shimpō* article that reported this incident highlighted the need to control the spread of sexually transmitted diseases by policing the practice and periodically testing women who had relations with multiple men through the activity.[91] This link between prostitution, syphilis, and loose women seeking pleasure was repeatedly made in newspaper articles around this time and reinforced the notion that young women were constantly in danger of slipping into prostitution and compromising the sexual health of entire villages. It was crucial for reformers to control the play between men and women that took place at night as it, like the women who appeared so hard working on the surface, could destroy whole communities. As was the case during the witch hunts in Europe investigated by Maria Mies, reformers "denounced female nature as sinful, as sexually uncontrollable, insatiable and ever ready to seduce the virtuous man."[92]

Reformers throughout Okinawa also deliberated the reform of a yearly event called the *sangatsu asobi*, which referred to days in March when women gathered to picnic and relax at the beach. Here, women were painted not as vixens whose amorous nature threatened the health of entire villages but as potential victims whose chastity had to be defended. Apparently, the fact that the sangatsu asobi was a daytime event diminished the threat that female sexuality posed to men, and reformers recommended measures such as requiring chaperones to "protect the bodies of these virgins" from drunks, shortening the length of the event from one week to one day to guard against "a flow toward decline and laziness," and prohibiting the singing of vulgar songs and disallowing men and women to dance in large circles together.[93] These restrictions sought to remake the sangatsu asobi into a strictly orchestrated piece of healthy entertainment and, thus, to transform it from a momentary escape from the rigors of everyday life into a sterile event that reinforced the rules, moral codes, and hierarchies that the reformers wished to instill into the community.

This becomes very apparent when we turn to an article about sangatsu asobi by an anonymous female contributor. She emphasized to her readers that the proper orchestration of the sangatsu asobi was an integral component of any project to improve society and emphasized that this important task should "by no means be left to the course of nature."[94] She encouraged her readers to submit to the newspaper the names of girls and their villages of origin in two categories: those who were especially good at performing elegant songs and dances and those who brought shame to their communities by engaging in vulgar forms of play. Public shaming was necessary to create an atmosphere of self-surveillance: "The girls and the villages that are listed in the paper will become the sacrificial lambs and will receive penalties for the good of society."[95]

In addition to public shaming and policing play, the transformation of gender relations and norms also required violent campaigns to diminish the authority of women who had once served important political, spiritual, and economic roles in the kingdom. Two key groups that were targets of such campaigns were Okinawa's female priestesses and oracles, called *noro* and *yuta*. In particular, female priestesses who enjoyed key positions in village communities as subordinates of the *Kikoeōgimi*—the title granted to the chief priestess, oracle, and highest ranking spiritual advisor to the king—lost much of their legitimacy in the transition from kingdom to prefecture.[96] During much of the early modern era, the noro had been women who performed monthly religious ceremonies in their villages and oversaw the spiritual health of the countryside.[97] They were granted official lands, called *norokumoi* lands, and were allowed to supplement their stipends by growing crops on them. The disposition of 1879 forced prefectural authorities to come to a decision about the treatment of the noro. They understood the important role that these women played in the spiritual life of village communities and decided to hold off on reforms to their lands until they could formulate a clear plan of action.[98] After 1879, the noro continued to perform their usual tasks of praying for the peace and prosperity of the village community and villagers' safety at sea and continued to lead annual ceremonies and festivals associated with harvest cycles.

This tolerant attitude began to change beginning with enactment of the Civil Code (Minpōhō) in 1898, which reinforced male leadership in the family. The principle of male primogeniture weakened the control that the noro had over their lands.[99] In conjunction with these new codes that took away her ability to manage her lands, attitudes of village leaders cooled considerably. Reformers began publicly criticizing the noro for offering ineffective spiritual advice and accused them of deliberately confusing ignorant people. Local elites were particularly critical of the noro's willingness to offer prayers on behalf of young men of conscription age to avoid being drafted and recommended stricter policing of her activities.[100]

Even more common than efforts to delegitimize the spiritual authority of the noro were broader and indirect attacks on the rationality that governed the ritual calendar within which these women occupied a central position. For example, local reformers in the Nakagami region were especially vigilant in limiting the resources that were expended in religious ceremonies, including those to mark births and deaths. A report on local conditions announced new regulations that restricted the number of days that families could devote to the celebration of a birth to just one day, which had to be exactly seven days after the child was born.[101] Contrary to common practice, singing and dancing were prohibited during the first six days after the birth, and only close relatives and those people approved by the head of the village were allowed to participate in the festivities. An article that reported the decisions reached by the committee to reform old customs in central Okinawa's Katsuren Village described how families also had to comply with regulations that limited the amount of money they could spend on alcohol during birth and funeral ceremonies.[102] These attempts to curb the spending of time and resources during these ceremonies and village festivals—which were unproductive from the perspective of capitalist rationality—went hand in hand with efforts to eliminate the influence of the noro in village communities.[103]

Yuta were also central figures in the spiritual life of village communities from the kingdom era. In contrast to the noro, they were not incorporated into the bureaucratic structure of the kingdom government, nor were they responsible for the village as a single unit. They served as fortune-tellers and interlocutors between the living and the dead, performed a wide variety of services for individuals and families, and responded to unfortunate events in people's lives. Unprotected by the kingdom government, they did not enjoy the same status or privileges that the female priestesses received as bureaucrats of the spiritual realm and were periodically targeted for policing.[104] In particular, King Shō Tei found the yuta's influence on the noro a problem for the kingdom government, which had its hands full mediating conflicts between the Kikoeōgimi and the male Council of Three (Sanshikan) over annual festival schedules.[105] The yuta, who were not involved in high-level kingdom decisions, were accused of spreading superstitious beliefs and offering incorrect medical advice. The kingdom government passed stringent laws against consultations with yuta throughout the eighteenth and early nineteenth centuries, claiming that these measures were designed to protect the people from being duped into offering expensive gifts to calm angry spirits.[106] In some regions, yuta became targets of full-fledged witch hunts. And they were rounded up and publicly humiliated at the open market in Shuri, with an ashiguruma tied around their necks as punishment for refusing to stop their banned practices. Despite these measures, the yuta remained a strong presence into the Meiji period.

Newspaper articles that appeared during the Movement to Reform Old Customs reveal the frustration that many reformers felt about these women. A common theme that emerged in these articles was the village yutas' connection to prostitution rings in the three pleasure quarters of Naha: "These yuta lie, trick people out of their money, cause the demise of businesses, and disrupt public morals. . . . We have heard that one woman, fifty years old, who was once a mistress in Unten works as a middleman [for yuta and their customers] and secretly sells herself on the side."[107] A large portion of this article was devoted to publicly outing these women, many of whom lived in the Tsuji District, by printing their names and addresses for all to see. Yuta were accused of being quacks who collected significant fees to make divinations for the sick, only to collect additional payments when their divinations proved ineffective.[108] Reformers believed that a vicious cycle existed, wherein superstitious reliance on the yuta during illnesses created debt, which in turn rendered villagers even more vulnerable to the prostitution rings that the same yuta operated.

Local reformers sought to remove female leaders like the noro and yuta from their central position in the spiritual, cultural, and economic lives of village communities at the turn of the century.[109] Attacks against priestesses, oracles, and women of loose morals show striking similarities to witch hunts in Europe during the primitive accumulation process of the sixteenth and seventeenth centuries that led to the confiscation of women's property, their removal from communal lands, and their loss of control over their bodies.[110] In Okinawa, a violent expropriation of priestesses from their lands and attacks against female property accompanied the recoding of gender norms and rationality through strict surveillance of women's activities in agrarian villages, all under the guise of modernizing old customs.[111] Lands were confiscated from the noro in the land reorganization project at the same time that the Movement to Reform Old Customs prohibited women from the practice of tattooing (figure 3.3), singing outdoors and playing the *shamisen* in the streets, viewing plays and renting out rooms to actors, and even communicating with people from other villages.

Taken as a whole, it is hard to deny the existence of a systematic project to subordinate women—who, according to Mies, "in their economic and sexual independence constituted a threat for the emerging bourgeois order."[112] They had to be discredited for embodying a certain type of irrationality and were labeled crazed, possessed, and capable of driving their peers, clients, and neighbors to act in the same way. It is in light of this demonization of female figures integral to village life that we must evaluate the significance of female weavers' refusal to comply with the prefecture-led project to modernize the textiles industry as a powerful form of anticapitalist struggle. These refusals constituted a rejection of the discourse of Okinawan community that local intellectuals and politicians mobilized to take hold of the surplus value that the prefecture's producers created.

Ryūkyūan Brand Textiles and Unruly Weavers

As we have seen, the main motivation for the Movement to Reform Old Customs was to ensure that the wealth created in the prefecture remained in the hands of Okinawa's bourgeoisie. After a long history of outsiders taking away the prefecture's resources and taxes, local leaders wanted to make certain that they would be allowed to keep what they felt they were entitled

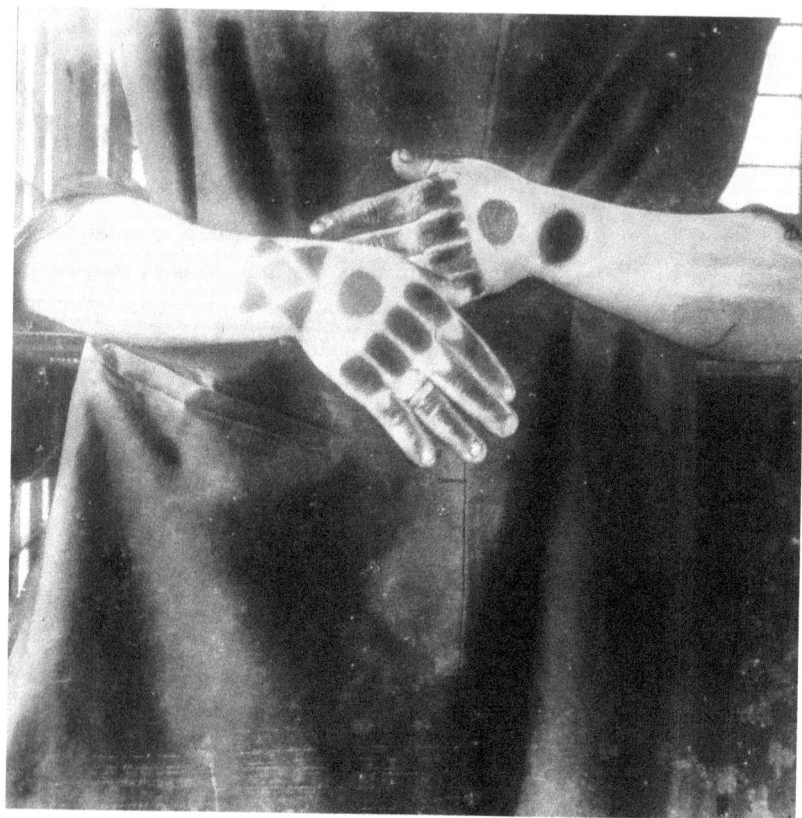

Fig. 3.3 The practice of tattooing was officially prohibited in 1882 with the enactment of the Criminal Code, but women continued to etch themselves through the Taisho era. Tatoo-marks on the hands of Loo Chooan Women, E. R. Bull's photographic plates, no. 26, Taisho era, Bull Collection, University of the Ryūkyūs.

to. In order to realize their self-exploitation—or, rather, their exploitation of the surplus value that was created by members of their purported community—local bourgeoisie began establishing their own financial institutions. The first two banks founded by Okinawan capital—the Okinawa Agricultural Bank and the Okinawa Bank—both were established in 1899. Soon thereafter, the Kunigami Bank (1905) and Okinawa Commercial Bank (1912) opened their doors.[113] These banks were connected directly or indirectly to the brown sugar industry and were attempts by Ōta, Nakayoshi Chōkō, and other local industrialists to establish stronger links between the small-scale brown sugar manufacture that existed at the village level, prefecturewide industrial associations, and finance capital. Ōta and Nakayoshi also founded consignment businesses like the Marushichi Shōten and selling associations to buttress the position of Okinawa's sugar vis-à-vis merchants in Osaka and Kagoshima.[114] Local leaders transformed themselves into merchant and finance capitalist rivals to mainland sugar merchants and succeeded in taking over a portion of the sale of brown sugar, which until that time had been monopolized by mainland merchants.

They also called on the prefecture to take more initiative and implement policies to encourage economic development. In an article published in the *Ryūkyū Shimpō* on June 27, 1901, Ōta clearly expressed this desire. He argued that a comprehensive vision and strategy for Okinawa's economic development had to be formulated, since a higher degree of organization distinguished a civilized society from a feudal one. He used the steam engine as an analogy for modern society: "Since the machines are organized in an orderly fashion, a small amount of steam can move a several-thousand-ton vessel. In this way proper organization can increase the amount of work accomplished while decreasing the amount of power necessary to complete it."[115]

Ōta's emphasis on the importance of organizing the whole society under a comprehensive and consistent policy carried over to the way that he thought specific industries such as sugar should be reorganized. Along with local sugar experts, he argued that the industry had to be rationalized in order to make it competitive in the external market. They regarded the establishment and enforcement of stringent quality standards and improved efficiency in the production process as urgent matters in light of recent events: mainland sugar brokers had been caught filling just the top of the sugar barrels with good-quality sugar and the rest with a lower grade to fool Japanese buyers into thinking that they were purchasing a full barrel of the superior product. Such cunning measures by those who cared little about protecting the industry's reputation made "a loss of confidence in the prefecture's most important industry" inevitable.[116] This was particularly detrimental since the prefecture was facing stiff competition from Taiwan.[117]

In response to these external threats to the well-being of Okinawa's most important export industry, local sugar merchants called on the Naha chamber of commerce to police sugar transactions more strictly in both "legal and social terms." If not, a *Ryūkyū Shimpō* article warned, this bad practice would become a virus: "The prefecture's social sanctions will become loose and more people will think that it is all right to be unethical."[118] A swift response seemed necessary for the very survival of the prefecture. If adjustments were not made quickly, Ōta feared, "the prefecture, like China, will step by step fall into a decline. If this worsens, it will be impossible to even retain the appearance of a prefecture. The region will become Kinawa County, Kagoshima Prefecture."[119]

In addition to sugar, reformers focused on textiles as a problem industry that was a microcosm of all that was broken in Okinawa. An 1888 report by an anonymous mainland observer described the conditions in Shiohama District, the center of commercial activity where a large proportion of the textiles produced in Okinawa was sold to individual buyers (figure 3.4). After introducing it to his readers as the Okinawan equivalent of Tokyo's Nihonbashi District, the author painted the following picture: "They [the sellers] do not abide by any rules and stalls are set up in a large area, some facing forward, others facing backward, and still others facing sideways. The women who run these stalls set up shop as they please. The conditions are extremely noisy; at times, their barbarism is unbearable." The author continued that it was at Shiohama that he was finally able to see an Okinawan woman up close for the first time, since upper-class Okinawan women were strictly forbidden from interacting with strangers: "They walk around mostly on the bare ground like beasts. I heard somewhere that the feet of Okinawan women are very solid, like that of cats and dogs. This is understandable since they have to carry around trees, rocks, sand, dirt, rice bales and sugar barrels. . . . They have tattoos on the back of both hands. Their words are incomprehensible though they do speak in broken Japanese or, at the very least, can understand it."[120]

A description that Ichiki presented in his 1894 report to the Home Ministry was slightly more sympathetic. Of these petty merchants he wrote: "There is much that can be learned from Okinawan women. Those who sell woven cloth in the inns, those who go to the market and sell miscellaneous items, those who sit in shops and sell its wares, those who carry important

Fig. 3.4 Markets such as this one in Naha, where female weavers peddled their wares, popped up throughout Okinawa's cities following the disposition of 1879. These became the target of policing and management as prefectural authorities tried to establish a more modern and mechanized industry, starting in the first decade of the twentieth century. Naha cloth market, Naha City Museum of History photo no. 02000219.

goods on their head and travel around selling them—all of them walk along the dirt roads carrying products on their head. Men carry umbrellas and stroll along slowly along the same road."[121] These merchant women who sold their textiles and miscellaneous wares at small markets like Shiohama also became targets for reform by Okinawa's aspiring bourgeoisie in the years of the land reorganization project. Reforms were not simply focused on transforming commercial practices or manufacturing techniques, but were part of a much more ambitious project of reconfiguring the sexual division of labor in a manner that reformers believed to be most conducive to their vision of modern Okinawa.[122]

As previous chapters have shown, woven cloth manufactured by Okinawan women were recognized as highly sophisticated and technically advanced works of art and were coveted by officials of the former Satsuma domain as tribute items to be collected from the kingdom government. Both the quality and quantity of these textiles increased through the years of Satsuma rule, as village officials were charged with maintaining strict control over the production process to uphold the value of the cloth on the market. Only women submitted cloth as tax payments, and they often substituted

Fig. 3.5 Weaving was exclusively a woman's task during the early modern period in Okinawa. Woven cloth was submitted for taxes or sold to mainland consumers. Female weaver, The University of Hawaii at Manoa Library Sakamaki/Hawley Collection, from *Bōkyo Okinawa*, vol. 5, 92.

it for rice and millet (figure 3.5). As the kingdom's economy became embedded into the China–Southeast Asia trade network in the fifteenth and sixteenth centuries, Ryūkyū's woven cloth came under even stricter surveillance, and the dingy weaving huts that Sasamori Gisuke observed in 1893 were built in villages. The most skilled weavers were confined in these huts until the quota was met.[123] Women who managed to escape this existence were still expected to weave tribute cloth for eight or nine months of the year in their homes.[124]

With the incorporation of the former kingdom into the Japanese nation-state, weaving women came to have greater opportunities to produce and sell their cloth for profit rather than to fulfill tax obligations. Still, as late as 1894, Ichiki cited cases of women who wove to meet their tax obligations and supplemented their household incomes by selling leftover pieces to mainland enthusiasts. Transforming these conditions of weaving into a modern, mechanized large industry fueled by waged workers required an overhaul of societal expectations, roles, and rhythms of life in Okinawa's agrarian villages. Reformers were quite optimistic that this herculean task could be completed with proper leadership and the establishment of clear guidelines. They envisioned that in time, reforms would eliminate the problems that currently plagued textile production, like petty thefts of raw materials, the pawning by individuals of communal tools, and the failure to meet externally imposed deadlines. These maladies, which reformers characterized as individual workers' theft of the collective profits of their villages, would necessarily decline with the start of large-scale factory work: if women attempted to steal from the community, they would be fired immediately.[125]

To create a modern textiles industry, reformers first targeted "the large number of ignorant island people who call themselves experts and are recognized by society as such."[126] Their disorganized activity had to be curbed and prominent position in the industry downplayed because their carelessness threatened to soil the reputation of Okinawa's textiles, which faced fierce competition from the new textile-producing region of Kurume in Fukuoka and from Kagoshima.[127] They instituted measures to control quality and inspect textiles produced by weavers and spinners in order to prevent the sale of products that could damage the reputation of the Okinawan brand.

The prefecture approved the formation of the Ryūkyū woven cloth dealers' association in the winter of 1898 as part of its efforts to modernize Okinawa's textile industry. The third article in its statement of purpose clearly outlined its objectives: "The association aims to reform the bad-quality woven cloth that is churned out in the prefecture. This should lead to gradual reform and the development of eternal trust in our woven cloth."[128] They reasoned that inspections would become easier to carry out once production had been concentrated in several central sites and envisioned a setup similar to the one that had been implemented by the Isesaki textile association, which established regular dates for transactions related to textiles. Specific days were set aside every month for individual manufacturers to bring the small quantities of cloth that they produced to the office to have them inspected. Once the cloth passed rigorous standards of inspection, weavers purchased a ticket that they then tacked onto their product. Only then could they take their textiles to the market to sell. This step ensured that transactions on quality products were conducted during the daylight hours and provided a structured system of inspections that enabled buyers to receive refunds if they were not happy with the quality of the pieces they purchased.[129] The Naha chamber of commerce hoped to implement this system in Okinawa, starting with a declaration that woven cloth could not be bought or sold after six o'clock in the evening. Any person caught engaging in transactions after that time would receive a harsh fine of five yen.[130]

In addition to transforming the work process of Okinawa's textile producers, reformers targeted the buyers of Ryūkyū textiles—mainland consumers—to make sure that they bought Okinawa's products properly. The Ryūkyū woven cloth dealers' association began a campaign to inform potential buyers that woven cloth from Okinawa that did not have an official seal of approval was inauthentic. Notices were posted in stores, restaurants, bathhouses, inns, newspapers, and journals in Tokyo, Osaka, Kobe, Kagoshima, Kumamoto, Nagasaki, and Taiwan to warn people not to be fooled into purchasing "fakes."[131] The reformers' resolve to control the flow of all textiles from Okinawa and their commitment to making sure that every piece that escaped their circuits of distribution was deemed inauthentic reflected their strong desire to wrest control away from Okinawa's traditional producers.

The textile industry's female producers remained unconvinced that these changes were necessary. Their refusal to cooperate with the guidelines set forth by the association led the *Ryūkyū Shimpō* to proclaim that these women were the gravest threat to the establishment of capitalist relations of production in the industry. An article published in November 1901 described the "carefree action of the small capitalists"[132] who walked around barefoot carrying their homemade wares on their heads and skillfully hawked their merchandise to unsuspecting travelers. The problem with these peddlers was that they were focused on their immediate profits and were unwilling to make sacrifices for the good of the industry as a whole. Since their activities involved very little in the form of capital investment, they were able to quit whenever they desired.[133] The article blamed the decline of the textile industry vis-à-vis its mainland rivals on these customary producers and sellers: "Thus, there is nothing in their heads that naturally leads to prizing trust or credibility. They try to fool people and absorb as much of the small profits as they can. They do not think about long-term fluctuations and have led the industry into its current nadir."[134] It was a great disappointment "that such an important industry [was] left in the hands of this ignorant and uneducated lot."[135]

The smooth-talking barefoot peddlers ignored these insults and continued to circumvent the sales routes that the association established. Unfortunately for Okinawa's reformers, thirty-three of the ninety-three members of the cloth weavers' association were women.[136] Though they were mocked as illiterate and uncivilized in the newspapers, they were hard to ignore, as they regularly spoke out against policies and regulations that they found objectionable. On one occasion they confronted Kuniyoshi Masayoshi, the president of the Naha chamber of commerce, about the restrictions that the chamber had recently imposed on selling.[137] A few days after this confrontation, a large group of protesters went to Kuniyoshi's home and threatened to break down his doors if he did not rescind these regulations. At a general meeting of the Ryūkyū woven cloth dealers' association on the afternoon of October 31, 1901—attended by Governor Narahara, the administrative head (kuchō) of Naha, and other prominent members of the prefectural administration—several women stood up and expressed their opposition to the association's attempts to regulate the quality of their products and collect fines for violations. They stormed the waiting rooms, offices, and houses of the association's officers to make sure that their displeasure was duly noted.[138]

It must have been quite an outrage for Okinawa's leaders, recipients of the highest level of education available in the nation, to witness these hordes of barefoot, sloppily dressed, tattooed women who could not even speak proper Japanese stand up to the political and commercial leaders of the prefecture and declare that they would not pay the outrageous inspection fees, membership dues, or fines levied without their consent. Not just that, they continued to sell their inferior products without any concern about upholding the reputation of the prefecture's industry. For the men who spent their days and nights racking their brains over how to improve an industry they believed to be under attack, this behavior was unbearable. The *Shimpō* reported on November 17, 1898: "If [the women's] obstructive acts were due to their stupidity and foolishness we would have reason to believe that proper enlightenment could bring forth improvements. However, since they are engaging in this behavior as bad businesspeople obstructing the development of industry, they should be driven out of this society."[139]

Men of the prefecture also posed serious obstacles to the success of the new textiles policy because they thought of weaving as women's work and were reluctant to take jobs in these newly established factories. Only after these stereotypes had been demolished could real advancements be made. The Movement to Reform Old Customs' efforts to correct the gender roles that had become inverted during the Ryūkyū kingdom period— "the men just lounge around at home while the women engage in commerce outside"[140]—has new meaning in light of this conflict within one of Okinawa's key industries. Implicit in these and other moves that blamed the selfishness and backwardness of local producers and merchants for Okinawa's economic weakness was the belief that Okinawa's traditional culture was the root of the problem. Like similar modernization discourses that scholars such as Manu Goswami and Kathy Le Mons Walker have observed in different historical contexts, this assumption reinforced elites' belief in the cultural deficiencies of the Okinawan peasantry and occluded the structural relationship between the Japanese state and Okinawa prefecture that promoted uneven development.[141]

In response to the vast cultural obstacles to their visions of modernization, local reformers tried to transform the prevailing image of cloth weaving as women's work and drive women out of the industry by offering high wages to male weavers. The November 1901 article cited above explained this decision. According to the article, in September 1900 a factory that the prefecture had built in Naha to encourage the modernization of Okinawa's textile industry employed 20 male and 150 female full-time factory workers, whose wages were determined by the difficulty and pattern of the work and the skill level of the weavers. Wages were also determined by gender: male workers received 14–20 sen per woven *shaku*, while female workers received 2–6 sen for the same work.[142] The article did not explain this discrepancy in wages between male and female workers, but it was clearly a manifestation of reformers' desire to wrest the industry out of the hands of the female peddler weavers. Time after time they disparaged the "small woven cloth sellers who only looked to their immediate measly profits" while admitting that textile production was "completely a woman's industry" that depended on the skill that women had acquired over generations of forced weaving.[143] The reformers' desire to expand the scale of production by mechanizing the industry while preserving the reputation of Ryūkyū woven cloth led them to declare that the old rules governing all facets of life had to be abandoned. They repeated the calls of the Movement to Reform Old Customs for men to work and urged women to assume their proper place in the home as good wives and mothers. The encouragement of waged work in textiles for men was part of this new economy and society that Okinawa's leaders were trying to mold into existence.[144]

The problem with this tactic was that a successful conversion to factory-style production could not take place by compensating the most skilled craftspeople the least or by excluding them altogether. The average output of the factory in Naha was just ten *tan* a day, despite vigorous efforts by reformers to recruit workers.[145] They blamed the low output on the workers' lack of devotion to factory work and lamented that neither men nor women differentiated between business hours and break times because they "lacked a concept of rules in their minds."[146] In fact, the workers did not lack discipline, but wages were a foreign concept to women who understood weaving as something they dabbled in while completing their other responsibilities in the household economy or as a coerced activity that they were required to engage in to fulfill their tax obligations.[147] Reformers had hoped that the establishment of the factory would automatically result in the creation of full-time factory workers, but this did not happen. Female weaver-peddlers were much too entrenched in the textile industry to fade into the background as cogs of a machine.

As we have seen, Okinawan intellectuals made the ill-behaved but skilled women of the villages their main target of attack at the turn of the century. These women, who favored the establishment of an association one minute and changed their minds the next, and who dared to express their discontent and engaged in behavior that threatened the prefecture's brand, needed to be driven out of the marketplace as well as the comfort of their homes. Their homes, which doubled as their workplace, were different from the modern factories that reformers advocated because there they could weave in their spare time or when tax collection season arrived. Before teaching these women how to be thrifty or how to balance their household budgets, local leaders had to place them in factories where regular workdays, hours, breaks, and quotas prevailed over their individual whims or family obligations. Once there, they had to be locked in and forbidden from roaming the streets barefoot and tattooed, so as to keep the evidence of Okinawa's barbarism hidden from public view.[148] This was not an easy task, since neither women nor men were ready to give up the roles that they had fulfilled for so long. These habits and relations were rooted not only in the economic structure of the region but also in people's social and cultural consciousness and their daily lives.

Conclusion: Female Shamans and Tattooed Barbarians

In his 1935 poem, "Kaiwa" ("A Conversation"), Yamanokuchi Baku imagined an encounter between a Japanese woman and an Okinawan man in mainland Japan.[149] In the first verse, Yamanokuchi lamented the way that Okinawa, his hometown, conjured up the image of an exotic South both temporally and spatially removed from modern Japan and criticized the propagation of this image by Japanese social scientists such as Yanagita Kunio, whose "discovery" of Okinawa in 1921 was instrumental to the development of native ethnology in Japan.[150] "Kaiwa," which is often read as a critique of Japanese intellectuals and observers of Okinawa—who considered the prefecture to exist in a time and space fundamentally different from those of the rest of the nation—can alternatively be read as a critique of local leaders' transformation of all the customs and practices of daily life into signs of barbarism and incivility. This chapter has shown that the Okinawan reformers and intellectuals associated with the *Ryūkyū Shimpō* faction aggressively sought to relegate existing practices, dress, cultural forms, and social relations to the past, in preparation for the completion of the land reorganization project in 1903.

Despite the necessarily incomplete and inadequate nature of the project to establish modern industry in the prefecture, this period is notable because it was the first time that self-professed leaders of Okinawa pursued the aggressive rationalization of industry as a tactic of resistance against the onslaught of global competition, mainland merchants, and state expropriation. For the first time, they advocated the dismantling of old economic structures and ways of life in the name of modernization: a synonym for capitalist relations of production. The reforms undertaken under the banner of reforming old customs as well as the simultaneous attempts to capitalize Okinawa's major industries must be understood as part of a general effort to dismantle old knowledge, techniques, and ways of life, an undertaking prompted by leaders' changed awareness of Okinawa's place in the global economy, the Japanese empire, and the modern era.

Ōta articulated this stance most clearly. For him, despotic methods were sometimes necessary, because the people had not yet internalized the values that were required to succeed in a rapidly changing world. He applauded when agrarian village elites took the initiative to impose regulations that they deemed necessary for restoring the economic and moral health of their regions. He explained: "Though these tactics may seem coercive and unfree, there is nothing more unfree than being employed by someone else. If the degree of oppressiveness is compared, the oppressiveness of the employer toward the employee is much greater than these rules. Violent or not, these regulations have advanced these villagers from people used by others to the ones doing the using."[151]

The aspiration to become "the ones doing the using" summed up the final goal of Ōta's faction, the dominant intellectual group of local leaders in the late nineteenth century. In light of the rapid influx of people from outside the prefecture and the intensifying degree of bureaucratization by the state, the assertion that "there is nothing more unfree than being employed by someone else" held great significance. Ōta's belief that any measures were tolerable if they served the goal of maintaining Okinawa's freedom and current position in the Japanese empire was shared by large numbers of local leaders in this period. Taiwan was firmly on Ōta's mind when he expressed his greatest fear that if people did not adjust quickly to changing conditions, "it will be impossible to even retain the appearance of a prefecture."[152]

Demotion to a colony was not just a hypothetical fear in the first decade of the twentieth century. In December 1908, thirty years after the establishment of Okinawa Prefecture, a proposal to transfer direct control of Okinawa to the Office of the Governor General of Taiwan was submitted to both houses of the National Diet. Though the rationale behind this suggestion is not completely clear, the proposal's gist was for Okinawa to be transferred to Taiwan as compensation from the state for the customs duties that it imposed on the colony. Newspaper accounts indicate that this proposal for direct control by the governor general's office was one of many possible political statuses that mainland politicians considered for Taiwan, Okinawa, and Amami Ōshima during the first decade of the twentieth century. This was part of a broader debate on the way to expand the empire and would have created a Nanyōdō in the south that was the equivalent of Hokkaido in the north.[153] The southern islands would be under a single administrative structure like the governor general's office in Taiwan. Advocates believed that this was the most efficient way to maintain control of and organize industrial policies for these regions that would support the development and defense of Japan proper.[154] Finally, they envisioned the Nanyōdō as a fortress from which the Japanese empire could mount its southward expansion in the future.

In the urgent calls for progress, modernization, and civilization of the prefecture that Okinawa's leaders issued to prevent the region's colonization, women became the metaphor for looseness, regression, and barbarism. It is no coincidence that the demonization of female oracles and the prohibition of female tattooing were undertaken with unparalleled vigor at the start of the land reorganization project, at the same time as the Movement to Reform Old Customs.[155] Women who received tattoos communally in order to inscribe names of hometowns, weaving skills, or other occupations on the back of their hands as a type of coming-of-age ceremony and yuta who held a privileged place in decision making about marriage, health, and family relations had to be reeducated or eliminated altogether in order for local intellectuals and bourgeois to fulfill their visions of Okinawan autonomy.[156]

Measures to reform the behavior of women were met with fierce resistance, particularly from female textile producers who had no interest in molding themselves into efficient and obedient wage workers in the factory or thrifty managers of the household. Their actions reflect their desires to produce, live, play, reproduce, and make decisions about their bodies and their work on their own terms. When seen as part of broader attempts to transform gender roles and expectations in Okinawa, the collective refusal by female weavers to accept the terms of the proposed community take on deeper meaning: they were simultaneously an articulation of a new social configuration founded on contempt for everything and everyone who sought to mutilate their bodily rhythms and practices. As the following chapters reveal, the persistence of these rhythms, particularly in agrarian villages, reveal the difficulties that capitalist actors faced. The people they targeted understood exactly what they stood to lose if they capitulated to the leaders of the so-called Okinawan community.

CHAPTER FOUR

≡

THE IMPOSSIBILITY OF PLANTATION SUGAR IN OKINAWA

World War I and the Refusal of Enclosure

The prerequisites for the real subsumption of Okinawan labor into capitalist society were laid with the completion of the land reorganization project in 1903. The project clarified the boundaries of land ownership, classified lands according to their yield and function, and established private property relations on all the islands in the prefecture. The government distributed certificates of land ownership in order to make the assessment and collection of taxes more uniform and efficient. As a result, individual heads of households rather than the village as a whole became responsible for fulfilling tax obligations, and the customary practice of periodic redivisions of lands was formally abolished.[1] The purported goal of these reforms was to secure the government's financial foundation. Moreover, by commodifying the land, the project theoretically freed the Okinawan people from their locales and provided one essential prerequisite for the commodification of their labor power. As I argued in chapters 2 and 3, this transition was an outcome of the Miyako Island Peasantry Movement's struggles against existing policies that kept commoners in service of a corrupt local elite and, simultaneously, a reflection of the shifting importance of the region in the Japanese empire from a supplier of sugar to a supplier of labor power and taxes like the rest of the nation.

In addition to providing certificates of land ownership to individual households, the land reorganization project converted a range of lands into state-owned and -managed property, whether the lands had been held communally by villages, owned by local municipalities, or owned privately by individuals. Despite the best efforts of local intellectuals like Jahana Noboru to resist this process of enclosure, which had begun with the reclamation projects of the 1890s, the prefectural assembly decided in 1908 that all communal lands whose status had been deliberately left ambiguous during the land reorganization project would be transferred to the state or municipalities as public lands in order to facilitate their conversion into areas devoted to large-scale sugar cultivation. After 1908 most of Okinawa's communal lands became publicly owned, and individual farming households were formally deprived of access to forest lands and materials that had been vital components of their household economies in the past.[2] Small producers did not accept the expropriation of communal lands without a fight, and their struggles against this process informed the way that industrial development took place in the region.

In his chapter on so-called primitive accumulation in *Capital*, Marx traced the dissolution of the agrarian villages that accompanied the process of enclosure and understood the latter to be a tactic that bourgeois states deployed in order to drive people out of their communities and into industry. In the case of Japan and many other regions of the world, these two processes did not take place at the same time, with agrarian villages remaining intact despite the loss of communal lands that were vital to the survival of small cultivators. This phenomenon and the crises that emerged as a result were collectively called the agrarian question and required resolution in order for proper capitalist development to take place.[3] In his works on the agrarian question that spanned the wartime and postwar years, the Japanese Marxist Uno Kōzō warned against seeing Japan's version as an exception and pointed out that the process of capitalist development that Marx described was simply one historically and geographically grounded example that could not simply be grafted onto other national contexts. Uno explained, "capitalism does not demand the capitalization of the agrarian village any more than is necessary for its own development."[4] In cases where the development of capitalism was not accompanied by the dissolution of the agrarian village, he observed, villages functioned for decades as repositories of theoretically commodified labor power awaiting their free valorization by capital. That is, they contained the industrial reserve army that Marx defined as "a mass of human material always already ready for exploitation by capital in the interests of capital's own changing valorization requirements."[5]

In Okinawa, where conditions of incorporation into Japanese capitalism necessitated policies that strategically kept old administrative systems and tax collection methods intact, the agrarian question arose during the conversion of many small peasantry (shōnō) into sugar producers.[6] One major task of this chapter is to examine how Okinawa's small producers who lost access to their communal lands responded to their further inclusion into the commodity economy through the entry of mainland sugar companies around World War I. I argue that the specific appearance of the agrarian question in Okinawa was not simply a result of the different way that the prefecture was incorporated into the Japanese capitalist state, but was the outcome of small peasantry's struggles against their transformation into dead labor that enabled capital's realization of surplus value. These struggles, informed by recent memories of dispossession, were key rather than merely ancillary factors in shaping the contours of the prefecture's agrarian question.

Three axes of confrontation will be examined in order to illuminate the complexity of positions that emerged as Okinawa became embedded into the national and global economies in the early twentieth century. In the first axis, Okinawa's intellectuals elaborated new understandings of national community that affirmed the original unity of Okinawans and Japanese. Local political leaders mobilized this new definition of community to argue that Okinawans were fully capable of governing themselves—an assertion that gained urgency as the Japanese empire expanded its presence into the peninsula. Small producers responded to this new definition of Okinawa with a mixture of disinterest and cynicism.

A second axis of confrontation developed between the small peasantry in Okinawa who produced brown sugar and local industrialists who bought into the economic nationalism that Ōta Chōfu first articulated in the late nineteenth century. They rejected efforts of local bourgeoisie like Ōta and Miyagi Tetsu to formulate industrial policies based on their belief that reorganizing Okinawa into a capitalist gemeinschaft would enable the ideal condition of Okinawans benevolently exploiting their fellow Okinawans.[7] The failure of medium-sized reform-style factories advocated by proponents of an Okinawa capitalism for Okinawans reveals that the organic community—whose interests local industrialists were so desperate to protect—lacked a constituency that was invested in its own defense.[8]

Finally, small peasantry who resided in regions at the jurisdictional boundaries of large-scale sugar factories owned by Okitai Takushoku Seitō Gaisha (hereafter Okitai Seitō) and Tainan Seitō Kabushiki Gaisha (hereafter Tainansha) that entered the prefecture in the 1910s organized a series of nonselling alliances between 1916 and 1920 that seriously impeded the development of the prefecture's sugar industry.⁹ These struggles reflected small peasantry's rejection of both local industrialists' and mainland sugar capital's efforts to mold them and their social relations in the pursuit of broader economic goals. The scope of these alliances were quite small—even the largest case affected just 10 percent of the arable lands owned by Tainansha—and documentation regarding these events is almost nonexistent. However, a consideration of these alliances that developed during the peak years of Okinawa's sugar industry reveals the antagonisms that emerged between cultivators and mainland sugar capital during the last years of the Meiji era.¹⁰ The constant inability of large sugar companies to procure enough cane from cultivators limited the proletarianization of Okinawa's agricultural population and reflected their failure to dismantle deeply embedded networks of social, cultural, and economic ties that continued to exist as counterforces to enclosure, even as cultivators became integrated in the broader commodity economy.

Instead of considering the relatively low levels of proletarianization of agricultural labor as evidence that an extreme version of the agrarian question existed in Okinawa, we should see the difficulty that mainland sugar capital had in transforming small producers into pure cultivators of raw material as an example of the antagonisms inherent in any process of converting people's labor into surplus value. As I explained in earlier chapters, these antagonisms have been theorized by autonomists as struggles between living labor—that part of labor associated with the needs and desires of workers and producers—and dead labor—the uncreative and unproductive part of the organic composition of capital. As such, these conflicts must be understood as a broad rejection of all social structures, relations, and ideologies that enabled capital's valorization of the surplus value of producers.

Iha Fuyū's Theory of Shared Origins

Marxist theorists argue that the establishment of private property relations in a territory is accompanied by a concealment of the true relationship between the state and the people through the idea of the nation. In Okinawa the state was not the most aggressive proponent of this subjection. After initially contesting Okinawa's incorporation into Japan, as we have already seen, by the end of the nineteenth century many of Okinawa's intellectuals had accepted a definition of the relationship between the Japanese and Okinawan people that called the disposition an integral part of the process of reunification of long-lost siblings. It is difficult to conclude that this was purely a strategic move that local leaders made in light of shifting geopolitical conditions, but it is necessary to consider just how much the propagation of this discourse was informed by the threat of colonization that loomed over them. In any case, in the twentieth century they became the most skillful manipulators of national ideology and the most active proponents of Okinawa's full inclusion in Japan even as they continued to hold onto their economic nationalism.

Iha Fuyū was instrumental to this call for inclusion. He returned to Okinawa in 1906 after receiving a graduate degree in linguistics from the Tokyo Imperial University, and in 1906 he published in the local newspaper a social-scientific elaboration of the historical relationship between the Okinawan and Japanese people called the theory of shared origins (*nichiryū dōsoron*).[11] Almost immediately the theory of shared origins replaced the theory of dual subordination to Japan and China that had been preeminent in explaining the relationship among Ryūkyū, Japan, and China during the second disposition in 1879.[12] Dual subordination was a useful notion for a former kingdom appealing to Chinese officials for aid, but calling for Okinawa's full inclusion into the Japanese nation-state required a radical reformulation. Iha made his first comprehensive argument about the shared origins of the Ryūkyū and Yamato people (*minzoku*) in "Okinawajin no Sosen ni Tsuite" ("Ancestors of the Okinawan People"), as noted above.[13] He agreed with the prominent Japanese historian Shiratori Kurakichi that the two peoples collectively composed the race of the descendants of the gods (*tenson jinrui*).[14] They were separated from each other and began their respective moves across Asia around 3000 BC. The faction loyal to the Jimmu emperor entered the Yamato region and conquered the indigenous Ainu people. In the meantime, the ancestors of the future Okinawans floated around until they finally arrived at the Okinawa archipelago, where they too defeated the Ainu and settled. A careful reading of their national histories—the *Kojiki* and the *Omoro Sōshi*—revealed to Iha that despite their long years apart, communication between the siblings never ceased completely.[15] He concluded that there was unequivocal proof that "the qualifications of the Okinawan people to be Japanese are fundamentally different from that of the Ainu or the Taiwanese barbarians (*seiban*)."[16] Their reunification under the emperor system through the Meiji Restoration was a fortuitous opportunity to restore a relationship that had weakened through time and distance. He concluded: "Now, we are united with our sisters from whom we were separated 2,000 years ago and live under the same political system as them."[17] In this skillful, yet forgetful, revision of the existing memory of the

1879 disposition as a violent second invasion, Iha erased the fierce struggle that took place between the Meiji state and former kingdom officials in the 1870s and 1880s from his narrative and chose to present the region's annexation as a triumphant reunification of siblings who had been separated for centuries by circumstances beyond their control.[18]

It should be clarified that reunification here did not mean the complete assimilation of the Okinawan people into Japan. That is, Iha did not advocate an elimination of all qualities or practices that were unique to the Okinawan people, nor did he call on the people to blindly adopt all Japanese practices. In fact, in several of his works, Iha advocated intermarriage or "the mixing of blood" between Okinawans and Japanese in order to physically reunite the two groups.[19] The ascendance of this theory of shared origins reflected a general shift in political allegiance by Okinawa's elite as well as a fundamental change in the way that the categories of Okinawa and Japan were defined. For local intellectuals who had accepted their inclusion into the Meiji political system by the end of the nineteenth century, this theory granted them the right to demand equal treatment and a rationale for differentiating themselves from subject populations that did not enjoy this relationship with the Japanese people. Previously they had been able to call for the enactment of identical laws and rights in Okinawa only on the basis of the Meiji state's benevolence and their constitutional right as subjects, but now Iha's scientific demonstration of the natural community of Okinawans and mainland Japanese gave local intellectuals a sense that it was their natural right to be treated equally. This made the differential treatment and discriminatory attitudes held by state actors even more injurious. Ōta was one Okinawan who was emboldened by Iha's theory of shared origins to argue for political equality during the late Meiji period.

As we saw in the previous chapter, Ōta believed that the most important task for the local bourgeoisie and intellectuals was to prevent the human and material resources of the prefecture from being exploited by mainland capitalists. Once they gained the "right to pay taxes," Ōta and other local leaders sought to win the right to send their own representatives to the National Diet, an urgent matter because political autonomy was a sign of their competence to make important decisions about matters that directly affected Okinawa's residents.[20] Ōta explained: "Minors, idiots and those with mental illnesses do not have the right or obligation to dispose of their property because they do not have the capacity to do so. Furthermore, those who have committed crimes and those who have been negligent are sometimes declared incompetent. These people are deemed incapable of taking care of themselves and are not considered full-fledged human beings. The term *autonomy* is nothing more than saying that one can take care of oneself. Regional autonomy means that people do not need others to intervene or take care of their region."[21]

He fiercely debated Jahana in the late 1890s over the timing of political reforms, but once the land reforms were completed, Ōta's main priority shifted to obtaining political equality with the mainland prefectures. The vast powers that the Okinawan governor held—which were above and beyond those enjoyed by his counterparts on the mainland—concerned him, particularly since the administration was in the midst of formulating aggressive plans for the modernization of the sugar industry. Its invitation to mainland sugar capitalists to enter the prefecture under favorable terms led Ōta to fear that those who entered the local industry would eventually parlay their economic advantages into control of policy making. He believed that if such conditions materialized because Okinawans still had not received voting rights, they would be no better than "minors, idiots and those with mental illnesses" or the Taiwanese people from whom he and his colleagues worked so hard to distinguish themselves. This concern about the need to separate themselves from these categories of inferior people who were incapable of making their own decisions conditioned the policies that Ōta and other members of the Okinawan bourgeoisie advocated for the sugar industry.

The Entry of Large Sugar Capital into Okinawa

The prefectural administration took an increasingly assertive role in developing a modern sugar industry in Okinawa after the land reorganization.[22] In 1907 it established a testing site—sanctioned by the Ministry of Agriculture and Commerce—in Nishihara Village, in the Nakagami region. In 1908 the prefecture used machinery it had procured from Glasgow to build at the site a factory that could produce a hundred tons of sugar a day. It also acquired a medium-size tract of land (2.75 chōbu) that served as a testing site for cane cultivation. The factory, constructed next to the Nishihara testing site, was designed to encourage rational cultivation methods like the selection of stalks, planting, fertilizer, irrigation, and extermination with the goal of improving yields.[23] In 1909 the Nishihara factory manufactured *bunmitsutō* for the first time.[24] The state's establishment of this large-scale modern factory transformed existing social and production relations in the area, as Nishihara's small producers became suppliers of cane for the factory.[25]

After conducting tests for two years, in 1911 the prefecture sold the Nishihara factory for 100,000 yen—to be paid over seven years, with no interest—to Okinawa Seitō, the first mainland sugar company to stake a claim in Okinawa.[26] Three men who had strong ties to the local political scene brought the company into the prefecture: Asabushi Kanjō, a career bureaucrat and head administrator (*gunchō*) of the Nakagami region at the time; Taira Hōichi, the president of Okinawa Kyōritsu Bank; and Hibi Shigeaki, the current governor.[27] They invited Yokohama's Abe Shōten, which had already established a branch office in Naha, to handle commercial transactions for the sale of brown sugar to mainland buyers and installed Narahara Shigeru, the former governor, as chairman of the board of directors.[28] Abe Kōnosuke represented Abe Shōten as president of the company, and Yano Keitarō, a well-known industrialist from the Kansai area, became its first CEO.[29] Under the management of Okinawa Seitō, the Nishihara factory expanded its capacity from 100 tons of sugar a day to 250 tons. Using the leverage that it had obtained from this transaction, Abe Shōten entered Taiwan's sugar industry through the purchase of a Japanese-run company already engaged in manufacture in November 1912. Following this foray into Taiwan, the company changed its name to Okitai Seitō and focused on expanding its operations in the empire's two southwestern territories. In Okinawa, Okitai Seitō continued to grow, particularly in the central and southern parts of the main island. After expanding the Nishihara factory (figure 4.1), it built a factory that could produce 400 tons of sugar a day approximately twelve miles northwest, in Nishihara's Kadena Ward; the new factory (figure 4.2) began operations in January 1912.[30] In its first year of operation, the Kadena factory manufactured many different types of sugar, but it switched completely to bunmitsutō in 1913.[31]

Following on the heels of Okitai Seitō, Tainansha—established by Abe Shōten's rival Suzuki Shōten, a sugar merchant company based in Kōbe turned Konzern—also set its sights on Okinawan sugar.[32] Tainansha was a relatively new company that began its operations in 1913 in Taiwan and entered Okinawa in August 1917 in dramatic fashion, purchasing Okinawa Seitō, a company that had just been founded, and acquiring all three of the factories of its rival, Okitai Seitō, in December.[33] In 1920, Tainansha also absorbed Miyako Seitō, which had been established on Miyako Island just the year before.[34]

Fig. 4.1 The Nishihara and Kadena factories came under the control of Tainansha following its takeover of the mechanized sugar industry on Okinawa Island in 1917. Nishihara sugar factory, The University of Hawaii at Manoa Library Sakamaki/Hawley Collection, from *Bōkyō Okinawa*, vol. 5, 85.

Fig. 4.2 The Kadena factory was the site of a tense confrontation between Tainansha and two hundred employees in the summer of 1930. Kadena sugar factory, The University of Hawaii at Manoa Library Sakamaki/Hawley Collection, from *Bōkyō Okinawa*, vol. 5, 84.

Though these mergers and acquisitions seem to indicate success for mainland sugar companies, from the start of their operations in Okinawa, their inability to secure supplies of cane from nearby cultivators threatened their ability to turn a profit. Acquiring enough cane to keep factories running at or near full capacity became the companies' biggest concern. Okitai Seitō took the first step toward creating a steady supply of cane in 1912 when it purchased a vast tract (400 chōbu) of fields and forest land in Yomitan Village in the Nakagami region that the former royal family had initially received from the prefecture to conduct reclamation.[35] It purchased all of the Shō family's holdings in Kudoku and Goeku Wards of the village and planned to convert these lands into small plots on which tenant farmers could cultivate cane for the Kadena factory.[36] The company encouraged movement onto these lands by offering rents at half the normal rate of 1.7 sen per tsubo to 250 families. These low rents indicate the company's intention to profit less from rents and more from forcing tenants to cultivate cane on these lands through a contract. A company manager who oversaw the cultivation supervised these tenants and was responsible for making sure that raw material of the highest quality was submitted to the factory after harvest. Tenants were also bound to the land by loans that the company extended to them for fertilizer and equipment.[37] Finally, the company managed a commission system in which profits that accrued from subsidiary industries were divided among producers after a certain number of years. Tainansha continued a similar arrangement in Yomitan after it absorbed Okitai Seitō in late 1917.[38]

In addition to binding tenants to the land through debt and surveillance, the companies hoped that small producers would eventually decide on their own that submitting the cane that they harvested exclusively to the factories was the most advantageous path for their household economies. The factory supervisor of Okitai Seitō expressed his company's vision for the future of Okinawa's sugar industry in a trade paper, the *Okinawa Jitsugyō Shimpō*, in 1914. He asserted that by investing capital to build factories and using advanced technologies, the company would bring about an economically complete division of labor under one order in Okinawa. As this change progressed, the company would eventually be able to fulfill the dream of all capitalists: to "employ large numbers of workers who engage in labor all day long."[39]

Okitai Seitō's lobbying efforts in Okinawa through the 1910s was consistent with this vision. The company appealed to the prefectural administration for financial assistance and political support for a comprehensive plan to promote the bunmitsutō sugar industry at the expense of brown sugar, which continued to employ the majority of Okinawa's small producers and cultivators. The company aggressively pushed proposals for laying railroad tracks between factory regions and Naha, where the market and port were located, and succeeded in convincing the prefectural assembly to approve a prefecture-operated railway that began operations in October 1914 (figure 4.3).[40] This resulted in the construction of a coastal line connecting Naha and the eastern coastal port of Yonabaru approximately two and a half miles south of Nishihara. This line transported charcoal and sugar barrels from Yonabaru port to Naha (figure 4.4). Soon after operations commenced, extension lines were built to connect the sugar companies' storage facilities and factories to each other. Additional factories and facilities quickly sprang up around the train stations.[41] Newspaper articles reported train cars filled to the brim with sugar going back and forth on the extension line between the Nishihara factory and Yonabaru station during the busy manufacturing season.[42]

In addition to lobbying for infrastructural development, sugar companies made road repairs, conducted irrigation projects, and tested new cane varieties to establish the foundations necessary for the healthy and con-

Fig. 4.3 Yonabaru station in Okinawa was completed in 1914. The Yonabaru line connected Naha and Shimajiri's Yonabaru, which was a center of bunmitsutō production. Yonabaru station and employees, Okinawa Prefectural Archive, document no. 0000036057.

Fig. 4.4 Brown sugar dominated Okinawa prefecture's sugar industry. Brown sugar manufactured by small peasants made its way to the poorer agrarian villages of mainland Japan, while more affluent consumers purchased the preferred white sugar. Loading of brown sugar barrels, Naha City Museum of History, photo no. 02000201.

tinuous operation of their factories. The stark contrast between these large, well-capitalized, steam-powered modern factories, which had the most advanced machinery and funds at their disposal, and the small sugar huts that were operated by the energy of humans and their livestock led Ōta to fear as early as 1912 that the prefecture's "46,000–47,000 isolated producers" would soon lose their autonomy in production and manufacture.[43] He predicted that Okinawa's small peasantry would be turned into cultivators who exclusively supplied these companies. Only the sugar producers' reluctance to transform themselves into nothing more than raw material producers kept Ōta's fears from being realized.

Local Intellectuals' Response to Mainland Sugar Capital

Despite their aggressive efforts to establish large-scale bunmitsutō factories and to construct the necessary infrastructure to facilitate the transport of their commodity, sugar companies regularly failed to collect enough cane from small cultivators in the nearby regions to operate their factories at full capacity. Furthermore, outside the Nakagami region, where many of these factories were located, few improvements had been made to the method of sugar production. Small peasantry in regions without bunmitsutō factories continued to manufacture their own sugar through small-scale, labor-intensive, unmechanized methods. The substantial increase in traditional brown sugar factories since the arrival of Okinawa Seitō indicated that although the entry of bunmitsutō in the prefecture stimulated cane production, the peasantry preferred to absorb as much of their increased yields as possible in their own communal brown sugar factories.[44]

The difficulties that the prefecture's bunmitsutō factories faced was of particular concern for Governor Ōmi, who arrived in the prefecture in June 1914, because the overall weakness of the prefecture's economy had led to higher levels of tax arrears and defaults on loans through the 1910s. Ōmi believed that a comprehensive plan for industrial development was necessary to improve conditions in Okinawa. To this end, he established a ten-year plan for industry and promulgated the Sugar Factory Laws (Seitōjō Kitei) in 1915.[45] The industrial plan stipulated that traditional brown sugar manufacturing huts be replaced with larger capacity, reform-type mechanized factories to gradually shift the emphasis in the prefecture's sugar industry from brown sugar to bunmitsutō, which Ōmi claimed would be more profitable to Okinawa in the long run.[46] It is not impossible that Ōmi had visions of great wealth for Okinawa's sugar industry, since around this time he witnessed mainland refining companies aggressively infiltrating Taiwan to fuel their refineries back home.[47] Conversion to bunmitsutō was necessary in Okinawa because these refineries accepted that, not the less pure ganmitsutō that small producers communally produced.

Ōta and other members of the local bourgeoisie reacted to Ōmi's prioritization of the conversion of Okinawa's sugar production to bunmitsutō with great discomfort. Inaka Akira, an industrialist who was not fundamentally opposed to increasing the production of bunmitsutō, explained why he opposed the governor's plan in a proposal that he submitted in December 1917 to the prefectural assembly.[48] His main concern was article 5 of the sugar factory law, which required anyone wanting to establish reform-type or machine-based sugar factories to get permission from the governor.[49] Inaka pointed to the similarity of this stipulation to laws passed in 1905 and 1912 in Taiwan that prohibited the formation of joint stock companies owned exclusively by natives under the rationale that "the Chinese are incapable of running a company by themselves."[50] Though Inaka's proposal did not refer directly to Taiwan's regulations of its sugar industry, he characterized Ōmi's proposed plan as unconstitutional and stated that such measures "may be acceptable in colonial areas but absolutely should not be permitted within a prefecture of the empire."[51]

Inaka's proposal, submitted during a prosperous time for Okinawa's sugar industry, revealed that mainland sugar capital's appeals to the governor had made local leaders fear that Okinawa would become a colony. This fear was exacerbated by the governor's condescending attitude toward the people of Okinawa, which the *Ryūkyū Shimpō* chronicled throughout 1915: the governor asked local officials if they had ever received an education, complained that many of them did not understand standard Japanese, called for mainland military officers residing in Okinawa to run for office, increased the police presence, and so on. Local leaders feared that unless they could find a way to curb Governor Ōmi's power, Okinawa would find itself in a predicament not dissimilar to that of its close neighbor in the southwest. An article in the *Ryūkyū Shimpō* expressed these anxieties: "His [Ōmi's] is a politics that looks at the land but does not look at the people. It is a politics that does not treat the indigenous people as Japanese subjects and instead treats them as a type of machine. It holds down the indigenous people and protects the rights and interests of the Japanese people. Since colonial politics needs only to use the land and the people, there is no need for harmony and cooperation between the indigenous people and the rulers. In order to attain their objectives, they must conduct superpolice politics and manage the indigenous people in a despotic manner."[52]

Ōmi's political despotism and favoritism toward mainland sugar capital radicalized local intellectuals, turning even those who favored full inclusion into anticolonial critics of mainland Japanese expropriation. They came to believe that the only way to counter these powerful forces was by strengthening cooperation and associations, starting at the village level. Resisting the political and psychological threat posed by the governor's policies necessitated refusing certain economic relations that facilitated the exploitation of the region by outsiders. These conditions made it impossible for many members of the local bourgeoisie to advocate the uncritical establishment of capitalist relations of production, even though they understood this to be the most advanced form of socioeconomic organization. In this period, Okinawa's leaders were forced to understand the treatment of the peasantry by mainland capital and politicians as an example of the way that Okinawa as a whole was being treated by the Japanese state and capital. The condition of the small peasantry—the main target of mainland sugar capital's exploitation—took on greater importance than ever before, and their defense became key to preserving Okinawa's independence.

It is in this light that we must understand Ōta's resistance to mainland sugar capital's intention to turn Okinawa's peasantry into a pure agricultural proletariat and his advocacy of a network of communally or prefecture-owned mechanized sugar factories that would use the cane supplied by each region's peasant households. He differentiated the system he envisioned from that of mainland sugar capitalists: "There are those who say that the prefecture's sugar industry will develop if large-scale factories are built in the agrarian villages and if cultivation and manufacture are completely separated. This opinion only looks at the development of the sugar industry and not at the interests of the peasantry. I believe that the interests of the peasantry will not be fulfilled if cultivation and manufacture are separated."[53]

Instead of a pure separation of cultivators and producers that worked to the advantage only of mainland capital, Ōta and Inaka proposed combining the existing sugar huts called *satō goya* that were communally operated by groups of neighboring families called *satō gumi* into larger-scale, medium-size factories that could produce more sugar more efficiently so the families would not have to become entirely dependent on large factories owned by big capital (figure 4.5). Ōta described what this arrangement might look like in a 1914 *Ryūkyū Shimpō* article. He explained that ten satō gumi could form a production association that would operate a reform-type sugar

Fig. 4.5 The sugar factory owned by the people of Takamine Village was the best known reform-type sugar factory that was communally owned by villagers. However, it was eventually taken over by mainland sugar capital. Takamine Village sugar factory, The University of Hawaii at Manoa Library Sakamaki/Hawley Collection, from *Bōkyo Okinawa*, vol. 5, 84.

factory that was approved by the Ministry of Agriculture and Commerce. This type of regionally based combination could keep production in the hands of the cultivators and strengthen the position of the 46,000–47,000 sugar producers. In contrast to the 400-ton daily capacity of Okitai Seitō's Kadena factory, the output of these factories would be closer to the 40 tons a day, but that would go a long way toward rationalizing production and reducing costs for the producers.[54] Ōta simultaneously advocated that the production associations use the prefectural agricultural bank, the Okinawa Nōkō Ginkō so they could get low-interest loans for the purchase of agricultural implements, machinery, and fertilizer and to facilitate irrigation, road repairs, and forestry projects.[55] Inaka also critiqued attempts by the prefectural administration to block efforts by local residents to establish their own reform-type sugar factories.[56]

Ōta argued that the success of the industrial associations hinged on greater harmony and cooperation—which he labeled *Okinawa-shugi*, an expansion of the economic nationalism that he had articulated during the land reorganization project—in the prefecture's agrarian villages and the end of petty conflicts over power and profits that had obstructed communal production based on industrial associations in the past. He explained that the long history of the Okinawan people's communal systems and internal village laws that emphasized mutual responsibility and assistance made it quite likely that a prefecturewide system of industrial associations could be successfully implemented. In this new context, Ōta had to pull back slightly from the enthusiasm that he had shown just a decade earlier for reforming old customs. Now he supported small cultivators' practices of mutual exchange and cooperation as a strategy to counter large mainland capital's attempts to proletarianize Okinawa's peasantry. Much to his disappointment, Okinawa's small-scale sugar producers were reluctant to organize production associations and establish reform-type factories despite a declining domestic demand for brown sugar that forced most to sell at least part of their cane as raw material to bunmitsutō factories. They continued to resist attempts to reorganize production on an expanded scale, even as the structure of Okinawa's economy was transformed to favor concentration following the outbreak of World War I.[57]

Brown Sugar Production in Okinawa's Agrarian Villages

The years immediately after the war brought an unprecedented level of prosperity to the prefecture because Europe's beet sugar production sites were destroyed by war and Taiwan experienced bad harvests. As a result of significantly reduced global supplies of sugar, the price of brown and bunmitsutō sugar on the Naha market spiked like never before. What the agricultural economist Mukai Kiyoshi called the "golden years of Okinawa's brown sugar industry" (1918 and 1919) corresponded to the period of the "dance of the millions" in Cuba.[58] In Okinawa's case, the price of first-grade brown sugar, which averaged 9.2 yen per picul in 1918, rose to the 22 yen mark in 1919 and peaked in January 1920 at 35.89 yen.[59] This sugar boom in Okinawa followed Tainansha's domination of the prefecture's industry in 1917. The consolidation of its monopolistic position in the realm of bunmitsutō production transformed the relationships that many small peasantry had to their lands.[60] The growth of bunmitsutō production effected by the company led to a gradual but significant decline in the amount of energy used by farming families to cultivate sweet potato for home consumption and a reduction in the amount of time and resources devoted to the maintenance of subsidiary industries among families that supplied cane to the factories.[61] The merger and the wartime boom pointed to a greater degree of class differentiation in the agrarian villages.

Despite the growth that the prefecture's sugar industry experienced, cultivators who lived as tenants on the lands directly owned by the company did not enjoy the fruits of this expansion. They continued to be subject to stringent regulations regarding their agricultural activity. They enjoyed relatively low rents, but the cash that they received for operating funds and living expenses from the company meant that between one-third and one-half of their harvest went to repay the company. According to the terms of a sample contract printed in a 1929 study of the conditions of Okinawan tenants conducted by the Home Division of Fukuoka's prefectural administration, following the settlement of their advance repayments, tenants were required to sell the remainder of their harvest to the factory at a price that the company determined each season. Disagreements over the price of the portion of their harvest that they sold to the factory as nonrepayment cane brought these tenants of Tainansha and brown sugar producers who resided in the same carrying-in region but did not live on company-owned lands together in a series of disputes that erupted in the Nakagami and Shimajiri regions of the main island between 1916 and 1920.[62] The central question that the remainder of this chapter investigates is why the latter group—cultivators living near large sugar factories who engaged in cane cultivation and small-scale manufacturing of brown sugar on their own—did not choose the path of proletarianization, even though the economic conditions of World War I seemed to favor increased submissions of cane to the large factories.

In cane cultivating regions, the method of brown sugar production continued as before and used preexisting modes of socioeconomic organization, although the revenues that flowed into the countryside during the sugar boom afforded savvy cultivators the opportunity to update their technologies. The satō goya that Ōta wanted so desperately to combine and rebuild into communally owned bunmitsutō factories remained important parts of the village landscape long after his suggestion to combine them into production associations. Data from 1917 reveal that there were approximately eight satō gumi in each single sugar-producing village, and an average of seventeen families in each satō gumi.[63] A single satō gumi was in charge of the management of the satō goya and the kiln, as well as creating a schedule for farming families to manufacture their harvested cane. The group collectively owned a single sugar hut and was responsible for managing all of the machinery, tools, additional cattle, and workers that were needed to complete the manufacturing process. In addition to the upkeep, management, and procurement of necessary inputs, the group was collectively responsible for deciding on the rotation of workers during the manufacturing season—approximately six people were needed for the entire process—and distributing payment to its members. After manufacturing was completed between April and May, the satō gumi would conclude its sugar-related tasks by settling accounts with each family in the group and would calculate the operating expenses that each family owed based on the amount of cane that each had manufactured. In this way, satō gumi members were inextricably linked to each other through collective labor, financing, and management.

Once the manufacture process had been completed and operating expenses had been calculated, each family received its share of the finished brown sugar and sold it at temporary markets (figure 4.6) or to middlemen between July and December. Middlemen handed off the sugar to brokers based in Naha or mainland Japan in exchange for commissions averaging 6–10 sen per barrel.[64] Brokers obtained additional sugar by collecting on the high-interest loans that they granted to producers through the sugar advance loan (satō maedai) system. These loans typically carried a 30 percent interest rate and approximately 20 percent of the total brown sugar pro-

Fig. 4.6 This postcard shows a temporary cane market in Naha that opened its doors during certain times of the year. These markets existed alongside more formal routes of buying and selling cane that were linked to large sugar capital. Sugar cane market, Naha City Museum of History, photo no. 02003600.

duced went to repayment.[65] Mainland sugar companies like Suzuki Shōten, Abe Shōten, and Masudaya, which entered the prefecture in the late Meiji period, doubled as these brokers, taking over this position from smaller operators who had links to the former kingdom's nobility.[66]

In addition to communally engaging in the manufacture of brown sugar, members of the satō gumi divided themselves into smaller groups of anywhere from five and eight people to complete tasks that were not directly related to manufacturing brown sugar. They entered into labor exchange agreements called *yuimaaru* through which farming families loaned each other labor power to complete the cutting of cane and its transportation to the sugar huts.[67] This arrangement was vital to the manufacturing process, as cane—an extremely sensitive plant—required cutting and transport in a timely manner to protect the quality of the final product.[68] The way that inequities in the process of labor exchange were settled remains a point of dispute among scholars, but the existence of ledgers containing transaction details indicates that there was some attempt to account for disparities either through the redress in labor at a later date or through payments in cash.[69] Furthermore, the existence of farming families of different scales in these groups reveals that this was not simply a process of communal exchange and mutual assistance but served to reinforce intercommunity hierarchies whose details are not completely clear to us today. In any case, because most families did not possess enough labor power to get through the busy harvest and manufacturing season on their own and did not have the resources to hire day laborers from outside the household, labor exchange arrangements were indispensable for most cane-growing households, so they could complete their tasks in each production cycle.

Higa Ryōzui, an Okinawan poet who achieved acclaim for depicting scenes of life in the countryside, wrote a poem called "Satō Goya" ("Sugar Hut") during the height of the sugar boom that depicted the conditions in these small-scale, communally held sugar huts:

> In front of the sugar hut
> Where the light warmly reflects
> The children make a racket.
> The movement of the compressor is driven
> By one skinny horse.
> The reverberations of the old worn whip,
> The shrieking of hysterical humans, and
> The suspicious echoes of gears.
> The sweet cane juices,
> Their faint scent,
> And the stench of smoke,
> And the dejected sweat of the humans
> Are all gifts sent from the gods.
> The indescribable drops of sweat.
> The faint smell of sweet cane juices.
> The wretched understanding of humans, their pity.
> In front of the sugar hut
> Where the light warmly reflects
> The children make a racket.[70]

Higa's depiction of the miserable conditions of a sugar hut that relied on a single horse to run the compressor during the dizzyingly busy period of manufacturing brown sugar provides a stark contrast to the large factories that enclosed the landscape of central and southern Okinawa and cast a cloud of black smoke over the island. The poem was one of the few works of its time to depict the life of sugar-producing families.

In contrast to Higa's description of the wretched conditions of brown sugar manufacturing, Iba Nantetsu—a poet from Ishigaki island, Yaeyama—

Fig. 4.7 Communal manufacture of brown sugar, including the use of mutual labor arrangements, was the main method of sugar production throughout the period before World War II in Okinawa. Sugar Mill in Loo Chooan Village, E. R. Bull's photographic plates, no. 17, Taisho era, Bull Collection, University of the Ryūkyūs.

wrote a piece called *Nangoku no Shirayuri* (*White Lilies of the South*) in 1927. This piece illuminated the embeddedness of sugar manufacture in village-level social relations and provides us with a better understanding of why it proved so difficult for sugar producers to transform themselves into pure cultivators to supply bunmitsutō factories. Iba's depiction of the sugar-producing countryside in the period between the world wars gives us valuable insight into the everyday concerns of cultivators living and working within a complex web of relations both old and new in their villages (figure 4.7).

In a section titled "Nōmin no Yorokobi" ("The Joy of the Peasantry"), Iba described a mesmerizing, almost ecstatic scene in which peasants were engaged in the communal production of brown sugar. He began with a sketch of the sugar-cultivating village during a normal season of harvest and manufacture: "Behind the pasture in spring that is like blue carpet laid out from corner to corner, young men and women become entangled . . . the young girls' towels peeking out from the stalks."⁷¹ He continued: "One hears the pure voices of young men and women singing folk melodies from behind the cane fields." Iba reported that he found this scene "irresistibly charming." Then he described the incredible skill that went into the harvesting of the cane: "How their hands move mechanically from years of experience . . . passersby stand still to watch, as the girls cut the cane without forgetting to sing their island folk songs."⁷²

Through his description of the dress of young men and women who tended the fields, Iba illuminated the gendered division of labor that governed the process of manufacturing brown sugar from cane during the winter months after a long year of tending to the fields: "The strong young men of the village wear blue vertical striped cotton shirts and white knit shirts with shorts. . . . [T]hey cut down the swiftly grown canes with a thick sickle and are in charge of transporting them to the sugar huts."⁷³ In contrast, the young women of the village "wear simple cotton indigo-dye (*kasuri*) kimono and on top, a vermillion kimono cord the color of flames. They wear black bracelets on the back of both hands and wrap a towel around their heads. . . . They take the cane that the men transport and separate the leaves from the stalks. They bind just the mesocotyl into bunches approximately two shaku in diameter. Passersby stop and watch how their hands mechanically cut the cane—a result of years of experience."⁷⁴ Although Iba pointed out that there were occasional accidents during the compressing process if kimono sleeves or hands got stuck in the gears, he described a well-oiled but living machine that involved young men, women, children, cows, and horses, all of whom soldiered through the arduous process of manufacturing that lasted all day and all night by singing folk songs and urging each other along.⁷⁵

Iba's work reminds us of the social character of production that entangled producers in small-scale credit and labor exchange relations that by design could not be settled in a single season or even with a single transaction between two parties. Work shaped much of the collective entertainment and play that villagers enjoyed during the busy seasons, beginning with songs that were performed during the planting, harvesting, and transport of sugar; the distribution of money to families after the sugar was sold; and the sharing of meals that were made with food that was purchased on a tab at the communal store. All of these activities remained part of a shared cycle of celebrations that accompanied each season of strenuous labor long after the official adoption of the Gregorian calendar and despite vigorous efforts by local reformers to restrict superfluous spending.[76] Although such an explanation risks romanticizing communal life if taken completely at face value, Iba's work points to the dangers of underestimating the importance of this type of shared experience for cultivators as they calculated the benefits and drawbacks to submitting cane to the nearby factory.

The Organization of Nonselling Alliances in Central Okinawa

Due to the socially embedded character of small-scale brown sugar manufacture described above, Tainansha's ability to increase the proportion of bunmitsutō in the total sugar production was frustrated even during the peak years immediately after World War I by difficulties in obtaining adequate supplies of cane from cultivators. Despite repeated injections of funds by the prefecture to increase production, bunmitsutō never exceeded 37 percent of total sugar production in any year before World War II and hovered around the 30 percent mark in most.[77] In many ways, communal production and mutual labor exchange arrangements enabled by membership in the satō gumi led cultivators to refuse the terms of purchase that Tainansha and other large sugar companies from the mainland tried to impose on them. The continuation of these village-level mechanisms long after large sugar capital's entry into the prefecture must be understood as a reflection of the desire of small peasantry to maintain as much self-sufficiency in their lives as possible. In this sense, their reluctance to transform themselves into pure cane cultivators was an act of anticapitalist refusal that obstructed the transformation of their work and lives into dead labor.[78] Small producers rejected cane submissions to factories as pursuits that brought short-term increases in cash income but also increased their vulnerability to external forces. As such, their refusals should be seen as much more than futile revolutionary acts or reactionary attempts to maintain feudal ways of life.[79]

In addition to the peasants' reluctance to transform themselves into pure cultivators, producers residing in carrying-in regions actively organized nonselling alliances in order to secure more favorable terms for the cane that they did choose to submit. The first of these alliances was organized in late 1916 and was spurred by a disagreement over the price that sugar companies set as small producers' cost of manufacturing brown sugar. Little documentary evidence exists about the alliance's leaders or members, but newspaper accounts indicate that the decision to boycott Okitai Seitō was supported by a large number of residents. Once representatives of the alliance and the company started negotiations, the former held open meetings in Shimajiri and Nakagami to keep interested parties abreast of the discussions and to discuss future strategy.

For participants in the nonselling alliance, the price that sugar companies set as the cultivators' brown sugar manufacturing expenses was key to deciding whether they would agree to submit their cane or manufacture it themselves. Brown sugar manufacturing expenses—what sugar companies calculated as the costs that small producers burdened when they produced brown sugar in their communal sugar huts—was a crucial component in calculating the price that bunmitsutō factories paid cultivators for their cane. Companies determined that payment by subtracting the production costs from the average price of grade-two sugar on the Naha market during the ten days before the date when cultivators were to submit their cane. From the perspective of the peasants, it was to their advantage to have brown sugar production expenses set as low as possible, while the companies benefited from calculating it as high as possible, regardless of whether or not cultivators had actually spent this amount.

An article in the *Ryūkyū Shimpō* dated December 25, 1916, reported the details of the negotiations between the alliance representatives and Okitai Seitō. According to the article, alliance representatives held a meeting at Shinkyōji temple—near the port at Naha, where thousands of sugar barrels awaited loading onto cargo ships for the mainland—to determine a response to the company's refusal to budge from the figure of 2.1 yen per barrel for brown sugar production expenses.[80] The alliance members decided that the highest figure they could accept was 1.7 yen per barrel, which was based on the calculations of the Okinawa Sugar Production Association.[81] This meant that the two sides had to bridge a 20 percent gap.

The company was simply unwilling to make this kind of concession. Instead of negotiating further on the price, it decided to shift tactics. According to a newspaper article published on January 12, 1917, it proposed a rebate system called *warimodoshi*, which made conditions more favorable for the peasants who submitted larger quantities of cane.[82] Those who supplied ten barrels or more received 0.3 yen per barrel; those supplying fifty barrels or more received 0.4 yen; and those who supplied all of their harvest, regardless of quantity, also received 0.4 yen back from the company as an incentive payment.[83] This incentive system was the company's attempt to bridge the gap of 0.4 yen per barrel that separated its proposed price from that of the alliance, while simultaneously securing larger quantities of cane from cultivators. It was also probably an attempt to divide the cultivators and break up the alliance.

Around the same time a nonselling alliance was also organized near the 250-ton capacity Nishihara factory also owned by Okitai Seitō. When this boycott began, company representatives met with prefectural authorities, who agreed to grant subsidies of 0.1 yen per barrel to cultivators as further incentive to submit large quantities of raw material cane to the company, in addition to the company's own payments.[84] The newspapers reported that these collective offers convinced cultivators to dissolve their nonselling alliances, but continued disputes in these regions following the takeover of Okitai Seitō by Tainansha indicates that these were merely temporary measures. Okitai Seitō's attempts to reverse some of the nonselling alliance's gains did not help its standing among the producers. Following its announcement that negotiations for a merger were in progress in October 1917, Okitai Seitō announced its intentions to revise its terms for purchasing raw cane for the 1917 season.[85] Instead of counting the sugar submitted to be grade 2, the company revised its guidelines downward so that they would only be accepted as grade 1.5, lower-quality sugar that was worth less on the Naha market.[86] This, along with the company's upward revisions of brown sugar production expenses, amounted to a substantial decrease in the value of the cultivators' cane. In the meantime, the incentive payment system would continue as it had in the past, with slight rate reductions. Those who submitted fewer than 20 barrels would receive 0.1 yen per barrel; those who submitted 20–49 barrels would receive 0.15 yen per barrel; and those who submitted fifty barrels or more would receive 0.2 yen per barrel from the company.[87] As a result of this sudden announcement of revised guidelines, many cultivators who resided in or near Okitai Seitō's factories refused to sign their tenant or supplier contracts.[88]

Following Okitai Seitō, Tainansha also published its regulations for cane purchases during 1917. The company announced its own encouragement monies to cane cultivators that increased in direct proportion to the length of contract they were willing to sign with the company. For a contract lasting one year, they would receive 0.1 yen per barrel; for two years, 0.25 yen; and for three years, 0.3 yen. As a further reward for ensuring a stable supply of cane to the company, Tainansha announced that once the Takamine factory reached a total output of 6,500 piculs and the Ginowan factory reached 3,500 piculs, 0.2 yen per barrel submitted would be distributed to all cultivators who delivered cane to the factories.[89]

The prefectural administration and sugar experts supported large sugar capital's aggressive efforts to entice cane cultivators to sell to their factories. However, cultivators in Mawashi, Tomigusuku, and Haebaru—all regions that supplied sugar to the 250-ton capacity Tomigusuku factory that was established in 1913—were not convinced of the advantages of selling raw material cane. For small producers, the conditions that Tainansha imposed, like longer contracts and incentives after quotas were met, left them further indebted to the sugar brokers, who offered high-interest loans in return for a promise of the bulk of a household's harvest by encouraging even more submissions to make up for the lower price. In addition, this system would leave peasants with little time to devote to brown sugar manufacture and subsidiary industries like livestock raising and sweet potato cultivation.[90] Their commitment to a single industry monopolized by large capital would also strip away from them the social and economic protections provided by their communities.[91] This rationale for remaining embedded in a village economy in which they performed agriculture as well as manufacturing indicates that although Okinawa's small peasantry may not have acted capitalistically according to Marxists who studied peasant behavior, they understood quite well the capitalist logic that governed decisions made by Tainansha.[92] Whether their responses were governed by economic, social, rational, or moral calculations is a complex question that cannot be answered by the sources at our disposal. However, examining the terms that small producers found acceptable can help illuminate their motives and desires.

Disputes between the cultivators and the companies finally ended in a truce in early January 1918, when representatives of the five villages that supplied the Nishihara factory finally decided to back down on the issue of the revised grade equivalents in exchange for extending the number of days after harvest during which cane could be submitted to the factory. The company had proposed sixteen days, but the representatives for the peasantry convinced the company to accept fifty days. This was a key point for small producers because the extra days gave them flexibility that would protect their ability to search for more advantageous conditions.[93] This extension would give them more time to decide whether to sell their cane to the factory or use it to manufacture brown sugar, which they would sell themselves.[94] In addition to increasing the number of days after harvest that cane could be sold to the factory, peasantry representatives succeeded in negotiating a lower quota for the cane that tenants living in factory-managed farms had to sell to the company.[95] No new disputes were reported in 1918, but in 1919 there were nonselling alliances that stretched over 10–20 chōbu, crossing two or three regions, and a 400-worker strike in a sugar factory in Daitōjima in November over wages.[96]

Despite the multiplicity of factors that governed small producers' decisions to organize nonselling alliances, observers attributed the peasants' resistance to transform themselves into raw material cultivators as a purely economic matter. In a report titled "Tōgyō Ikensho" ("Opinion on the Sugar Industry"), Miyagi Tetsu, a local sugar industry expert who worked for Tainansha, outlined the company's concerns and criticized farming households for focusing too much on their individual interests: "Because the peasants are always focused on the price of brown sugar they focused exclusively on the manufacture of brown sugar and waited for the price of sugar to rise so that they could sell at the most opportune time. They believe this to be the most profitable method and do not want to sell to the company."[97] On behalf of Tainansha, he requested the prefectural authorities to provide more resources to increase cane yields, provide encouragement for the sale of raw materials to the company, and restrict farming households from manufacturing brown sugar.

During its coverage of the 1916–19 nonselling alliances, the *Ryūkyū Shimpō* echoed Miyagi's view that the conflict between the cultivators and company was the result of the formers' obsession with squeezing even one sen more out of their crops. The newspaper reinforced the view that the peasantry's main objective was gaining the economic upper hand over the company. One article explained that once the company increased the rate of incentive payments that it provided to cultivators who sold a large amount of their sugar to the factory, "the peasantry fought to sell off, and in five days' time the company was able to obtain 20,000 barrels, which was an increase by 10,000 barrels from previous years."[98]

Representatives of the small peasantry who worked closely with the Sugar Production Association to come up with a more favorable calculation of brown sugar production expenses were no less guilty of the same simplification. One *Ryūkyū Shimpō* article mentioned above provides us with a glimpse into the detailed breakdown of expenses that peasants used to determine an acceptable figure. Wages were the highest, at 55 sen per barrel, followed by barrel costs (50 sen) and transportation costs (17 sen). Charcoal, rope, inspections, storage, maintenance, commissions, and association fees rounded out the items that were included in the expense column. The sum of these figures provided the alliance representatives with their figure of 1.7 yen per barrel. Although that was significantly lower than the 2.1 yen set by the company, the inclusion of wages is notable, since the process of sugar production at the level of the satō gumi discussed in this chapter did not include the exchange of money for supplementary labor.[99] Sugar producers surely resented the inclusion of labor costs that in practice were settled through the mutual labor exchange system or through the intensification of their own labor activity during the manufacture season, precisely because they could not afford to hire workers who required payment in cash. In addition to the conflict over the wage portion of production costs, the fact that a single number was published and applied to all peasants was probably a source of frustration.[100]

The fact that the wage was the largest part of the production expense allows us to examine the dispute from a completely different perspective and enables us to see the truly antagonistic position that the nonselling alliance took as it faced off with Japanese sugar capital. As we have already seen, under the satō gumi system, brown sugar producers did not approach the exchange of labor in the same way as sugar capital did. For members of the satō gumi, labor transactions did not take place through a contract but were a messy process of exchanges that could not be squared away in a single season. The peasants' embeddedness in two very different economies and wage regimes enabled them to identify the sugar companies' uncritical inclusion of the wage as part of the brown sugar production expenses as an act that did not reflect the way that labor was exchanged in their everyday lives. They saw right through the sugar companies' attempts to naturalize the wage form—an act that performed a powerful societal function of concealing exploitation through what Marx calls the legal fiction of the contract.[101] Thus, though there were few nonselling alliances, the ones that appeared at the height of the global sugar boom were a sign of small producers' clear refusal of the extension of what some theorists have called the "code of abstract labor" into Okinawa's agrarian villages.[102] In opposition to "the extraction of wealth from a multitude of subjects that are constituted as basically interchangeable"[103] that the extension of this code enables, participants in the nonselling alliances rejected the extension of the field of abstraction into Okinawa's agrarian villages.[104] Large sugar capital came up short in this struggle over subjectivities.

Ōta's Calls to Counter Proletarianization in the Countryside

Okinawa's small producers also rejected the combination of sugar huts into the larger reform-type factories that Ōta and other local leaders pushed as alternatives to the large factories owned by mainland capital. The main reason for the peasants' rejection of these midsize, village-level factories and the industrial associations charged with facilitating the financing of the transformation, procuring materials, and selling of the product was largely the result of their suspicion of village officials. Though local officials were less able than they had been to extract funds or overcollect taxes from inhabitants, reports of misused funds and corruption in the village offices were widely covered by local media outlets. Ōta was not unaware that village officials' blatant misuse of association funds for their personal use hurt the credibility of his proposals for a village-led organization of peasants. But he attributed the main cause of its failure to the peasants' inability to understand that it was the only organization that could make Okinawa's sugar industry competitive in the world while also preventing them from becoming an agricultural proletariat exploited by outside capital. In a desperate appeal to small producers, he called for increased harmony and cooperation—Okinawa-shugi beyond the village unit—and an end to the petty conflicts over power and profits that obstructed the organization of communal production based on industrial associations. Ōta argued that if Okinawans could not work together to keep out mainland officials and capitalists, they would be right back where they started in 1609: "Unless we can stand shoulder to shoulder with the other prefectures, no matter what form the system takes, in reality we must be considered the indigenous people of a colony."[105] Like the author of the *Ryūkyū Shimpō* article cited earlier, Ōta failed to understand that the policies that he advocated were rooted in an abstract category—Okinawa—that had not taken hold among small peasantry who continued to work, celebrate, mourn, and struggle together with the other residents of their small satō gumi communities.

Finally, the social and economic difficulties of extracting oneself from brown sugar production based on the *satō gumi* stemmed from the notion of community that A. V. Chayanov described as "eating from the common pot."[106] This fact can help to explain why Ōta's vision of large-scale production based on a prefecturewide industrial association that implicitly required producers to accept their membership in a larger, organic Okinawan community also failed to take hold in the prefecture.[107] Despite Ōta and Inaka's attempts to alleviate the burdens for cultivating families through the formation of broader associations linked to more advantageous financing sources, the number of satō goya increased from 1,657 factories in 1903 to 3,320 in 1909 and 4,329 in 1917.[108] This increase took place as the number of farming households that manufactured sugar declined, reflecting increased productivity on the part of individual farming households and a contraction in the number of families involved in a single communally held factory.[109] The so-called community that Ōta envisioned was too large and ungrounded in the daily cycles of work, rest, play, and struggle for producers to wholeheartedly embrace, even at times that seemed opportune for prefecturewide organization.

Conclusion: Continued Struggles against Mechanized Sugar Production

As we have seen, the small but determined nonselling alliances that small peasantry organized during the sugar boom in World War I reveal their reluctance to abandon the entire web of communal resources, social relations, and supplementary activities at their disposal in exchange for their transformation into tenant farmers who produced raw material for factories. This can be seen in the way that agricultural household composition was transformed in the Nakagami region, the center of Tainansha-led factory sugar manufacture. There, the percentage of jisaku farming families—which owned land that they farmed with family labor—increased, from 61.25 percent in March 1914 to 68.6 percent in June 1917. In the same period, the percentage of half-tenant farming families (jikosaku)—which owned some lands and rented additional lands from others, using family labor to work all the lands—fell, from 29.02 percent to 26.15 percent.[110] These changes can be attributed to the peasantry's turn to temporary migrant work and immigration to exhaust family labor instead of renting additional plots of land to continue agricultural production.[111] Many factors need to be taken into account to properly analyze these changes. However, it is important to note that amid these shifts in Nakagami's farming household composition, Tainansha and the prefecture continued to struggle to convert sugar manufacturers into cane cultivators. If additional family labor needed to be exhausted, farming families preferred to send a family member outside of the village, prefecture, or country rather than convert all the family's operations into supplying raw materials to Tainansha.[112]

Instead of being seen as evidence of the pervasive nature of feudal thought, sentiments, and customs among small peasantry and as a reflection of a drive to increase property through overwork, underconsumption, and exhaustion, the continuation of mechanisms below the village level long after large sugar capital's entry into the prefecture can be read as a manifestation of small peasantry's desire to remain embedded in communal forms of production, manufacture, and exchange. If read this way, the peasants' reluctance to transform themselves into pure cultivators of cane must be understood as a significant act of anticapitalist refusal that obstructed the transformation of their work and lives into dead labor, a process that would have remade them into alienated producers of raw materials or sellers of their labor power. Specifically, the struggles between mainland sugar capital and Okinawa's brown sugar producers reveals the necessity of understanding these refusals as conscious decisions that small peasantry made to reject pursuits that brought short-term increases in income but embedded them in the regime of abstract labor, rather than as reactionary attempts to maintain outmoded ways of life or holdouts designed only to extract more money from the companies.

The common thread that united these nonselling alliances and subsequent disputes that erupted in the interwar period between large sugar capital and Okinawa's small peasantry was that they revolved around the valorization of living labor—in the rejection of the wage form, disputes over rents, or strikes that demanded shorter working days and higher wages. Large sugar capital, which attempted to achieve stable procurement of cane by signing long-term contracts and providing incentives for large submissions of raw material, fought with small cultivators who understood that completely embedding themselves in this system would destroy the social and economic protections provided by their existing networks of communal production and lending—mechanisms that granted them the possibility of self-valorization and, most crucially, reminded them that a different type of rationality was possible.[113]

Finally, the small successes that the disputes against Tainansha from 1917 on achieved transformed the possibilities of belonging and action that Okinawa's small peasantry could imagine. Their resistance to incorporation into a prefectural industrial association advocated by the local bourgeoisie around the same time constituted a rejection of the idea of a natural community of Okinawans with shared interests and revealed the impossibility of Okinawa-shugi to satisfy the desires of everyone included in this category. The deeper impact of these wartime struggles can be found in the radicalization of the same agrarian village societies in the late 1920s and early 1930s, as the prefectural economy approached crisis conditions.[114]

CHAPTER FIVE

≡

UNEVEN DEVELOPMENT AND
THE REJECTION OF ECONOMIC NATIONALISM
IN "SAGO PALM HELL" OKINAWA

The Uneven Consequences of Economic Crisis

The transformation of Okinawa's sugar industry and the creation of its labor market at the end of the nineteenth century allow us to witness the process through which the region flexibly absorbed the crises of Japanese capitalist development both inside and outside the formal boundaries of Okinawa Prefecture.[1] This chapter considers two attempts at political mobilization and organization that took place in the crisis conditions of the early 1930s, the Ōgimi Sonsei Kakushin Undō (Ōgimi Village Reform Movement) and the Arashiyama Jiken (Arashiyama Incident). Despite important differences, both constituted a rejection by northern Okinawa's peasant activists and Marxist intellectuals of the economic nationalism espoused by the prefecture's leading intellectuals, attempts to absorb the economic crisis that plagued the prefecture since the end of World War I, and a reflection of their desire to create new sites of cooperation. Their demands for the reinstatement of communal lands and resources and their organization of consumer cooperatives reflect these common objectives.[2]

The disturbances that engulfed the northern part of the main island of Okinawa cannot be understood without clarifying its peripheralization within the prefecture.[3] Like the Miyako Island Peasantry Movement analyzed in chapter 2, the demands of these cultivators may seem from the classical Marxist understanding of anticapitalist struggle like the result of their desire to become fully subsumed by capital—a position that small peasantry (shōnō) in southern and central Okinawa were vehemently refusing around the same time through nonselling alliances and strikes against Tainansha.[4] Past studies have lumped all struggles that erupted after the outbreak of World War I through the early 1930s together under the broad category of resistance, in spite of their contradictory stances toward capitalization, in an effort to construct a celebratory narrative of Okinawans' struggle against generalized oppression.[5] However, the divergent stances vis-à-vis capital that emerged in the period of transition from Taisho to Showa by small-producing peasants and tenant farmers in the southern, central, and northern parts of the main island of Okinawa require a more nuanced analysis, one that neither collapses all mobilization into resistance against a monolithic enemy or adheres too stringently to methodologies used in traditional class analysis that have struggled to ascribe meaning to the divergent desires of people in a single social category like the peasantry. Instead, we need an analysis that accounts for the multiple and contradictory responses to exploitation and expropriation that emerged from the specificities of uneven development within the prefecture.[6]

Taking uneven development in Okinawa seriously can provide valuable insights into why the Okinawa-shugi that developed out of an earlier economic nationalism, that intellectuals like Oyadomari Kōei and Ōta Chōfu articulated from World War I on, could not give the inhabitants of Ōgimi and Arashiyama a rallying cry against the semicolonial policies imposed by the central government. It was not an identification with an organic community of Okinawans that enables us to link these divergent struggles. Instead, their rejection of the notion implicitly held by local bourgeoisie that "it is better to be exploited by your own countrymen than to be exploited by that of another"[7] places participants in these two struggles in a trajectory of anticapitalist struggle that we can trace from the Miyako Island Peasantry Movement to the female weaver-peddlers and the brown sugar producers who participated in nonselling alliances. This common stance was inextricably linked to peasant activists' acute recognition of unevenness within the prefecture's agrarian villages and beyond.[8]

The Reaction Crisis in Okinawa after World War I

The transformation of Okinawa's economy accelerated with the outbreak of World War I. Both positive and negative impacts of the war were felt acutely in Okinawa and revealed the prefecture's indissoluble relationship to the rest of the world as a monocultural producer of a global commodity.⁹ The Naha market saw an unprecedented rise in the price of both brown and bunmitsutō sugar immediately after World War I. The boom, described by one scholar as "one of the shortest and sharpest booms ever recorded," was followed by a precipitous fall in prices.¹⁰

The sugar industry was not the only casualty in this sudden turn of events. The Tokyo Stock Market collapsed on March 15, 1920.¹¹ After one week, the price of rice and silk had fallen by 55 percent and 75 percent, respectively.¹² Share prices also dropped as much as 70–80 percent in the next six months. Because banks had become extremely generous with their lending practices during the boom and had held their own shares of commodity bills, they immediately felt the effects of the collapse. In April 1920 banks began to shut down and the government was forced to intervene, with the quasigovernmental Bank of Japan issuing loans totaling over 360 million yen.¹³ These financial difficulties continued into the 1920s, and many local banks—even the mighty colonial banks of Taiwan and Korea—found it difficult to continue operating. After a run on banks that occurred throughout the nation in late 1922, the government enacted the Ginkō Gōdō Seisaku (Bank Combination Policy) that closed, combined, or merged small regional banks and established stronger ties with the Bank of Japan.¹⁴ The government responded to this crisis by aiding the formation of monopolies in finance and industry.

The postwar boom was extremely short-lived for the global sugar industry. In the United States, sugar prices climbed to twenty-four cents per pound in the period immediately after World War I but fell to less than five cents per pound over the next year.¹⁵ The industry found it difficult to recover from this sharp decline because the destruction of the beet sugar industry in Europe and the ensuing shortages forced sugar-exporting countries to increase their technological capacity to respond to the lack of supply. Sugar's recovery through increased capitalization, combined with the overall increase in production levels, resulted in overproduction.¹⁶ Since sugar was such a capital-intensive enterprise, it was not easy to cut production when surpluses emerged. As Uno Kōzō explained, "with the increase in fixed capital that accompanies mechanization, the ability to transfer capital to other industries immediately because of a decrease in demand is obstructed . . . there is no alternative but to continue to supply in surplus."¹⁷ He observed that sugar-producing countries' turn to policies of self-sufficiency after the war exacerbated the so-called agrarian problem in these regions by encouraging oversupply relative to demand.¹⁸

The global postwar recession and efforts by states to restructure their economies in response had immediate impacts on Okinawa. The prefecture's main export industry, brown sugar, saw market prices climb to historic peaks and then collapse in a matter of months. It reached its highest price of 35.89 yen per picul in January 1920, began its decline in August, and finally dropped to below the 10-yen mark by year's end. Three of the prefecture's banks whose capital was mainly local collapsed in 1924. The failure of the local industrial bank was particularly devastating because the prefecture's funds were deposited in it, and its collapse effectively bankrupted the prefecture's economy.[19]

It must be pointed out that although the postwar recession was acutely experienced worldwide, its effects were dramatic in Okinawa because of local capital's structural relation to Japanese capital, the weakness of the prefecture's sugar industry compared to colonial plantation systems in other parts of the world, and the predominant place sugar occupied in the prefecture's economy. The sugar industry, which consisted of a dual structure of small-scale household manufacture of brown sugar and the large-scale mechanized factories of Tainansha, was in an extremely disadvantageous position relative to its global competitors.[20] It was impossible for Okinawa's industry to compete against producers that mobilized colonial labor power and relied on heavy protectionist policies, especially since the Japanese state had begun to favor the import of inexpensive sugar from Java to supply the growing demand in its cities over the protection of the domestic sugar industry after World War I.[21] Compounding this situation was the lack or failure of other industries that could fill in for the sugar industry in its time of weakness. The sugar-centered policy that the state and Japanese capital had promoted with renewed vigor in the early Taisho period had obstructed the development of subsidiary and secondary industries like the production of Panama hats and the cultivation of vegetables to the detriment of Okinawa's small peasantry.[22] Furthermore, the existence of a large labor force engaged in family-based agriculture meant that there was a very limited labor market in the prefecture that could absorb these people in times of recessions that affected agriculture.[23]

Diagnosis: Sago Palm Hell

Prompted by this emergency situation, Governor Kamei Mitsumasa petitioned the Finance Ministry for emergency funds and organized a bipartisan, official, and civilian-based committee, the Okinawa Ken Keizai Shinkōkai

(Okinawa Economic Promotion Committee) in the winter of 1924. He charged the committee with formulating strategies, compiling statistics, and drawing up proposals to raise much-needed funds for Okinawa's relief and recovery. Its submission of its first petition for the relief of the prefecture to the Home Ministry in January 1925 began a nationwide offensive by policy makers and Okinawa's sympathizers to procure funds to rebuild the ailing prefecture, which continued until 1931.

Mainland journalists who covered the plight of Okinawa emphasized its difficulties in order to raise funds for the prefecture's relief. One reporters used the phrase *Sago Palm hell* (*sotetsu jigoku*) to express how dire the situation was in a 1925 essay titled "Hinshi no Ryūkyū" ("Ryūkyū on the Verge of Death").[24] This phrase was quickly appropriated by others who felt it impossible to do justice to the depth of Okinawa's suffering through descriptions alone. Okinawa's conditions, which were "too miserable for words," required the use of the expression *Sago Palm hell* to capture the desperation that pervaded every corner of the prefecture.[25] Reporters traveled around the island, spent time speaking with residents (through interpreters, of course), and recorded their encounters with these barefoot, destitute people who were driven to eat the potentially deadly sago palm fruit out of desperation. Although the impoverishment of the region may have been a violent interruption of the image of utopia that some people had of this faraway land, stories that reporters brought back merely confirmed the existence of an unmodern, unalienated people who were now in need of rescue.

Though well-intentioned, the portrayals of Okinawa in many of these pieces revealed the prejudices of even its most sympathetic observers. In their desire to show the readers the "naked truth about Okinawa's current conditions" and to expose the structural imbalances that existed between the prefecture and the state in the realm of finances, they tended to paint as bad a picture as possible.[26] Along with a barrage of statistics and chronological comparisons of inputs and outputs, journalists described the consequences of these imbalances as vividly as they could. One example is a piece by Shimoda Masami of the *Ōsaka Mainichi Shimbun*. After going through all of the objective explanations for the prefecture's impoverishment, he resorted to an all-too-familiar conclusion. The main problem, Shimoda wrote, was that the climate had made the people lazy. They passed their days making sweet potato and their nights drinking *awamori* (a spirit made from rice produced in Okinawa) and listening to soft melodies played on the *shamisen*.[27] This easy life lulled Okinawans into complacency and left them ill-equipped to handle the current crisis on their own.

Although the phrase *Sago Palm hell* was sympathetic, its use to describe Okinawa's conditions in the mid-1920s exceptionalized the prefecture and gave credence to viewpoints that blamed the laziness and backwardness of the people for the prefecture's financial collapse. In addition to completely negating their own descriptions of the uneven structural relationships and historical conditions that led to such a violent crisis in the first place, this characterization completely erased the refusals on the part of weavers and sugar producers to convert themselves into an industrial and agricultural proletariat from Okinawa's story. The energy that these Okinawan men and women expended to gain fair terms and their careful calculations regarding production, which kept flexibility at the forefront of their decision-making processes, were not, of course, acknowledged by authors who labeled local conditions Sago Palm hell. If their efforts were mentioned at all, it was as evidence of feudal remnants in countryside that continued to thwart the modernization of the prefecture's economy.

Okinawa's policy makers eagerly adopted this depiction of the conditions of the prefecture. Although the first petition that the relief committee submitted to the National Diet, the Okinawa Relief Bill did not invoke the phrase directly, it did rely on a tragic image of people who had to eat the fruit of the sago palm even though they knew that it was poisonous to illustrate the gamble with death that the prefecture was currently waging.[28] The people of Okinawa were so starved that they had to risk death by liver failure to assuage their immediate hunger. Okinawa's papers corroborated these reports by occasionally publishing accounts of families who, along with their pets, died after consuming the poisonous plant.[29] The bill echoed mainland journalists' argument that the people of Okinawa were not equipped to handle the process of development and modernization on their own. In fact, they were to blame for the current crisis because they could not carry their own weight. It advocated a familiar solution: "Some kind of colonial administration in the realm of finances such as the establishment of special accounts or the return of all treasury surpluses that are paid by Okinawa back to the prefecture is necessary under present conditions."[30]

Although the difficulties that people faced as they were forced to default on their taxes cannot be denied, it was a misrepresentation to attribute the bankruptcy of the banks and the decline in commodity prices—the specificity of the late Taisho crisis—to the shortcomings of the peasantry. The widespread impoverishment and indebtedness of the small peasants was nothing new, but their suffering was exaggerated by the prefecture's politicians as Sago Palm hell to secure a reprieve from the financial debacle specific to the recessionary conditions that followed the postwar boom. On closer examination, responsibility for Sago Palm hell's conditions was attributable chiefly to the speculative activity that the prefecture's capitalists engaged in immediately following the World War I sugar boom that Ōta described in *Okinawa Kensei Gojūnen*: "In the following two years [1919, 1920], for no apparent reason people in both city and countryside became intoxicated with business. One could turn a profit just by purchasing horse and dog manure. There was a frenzy of speculative activity on land and capital and small moneylenders appeared in various places . . . the general economy was enflamed to the highest degree. City and countryside were both enraptured."[31]

That is, although the collapse of the banks was part of a national and global crisis of capitalism, in many cases bank executives who either exercised favoritism when extending loans or used their position to profit from the financial bubble played a large part in the failure of these institutions. Just as banks throughout Japan overextended themselves in making loans during the boom immediately after World War I, Okinawa's banks also loaned too much money. As Ōshiro Kaneyoshi—the CEO of Okinawa Jitsugyō Ginkō, one of the failed banks, and a member of the House of Peers of the National Diet—pointed out in a House of Peers diet session on March 24, 1926, banks loaned a total of 15.2 million yen as of April 1924, but their total deposits were just 5.7 million yen.[32] Things seemed to be going smoothly during the boom, but the recession made it impossible for these banks to collect on their loans.

The language of relief for Okinawa masked the content of the proposals, but a careful analysis reveals that the only recipient of relief was Tainansha. The common thread that ran throughout all of the proposals for the relief of Okinawa's economy was a vigorous call for funds that could support the sugar industry's switch from brown sugar to a more advanced and profitable type: "The final objective of the reform of the prefecture's sugar industry is to convert the production to bunmitsutō. . . . The demand for brown sugar and low-grade white sugar will not grow any more. Thus, we should encourage the production of bunmitsutō."[33] Ōshiro explained that the prefecture's long-term goal for the sugar industry was to reverse the ratio of brown sugar and bunmitsutō production, currently 2:1, to 1:2 by the time industrial reforms were completed. To achieve this goal, he requested two things: the protection of brown sugar producers through reductions in the consumption tax rate exclusively for brown sugar, and the promotion of the bunmitsutō industry through direct subsidies for peasants who sold cane to the factories run by Tainansha. He and other prefectural leaders hoped that the second item would improve the prefecture's economy by enabling Tainansha to run its factories at full capacity. Ōshiro criticized the unfairness of the state's sugar policy, which historically provided Taiwan with thirteen times more subsidies and more protection than Okinawa although its production was only three times greater. He believed that because Okinawa's sugar industry was constrained by the fact that coercive colonial policies could not be implemented in the prefecture, the industry should at least be compensated through additional direct subsidies from the state.[34] He noted that "Okinawa's bunmitsutō factories are also having difficulties because of the high rates at which they [Tainansha] purchase [raw material]. We cannot ask them to purchase for any higher [price]. . . . If things are left as is the bunmitsutō industry will collapse."[35]

To the frustration of Ōshiro and other supporters of the Okinawa Relief Bill, the central government's response to their recommendations was tepid at best. It did provide some aid, but relief was not as intensive as many had hoped. The state wanted Taiwan, not Okinawa, to take the lead in making Japan self-sufficient in sugar. The colony provided the political conditions that the state and capital needed to succeed in the industry, which generally required coercive tactics. Okinawa's regional administrator, Ida Kenji, described the obstacles that existed to developing this competitive global commodity in a region like Okinawa Prefecture: "We cannot force the peasants to switch [over to bunmitsutō] so we have to convince them that it is more profitable in terms of production to carry the raw material to the bunmitsutō factory. In a colony like Taiwan [in contrast], it is possible to force the people to some extent . . . in this prefecture, we can only try to convince them by appealing to their interests."[36] The state considered the political costs of coercive policies to facilitate the procurement of cane in Okinawa too burdensome to attempt.[37] The final version of the relief plan focused on increasing mainland sugar capital's monopolistic control of Okinawa's economy while protecting the state from significant losses. Though the state would not enact colonial policies in Okinawa, it did grant it the type of subsidies that gave the peasants no alternative but to sell a large part of their cane to Tainansha.[38] It achieved this under the guise of providing relief to ailing cultivators in Sago Palm hell conditions and implied that they had gotten themselves into their current situation through pure laziness.

The Reemergence of Economic Nationalism as the True Path to Recovery

Ōta and Oyadomari, long-time proponents of greater local autonomy, opposed what they believed to be the relief policy's pursuit of an unsustainable path. In particular, both opposed the overprioritization of the bunmitsutō industry. In the eyes of local intellectuals who favored self-sufficiency, true recovery could never take place unless the entire machinery of Okinawa's economy, including the people, was transformed into a rationally organized and efficiently functioning machine. Throughout the 1920s, Ōta consistently advocated a strengthened local autonomy to keep capital produced in the prefecture in the hands of the Okinawan people.[39] I will consider first Oyadomari's work, which expressed interests that were slightly different from Ōta's but shared his concern that too much of Okinawa's wealth and resources flowed into other people's pockets.

Oyadomari's criticism centered on the state's aggressive immigration policy for the prefecture. He argued that as a result of the reckless promotion of immigration, "the best assets of Okinawa are all being transported outside the prefecture and must be considered an accompaniment to the impoverishment of Okinawa." He continued: "When we consider immigrants who come back after failing in foreign development and male and female workers who come back after suffering from unemployment we see that this accelerates the gears of impoverishment in Okinawa."[40] For Oyadomari, relief policies directed toward Okinawa's economic recovery should not neglect the mutually reinforcing relationship between impoverishment, particularly in the prefecture's agrarian villages, and the rapid outflow of people as cheap labor power in times of financial crisis. He lamented: "If brain power and labor power are going abroad and if only the elderly and people without ability are left inside of the prefecture what will become of the future of Okinawa?"[41]

To alleviate some of the conditions that left Okinawa's agrarian villages impoverished, Oyadomari advocated the establishment of cooperatives consisting of consumers' associations and productive associations inspired by Robert Owen's example in Rochdale, England.[42] Like Okamoto Rikichi and Gondō Seikyō, advocates of cooperatives in mainland Japan, he argued that cooperatives similar to those in Rochdale could alleviate the economic and spiritual crises that plagued Okinawa.[43] He explained that the cooperative spirit that would develop out of organization and the mutually beneficial connection between seller and producer would "do away with thinking about production as a means through which personal desire is fulfilled, would instead create an ideal where production took place for the progress of humanity, livelihood, association, and society."[44] Then "the cooperative will not just be the combination of capital's power but will become a union of people apart from capital's power. This will lead to real abundance for the workers, peasants, and [other] commoners."[45]

It is not clear what would happen to large capital in this type of society, or how Oyadomari expected capitalists to give up their dominant position.[46] His call to the state to prop up Okinawa's banks and to mediate relations between the people and finance capital indicate that he held a notion of the state-capital relationship criticized by Michael Hardt and Antonio Negri in *Labor of Dionysus* as a "mechanical and instrumental conception of the relationship between monopoly capitalism and the structure of the state."[47] Oyadomari called on the state, as the central actor that had control over power and resources, to step in and help Okinawa's agrarian villages. He also urged the prefecture's youth to stand with the state to "fight against the political inequalities, economic exploitation and bad conduct of finance capital that presently oppress Okinawa."[48] His vision of the state and young men and women from cultivating sectors of the economy cooperating to form a protective barrier in Okinawa against finance capital's monopolization of profits in the countryside and cities reveals his fundamental misperception of the role that the state had played for the last half-century in peripheralizing the region.[49] Furthermore, his version of state-organized cooperatives overlooked existing forms of cooperation and mutual assistance that small producers in the prefecture's agrarian villages had maintained in the face of efforts led by the state and large sugar capital to dismantle them for the preceding two decades.[50] Thus, Oyadomari promoted state-protected cooperatives as organizations that could counter the destabilization and weakening of agrarian villages that had been going on since the end of World War I.

In contrast, Ōta continued to advocate for greater organization and unification of industry.[51] His concern for strengthening the position of Okinawa as a whole against other regions distinguished him from Oyadomari, who was more concerned about the relative strength of the prefecture's peasants and workers and that of mainland and local capitalists. In the 1920s and 1930s, Ōta reiterated the need that he had first expressed in the early 1900s for a prefecturewide network of industrial associations that would join villages together under an umbrella-like structure to place Okinawa's producers in a stronger position compared to their global competitors.[52] He proclaimed, "to stand in the economic battlefield of the postwar period without this [network] is like being caught in battle without a gun."[53] The description of Okinawa's relations with other regions as akin to war was contrary to dominant characterizations of the prefecture during the Sago Palm hell period as already defeated—a place and a people who never had a chance to do battle. The uniqueness of Ōta's perspective is highlighted in his prescriptions for development rather than relief after World War I.

With regard to the claims made by politicians and journalists that Okinawa's conditions were "too miserable to describe with words," Ōta asked, "At one point Okinawa was treated like a natural disaster region. As a result, the prefecture's plight was known inside and out and was named 'Sago Palm hell.' However, was the condition that came to be known as such the real condition of Okinawa Prefecture? Was the prefectural people's economic life as miserable as the words suggest?"[54] In contrast to descriptions of an Okinawa in need of immediate salvation, Ōta downplayed the severity of the region's impoverishment to avoid attracting the sympathy of outsiders. He insisted that "Kunigami is considered the home of 'Sago Palm hell' but when I traveled there it was not clear where this hell was."[55] This stemmed in part from his awareness that such sympathy was fleeting and could not provide a lasting path to prosperity. He observed: "I became painfully aware that relief really depends on the efforts of the people of the prefecture themselves. Whether that amount is half a million, a million or ten million yen, if it is injected into a starving hamlet it will only quicken that area's death."[56]

In addition to his rejection of the notion that charity could bring recovery to the prefecture, Ōta feared the psychological consequences of repeated calls for salvation. He criticized Okinawan and mainland politicians for treating subsidy procurements like a game—a way to increase the popularity of their own party or faction rather than a matter of life or death. He believed requests by the prefecture for funds in the absence of a clear plan for the fundamental reorganization of its industrial structure only guaranteed failure. He wrote to Kamiyama Seiryō, the director of finance at the prefecture's Monopoly Bureau, that the more subsidies were granted, the more the people would become dependent on them.[57] The constant requests for funds by Okinawa's politicians to the state or the Diet would only breed antipathy and irritation toward the people of the region, once initial sympathies wore off.

Finally, Ōta vehemently opposed the proposals for relief mentioned above that requested the implementation of a special accounts system like the one used in Taiwan. He rejected the request by the Okinawa Economic Promotion Committee to the government to implement colonial administration in the economic realm and resigned from the committee as soon as its position became clear.[58] The measures that removed Okinawa's ability to govern itself in exchange for relief threatened to undo all of the hard work that he and other local leaders had been engaged in since the First Sino-Japanese War to gain full acceptance in the Japanese nation-state. For Ōta, a plan that exchanged political autonomy for material assistance was totally unacceptable. His alternative was cooperation. He presented Denmark as a successful example of what organization in small-scale industry should look like and urged Okinawans to draw on their strengths—their spirit of coexistence and the prosperity embedded in their old laws and forms of social organization—to create a form of industrial organization that would enable individual families to secure reasonable profits.

As we have seen, although the committee and the state focused on increasing mechanization and securing the people's ability to pay taxes, Ōta and Oyadomari asserted that the proposed relief measures would only weaken local control and autonomy. The very thing that politicians and state authorities lamented about Okinawa—that its noncolonial status meant they could not force the peasantry to grow cane to sell to the sugar factories or peg prices to other agricultural products—was what Ōta and Oyadomari felt it absolutely necessary to protect.[59] Both men believed that strengthening the industrial mechanisms to promote cooperation among people who were united by their economic and spiritual position as Okinawans against outside capitalist exploitation was the only way to make sure that the prefecture could keep its noncolonial status in the ever-expanding Japanese empire.

It was naive, not to mention inaccurate, for Ōta and Oyadomari to assume that an Okinawa controlled by Okinawan capital would be more benevolent and prosperous than one ruled by Japanese capital. However, it is important to note that this call for increased control of Okinawa's economy by Okinawans was being echoed by many leaders of colonized and semicolonized regions throughout the world.[60] Ōta's and Oyadomari's critiques, based on Okinawa's rightful position in the Japanese nation-state and reflecting their disappointment at the state's willingness to sell the freedom of the Okinawan people to capital, exposed how colonial policies themselves were often masked as benevolent measures of relief. Thus, Ōta's and Oyadomari's economic nationalism, or Okinawa-shugi, was theoretically wedded to Okinawa's position as a self-governing prefecture in the Japanese nation-state and had as its primary objective the maintenance of this position at all costs.[61]

The Spread of Marxist Thought and Organization in Okinawa

The conflicts that erupted in the northern region of Kunigami in the early 1930s posed serious challenges to the concrete strategies proposed by Ōta and Oyadomari and to the policies articulated in the Okinawa Relief Bill. They were intimately linked to the intensification of Marxist activism in Okinawa that began with the organization of the Okinawa Seinen Dōmei (Okinawa Youth League) by mainland and Okinawa-based young activists and intellectuals in February 1926.[62] The sparks of residents' discontent with various aspects of village life and leadership were fanned by these activists and burst into flames in the Kunigami region. There was a determined standoff in Ōgimi in the fall of 1931 between residents and local officials. Then an already smoldering fire burst out in nearby Haneji. Before turning to these movements, I will briefly outline the spread of Marxist thought and activity in Okinawa. The flows of labor power to, from, and inside Okinawa were accompanied by flows of thought and strategies of anticapitalist resistance that were led by a younger generation of Okinawan activists and intellectuals who came of age after the recession that followed World War I.

As the prefectural authorities and the state debated relief proposals to respond to the collapse of Okinawa's economy, many people were left with no alternative but to abandon their homes and seek their livelihoods in other regions and countries. Particularly conspicuous was the accelerated outflow of female labor as many people left Okinawa to work in mainland spinning factories in the first half of the 1920s. They and male laborers from Okinawa (along with Korean workers) grew in numbers while the mainland labor market contracted overall, which reflected the differential pay scale that Japanese capital used for these precarious workers.[63] Despite low wages, the recessionary conditions in the sugar industry—compounded by the total collapse of Okinawa's other export industry, the Panama hat industry—led workers to leave their hometowns in search of a wage, no matter how small.

As discussed in the previous chapter, men and women preferred to leave the prefecture rather than convert themselves into tenant farmers of Tainansha's large sugar factories on Okinawa's main island. Similarly, Yaeyama's cultivators preferred to forge new lives in Taipei and the South Seas rather than work for large sugar factories or mines that began operations around World War I. These decisions that small producers made to leave their hometowns to become industrial laborers, maids, fishermen, and so on in mainland Japan, colonial cities, and beyond instead of remaining to form part of an agricultural proletariat reveals the harshness of life under large sugar capital-operated farms and the small producers' rejection of a definition of Okinawan community grounded in the territorial boundaries of the prefecture. With the exception of wealthy families, most unmarried women in the Taisho period abandoned agriculture and were recruited as workers by spinning factories in the cities.[64]

This increase in immigration destabilized the social structure and the material world of the prefecture—"an agrarian village with no girls!"[65]— and also forced people from Okinawa who were living on the mainland and overseas to form new communities. As a growing number of people from Okinawa settled in the cities and formed their own neighborhoods, they established organizations, united by their homesickness and the discrimination they faced in their everyday lives. As Tomiyama shows, organizations formed by young activists from the prefecture in their sites of migration had the goal of providing a safe haven for Okinawans experiencing shared challenges in work and life, as they were harassed by their Japanese employers and colleagues for being from the south. In fact, the discrimination that thousands of workers from Okinawa endured when they left the prefecture expanded the community of negatively defined Okinawans on a scale and with an intensity that had not existed before.[66] The daily experience of being discriminated against and belittled by virtue of being Okinawan while they labored alongside workers from other prefectures in the factories was something that the emigrants had not experienced outright in their agrarian villages. Mainland factories were spaces in which workers from Okinawa were confronted with their Okinawanness each day. These were spaces from which new subjectivities and alliances emerged simultaneously.

The significance of these new organizations for Okinawan workers residing in mainland cities can be seen in the example of the Kansai Okinawa Kenjinkai (Kansai Okinawa Prefectural Association), which was founded in February 1924 and organized over 50,000 factory workers in the western Japanese regions of Osaka, Hyogo, Kyoto, and Wakayama.[67] Its success in gaining members was linked to its broad goal of promoting "the mutual relief of the members, the integration of the people of the prefecture and their progress."[68] Its projects included providing refuge from natural disasters, treating illnesses, providing introductions to potential employers, providing help during periods of unemployment, maintaining communications with Okinawa, holding funerals, and officiating at weddings. At the same time, its leaders educated workers in Marxist-Leninist thought so as to equip them with knowledge of the importance of participating in strikes and fighting against their employers.[69] A critique of capitalism joined with the specifically Okinawan experience of discrimination to give the prefectural association's leaders, like Inoguchi Masao and Maeda San'ei, a complex understanding of the nature of capitalist exploitation. In reality, this exploitation was not an abstract concept but a violent relationship reenacted daily between Okinawans and Japanese capitalists, who rationalized their mistreatment of workers from Okinawa by assuming they were naturally inferior. Their working-class struggle against capitalism had to address the ethnic or racial component usually reserved for anticolonial movements.[70]

The multilayered character of Okinawa's Marxist movement grew even more complex as the main site of struggle shifted from the Kansai region back to Okinawa Prefecture following the organization of the Okinawa Youth League in February 1926.[71] The alliance leaders' strong links to the Rōdō Nōmintō (Labor-Farmer Party) as opposed to the Japanese Communist Party reflected their advocacy of a broad-based organization of Okinawa's workers and peasantry and a united front of left-wing thinkers in revolutionary struggle.[72] The league's formation signaled the beginning of an organized, anticapitalist labor movement in the prefecture. In the face of Tainansha's dominance in the prefecture and the mainland Japanese who held positions of political authority there, the activities of the Okinawa Youth League focused on highlighting the link between economic exploitation and discrimination. Its definition of exploitation expanded beyond the unequal wages and hiring practices that had been the main concern of the Kansai Okinawa Prefectural Association to include different levels of exploitation that the majority of Okinawans were subjected to: the dependent nature of the small-scale farming-based monoculture economy, global fluctuations in the price of sugar, and the way that Okinawa's small producers were exploited and left indebted by large mainland capital. Thus, they focused on alleviating the conditions of Okinawa's small producers while simultaneously organizing strikes in the prefecture's factories.[73] The rest of this chapter will examine how working-class struggle in the prefecture came together with agrarian struggles that erupted in the northern region of Okinawa's main island. It will also clarify the demands of the small peasantry who were the participants in these struggles, which shattered any visions of a peaceful and harmonious path to village reorganization that intellectuals like Oyadomari and to some extent Ōta held.

Trouble in the North: Precursors to the Struggles of the Early 1930s

Marxist activists who gathered around the Okinawa Youth League focused on the mutually reinforcing relationship between the Japanese state and capital as the main culprit behind the suffering experienced by Okinawa's cultivators and workers. Okinawa's Marxists did not believe that the state or the prefecture's self-proclaimed leaders could be trusted to alleviate this suffering. Their organizational strategies and experience, combined with the energy and demands of residents of two villages in the Kunigami region produced fierce struggles beginning in the spring of 1931 that could not be calmed even after the main leaders were forced underground following the state's crackdown on Marxist thought shortly after the outbreak of these disputes. The specificity of Kunigami's experience of incorporation into the Japanese nation-state following the completion of the land reorganization project shaped the concrete contours of the early 1930s struggle.

By 1928, the Kunigami region was considered something of a backwater compared to its flourishing counterparts of Nakagami and Shimajiri, which benefited from their relative proximity to the prefecture's cultural center, Shuri, and its commercial and political center, Naha.[74] The northern region had always suffered as a result of its distance from these centers of power, but played an important role as a transporter of lumber, livestock, and agricultural products to the rest of Okinawa. Until the entry of mainland shipping and transport companies into Okinawa in the Meiji period, its small, municipally owned boats called Yanbarusen (figure 5.1) carried lumber, charcoal, daily goods, and specialty items extracted or produced in the region and the Sakishima islands to Naha for sale.[75] The entry of the steamships owned by the Ōsaka Shōsen Kabushikigaisha (OSK) in 1884 made it difficult for the Yanbarusen to control coastal shipping and reflected a turn to trade and transport between Okinawa, mainland Japan, Taiwan, and the South Seas rather than intra-Okinawan exchanges.[76]

The way that communal lands were disposed of in Kunigami beginning in the 1880s exacerbated the region's economic challenges and made it particularly ripe for peasant unrest and struggle under the so-called Sago Palm hell conditions. In 1895, a year after the Yaeyama reclamation project discussed in chapter 3 began, Jahana Noboru visited Kunigami to investigate the conditions of its communal mountains and forests. When he arrived in Motobu Village, he met with village representatives to investigate why these lands were ravaged despite the presence of officials who were in charge of monitoring and managing them.[77] He encouraged villagers to take

Fig. 5.1 Yanbaru boats served an important function, particularly for inter-Okinawa trade. Yanbaru boat, The University of Hawaii at Manoa Library Sakamaki/Hawley Collection, from *Bōkyo Okinawa*, vol. 5, 15.

better care of their communal lands and reassured them that the prefecture was not planning to turn over all of the lands classified as communal to the former nobility. After returning to Naha, Jahana submitted a report to the Narahara administration in which he outlined the obstacles to the healthy management and use of communal mountain and forest lands by the people of Kunigami.[78] He explained that despite his best efforts to convince village representatives to encourage residents to use these lands wisely, he could not guarantee that his advice would be heeded because conflicts over their use and management had exacerbated tensions between the peasants and local officials. The main problem between these two groups, Jahana explained, was that the former nobles had been cutting down trees without regard for the rules and regulations that villagers had abided by for generations and had been selling these resources to outsiders for personal profit. Still others had formed corporate groups and had applied for access to lands to conduct reclamation projects. However, once they received permission, they did not engage in clearing or cultivation and instead loaned the lands out to villagers as tenant lands.[79] It was extremely difficult under such conditions for local officials—even those who were not engaged in this kind of deforestation—to convince the peasantry to cooperate with their efforts to reforest and protect these holdings.[80] As we saw in chapter 3, one of the main reasons for Jahana's resignation from the prefectural administration was to fight Narahara's conversion of communal lands into state-owned properties during the land reorganization project of 1899–1903. Despite his efforts, the thirteenth National Diet decided that the communal lands in Okinawa would be disposed of as the prefectural administration had proposed (figure 5.2).

The actual disposal of these lands did not begin until three years after the completion of the land reorganization project in 1903. At the first meeting of a special committee in the House of Peers charged with establishing guidelines for the disposal of these lands, in January 1906—seven years after prefectural authorities had provisionally converted them into state-owned lands—the members decided to hold a comprehensive investigation to determine which lands should remain officially owned and which should be sold off to villages and individuals. News of the start of this investigation to determine the classifications of communal mountains and forests brought anxiety to Kunigami's cultivators, who depended more than their counterparts in the southern and central regions of the prefecture on access to these lands. These surveys to determine what the state would sell and what it would keep, which conveniently ignored the fact that these lands were not the state's to sell in the first place, began in April 1906.[81]

Fig. 5.2 The prefecture targeted the lush forests of northern Okinawa as valuable sources of lumber during the period before World War II. Residents in these areas fought against these efforts by proposing their own projects to manage and develop these lands. A home in Yanbaru, The University of Hawaii at Manoa Library Sakamaki/Hawley Collection, from *Bōkyo Okinawa*, vol. 4, 46.

The method that the state used to determine which lands it would own and which it would turn over to the villages was based on a simple calculation of profitability. This emerged clearly during deliberations in the House of Peers on a proposal by the government to reform the laws concerning state-owned forest lands in the prefecture.[82] Kume Kinya, the government's representative to the session, reassured members of the Diet who were concerned that a large-scale reorganization of lands on Okinawa would be too costly: "When one manages the mountains, there is always an income. It is clear from the mainland experience that there is an income in relation to expenses. This is why all of the mountains are state-owned."[83] In Okinawa, the government had made sure in its division of lands into those owned by the people and those owned by the state that "the parts in the red are civilian-owned and the profitable parts are taken by the government."[84] Kume buttressed his argument in the next session two days later by emphasizing that the state had no intention of keeping the large areas near local inhabitants where all the trees had already been cut down and the land was ravaged. He explained that according to the disposal stipulations, the state would keep all of the large tracts of land (a thousand chōbu or more) on which future reclamation was anticipated. Once reclamation was completed and hefty profits were made from the sale of lumber, the state would fund the construction of large-scale sugar cultivation and manufacturing areas.[85]

Peasant opposition to this state-led plan to nationalize the best parts of Okinawa's communal lands was especially vocal in Motobu Village and led to the organization of a movement to refuse to pay taxes in the summer of 1907. According to a report published in the *Ryūkyū Shimpō* on October 9, residents refused to submit their taxes until the village tax collection law was reformed.[86] In November, when the prefectural office's tax collectors arrived in the village to investigate sales of salt and tobacco on the black market, between forty and fifty people armed with sticks and stones gathered outside the village office where interrogations were taking place and sounded whistles to disrupt the sessions. They also set fire to some structures around the office. Police officers had to be dispatched from Nago to calm the protesters and restore order.[87] Repeated struggles by peasants protesting their increasing expenses and loss of access to communal lands throughout the late Meiji period reveals the difficult economic conditions that Kunigami's small cultivators endured after land reorganization. In October 1911 peasants in Kunigami had to pay close to 57 yen a year per household in taxes—60 percent more than their counterparts in Shimajiri and over 30 percent more than those in Nakagami.[88]

In that year, less than a decade after the completion of the land reorganization project, an Okinawan writer Yamagusuku Seichū introduced the plight of Kunigami's residents to readers nationwide in "Kunenbo," a story set in Okinawa during the First Sino-Japanese War. In it, he depicted the life of an elementary school teacher from Japan who was arrested for taking advantage of the confusion surrounding the former kingdom's political relationships with Japan and China and plotting against his country. He described the state to which the Yanbarusen had been reduced by the mid-1890s: "It had a broken mast that had drifted ashore and the boat itself was tipped to its side, its red stern split in two." The wrecked ship blended into the background of the neglected beach, which was "littered with white shells, sea urchins, the carcasses of red crabs and corpses of sea anemones that were tangled up into brown weeds and scattered everywhere." As people gathered around to examine the wrecked ship, "the color of the sun cast a thin veil of light over everything and emitted a light that was weak like a kerosene lamp in the winter."[89] Already, the Kunigami region and the Yanbaru boats that connected it to Naha and the outer islands were depicted as the backward remnants of an earlier time destined to fade away or remain only in faint light and isolation.

The construction of the first railways in the prefecture in 1914, which connected the sugar-manufacturing regions of Nakagami and Shimajiri to Naha, exacerbated the isolation of Kunigami and made it difficult for the region's cultivators—who, with the rest of the prefecture, had turned to small-scale, labor-intensive methods of brown sugar manufacture—to compete with both bunmitsutō production and small-scale production in regions that had relatively lower expenses because their products did not have to travel as far to reach market. Mainland sugar capital's lack of interest in establishing factories in the Kunigami region spared cultivators there from being separated from their means of production and transformed into an agricultural proletariat. However, their isolation, particularly from convenient modes of transport, made it difficult for them to make ends meet in an increasingly cash-dependent economy. As brown sugar producers in Shimajiri and Nakagami organized nonselling alliances against Okitai Seitō and Tainansha, cultivators in Kunigami welcomed Ryūkyū Seitō's announcement in 1916 that it would build a 350-ton capacity sugar factory in the north, which would initially use cane from Haneji and the wards of Onna, Nago, Haneji, and Kushi and would gradually expand to receive cane from Ōgimi, Kunigami, and Nakijin.[90] But both this initiative and plans for a fifty-ton steam-powered communally owned factory in Nago approved by the prefecture in late 1917 failed to gain traction and fizzled out by the mid-1920s.[91]

The region missed out on the opportunity to suffer directly from the exploitation of Tainansha, but its residents felt the effects of the economic crisis after the sugar boom that followed World War I, perhaps more acutely than others. The declining strength of the brown sugar industry caused by the prefecture's promotion of bunmitsutō hastened the north's peripheralization. The relief petition, which promoted the development of bunmitsutō, was completely antithetical to the well-being of people there, particularly since the plan for the establishment of a large-scale factory had fallen through. In 1929 a second plan for the establishment of a bunmitsutō factory in Kunigami operated by Tainansha was floated, but it quickly died because the Nihon Kōgyō Ginkō, their bank, refused to loan the company 1.35 million yen to build the factory.[92] The failure of Tainansha to gain financing for the Kunigami factory in turn delayed the completion of the prefecture-operated Motobu railway line that was supposed to link Nago with Naha.[93] Political tensions intensified when Motobu and Kin Villages decided to leave Kunigami region's municipal association (*chōson kumiai*) in the spring of 1929 because they did not want to burden the high costs of the repairs of prefectural roads and construction fees to improve infrastructure and schools.[94]

The Ōgimi Village Reform Movement

It was under these difficult economic conditions and political tensions that governed life in northern Okinawa that the Ōgimi Village Reform Movement, a broad-based movement involving 90 percent of Ōgimi Village's population erupted in August 1931.[95] It was intimately linked to the indebtedness of the northern region; the influx of Marxist activists who returned to their hometowns from mainland cities to lead a struggle in the agrarian villages; and measures deployed by Kinjō Tansuke, the first publicly elected village head (*sonchō*) of Ōgimi to facilitate capitalist development in the region.[96] The confluence of these factors resulted in an intense struggle over village leadership in Ōgimi, a region that up to that point had escaped the tumultuous disputes that had plagued the nearby villages of Haneji, Motobu, and Kin in earlier decades. The measures that Kinjō implemented following his election brought to the surface all of the anxieties, discontent, and anger that had been brewing since the completion of the land reorganization project.

Three projects transformed Kinjō and his ally Taira Shinjun—who concurrently held the lucrative post of village physician, was a member of the prefectural assembly, and headed of the branch of the Seiyūkai (Friends of Constitutional Government) Party in Okinawa—from hometown heroes into their neighbors' most hated enemies.[97] Kinjō's main projects discussed below—the relocation of the Ōgimi office (*yakuba*), economic rationalization plans, and a thrift campaign (*shōhi setsuyaku undō*) to limit excessive consumption by families—were part of his efforts to bring development to the village, but they were not looked upon favorably by residents who saw local authorities growing fatter by parlaying their posts into lucrative opportunities to increase their personal wealth. In each project, the monopolization of decision-making power by village officials bred resentment among residents, who had grown accustomed to the rituals of democratic practice following the extension of the election laws to Okinawa in 1920.

The first source of tension emerged out of a longstanding project to transfer the village office from its original location in Shioya Ward, in the southwestern part of the village, to a more central location in Ōgimi—a decision that had been made unilaterally by the first village head, Yamakawa Bunkō in the summer of 1911. Residents of Shioya rejected his sudden announcement and discussed the possibility of seceding and forming their own village, prohibiting the entry of vessels from northern wards into the port of Shioya, refusing to buy pigs and fish from the north, and so on.[98] This dispute was settled the following year after Yamakawa agreed to provide funds for a school expansion in Shioya and to exempt its residents from the majority of costs associated with the transfer and construction of the new village office.[99] Still, for the next eight years, the village office operated out of Shioya elementary school as officials scrambled for funding to construct the new office. After Kinjō was elected, he began construction of the village office in the middle of the recession and made the northern wards of the village bear 80 percent of the construction expenses, as his predecessor had promised in 1912.[100]

In addition to completing the relocation of the village office, Kinjō's main objectives included developing the village's industry in order to increase the amount of cash crops and commodities that Ōgimi's residents produced. He zeroed in on the sugar industry but found it difficult to convince villagers to plant more cane when they had so little cash. He turned his attention to the effective management of the village's forests, which formed the basis for the region's most important export: lumber.[101] Because of the importance of forestry for Ōgimi's export economy, Kinjō focused on bringing the vast mountain and forest lands under tighter surveillance and management. He also proposed an afforestation project that was designed to expand lumber exports and limit the ability of residents to continue their practice of entering the forest, cutting down trees, and selling the wood to their local store in order to purchase rice and daily necessities. This proposal sparked immediate opposition from local residents, who feared that a state-run afforestation project would restrict their ability to access and control communal resources.[102]

The third major undertaking that Kinjō embarked on after taking office was a thrift campaign to limit excessive consumption, particularly for celebrations and festivals. Detailed regulations of this sort were not unique to Ōgimi Village and had begun during the turn of the century in the form of a prefecture-wide push to reform old customs. During these earlier campaigns, Kunigami was one region where local reformers had exercised caution in limiting the practices of mōasobi and yagamaya for fear of unnecessarily upsetting village inhabitants.[103] Once he took office, Kinjō veered from this moderate approach and pursued an aggressive reformist stance. He organized and mobilized committees in each ward to strictly enforce his new measures. In January 1930, ward representatives deliberated and passed twelve items that included restrictions on participation in coming-of-age celebrations to immediate family members and prohibitions of minor or subsidiary celebrations before and after the primary event, strict regulations on the amount of money that could be given as celebratory gifts, limitations on the quantity of sake and food that could be consumed during celebrations, and so on. These measures attempted to reduce the frequency, scope, and length of interactions between people and therefore, costs that were incurred during annual celebrations.[104] Although it is not possible to trace a direct link between this component of Kinjō's restrictions and village anger over his economic policies, the destructive nature of the restrictions—particularly for social relations in local communities—cannot be ignored when considering the broad feeling of resentment that developed against him.[105] These policies—which emphasized development and rationality at the expense of the social, religious, and economic practices of local communities, while his industrial policies reduced the political and economic autonomy of villagers—must be weighed as heavily as the organizational experience of the young activists who returned to Ōgimi in explaining why 90 percent of its residents participated in the struggle against Kinjō that began in the summer of 1931.

Finally, the fact that large numbers of workers left Ōgimi Village for other parts of the prefecture, mainland cities, and abroad must be considered when accounting for activists' successful mobilization of villagers against Kinjō. Since the early 1900s, much of Ōgimi's skilled workforce—most notably fishermen, construction workers, and fishmongers—had departed in search of waged work, as expenses requiring cash outgrew the ability of residents to earn it.[106] The cash-poor region became dependent on remittances that workers sent home from their places of work in Naha, Osaka, and the South Seas to keep up with the ever-increasing public expenses and taxes levied on them each year (figure 5.3).[107] Considering the strong economic ties that bound together the people who called Ōgimi home, it is not surprising that activists found a receptive audience in many of the villagers who had remained behind.

The Ōgimi Village Reform Movement formally commenced with the return home of these activists from the mainland in the summer of 1931. A first-person account written by one of the participants, Yamashiro Zenkō, recounts the early stages of the movement. In Yamashiro's case, after his

Fig. 5.3 Many people who left Ōgimi went to Yaeyama, where they worked in the bonito industry. The establishment of a fishery association in 1921 spurred growth of the industry, and by the late 1930s factories that produced dried bonito flakes lined the streets of the coastal city of Arakawa on Ishigaki Island. Yaeyama's bonito factory, Naha City Museum of History, photo no. 02004756.

return to Ōgimi, he and several of his friends met on the beach with the leader of the movement, Uezato Haruo, to strategize.[108] Uezato, who had achieved a small degree of fame as a poet, had just recently returned to his adopted hometown of Kijoka Ward in Ōgimi to lead his comrades in a movement to reform village administration. This was tied to a broader vision that he had of bringing anticapitalist struggle to the agrarian villages of the northern region of Okinawa. At that initial meeting on the beach, the men agreed that their immediate goals were to force Kinjō and Taira out of their positions. Kinjō's socializing expense fund of 480 yen a year that kept him traveling for most of the year and Taira's 150-yen annual salary as village physician angered Uezato and the alliance members, who saw these sums as measures that enriched the two leaders as they extolled the virtues of thrift and urged their constituents to severely restrict their own spending.[109] They drew inhabitants into their movement by creating an alliance flag and song that they taught the people who listened to the lectures that they delivered throughout the village.[110] The movement was particularly successful in attracting men and women between the ages of eighteen and twenty-five, despite prohibitions on people under twenty-five from engaging in political activity.[111]

Following a round of lectures and organizational activities, on August 22, 1931, the alliance drafted a list of twenty-two demands to be presented to the village administration. The draft proposal was signed by representatives of seven of the ten wards in Ōgimi Village. The list was wide-ranging and included demands for a reduction of village administration expenses and tax rates; the abolition of the corvée; the return of fishing rights to villagers; an end to the practice of selling off state-owned communal forest lands; the reestablishment of villagers' control of the pawn shop and the communal use of its profits; greater transparency of finances; the establishment of a free clinic; a public election for the post of head of ward administration (kuchō); and lowering the salaries of officials.[112]

The nature of the demands illuminates the comprehensive nature of the movement's objectives and reveals that a major component of this agrarian struggle was the residents' desire for increased economic and political control of village affairs. The reestablishment of collective control over former communal lands, access to fisheries, and mechanisms of mutual financing were all part of a broad effort on the part of Ōgimi's small peasantry to regain many rights that they had lost as a result of the prefecture's modernizing reforms and constituted a clear rejection of the type of development that Kinjō envisioned. The privatization of property and the enclosure of the commons in Ōgimi in the name of development, particularly of the sugar industry, had already brought heightened levels of indebtedness and vulnerability to market fluctuations for many of its residents. Furthermore, Kinjō's promotion of the thrift campaign implicitly blamed the sloppy spending habits of villagers for their current state of impoverishment. It was the combined consequences of development and austerity that Kinjō implemented in Ōgimi that led residents to throw in their lot with the young activists, even at the risk of arrest or social ostracization.

The circle of organizers widened throughout September 1931, from twenty representatives of the various wards to twenty-five who submitted their collective demands to Kinjō. The scope of the alliance's demands also expanded over time. At the villagers' assembly (sonmin taikai) on September 23, a decision was made to formally demand Kinjō's resignation from the post to which he was first elected over a decade earlier. Furthermore, the initial call for the establishment of a free clinic grew into a demand for the construction of a village hospital and the abolition of Taira's post of village physician. These escalating demands and the widening circle of participation finally led

Kinjō and prefectural authorities to order the dissolution of the alliance on October 7 for violating the terms of the Peace Preservation Law. The alliance responded by conceding to an expulsion of all members younger than twenty-five but increased the frequency and intensity of its demonstrations and attacks against Kinjō.

Okinawa's local papers, which had ties to either the Seiyūkai or Minseitō (Constitutional Democratic Party), consistently dismissed the legitimacy of the movement and presented the village-level class struggle as just another example of a national political contest between the major parties that was destroying the social fabric of an otherwise peaceful community. In order to depoliticize the dispute and, in some cases, co-opt it for their own ends, Okinawa's newspapers spun this movement into a political confrontation between the Seiyūkai and the Minseitō and urged politicians from the latter party to stop toying with naive peoples' sentiments in an attempt to destroy the stability of the Seiyūkai stronghold.[113] In this story told by the Seiyūkai-backed *Ryūkyū Shimpō*, not only were the common people deceived by evil politicians, but even the Marxist leaders Uezato and Yamashiro were manipulated by politicians of the Minseitō, who saw this conflict as a perfect opportunity to weaken an important Seiyūkai base.[114] In this way, the will and political consciousness of villagers who participated in the movement and their concrete demands were dismissed, and the parties' successful manipulation of their emotions became the focal point in the press.

In a strange turn of events, in the prefectural assembly this conflict was turned into an example of the "energetic spirit of the youth" that could become the driving force for national growth and rejuvenation.[115] The propagator of this view was Shibata Komezō, a representative who celebrated the enthusiasm of the movement's youth for reforming the conditions of their villages. He incorporated the actions of the Ōgimi youth into a national narrative of rebirth by comparing it to what the "nameless youth" did to bring about the Meiji Restoration: "The Japan of today exists because the nameless youth burned with the spirit of nation building and moved under this spirit of advancement to build a new Japan . . . they are the motive force of the advancement of the state."[116] He also compared their activity to the organization of the National Socialists by Adolf Hitler: "The party is now the great leader of Germany . . . but we must be reminded that this all began on the second floor of a café in Munich by six unknown youth."[117] Shibata begged the state not to destroy the spirit of revolution displayed by the youth of the Ōgimi movement, but to simply get rid of the Marxists who were at its helm.

Despite the desire of the papers and the prefectural authorities to understand the movement as either a manipulation of the sentiments of the people by ill-intentioned leaders or an inspirational movement that could realize a higher form of state organization, pamphlets and letters of support confirm what a close analysis of the impact of Kinjō's attempted policies on agrarian households points to—a much wider circle of involvement and deeper political commitment than what the papers reported. Pamphlets that the alliance published reported a gathering of seven thousand people that took place at the Ōgimi normal school to express support for the movement. By this time, news of the alliance had spread throughout the prefecture, and supporters came from as far away as Naha (fifty-five miles distant) and Kadena (the center of Tainansha's bunmitsutō industry) on foot or by bicycle in the rain to participate in a rally. The scope of participation and willingness to gather in the rain despite fears of malaria transmission revealed the depth of determination and anger that inspired this movement to remove Kinjō from his village head seat: "A grudge runs through the marrow of the villagers. In order to live a more human life the villagers have risen up and have united in order to drive him out."[118]

Most important, the actions of the villagers illustrate the strong commitment that they had to the movement. The women's associations (*fujinbu*) of Janagusuku and Kijoka wards organized and placed themselves in charge of collecting donations, primarily of foodstuffs from farming households and merchants, which they used to cook meals for the 20–30 alliance members who met each night to strategize and hold study sessions led by Uezato.[119] Although existing accounts do not give us access to the motivations of each member of the women's associations, their unflinching support of the alliance despite repeated roundups and constant surveillance by the regular police and the Special Higher Police (Tokkōka) reveals the strength of their collective commitment. The movement was clearly much more than a local inflection of a national contest or a desperate response to economic suffering. Instead, it indicated the deep desire by many people to eliminate the forces that threatened their material survival and stood in the way of their full participation in political and economic life. This recognition requires a type of analysis that Jacques Rancière has used to describe another place and time: "Leaving the field open, for once, to the thinking of those not 'destined' to think, we may come to see that the relationship between the order of things and the desires of those subjugated to it is a bit more complicated than scholarly treatises realize."[120]

Confronted with this widespread and sustained commitment to the alliance, prefectural authorities responded first with police suppression and arrests of its leaders, most notably Uezato. In an attempt to neutralize the situation and respond to the impoverishment that they believed to be the reason for the widespread participation of villagers in the movement, Kinjō decided to concede to some of the alliance's demands. He held an emergency meeting on November 5 and reached a compromise with the now leaderless alliance.[121] Backed by the prefectural administration, Kinjō agreed to a 30 percent reduction in the salary of all village officials, a 30 percent reduction in the pay for village assemblymen, the abolition of the posts of village physician and midwife, and a reorganization of industrial expenditures. All of the money saved by these cuts would then be applied to a reduction of taxes by 1,343 yen. As these concessions indicate, Kinjō focused on the reduction of economic burdens and did not address the alliance's political demands, such as increasing fiscal transparency and transferring decision-making power to the residents.[122]

These partial measures failed to eliminate the discontent or stop the activity of the villagers. The alliance, seeing that the strategy of directing their demands to the government had reached a dead end, set their sights on a new task in the village: organizing a consumer cooperative movement that was directly linked to the Japan Proletarian Consumer Cooperative Alliance.[123] In November, as Kinjō announced his concessions to the village assembly, the alliance sent a representative to Hyogo Prefecture—where the radical consumer cooperative movement had been active for some time—to receive training in the management and operation of cooperatives. The alliance began cooperative buying (*kyōdō kōbai*) in December and officially formed the Ōgimi Shōhi Kumiai (Ōgimi Consumer Cooperative) with 500 members in early March 1932.[124] They began operations in spite of police suppression of their activities in June of that year. An examination of the activities and ideological connections of the Ōgimi Consumer Cooperative will bring to light the fundamental difference between the goals that the participants in the movement were working toward, the alliance's demands as Kinjō and the prefecture's policy makers understood them, and the type of cooperation that local leaders like Ōta and Oyadomari envisioned.

The Ōgimi Consumer Cooperative's affiliation with the Japan Proletarian Consumer Cooperative Alliance—the more radical of the two main national consumer cooperative bodies—indicates its organizers' commitment to the consumer cooperative as a way to distribute daily necessities and other material to the residents of Ōgimi without exploitation by middlemen and to heighten the peasantry's political consciousness and assertiveness vis-à-vis existing power holders like Kinjō and Taira. The immediate concern of the cooperative was to strengthen its members' ability to control and manage the distribution, sale, and exchange of their own products with other cooperatives in cities and agrarian regions domestically and abroad. This put the cooperative's stance close to that of the Japan Proletarian Consumer Cooperative Alliance, which split from the Shōhi Kumiai Rengōkai (Federation of Consumer Unions) because the latter envisioned a Rochdale-inspired consumer cooperative movement to better the livelihood of consumers but made no mention of using the movement as a weapon in class struggle.[125] The Ōgimi Consumer Cooperative was formed right before the official founding of the Japan Proletarian Consumer Cooperative Alliance in late March 1932, and one of the former's key members, Kinjō Kanematsu, served as an officer on the latter's central committee.[126]

Ōgimi's cooperative had a twofold character, as a distributor of communally purchased daily necessities such as firewood, matches, and oil and as an educational organ that spread Marxist thought to young students in communal learning areas.[127] Their economic aims remained the same as those of the earlier phases of the movement—alleviating tax burdens and transferring the control of communal resources to the people. Villagers who joined the cooperative were able to procure their daily necessities without depending on middlemen and were responsible for distributing these goods to each other. Notably, though the political agitation and petition-writing activities did not lead to Kinjō's resignation, he finally capitulated on June 14, 1932, exactly one week after the pioneer wing of the consumer cooperative alliance—the Nakayoshikai, modeled after the Soviet Young Pioneer Organization—was formed with 120 fifth graders from Kijoka elementary school as its members.[128] The successful establishment of the consumer cooperative and pioneer wing—which showed that cooperation was not just a response to economic impoverishment or an expression of Okinawans' primordial community, but a reflection of their desire to exercise collective control over the management, circulation, and distribution of resources, produce, finance, and information—provides a stark contrast to the type of communality envisioned by both Ōta and Oyadomari, which implicitly saw the local bourgeoisie as the stratum in charge of maintaining order in the village economy and society.

The police disbanded the Ōgimi Consumer Cooperative shortly after its organization, and authorities were able to reestablish some stability in the region by implementing the economic rehabilitation plan in Ōgimi (and the rest of Okinawa and Japan).[129] The alliance's disappearance should not be seen as its defeat but as a fulfillment of its objectives. Its effectiveness was revealed in the forcefulness of the counterattack by prefectural authorities and in the exposure of the inability of any of the relief proposals to fulfill the desires of Okinawa's peasantry. Finally, the decision of the members of the alliance to separate themselves from the old community was not simply a strategy of refusal but a moment of creative construction. As Deleuze and Guattari remind those who are discouraged by the revolutionary moment that never comes, "practice does not come after the emplacement of the terms and their relations, but actively participates in the drawing of the lines."[130]

The Arashiyama Incident

Around the same time that the Ōgimi Village reform movement was unfolding, just ten miles southwest, residents of Haneji Village were mobilizing in droves with what appeared on the surface to be a completely different agenda. Beginning in March 1931, residents of Haneji organized a movement to stop the construction of a leprosy sanatorium at Arashiyama, a mountain that served as a watershed for rivers that ran through the villages of Haneji, Nakijin, and Nago. Arashiyama became a site of contention immediately after the top-secret construction site was discovered. Five village leaders—including the village head of Haneji, Taira Masao—led the opposition movement. They traveled to Naha in early May 1931 to submit a petition expressing their opposition to this construction to Governor Iino Jirō and the prefecture's chief of the Division of Health, Nishimura.

It might seem easy to dismiss this movement as nothing more than an irrational response by villagers to the fear of infection. But it becomes more difficult to do so when the early phase of the opposition movement is examined in conjunction with proposals in the early Taisho era for stimulating the village economy. Haneji emerges in reports published in the *Ryūkyū Shimpō* as being particularly entrepreneurial and adaptive to change, compared to other villages in Kunigami. Articles about Haneji reveal that local leaders proposed reforms and blueprints for the development of the village. For example, in August 1915, the *Ryūkyū Shimpō* reported that the prefecture had targeted thirty-three chōbu of land in Haneji for reforms to improve agricultural productivity. The reform of these lands in Isagawa Ward was part of a prefecturewide project to improve and reorganize arable lands that began in March 1915 under the direction of Governor Ōmi

Kyūgorō.¹³¹ According to this plan, seventeen of the thirty-three chōbu were to be transferred to village ownership and turned into tenant lands. Though this process would increase the rents for tenants in Haneji, an August 21, 1915, article in the *Ryūkyū Shimpō* predicted that these lands would be in high demand because the irrigation and draining system in place would be extremely convenient for cultivation.¹³² Around this time, Haneji's leaders responded enthusiastically to plans proposed by the Ryūkyū Seitō to build a large-scale bunmitsutō factory. Even after that proposal fizzled out, local leaders continued to adapt to the prefecture's prioritization of bunmitsutō by purchasing 23,000 stalks of the Proefstation Oost Java variety of sugarcane from Taiwan in 1925 and planting them on village lands.¹³³

Two proposals, one to turn Haneji's Genka River into an artificial incubation site for sweetfish (*ayu*) and the second to transform its arable lands into rice paddies for the cultivation of a new strain of high-yielding rice, were floated in the two years prior to the Arashiyama incident, which further illustrates the village administration's enthusiasm for reforms that could reduce its dependence on external market fluctuations. With regard to the first proposal, village authorities and villagers who lived near the river planned to take advantage of the abundance of sweetfish and formulated a plan to export large quantities to the Naha market through artificial incubation. They formulated and submitted a proposal to the prefectural office in charge of fishery policy, which determined after conducting investigations that the Genka River was in fact a suitable breeding ground for sweetfish. The office concluded that as long as a suitable artificial incubation method could be implemented, the project would be successful, and the prefecture gave the office permission to work with the village to develop this project.¹³⁴ With regard to the second project, in late 1929 Haneji was selected as one site for prefecture-directed rice cultivation improvements. Following this selection, local leaders formed a rice cultivation reform alliance consisting of two hundred families from Genka, Makiya, and other grain-producing wards in the village.¹³⁵ The alliance was so successful in cultivating a new strain of rice in 1929 that in the following November the prefecture decided to continue providing encouragement: it gave farmers in Haneji subsidies to expand cultivation and to encourage cultivators to use a more effective type of synthetic fertilizer. Any surplus rice was to be sold communally and the profits used to reform agricultural operations.¹³⁶ For village authorities and residents who had engaged in these projects to compensate for the challenges to industrial development posed by the region's distance from Naha, the prefecture's proposal to build a sanatorium for leprosy patients at the source for their rivers, which were crucial for the success of both endeavors, heightened the fear they already held of being left behind.[137]

The petition activity by village authorities marked the initial phase of the opposition to the construction of a sanatorium in Arashiyama, but the movement soon expanded and recruited hundreds and then thousands of villagers. The process by which this transformation took place is unclear due to the paucity of existing documents. However, what is certain is that local officials, primarily from Haneji and Nakijin, worked with young Marxist activists from both villages who had been energized by the successful mobilization in Ōgimi to gather support.[138]

Opposition grew rapidly. Over three thousand residents participated in a demonstration in Nakijin on March 16 that resolutely opposed the establishment of the sanatorium, despite the fact that it was the busiest season for farming.[139] This demonstration was followed by a gathering of over a thousand people, who surrounded the Nago police station to demand the release of the Okinawa Youth League members who had been arrested on May 28 following an assembly that had been broken up by the police (figure 5.4). Opposition culminated in an demonstration of eight thousand people on July 5 at the Arashiyama construction site, which brought villagers from Haneji and Nakijin together again, bamboo sticks in hand, shouting slogans like "solidarity is power" and "no to the establishment in Arashiyama." After the demonstration, the participants split into two groups. Residents of Nakijin formed a line—with a drummer and a man carrying a large flag at the front—and marched home, taking detours along the way in an effort to draw attention to their activities. Residents of Haneji marched, bamboo sticks in hand, to Nago, where they paced back and forth in front of the Nago police station as the police chief helplessly looked on.[140] The scanty documentary evidence makes it difficult to form a clear picture of the range of motivations of the thousands who participated in these demonstrations, but it is noteworthy that significant numbers of people joined in, despite a constant police presence at all of the gatherings. It cannot be doubted that the opposition was legitimated by the leadership of the village elite and was at least partially motivated by their prejudice against leprosy patients, but we must also keep in mind that the slogans that they mobilized around were similar to those that inspired the participants of the Ōgimi movement.[141]

In response to the demonstrations, mass resignations submitted by Taira and his entire staff, and the formation by students of Haneji and Nakijin Villages of a consumer cooperative alliance modeled on the Nakayoshikai in Ōgimi, the prefecture appointed an interim village head, Kamejima Zoku,

Fig. 5.4 This large road ran through Nago, which had seen impressive growth since the late nineteenth century. By the end of the century, Nago had developed into the entertainment center of northern Okinawa. The main road in Nago, Naha City Museum of History, photo no. 02003693.

and dispatched him to Haneji to restore order.[142] When he arrived in mid-June 1932, he was shunned by villagers, who refused to sell him any food or rent him a place to live. In the end, he had no choice but to commute from Nago, approximately two and a half miles away. When he reported to work at the village hall, he found that his office had been occupied by the oppositional alliance and transformed into their headquarters. Things came to a head on June 25, 1932, when several young men from the village who were armed with sickles and spades physically threatened Kamejima and demanded that he leave town. In response, four days later the prosecutor's office at Nago rounded up a hundred people thought to be involved in the attack or its planning, including the leaders of the alliance.[143] The Arashiyama Incident officially ended with the prosecution of fifteen men, but disruptions to village administration continued until at least 1934.

For better or worse, the movement did achieve its goal of suspending the prefecture's construction of the leprosy sanatorium in Arashiyama.[144] Although it is tempting to dismiss the movement as an ugly chapter in the long history of prejudice against leprosy patients, it is important to place this movement also in the long history of northern Okinawa's peripheralization from the perspective of the prefecture's industrial policies, a history that began with the granting of large swaths of communal lands in the northern region in the early Meiji period to former Ryūkyū kingdom elites and mainland entrepreneurs for reclamation. Just as the mobilization of thousands of people during the movement to oppose the construction in Arashiyama revealed the residents' anger at yet another attempt by prefectural authorities to make important decisions regarding their land and resources without any consent or discussion, the lack of a single voter's participation in elections for the village council that were held in late November 1932—months after the movement's most radical members had been jailed—expresses the residents' rejection of the legitimacy of the Japanese state's political mechanisms that were most immediate to them.

Conclusion: The Limits of Okinawa-Shugi

The small successes of both movements against the prefectural administration were particularly important in transforming the realm of possibilities of belonging and action that Okinawa's small peasantry could imagine. In particular, their self-organization into cooperatives indicates that the villagers of Kunigami who participated in the two drastically different movements outlined in this chapter had a common goal—perhaps one that emerged in the course of the struggle—of finding a method of social organization drastically different from the type of modernization of Yanbaru that they had desired in the beginning. The political victories that these participants were able to win, and the transformation of their demands and desires through the process of struggle, created enormous difficulties for state leaders who hoped that the northern periphery of Okinawa would remain nothing more than a source of cheap labor power that could be funneled into factories during times of labor shortages in the prefecture and beyond. The nature of these struggles warrants a reconsideration of the dominant characterization of Okinawa's agrarian villages as model villages that were smoothly incorporated into the project of total war from 1932 onward.[145]

Finally, they reveal the limited usefulness of the idea of Okinawa-shugi—as a classless, timeless organic community of Okinawans with shared interests—to fulfill the desires of the vast majority of the people of Okinawa Prefecture. Appeals to an abstract community failed to provide comfort to the cultivating peasantry and workers of northern Okinawa, who by the beginning of the 1930s were equipped with a language that enabled them to envision an alternative version of the relationships among themselves, the state, and capital in which they had the power to make decisions that affected their own lives. Neither Ōta nor Oyadomari could have anticipated the way that residents united strategically along and across geographical and class boundaries to form temporary alliances based on their specific experiences of discrimination and exploitation by the state and capital.

CONCLUSION

三

LIVING LABOR AND THE LIMITS OF OKINAWAN COMMUNITY

In "Horobiyuku Ryūkyū Onna no Shoki" ("Memoirs of a Declining Ryūkyūan Woman"), a short story published in the June 1932 issue of the *Fujin Kōron* magazine, Kushi Fusako, a young writer from Shuri, explored the consequences that incorporation into the Japanese nation-state in 1879 had on the material and psychological well-being of the people of Okinawa. The subtitle of the story, "Please Hear the Cries of the People who have been Pushed to the Corner of the Earth" was selected by the editors of the magazine who wanted to take advantage of the national audience that they expected would be sympathetic to the pleas of an Okinawan writer vividly describing the distress of her people.[1] As Keiko Katsukata-Inafuku has written, the editorial board likely wanted to ride the wave of the great interest that had developed after the Sago Palm hell and folk arts boom had drawn dozens of prominent mainland social scientists, journalists, and artists to the southern islands, a group that had gone on to publish hundreds of articles recounting their adventures.[2] Readers likely anticipated a story that would confirm what they already knew about Okinawa—that its people should be an object of their pity and a target of relief efforts.

Contrary to these expectations, Kushi's gaze was firmly fixed on her hometown as she—like Walter Benjamin's angel of history—stood still while wreckage piled up in front of her eyes.[3] Her short story was an attempt to capture this wreckage before the storm of progress scattered it and rendered it a mere casualty of the universal history of linear development. In recording her testimony about this wreckage, Kushi posed many difficult questions to the people who identified themselves as Okinawan about this category that loomed so heavily in their minds and hearts. She called on her readers from Okinawa to search within themselves and their communities for a different story—one of dignity, rather than of alienation and self-loathing.

In the opening lines of Kushi's story, the narrator, a young woman from Okinawa living in Tokyo, asks her friend—who had recently been home in Okinawa—about the health of the narrator's mother.[4] Lest the reader think it strange that the narrator had to ask her friend about the health of her own mother, the narrator reassured the reader that her situation was not unique; all Okinawans who lived outside the prefecture could relate to it. Yet in the same breath, the narrator explained that not all Okinawans experienced tragedy to the same degree. Those who suffered the most, she explained, were women of her mother's generation. Their tattooed bodies rendered them immobile and required them to be hidden from view. Theirs was a life of silent waiting: "Their tragedy is that the older ones cannot even leave Okinawa because of their tattoos. As a result, they cannot lay eyes on their grandchildren."[5]

Kushi's young narrator blamed Okinawa's intellectuals and educators for this tragic situation. They were overly sensitive to the gaze of mainland Japanese and could not bear the sight of these women, who exposed the barbarity of Okinawa's culture on the back of their hands. Here, we cannot help but recall the decision by the Prefectural Association in 1916 to demand that all tattooed women who immigrated to the Philippines immediately return to the prefecture because they were bringing shame upon the Okinawan people. These women, who had joined their husbands in their new place of residence, were ridiculed by the Japanese community in the Philippines for their barbaric customs. The horrified members of the Prefectural Association demanded their return to Okinawa because they believed that these women would damage the interests of properly civilized Okinawans, who had been working so hard to blend in as Japanese in that foreign land.[6] Those intellectuals, like their counterparts in the early 1930s whom Kushi criticized, were responsible for keeping Okinawa's women trapped in the miserable conditions of their hometowns because they were deathly afraid, she wrote, of "exposing themselves to others."[7]

Ordinary Okinawans who lived in mainland Japanese cities were affected by these assimilatory impulses expressed by the Prefectural Association and the Okinawa Student Association, which registered a strong complaint about Kushi's story. In return for discarding bodily and linguistic markets that might expose their ultimately incurable condition—being Okinawan—they had absorbed large doses of self-loathing and shame because of their origin. As they sought to escape the marks of their original sin, they ironically came together again. That is, they developed a commonality of the most unfortunate kind: "We have loneliness in our hearts in common . . . we waver and mend our appearances, living day by day." The pursuit of assimilation secured Okinawans' fate of becoming united in their loneliness at being forsaken by the Japanese community to which they longed so desperately to belong. They sought protection from their loneliness in numbers, "living clumped together like mushrooms in the large city" despite being encouraged to assimilate.[8] Their collective destiny, Kushi lamented, was to "eternally cater to the rear of history and live, dragged along the road that others have already walked on or sullied."[9] Her story constituted a powerful critique of the tendency of intellectuals who identified themselves as Okinawan to impose strict standards of conduct on their targets of reform in the name of the abstract Okinawan community—something that we saw commence around the First Sino-Japanese War—and a vivid description of the heavy consequences that their assimilatory tendencies had on the mental condition of the people from the region.

It is this condition that Kushi bore witness to in "Horobiyuku Ryūkyū Onna no Shoki." Her story pinpointed an important problem that all people writing about Okinawa around that time had to address: how to reaffirm the existence of Okinawa and Okinawans while believing it necessary to transcend those categories to have some sort of value in Japanese society. The problem was impossible to resolve because the categories were born out of a forceful annexation and from the start were imbued with unequal relations of power. The category of Okinawa that Kushi's intellectuals fought so hard to uphold was bound to remain inferior as long as it required the category of Japan to exist.

Kushi's work and her apology for it to the Okinawa Student Association expressed a complete refusal of such attempts to create a singular Okinawan cause. She believed that upholding an organic, transhistorical Okinawan community was inadequate for the effacement of internal unevenness and difference. The primary targets of her vitriol were groups like the Prefectural Association and the Okinawa Student Association, whose members took it on themselves to police the words, actions, lifestyles, and thoughts of the people in an effort to win respect for the community. She wrote of the difficulty that those who faced this surveillance underwent: "It is the rule in Okinawa that only men with power are supposed to express their opinion, while people without power and formal education have no alternative but to follow behind them. As long as those with power control us, we who are powerless have no hope of salvation."[10] Her own silencing in the years following the publication of both pieces in 1932 and her depictions of Okinawa's mothers, workers, uncles, and daughters as emasculated objects of disdain and targets of reform may signal the difficulty that she ultimately encountered in speaking in her own name.

The dilemma that Kushi faced in trying to tell a different story is revealed in the ambivalent conclusion to her piece. She ends the story with her narrator hoping that one day she can discover something comparable to the "declining beauty" that she ultimately discovered in the battered landscape of her hometown and in herself.[11] As for her mother and her uncle, it appears unlikely that they will have a new story to tell. What appears to be Kushi's resigning herself to the facts that everyday Okinawans were passive victims of misrepresentations, discriminatory policies, and mistaken strategies by their leaders and that they had no choice but to find beauty in the miserable conditions in which they lived, limited the realm of possibilities that she could envision or provide testimony for.

If Kushi had turned her gaze to the antagonisms that repeatedly electrified different regions of the prefecture since the 1890s over precisely the question of who was qualified to articulate and represent the interests of various communities in Okinawa, she might have been encouraged to see that she was not fighting a solitary battle. Her critique of the assumption that some Okinawans were more qualified than others to speak for the whole (and the assumption that all Okinawans could share a single cause) echoed the sentiments of small peasantry in Miyako who called for reform of old taxation systems that privileged local officials prior to the First Sino-Japanese War, the weaving women of Naha who resisted attempts to transform them into factory laborers during the land reorganization project, the brown sugar producers of Nakagami and Shimajiri who formed nonselling alliances to resist mainland sugar capital's attempts to transform them into suppliers of raw material during World War I, and residents of Kunigami who sought to define development on their own terms during the early 1930s. Each of these efforts, though minor events when seen from the perspective of Okinawan labor history or anticolonial resistance, were profoundly transformative for the people involved in them and challenged the existing order of things—acts that Jacques Rancière called claiming "the status of fully speaking and thinking beings." Just as this act led to a "rupture in the traditional division assigning privilege of thought to some and the tasks of production to others" in nineteenth-century France, in Okinawa the challenges that small producers, merchants, and weavers mounted time and time again to attempts by mainland Japanese and Okinawan capitalists to valorize their labor in service of accumulation as living labor transformed subjectivities, interrupted accepted social hierarchies, and provided serious obstacles to the self-valorization of capital.[12] An examination of modern Okinawa's experience from the perspective of these moments of antagonism might have convinced Kushi that a story of rising, rather than one of decline, could be told about her hometown. This book is an attempt to narrate these performative acts of reclamation.

The book also investigated the tensions among our protagonists—local small producers—and the Okinawan bourgeoisie and the Japanese capitalist state. It traced how the category of Okinawa, an entity that came into existence as a territorial and political category only in the late 1870s through the region's annexation by the Meiji state, was transformed by the early 1930s into a diasporic cultural community included in, but distinct from, the Japanese nation-state. Instead of taking the belief in Okinawa as an organic, transhistorical community as a given, the book traced the creation of that belief by focusing on moments of crises in the reproduction of capitalist society that were temporarily resolved by appeals to Okinawan community. The emergence of a singular Okinawan difference from mainland Japan by the early 1930s was inextricably linked to multiple confrontations between dead labor and living labor after the prefecture was violently incorporated into the empire by the Meiji state. More specifically, it was the outcome of the role that Okinawa's economy was asked to play in the establishment of capitalism in Japan. The local bourgeoisie tried to resolve the social and political movements that erupted in the prefecture in response to the heavy burdens that Okinawans were asked to shoulder and tried to secure their share of the pie by invoking the cultural community of Okinawa. Despite the best efforts of the bourgeoisie to construct an Okinawan community that could resist the Japanese capitalist state's attempts to differentiate the region for its own economic and political interests, the category's stability was constantly challenged by anticapitalist struggles waged by small producers who did not care whether the owners of capital were Japanese or Okinawan. The repeated invocations by members of the bourgeoisie of the Okinawan community as an economic space over which they had exclusive rights, especially after their calls failed to convince these unruly subjects to cooperate, gave the category a fullness that it did not hold in the years immediately following the kingdom's annexation. The constant failure of these invocations reveals to us the limits of Okinawan community as a naturalized cultural and economic category.

This story allows us to reconsider dominant narratives of the region from the mid-1930s on that focus primarily on the psychological and material implications of wartime mobilization for the people of Okinawa. While heeding Tomiyama Ichirō's warning that we must not dissolve the specificity of wartime mobilization into a narrative of the continuity of the kitchen, our perspective—which examined small-scale anticapitalist struggles that erupted time and time again as workers and producers refused capital's attempts to transform them into dead labor and that constructed new communities in the process—lends itself to an examination of similar struggles during the extraordinary conditions of total war.[13] That is, only a close examination of the subtle and often contradictory ways that men and women residing in Okinawa's agrarian villages in the 1930s and 1940s positioned themselves vis-à-vis the Japanese empire, local intellectuals, and capital enables us to challenge apocalyptic histories that render all struggles futile in the face of overwhelming external forces.[14] No force in modern Okinawa's experience was more overwhelming than mobilization for World War II. Tracing the way that Okinawans—in the prefecture's agrarian villages and in factories and plantations throughout the empire, to which many of them immigrated—employed various strategies of refusal such as crop choices, work delay tactics, and the organization of play that frustrated the project of wartime mobilization can help construct an alternative to existing histories that treat Okinawa's wartime experience as a black box in which no significant anticapitalist struggle was possible.[15]

This reconsideration of narratives of wartime Okinawa can lead to a rejection of the notion that small cultivators in the prefecture were successfully reorganized into agents of Japanese fascism beginning in the early 1930s.[16] Such a conclusion, which is tied to studies of Japanese agrarian villages that debate the continuities and discontinuities among the prewar, wartime, and postwar contexts, effaces the long history of anticapitalist struggle in the prefecture that may not have crystallized into a single revolutionary moment but that helped draw the contours of policies and relations that governed small producers' everyday lives.[17] At worst, the conclusion that follows such a perspective is that Okinawans, because of their longing to be truly Japanese and because of the strength of their communal organizations stemming from premodern times, were in fact the most enthusiastic proponents of Japanese fascism—and hence, the population most brutally betrayed at war's end—in the entire empire.[18]

NOTES

≡

Introduction

1. "Disposition" is the word commonly used to describe the Ryūkyū Shobun process that began in 1872 and ended in 1879. Details of this process are provided in chapter 1. Iha Fuyū, the father of Okinawan studies, first expressed the idea of the disposition of Ryūkyū as a process of national reunification in his theory of shared origins during the early years of the twentieth century. See Iha, "Okinawajin no Sosen ni Tsuite." For an explication of this theory, see chapter 4.
2. Kawada's approach is similar to Karatani Kojin's in *History and Repetition*.
3. Kawada expressed his views in a series of articles between 1970 and 1973, including "'Hangyaku Bōkoku, Kokkyō Toppa' no Shisō," "Nihon Teikokushugi to Okinawa," and "Nihon Rōdō Undō no 'Kokkyō.'" Kawada explicitly linked different moments of subjugation together as moments of capital's primitive accumulation process.
4. Theoretical work on the concept of primitive accumulation has a long and complicated history that began with Marx's elaboration in *Capital*, volume 1, chapter 26, "The Secret of Primitive Accumulation." Recent critical analyses can be found in Bonefeld, "The Permanence of Primitive Accumulation"; De Angelis, "Marx and Primitive Accumulation"; Mezzadra, "The Topicality of Prehistory"; Tomba, "Historical Temporalities of Capital"; Perelman, *The Invention of Capitalism*.
5. We see here that Kawada implicitly embeds himself into the debate about the transition from feudalism to capitalism.
6. Details on this process and the impact it had on policies regarding the countryside are included in chapter 1.
7. The focus on small peasantry, in Japanese, the category of shōnō, inserts this study into debates about the nature of Japan's agrarian question that began in the 1930s and continued through the period of American occupation. Shōnō is an unwieldy term but in Okinawa's case it refers to a family farm that is run and at times owed by a farming household without the use of outside hired labor. This is similar to the way that *jisaku* (owner-farmer) is defined in mainland Japan—a jisaku usually depends on hired labor, though in Okinawa even jisaku lands were too small to require the use of hired labor. The significance of these differences in understanding the specificity of Okinawa's so-called agrarian question will be explored in chapter 4.

8. Of course, these changes would not lead to the removal of military bases that the Americans had built during their occupation of the islands. Kawada was mistaken in his view that reversion would realize parasitic landlordism for the first time. The rents on military lands that had begun to be paid to landowners in 1952 increased over time. By the early 1970s approximately 24,000 former cultivators had been transformed into parasitic recipients of very high ground rents paid by the U.S. government and mediated by the local civilian government. Reversion continued the dissolution of the agrarian villages. Today the number of landlords receiving these types of rent payments remains around 24,000. The total rent on military lands has risen sixfold since 1972. For these figures, see Kurima, "Gunyōchiryō Hikiage no Keika to Genzai."

9. Living and dead labor will be defined in greater detail below in this chapter. For elaborations on these concepts, see Read, *The Micropolitics of Capital*; Baronian, *Marx and Living Labour*; Bensaid, *Marx for Our Times*. My understanding of the immanence of struggles to the capitalist mode of production is similar to the way Deleuze and Guattari explained crises: "capitalism for its part was able to interpret the general principle according to which things work well only providing they break down, crises being 'the means immanent to the capitalist mode of production.' If capitalism is the exterior limit of all societies, this is because capitalism for its part has no exterior limit, but only an interior limit that is capital itself and that it does not encounter, but reproduces by always displacing it" (*Anti-Oedipus*, 230–31).

10. This is similar to Althusser's notion of immanent causality.

11. There was no historical inevitability or well-thought-out concrete plan that governed the Meiji government's treatment of Okinawa. The decision to incorporate it into the national territory was made in the context of a particular set of geopolitical relations whose end was not clear even to the participants who were directly involved. The tragedy of such decisions is that they are not erasable and that the traces or scars of every decision exist—if not in a concretely observable legacy, at least in the realm of collective memory.

12. For more on the way that Hokkaido functioned during the period of national consolidation, see Harootunian, "Economic Rehabilitation of the Samurai in the Early Meiji Period"; Mason, *Dominant Narratives of Colonial Hokkaido and Imperial Japan*; Komori, "Rule in the Name of 'Protection.'"

13. Hardt and Negri, *Labor of Dionysus*, 226. Okinawa's example can provide a critique of dominant approaches to the process of nation-state formation in the Meiji era since Gluck's *Japan's Modern Myths*, which focuses on the standardization of systems nationwide. The Meiji state was quite reactive and flexible in its early policies and often found it advantageous to maintain or use differences for political or economic purposes in combating internal or external threats to its legitimacy.

14. The works of these scholars were not linked to a clear colonial project of surveying boundaries or assessing loyalty. Instead, they indicate an interest in Okinawa's arts, wedding and funerary practices, and village social relations. For example, see Shōzan, *Okinawa Fūzoku no Zu* (a set of drawings on Okinawan manners and customs published in 1889); Watanabe, *Ryūkyū Manroku* (a compilation of writ-

ings on Okinawan customs, arts, and religion published in 1879); "Okinawaken no Konin oyobi Sōshiki" and "Okinawaken Naha no Seibo Shinnen Kiji oyobi Zu" (two articles published in the magazine *Fūzoku Gahō* in the 1890s that described marriage, mortuary, and gift-giving practices in the prefecture).

15. Sasamori Gisuke was one of the early visitors to the islands. His visit to Okinawa in the early 1890s was linked to the establishment of the Tokyo Anthropological Association in 1886, and his works piqued Yanagita's interest in the region. His work will be examined in greater detail in chapter 2.
16. For more on this process of land redistribution that took place in most villages of the former kingdom, see chapter 1.
17. He was charged with determining just how much class differentiation had resulted from the distribution of land titles during Okinawa's major land reform that begin in 1899.
18. See Higa S., *Okinawa no Saigetsu*, 57.
19. The speech was defended in two articles in the *Okinawa Mainichi Shimbun* ("Kawakami Sensei o Okuru," April 9, 1911; and "Okinawa Seinen Dōshi Kurabu o Setsuritsu Shite wa Ikani," April 11, 1911), both of which were reprinted in *Okinawa Kenshi* 19:485–89.
20. Kawakami, "Ryūkyū Itoman no Kojinshugiteki Kazoku," 318. All translations are mine, unless otherwise noted.
21. Kawakami, "Ryūkyū Itoman no Kojinshugiteki Kazoku," 321.
22. Itoman became one of two centers of anarchist activity in Okinawa the early 1920s. For details, see Urasaki, *Gyakuryū no Naka de*, chapter 2.
23. Miki, *Yaeyama Gasshūkoku no Keifu*, 48.
24. In addition to Yaeyama, Itoman's fishermen had settled in small villages in Amami Ōshima and Taiwan in pursuit of new fishing sites before Kawakami's visit. This was not unrelated to a state project of expansion, evidenced by the Ministry of Agriculture and Commerce's granting of 46,000 yen to the Itoman Pelagic Fisheries Company that was established in 1905 as part of an aggressive policy to encourage movement into southern China and to develop export trade with China. Japanese officials believed that if Itoman's fishermen could gain a foothold in the southern Chinese market, it could be the "key to opening one treasure trove of the empire." This quote comes from Kondō, "Gyogyō, Nanshin, Okinawa," 156.
25. "Taiwan no Kinkyō," *Ryūkyū Shimpō*, September 21, 1900, *Okinawa Kenshi Shiryō Joseishi (Jyō)* 16(1):118 describes Okinawan women who traveled to Taiwan as Japanese aborigines. Yamanokuchi Baku, Okinawa's most famous modern poet, wrote under the pen name Samuro when he first published his poems in the *Yaeyama Shimpō*.
26. The phrase "Republic of Yaeyama" expressed the highly fluid and tenuous conditions of existence born of opportunity, exploitation, and the constant threat of disease that faced Yaeyama's residents. Life in the prefecture's southwesternmost region, where several hundred of Itoman's fishing families lived during the prewar period gave rise to numerous struggles and dangerous thought, which made its population highly unreliable to a state that desired a stable fortress against

imperialist rivals approaching from the south. The inability of extractive industries and large-scale agriculture to take hold in Yaeyama despite the visions that the Meiji state held for it as a Hokkaido of the south had as much to do with the unwillingness of its inhabitants to provide the necessary labor for these industries as with the devastating impact of malaria. Miki documents the struggles that inhabitants waged against Japanese capital's attempts to establish industry in the islands in *Yaeyama Kindai Minshūshi*. Like Hokkaido, the language of reclamation implied that the lands were uninhabited, unworked, and required the hands of outsiders to modernize them. For the operation of this discourse in Hokkaido, see Mason, *Dominant Narratives of Colonial Hokkaido and Imperial Japan*.

27. Figures from 1914 and 1932 indicate a huge fall in the percentage of *jisaku* (owner farmers)—from 81 percent to 69 percent—and a huge rise in *kosaku* (tenant farmers)—from just over 3 percent to over 17 percent. For more detailed figures, see Ishigakishi, *Ishigaki Shishi Shimbun Shūsei 1*; Okinawaken Yaeyama Shichō, *Yaeyama Gunsei Yōran*, 21.

28. In *Heritage Politics*, Tze May Loo examines the way that cultural heritage aided Okinawa's subordinate incorporation into the nation-state.

29. Marx uses this concept in his chapter on primitive accumulation in *Capital*. He writes: "This primitive accumulation plays approximately the same role in political economy as original sin does in theology. . . Its origin is supposed to be explained when it is told as an anecdote about the past. Long, long ago there were two sorts of people; one, the diligent, intelligent and above all frugal elite; the other, lazy rascals, spending their substance, and more, in riotous living" (873).

30. Marx also observed in *Capital* that "it is a notorious fact that conquest, enslavement, robbery, murder, in short, force, play the greatest part" in realizing the conditions for the capitalist mode of production (874).

31. The development of Okinawa's sugar industry was encouraged to resolve the state's balance of trade deficit. For details, see Kinjō I., *Kindai Okinawa no Tōgyō*.

32. For proponents of Okinawa-shugi, it was crucial that Okinawa remain a part of the Japanese nation-state as a prefecture. One of their main goals was to make sure that the region's political status would not be changed to that of colony.

33. Fanon, *Black Skin, White Masks*; Mariátegui, *Seven Interpretive Essays on Peruvian Reality*. For more recent work, see Goswami, *Producing India*; Park, *Two Dreams in One Bed*.

34. Ōta Chōfu said this in 1900 during the Movement to Reform Old Customs that will be described in chapter 3. Ōta Chōfu, "Jyoshi kyoiku to honken," *Ryūkyū Shimpō*, July 3, 1900, *Okinawa Kenshi Shiryō Joseishi (Jyō)* 16(1):104.

35. Hardt and Negri, *Labor of Dionysus*, 6.

36. What I mean by fullness here is that the definition of Okinawan community itself became more fully elaborated over the years. I aim to illuminate the process through which the notion of an organic, transhistorical Okinawan community with specific linguistic, cultural, and even spiritual characteristics emerged as Okinawan intellectuals and politicians responded to moments of crisis—in many cases, crises of accumulation.

37. Rancière, *The Nights of Labor*.
38. Excellent full-length manuscripts in English on Okinawa have been published in the fields of anthropology (Nelson, *Dancing with the Dead*) and politics (Tanji, *Myth, Protest and Struggle in Okinawa*) that illuminate the way in which Okinawan subjects, through performance, political protest, and commemoration in the period after World War II came to grips with their collective pasts and, in the process, wrote alternative histories of Okinawa. Although I share the commitment of these authors to a nonteleological understanding of Okinawa's modern history, my project seeks to go one step further by arguing that these struggles—understood as manifestations of living labor—did not just emerge as a result of Okinawa's incorporation into modern capitalist society, but rather constituted and shaped that society. This methodological distinction will be elaborated below.
39. Recent works on this include Taira Y., *Sengo Okinawa to Beigun Kichi*; Kabira, *Okinawa Senryōka o Ikinuku*.
40. Yakabi, "Kiso Shiryō Seibi to Hōhōteki Mosaku."
41. This debate has its origins in the period before World War II, when Okinawan and mainland Japanese thinkers like Kawakami Hajime, Nakayoshi Chōkō, Majikina Ankō, and Tamura Hiroshi debated the differences and similarities among Okinawa's land systems. For an outline of some of the prewar debates, see Taminato, "Kinsei Makki no Okinawa Nōson ni Tsuite no Ichi Kōsatsu." For a review of postwar debates, see Sakamoto, "Okinawa Kindai Keizaishi Kenkyū no Seika to Kadai." The main prewar texts include Nakayoshi, "Ryūkyū no Jiwari Seido (3)"; Majikina and Shimakura, *Okinawa Issennenshi*; Kawakami, "Shinjidai Kuru," *Okinawa Mainichi Shimbun*, April 5–6, 1911, *Okinawa Kenshi* 19:485–87; Tamura, *Ryūkyū Kyōsan Sonraku no Kenkyū*.
42. One example is the historian Nakahara Zenchū's essay "Okinawa Gendai Seijishi," which appeared in *Okinawa* magazine in 1952. He argued that despite the domination of the historical record by former nobles, who fiercely resisted incorporation into the Meiji state, the majority of Okinawans welcomed the process of incorporation into the Japanese empire because they believed that this political transformation would liberate them from the expropriative policies of the Ryūkyū kingdom and the Satsuma domain. He concluded that the disposition of Ryukyu could be characterized only as an incomplete revolution because of the former rulers' fierce opposition to incorporation and their wholesale rejection of membership in the new nation-state. The former elite's refusal to cooperate with the Meiji state impeded the implementation of modernizing reforms in the new prefecture and obstructed the Okinawan peoples' full incorporation into Japanese society. Nakahara's essay has been reprinted in his collected works, *Nakahara Zenchū Shū (Jyō)*. Higa S., Shimota, and Shinzato (*Okinawa*) agreed with Nakahara's assessment of the disposition but blamed Meiji leaders for not pursuing more far-reaching reforms from the start. They concluded that because the government kept a lot of the old administrative systems, tax collection methods, and land systems intact, the disposition had to be understood as a nonrevolutionary event. Although subsequent scholars of modern Okinawan history would build on or revise these

analyses, the 1879 disposition as an originary event gained a significance comparable to that of the Meiji Restoration in the prewar Japanese capitalism debate (*Nihon shihonshugi ronsō*). Like Japanese Marxists who continued to debate the so-called agrarian question in the immediate postwar period and directly participated in the occupation's land reforms, Okinawan scholars understood—much earlier than members of the Frankfurt school or Robert Brenner—that the path to liberation required an approach that did not separate the economic and cultural spheres. From the Kōza faction, see Yamada, "Nōchi Kaikaku no Igi" and "Nōchi Kaikaku no Rekishiteki Igi." From the Rōnō faction, see Sakisaka, *Nōgyō Mondai*; Inomata, *Nōson Mondai Nyūmon*. From the Uno faction, see Uno, "Hōken Ronsō no Sainen ni Tsuite," *Daigaku Shimbun*, November 11, 1945, "Waga Kuni Nōson no Hōkensei," *Bunka Shimbun*, February 17, 1947, "Iwayuru Keizaigai Kyōsei ni Tsuite," *Shisō* (January 1947) and "Nōgyō Mondai Joron," August 1948. All of Uno's works are reprinted in *Uno Kōzō Chosakushū* 8. For works in English, see Hoston, *Marxism and the Crisis of Development in Prewar Japan*; Barshay, *The Social Sciences in Modern Japan*; Sugiyama, "The World Conception of Japanese Social Science."

43. For examples of work in this field, see the essays in Okinawa Rekishi Kenkyūkai, *Kindai Okinawa no Rekishi to Minshū*.

44. See, for example, Hiyane, *Jiyū Minken Shisō to Okinawa*; Ōsato, *Okinawa no Jiyū Minken Undō*; Aniya, *Okinawa no Musansha Undō*; Taminato, "Kindai ni Okeru Okinawa"; Yoshihara, *Okinawa Minshū Undō no Dentō*. For a recent outcome of this in Okinawa, see Nishi and Hara, *Fukusū no Okinawa*.

45. The dependency theory of Immanuel Wallerstein and Andre Gunder Frank was part of a broader postwar reaction against the rise of development discourse and growing interest in the so-called peasant question by Western scholars who believed it necessary to correct the dominant notion of peasants as "unlimited supplies of labor" who remained locked in a traditional stage of human history, as articulated by W. Arthur Lewis and Walt Rostow. Dependency theory critiqued the very premise of the Dobb-Sweezy transition debate of the late 1940s by arguing that it was a mistake to understand capitalist production, particularly in agriculture, as a universally necessary condition that had to be achieved to bring feudalism to an end and avoid distortion in the process of development. Instead, dependency theorists argued that if we take the world economy as a single unit of analysis, we see that the continued existence of noncapitalist forms of production like small-scale peasant agriculture are not remnants of a past time but in fact enable advanced capitalist countries to accumulate capital. The establishment of core-periphery relations should not be seen as the result of some defect in so-called peripheral countries but as a natural outcome of capitalist development on a world scale. See Rostow, *The Stages of Economic Growth*; Lewis, "Economic Development with Unlimited Supplies of Labor"; McMichael, "Peasants Make Their Own History"; Wallerstein, *The Modern World-System*; Frank, *Capitalism and Underdevelopment in Latin America*; Amin, *Accumulation on a World Scale*.

46. According to this approach, only a politically measurable outcome could transform these moments of possibility into real struggle.

47. This is no different from the way that orthodox and Western Marxists have dealt with moments of struggle that erupted without the outcome of revolution. Such a critique is also applicable to much of labor history and works on peasant uprisings that do not take an autonomist Marxist approach.
48. Tomiyama, *Kindai Nihon Shakai to Okinawajin*, 42.
49. This was an Okinawan version of the debate between Rōnō- and Kōza-faction Marxists on the so-called agrarian question in Japanese capitalism, but it was also a debate over whether or not abstract Marxist categories could be used to understand relations in Okinawa. Tomiyama took Mukai's side in this debate and argued that significant changes in the landlord-tenant relationship did take place in prewar Okinawa, and that it was possible to recognize the dynamism of the prefecture's agrarian villages while also recognizing the structurally dependent nature of the Okinawan economy vis-à-vis Japanese capitalism. See Kurima, *Okinawa Keizai no Gensō to Genjitsu*; Tomiyama, *Kindai Nihon Shakai to Okinawajin*; Mukai, *Okinawa Kindai Keizaishi*.
50. Tomiyama's work echoed the observations made in the late 1930s by Uno on the global nature of the agrarian question but implicitly critiqued his framework for not seeing the movement of people as labor power as an integral component of capital's reproduction after World War I. See Uno, *Tōgyō Yori Mitaru Kōiki Keizai no Kenkyū*; Tomiyama, "From the Colonization of Outer Regions to Regional Economies." For a recent English-language work on prewar emigration from Okinawa, see Rabson, *The Okinawan Diaspora in Japan*.
51. Sugihara, *Kazokusei Nōgyō no Suiten Katei*.
52. Meillassoux, *Maidens, Meal and Money*. Meillassoux critiqued classical and structural anthropology from a historical materialist perspective and challenged the dominance of studies of kinship in these fields. He analyzed the domestic economy of African villages in conjunction with the problem of labor in the capitalist countries to which many villagers migrated. He emphasized that since colonialism had brought capitalism and domestic economies into direct contact, it was necessary to illuminate the workings of this relationship instead of being distracted by the formal existence of master-subordinate relationships. Women emerged as central agents of production and reproduction in his investigation.
53. We see an exemplary approach to this in Tomiyama's third book, *Bōryoku no Yokan*. His study of Iha Fuyū emphasized the difficulties involved in mounting significant resistance and sought to redeem Okinawa's intellectuals by showing that violence had been inflicted on them at a deeper level than previous works had recognized. Okinawa was not simply a backward part of the Japanese nation-state and could be better analyzed by referencing postcolonial theory. He was influenced by his reading of Fanon and treated Iha and other local thinkers as colonized intellectuals—colonized in the sense that their discourses and actions were prescribed by their latent anticipation of the state's swift and overwhelming violence. Mori Y. (*Tsuchi no Naka no Kakumei*) takes a similar approach but deals with the postwar context. For a work in English, see Shimabuku, "Petitioning Subjects."

54. We must heed Rancière's critique of Althusserian educational theories in *The Ignorant Schoolmaster*. As Ross explains, "by beginning with inequality, proves it, and by proving it, in the end, is obliged to rediscover it again and again" (quoted in Ross, "Ranciere and the Practice of Equality," 67).

55. The quote comes from Read, "The Age of Cynicism"; Deleuze and Guattari, *Anti-Oedipus*. This refers to the logic of capital that makes it appear that all resistance is futile and everything can be absorbed into its drive for accumulation.

56. A special issue of the *Radical History Review* paid attention to new enclosures (Chazkel and Serlin, "New Approaches to Enclosures").

57. Even Hardt and Negri, who prioritized anticapitalist struggles of workers in *Empire*, included a significant consideration of struggles that have emerged from beyond the most advanced sectors of the capitalist economy in their recent collaboration, *Commonwealth*.

58. For an example of this type of study see Negri, *Insurgencies*.

59. Deleuze and Sanbar, "The Indians of Palestine," 29.

60. Marx, *The 18th Brumaire of Louis Bonaparte*, 15.

61. This quote is from Read, "A Universal History of Contingency." In this essay, he traces Marx's writings about the contingency of the encounter in *Pre-Capitalist Economic Formations* and analyses Deleuze and Guattari's reading of this strand in Marx's thought. Read emphasizes that Deleuze and Guattari's reading is heavily indebted to Althusser and Balibar's *Reading Capital*.

62. This includes a critique of Frankfurt school theorists like Adorno and Marcuse, who understand capital as exercising power over all social relations through the culture industry's control over everyday life.

63. Their political and theoretical concerns were to understand the significance of the working-class struggle against the Italian Communist Party in the 1960s and 1970s.

64. Wright, *Storming Heaven*.

65. Negri, *Marx beyond Marx*. Tronti's *Operai e Capital* is also considered a classic in autonomist historiography. For an autobiographical account of his project, see Tronti, "Our Operaismo."

66. Read, "The Antagonistic Ground of Constitutive Power."

67. Brenner critiqued existing understandings and debates of capitalist transition as economistic. In particular, he critiqued the terms of the Dobb-Sweezy transition debate, saying that the "process of transition was explained either in terms of the dissolving effect of external trade on an otherwise static feudal economy, or the crisis of rent caused by long-term declines in productivity and by depopulation in feudal agriculture" ("Agrarian Class Structure and Economic Development in Pre-Industrial Europe"). He also rejected Dobbs's argument as deterministic in its presupposition that the technical superiority of one mode of production determines its victory. For Brenner class struggle was more important than transitions that took place in the economy or society. For a summary of Brenner's contributions, see Chatterjee, "More on Modes of Power and the Peasantry."

68. Marx writes: "The less his [the worker's] necessary labor time, the more surplus labor he can provide, so, in the case of the working population, the smaller the

portion of it is required for the production of the necessary means of subsistence, the greater the portion available for other work" (*Capital*, 648).
69. Read, "A Universal History of Contingency," 9.
70. Bonefeld explains: "Within capitalist society, this contradiction can be contained only through force (*Gewalt*), including not only the destruction of productive capacities, unemployment, worsening conditions, war, ecological disaster, famine, the burning of land, the poisoning of water, devastation of communities. . . etc." ("The Permanence of Primitive Accumulation," 11).
71. For more on this strand of Marx's thought and the concept of the perennial civil war, see Tomba, "Another Kind of Gewalt."
72. A point of debate among theorists loosely affiliated with the autonomists is the question of whether it is possible for actors who do not labor in capitalist industries or under capitalist relations of production to have these desires. De Angelis, Dalla Costa, and others whose views are presented in *The Commoner*, believe that it is possible.
73. For more on the antagonisms of dead and living labor, see Negri, *Insurgencies*; Wright, *Storming Heaven*; Read, "The Age of Cynicism."
74. See Harvey, *The Limits to Capital*.
75. Deleuze and Guattari, *A Thousand Plateaus*, 203.
76. Responding to Negri's characterization of the current conjuncture as one characterized by the hegemony of immaterial labor, Tomba asks in "Historical Temporalities of Capital," "to what fragment of the planet do these analyses refer?" (45).
77. Negri and Hardt have addressed some of these concerns in *Commonwealth*.
78. Banaji defines Lenin's concept of technical process of production in order to critique transition narratives: "For Lenin, this incipient 'industrial capitalism' which evolves out of the merchant's domination over the small producer is quite compatible with the 'system of production' inherited from small-scale handicraft industries. In this form of incipient capitalism, capital operates on an inherited labour-process" (*Theory as History*, 51).
79. For more on Marx and the Russian populists, see Kingston-Mann, *Lenin and the Problem of Marxist Peasant Revolution*; Shanin, "Marx, Marxism and the Agrarian Question I"; Wada, "Marx, Marxism and the Agrarian Question II"; Walicki, *The Controversy over Capitalism*. I would like to thank Harry Harootunian for these references and for his observation that Marx was aware of coexisting and uneven forms of primitive accumulation within one country—a reflection of the importance he gave to analyzing the current conjuncture.
80. There is disagreement over whether this strain of Marx's thought had always existed or if this was a revision that resulted from his encounter with the populists. Kevin Anderson argues the former position in *Marx at the Margins* by emphasizing the continuity of Marx's thought from the late 1850s on.
81. In the decades following Marx's death in 1883, Engels, Kautsky, and Lenin published works that investigated the place of the peasantry under capitalism, and these studies appeared for the first time as a distinct field of inquiry within political economy. All three implied that the continued existence of small farms, the

persistence of nonmechanized agricultural production, and the resultant impoverishment of the peasantry were products and signs of the backwardness, abnormality, or immature character of development—despite Marx's misgivings about such a characterization. These assumptions colored subsequent approaches to the question and led theorists and activists around the world to relegate the peasantry to a subordinate or secondary role in revolutionary struggle. For a critical review of this literature, see Akram-Lodhi and Kay's introduction to their edited volume, *Peasants and Globalization*, "The Agrarian Question: Peasants and Rural Change."

82. The quote is from a letter Marx composed to Vera Zasulich. All of Marx's draft letters to Zasulich are reprinted in Shanin, *Late Marx and the Russian Road*.

83. Both Shanin and Wada's essays are in Shanin, *Late Marx and the Russian Road*, 108, 116. Furthermore, Marx argued that the communal practices that continued to exist could provide a foundation for a transition to collective farming once the revolution was achieved (ibid., 121–22).

84. Mariátegui, *Seven Interpretive Essays on Peruvian Reality*. In particular, see the third essay, "The Problem of Land."

85. For more on Mariátegui, see González, "José Carlos Mariátegui."

86. Mao's prioritization of the peasantry over the urban proletariat in China's struggle is reflected in his notion of the mass line, which stated that communist cadres must become intimately involved with the peasant masses—their pupils—before they could lead them. See Meisner, *Mao's China and After*, 44.

87. Karl, *Mao Zedong and China in the Twentieth-Century World*, 31.

88. Peasant studies and colonial studies emerged in productive tension with dependency theory, which had provided an important critique of developmentalist discourse but had focused primarily on the way that advanced capitalist countries had underdeveloped the periphery for their own benefit. In contrast to dependency theory, scholars working in these fields sought to clarify how people in peripheral regions encountered, came to terms with, and struggled against the new forms of exploitation that accompanied capitalist penetration into noncapitalist communities.

89. Their differences would lead to a split between members of the Peasants Seminar and Shanin, one of its founding members. He left the group in 1975 over intellectual differences, including about how to read Chayanov's works.

90. Redfield, *The Little Community*. For an introduction of key early texts, see Wolf, "Peasants and Political Mobilization."

91. Shanin, "The Peasantry as a Political Factor."

92. Chayanov, *The Theory of Peasant Economy*. In addition to arguing that small farming families made decisions about production and reproduction that was to a large extent independent of macrolevel transformations in the global economy, Chayanov argued that small-scale production continued to survive because farming households were able to find a way to be more competitive than agrarian capitalism that was installed from the outside. For more on the reception of his work, see Bernstein and Byres, "From Peasant Studies to Agrarian Change."

93. For a critique of recent readings of Chayanov, see Shanin, "Chayanov's Treble Death and Tenuous Resurrection."

94. See Sivaramakrishnan, "Introduction to 'Moral Economies, State Spaces, and Categorical Violence'"; Edelman, "Bringing the Moral Economy Back In . . . to the Study of 21st Century Transnational Peasant Movements." James Scott applied the labor historian E. P. Thompson's concept of moral economy to the agrarian sphere and argued that the introduction of market forces into communities that operated for many generations on relations of reciprocity challenged shared moral expectations and led to collective action that often resulted in the retreat or tempering of these forces. The moral economy approach, which highlighted the socially constructed nature of markets and the importance of cultural norms in the way that economic relations were configured, challenged the economic reductionism of orthodox Marxism and the free-market discourse of classical political economists.
95. Wolf and Silverman, *Pathways of Power*. James Scott's project focused on merging analyses of everyday life with larger structural configurations. Two anthropologists whose work concentrated on peasant populations enmeshed in the rise of plantation economies worldwide, Sidney Mintz and Eric Wolf, rejected the treatment of peasants as isolated and backward figures lacking subjectivity and demonstrated the dynamism and conflict in peasant communities by narrating their struggles against the global forces that threatened existing social relations, livelihoods, rhythms of life, and worldviews. See Mintz, *Caribbean Transformations* and *Worker in the Cane*; Wolf, *Peasants*. Clifford Geertz's work in the fields of political and symbolic anthropology complemented Mintz's and Wolf's early works by treating peasant action as imbued with meanings whose political repercussions may not be detected by the untrained eye. See Geertz, *Agricultural Involution*. For a critical review of this field, see Ortner, *Anthropology and Social Theory*.
96. Tomich, *Through the Prism of Slavery*; Taussig, *The Devil and Commodity Fetishism in South America*.
97. Taussig's pathbreaking *The Devil and Commodity Fetishism in South America* explored the way that the transition from peasantry to proletariat, particularly in plantation economies, was mediated by a precapitalist consciousness that constantly served as a barrier to smooth capitalist operations. He argued that cultural practices, religion, and memory that persisted in peasant communities even after a region's incorporation into global capitalism demystified the mystifications of capital and exposed the violence of capitalism that Marx elaborated in his chapter on the colonies in *Capital*. It told a story of capital's attempt to overcome the economic, cultural, and social barriers to accumulation and communities' struggles to maintain them. Peasants were not irrational or ignorant beings who responded emotionally to some unknown threat; rather, they were historical actors who knew exactly what was at stake in their anticapitalist struggles. Though Taussig by no means underestimated the vast power differentials between capital backed by the state and these communities, his work granted the latter an intelligence that was less present in other works that stopped at narrating heroic, often instinctual acts of spontaneous resistance.
98. Subaltern studies emerged from the study of peasant societies in colonial contexts and granted peasants a powerful collective subjectivity, going further than Taussig

in giving their struggles an advanced, organized form. For example, by replacing the concept of rebellion with that of insurgency, Ranajit Guha's works that first appeared in the *Journal of Peasant Studies* in 1974 challenged the notion that anticapitalist or anticolonial struggles undertaken by the peasantry were merely an effort to maintain precapitalist relations and traditions. By reading the colonial archives against the grain, he simultaneously performed two tasks that were common to the subaltern studies project. First, he understood peasant insurrections on their own terms and not as a prehistory of national revolution or the result of manipulation on the part of traditional village elites. Second, he exposed the way that official knowledge erased the agency of colonial subjects through the violent act of translation. For critical praise for this approach, see Stoler, *Along the Archival Grain*, chapter 2.

99. Such attempts to see in uneven development and difference a potential for transformation was aided by innovations in Marxist theory that began in the mid-1960s, starting with those of French Marxists like Balibar and Althusser, and continued in the mid-1970s with Banaji's stringent critique of Brenner's Eurocentrism and stagism and more recently with Chakrabarty's expansion of Guha's critique of the colonization of indigenous thought by colonial historiography. See Althusser and Balibar, *Reading Capital*; Chakrabarty, *Provincializing Europe*; Banaji, *Theory as History*.

100. This statement is found in the second draft of a response that he formulated to Zasulich (Shanin, *Late Marx and the Russian Road*). See Wada, "Marx and Revolutionary Russia" in *Late Marx and the Russian Road*.

101. In fact, Dalla Costa, a central theorist of autonomia, broke with the camp after completing her study on housework. More recent splits that led to the establishment of the *Commoner* were the direct result of a split about the political strategy of refusal of work. See Caffentzis, "TPTG's Conversation with George Caffentzis"; Wright, *Storming Heaven*; Cuninghame, "Italian Feminism, Workerism and Autonomy in the 1970s." Dalla Costa coauthored a pamphlet that became one of the central texts of the Italian feminist movement. See Dalla Costa and James, *The Power of Women and the Subversion of the Community*.

102. Federici's *The Caliban and the Witch* is particularly informative on the relationship between capitalism and patriarchy.

103. Tomba, "Historical Temporalities of Capital," 55.

104. Bloch, "Nonsynchronism and the Obligation to Its Dialectics," 27.

1. The Birth of Okinawa Prefecture and the Creation of Difference

1. For details, see Takara, *Ryūkyū Ōkoku*; Uezato, *Umi no Ōkoku Ryūkyū*. In English, see Sakai, "The Satsuma-Ryūkyū Trade and the Tokugawa Seclusion Policy."

2. For more on these and other types of arrangements in premodern East Asia, see Howland, *Borders of Chinese Civilization*.

3. The Ryūkyū kingdom was placed under the rule of the Foreign Ministry in the period 1872–74.

4. Sakai, "The Ryūkyū (Liu-chiu) Islands as a Fief of Satsuma," 117.

5. On this trade, see Sakai, "The Ryūkyū (Liu-chiu) Islands as a Fief of Satsuma."
6. For details on this early period of annexation, see Smits, *Visions of Ryūkyū*, chapter 1. For the ways that annexation affected taxation policies in Okinawa, see Nakasone, "Kinsei Miyako no Jintōzei to Sono Haishi Undō"; Inoue and Hatate, "Okinawa to Hokkaido."
7. This figure is from Taminato, "Kinsei Makki no Okinawa Nōson ni Tsuite no Ichi Kōsatsu." For more on Amami Ōshima under Satsuma control, see Namihira, "Amami Ōshima Nanbu Sonraku ni Okeru Jinushi Keisei to Nōminsō Bunkai."
8. In 1699 the Satsuma domain prohibited the importation of weapons into the kingdom. For details, see Sakai, "The Ryūkyū (Liu-chiu) Islands as a Fief of Satsuma."
9. See Smits, *Visions of Ryūkyū*; Kamiya, "Edo Nobori."
10. The first record of this tributary relation dates from 1372 and is between China and the kingdom of Chūzan, one of the three principalities that governed Okinawa at the time. This relationship continued after the king of Chūzan, Shō Hashi, unified the principalities in 1429. See Sakamaki, "Ryūkyū and Southeast Asia."
11. Ta-tuan Ch'en, "Investiture of Liu-ch'iu Kings in the Ch'ing Period."
12. For details, see Sakamaki, "Ryūkyū and Southeast Asia."
13. Sakai, "The Satsuma-Ryūkyū Trade and the Tokugawa Seclusion Policy," 395. The Satsuma domain's policy prohibiting the Japanization of Ryūkyūan practices and customs did not really begin until 1616 when the domain failed to negotiate the re-opening of trade relations with the Ming. See Smits, *Visions of Ryūkyū*, 19.
14. For a description of the procession, see Kamiya, "Edo Nobori."
15. For specifics on the taxes and tributes that cultivators had to pay to the kingdom and the domain, see Higa S., *Shinkō Okinawa no Rekishi*.
16. Shadanhōjin Tōgyō Kyōkai, *Kindai Nihon Tōgyōshi (Jyō)*, 31. This system refers to the official purchase of sugar at below-market prices that began in the kingdom, which was accompanied by the prohibition of the personal buying and selling of surpluses.
17. Shadanhōjin Tōgyō Kyōkai, *Kindai Nihon Tōgyōshi (Jyō)*, 6.
18. This position was created in conjunction with a shift in the Shuri government's administrative structure that abolished the post of *aji*—relatives of the royal family who were dispatched to far-flung parts of the kingdom to enact the policies of the central government. See Higa S., *Shinkō Okinawa no Rekishi*; Nakachi T., "Kinsei Ryūkyū no Sonraku to Hyakushō."
19. This was in contrast to unemployed nobles, who had to form separate communities called *yadori* when they moved from Shuri to the countryside and who were not entitled to participate in these distributions. To make up for this, the kingdom granted them plots of land and exemptions from taxes and tributes. Higa S., *Shinkō Okinawa no Rekishi*, 251.
20. For the types of taxes that were paid by local farmers during the early modern period, see Higa S., *Shinkō Okinawa no Rekishi*, 255–66.
21. Higa S., *Shinkō Okinawa no Rekishi*, 266.
22. It is not clear whether this right was also granted to the *noro*, female officials and priestesses in villages.

23. Namihira, *Kindai Shoki Nantō no Jinushizō*, 105.
24. On the mechanisms that the kingdom used to supervise and control agricultural production, see Kurima, *Okinawa Keizai no Gensō to Genjitsu*. The most comprehensive controls were enacted in the first half of the eighteenth century during Sai On's tenure as a member of the powerful Council of Three. Umeki outlines the creation of a ledger called *magiri kōjihyō* in 1735, a list of detailed rules and regulations concerning the daily tasks of officials of the village ("Kinsei Nōson no Seiritsu").
25. This dependence grew even stronger in the late eighteenth century. For details, see Nakachi T., "Kinsei Ryūkyū no Sonraku to Hyakushō."
26. Namihira, *Kindai Shoki Nantō no Jinushizō*, 140.
27. Namihira, *Kindai Shoki Nantō no Jinushizō*, 157. The name given to people who sold themselves in this way is *naagu* (the Okinawan equivalent of *nago*, a term used in early modern Japan).
28. Namihira, *Kindai Shoki Nantō no Jinushizō*, 157.
29. Kinjō S., "Ryūkyū Shobun to Nōson Mondai," 116.
30. Kinjō S., "Ryūkyū Shobun to Nōson Mondai," 116.
31. Namihira, *Kindai Shoki Nantō no Jinushizō*, 157.
32. Nishihara, *Okinawa Kindai Keizaishi no Hōhō*, 3.
33. Iha refers to the earlier period, when Okinawans were adventurous seafarers but became slavish and subordinate as a result of Kawada's first disposition, in "Ryūkyū Shobun wa Isshu no Dorei Kaihō Nari." All translations are mine, unless otherwise noted.
34. Uehara, *Sakoku to Han Bōeki*, 289.
35. Ōhata, "Okinawa no Ichi," 63.
36. Uehara, *Sakoku to Han Bōeki*, 296–98.
37. The debates within the kingdom's government over how to respond to Nariakira's demands drew on a rich tradition of Confucian studies beginning in the first half of the 1700s and indicate that kingdom leaders believed that Ryūkyū was an autonomous state, despite its tributary relations with China and Japan. Far from compromising the kingdom's sovereignty, its relationships with the Qing and the domain legitimized the king's status as ruler. For Sai On's thoughts on this matter, see Smits, *Visions of Ryūkyū*.
38. Uehara, *Sakoku to Han Bōeki*, 301.
39. Uehara, *Sakoku to Han Bōeki*, 306.
40. As Umegaki has argued, the new government was largely limited to its own territories. Despite changes to official policy, domains were still responsible for managing their own foreign relations (Umegaki, "From Domain to Prefecture").
41. The government preferred to leave negotiations with Korea to the Tsushima domain as it transferred management of the latter to the Foreign Ministry. Even those in the new government who believed that aggressive action toward Korea was necessary did not favor a more aggressive policy by the state just yet. See Kim, *The Last Phase of the East Asian World Order*, 112.
42. Inoue and Hatate, "Okinawa to Hokkaido," 337.

43. Hokkaido became the place where samurai, who no longer received stipends, were molded into a modern army or modern farmers, as well as a test site for the state's establishment of capitalist industry from above. In addition, it was reconfigured into a utopic site that could contain the desires of Japan's new modernizers. On concrete policies toward Hokkaido see Inoue and Hatate, "Okinawa to Hokkaido"; Harootunian, "Economic Rehabilitation of the Samurai in the Early Meiji Period." For more on cultural policies toward the northern territories and their indigenous populations, see Mason, *Dominant Narratives of Colonial Hokkaido and Imperial Japan*; Komori, "Rule in the Name of 'Protection.'"
44. According to Kerr (*Okinawa*, 356), Iwakura's mission report of November 1871 states that this was one of the more important issues to take care of. Kim (*The Last Phase of the East Asian World Order*) explains that a rearticulation of the relationship between Japan and these territories was part of a general movement for the former to insert itself into the community of Western nations.
45. When prefectural officials of Kagoshima, Ijichi Sadaka and Narahara Shigeru traveled to the kingdom in January 1872 to explain the impact that the changes taking place in the central government would have on Ryūkyū-Kagoshima relations, they emphasized the continuity of the Meiji and Tokugawa states by reiterating the equivalence of Kagoshima Prefecture and the Satsuma domain. For details, see Mizuno, "Early Meiji Policies Toward the Ryukyus and the Taiwanese Aborigines."
46. Ryūkyūan and Korean issues should not be conflated. Although the latter was considered by those who favored its annexation as a gold mine from which labor, minerals, and food could be transported to Japan to aid capitalist development, people held no such hopes for Ryūkyū. The kingdom's integration into the territory of the Japanese state was necessary to make sure that no other state laid claim to it. For details on economic motivations for Korean annexation, see Duus, *The Abacus and the Sword*, 35.
47. Ministry of the Left to Inoue, "Ryūkyū Koku Shisha Jitai Narabini Sono Kuni o Shochi Suru no Gi," June 1871, *Okinawa Kenshi* 12:2.
48. Ministry of the Left to Inoue, "Ryūkyū Koku Shisha Jitai Narabini Sono Kuni o Shochi Suru no Gi," June 1871, *Okinawa Kenshi* 12:3.
49. In an article on the beheading of the statues of the Ashikaga shoguns, Walthall sheds further light on the boundaries of the imperial realm in the eyes of the loyalist activists. Hirata disciples who beheaded the statues at the height of the *sonnō-joi* (revere the emperor, expel the barbarians) movement in 1863 use the traitor label that already existed to describe the Ashikaga shogun who had "usurped imperial authority by calling himself 'king' in paying tribute to China" ("Off with Their Heads," 166). The problem with this was that calling oneself king instead of feudal lord constituted a serious blasphemy, implying that the shogun had a status equivalent to that of the Japanese emperor. According to a precise definition of the imperial realm as implied or articulated by the nativist loyalists, the relationship between the Ryūkyū kingdom, whose king paid tribute to the shogunate in Edo every other year (and in this way expressed his subservience to the court),

and the imperial court was of a completely different nature than that between the domains' feudal lords and the imperial court.

50. Ministry of the Left to Inoue, "Ryūkyū Koku Shisha Jitai Narabini Sono Kuni o Shochi Suru no Gi," June 1871, *Okinawa Kenshi* 12:3.
51. Ministry of the Left to Inoue, "Ryūkyū Koku Shisha Jitai Narabini Sono Kuni o Shochi Suru no Gi," June 1871, *Okinawa Kenshi* 12:3.
52. Ministry of the Left to Inoue, "Ryūkyū Koku Shisha Jitai Narabini Sono Kuni o Shochi Suru no Gi," June 1871, *Okinawa Kenshi* 12:3.
53. Inoue to Council of State, "Ryūkyū Koku no Shobun o Gisu," May 30, 1871, *Okinawa Kenshi* 12:1.
54. Inoue to Council of State, "Ryūkyū Koku no Shobun o Gisu," May 30, 1871, *Okinawa Kenshi* 12:2.
55. Inoue to Council of State, "Ryūkyū Koku no Shobun o Gisu," May 30, 1871, *Okinawa Kenshi* 12:2.
56. Gabe, *Meiji Kokka to Okinawa*, 30.
57. An *oyakata* (also referred to as *ueekata*) is a title designating the highest-ranking official in each of the districts of the Ryūkyū kingdom. For more on early modern thought and politics in the Ryūkyū kingdom, see Smits, *Visions of Ryūkyū*.
58. Kishaba, *Tōtei Zuihitsu*, 199.
59. Kishaba, *Tōtei Zuihitsu*, 200.
60. Despite evidence of these internal debates, the dominant historiographical interpretation of the kingdom's response is that it did not understand the significance of the changes that were taking place. This underestimates the kingdom's central role as a supplier of information about conditions in East Asia after Western encroachment.
61. For an English translation of the decree, see Kerr, *Okinawa*, 364.
62. Council of State order declaring King Shō Tai's conversion into feudal lord and peer, September 13, 1871, *Okinawa Kenshi* 12:9.
63. Kerr, *Okinawa*, 363.
64. Gabe, *Meiji Kokka to Okinawa*, 34.
65. The signed agreement seems to have represented a compromise—the Chinese government agreed to recognize the Japanese state's right to defend their subjects (the Ryūkyūans) in return for its right to keep Taiwan under its jurisdiction. Though it refused to relinquish its position as suzerain over the Ryūkyū kingdom, the Chinese government had no choice but to acquiesce to the Japanese state's claim that it had the right to defend the Ryūkyūan people as Japanese subjects from attack.
66. Gabe, *Meiji Kokka to Okinawa*, 48.
67. Eskildsen, "Of Civilization and Savages: The Mimetic Imperialism of Japan's 1874 Expedition to Taiwan."
68. Kerr, 3 *Okinawa*, 67.
69. Gabe, *Meiji Kokka to Okinawa*, 56.
70. The Ryūkyū House (Ryūkyūkan) was located in Fuzhou and was a gathering place for Ryūkyūan emissaries, merchants, scholars, and others who were engaged in Ryūkyū-China exchanges during the early modern period.

71. Kikuyama, "Chikengo ni Okeru Okinawa Tōji Kikō no Seiritsu," 59–60.
72. Kishaba, *Ryūkyū Kenbunroku*, 20.
73. Kishaba, *Ryūkyū Kenbunroku*, 50–51.
74. Ito replaced Ōkubo Toshimichi—an earlier key negotiator of the Ryūkyū issue with China—as home minister after Ōkubo was assassinated in May 1878.
75. Matsuda M., "Ryūkyū Han Shobun An," 201–4.
76. Matsuda M., "Ryūkyū Han Shobun An," 202.
77. Matsuda M., "Ryūkyū Han Shobun An," 202.
78. Matsuda M., "Ryūkyū Han Shobun An," 202.
79. Matsuda M., "Ryūkyū Han Shobun An," 204.
80. Kishaba, *Ryūkyū Kenbunroku*, 151.
81. Kishaba, *Ryūkyū Kenbunroku*, 152.
82. Nishizato, "Ryūkyū Kyūkoku Undō to Nihon Shinkoku," 48.
83. Quoted in Nishizato, "Ryūkyū Kyūkoku Undō to Nihon Shinkoku," 48–49.
84. Gabe, "Meiji Shoki no Seifu to Okinawa Chihō," 91.
85. Gabe, "Meiji Shoki no Seifu to Okinawa Chihō," 91.
86. Quoted in Kishaba, *Ryūkyū Kenbunroku*, 176–77.
87. Often, this rejection took the shape of flight to China. The following works discuss the activities of officials who fled to China during the late 1870s and early 1880s: Gabe, "Tōchi Katei ni Okeru Kokka to Shūhen Chiiki: Keppan Seiyakusho Keisei Katei no Seijiteki Igi"; Mori Y., "Ryūkyū Wa 'Shobun' Sareta Ka"; Nishizato, "Ryūkyū Kyūkoku Undō to Nihon Shinkoku."
88. Nishizato, "Ryūkyū Kyūkoku Undō to Nihon Shinkoku," 50.
89. Mori Y., "Ryūkyū Wa 'Shobun' Sareta Ka," 50.
90. Hentona, "Karoku Shobun to Shizoku," 151. This was much more generous than the stipends that former nobles of other domains with equivalent ranks received.
91. As James Scott writes in his foreword to the Duke edition of *Elementary Aspects of Peasant Insurgency in Colonial India*, Guha examines the "mentality, values, ideas and structure" (*Elementary Aspects of Peasant Insurgency in Colonial India*, x) behind peasant insurgencies in colonial India between the late eighteenth century and the twentieth. He understands the special character of these insurgencies to be motivated by a condition of domination by the colonial state without hegemony and describes the political economic relationships that exist among peasant communities, local power, and the colonial state as "a political relationship of the feudal type, or as it has been appropriately described, a semi-feudal relationship which derived its material sustenance from pre-capitalist conditions of production and its legitimacy from a traditional culture still paramount in the superstructure" (ibid., 6). Similar conditions existed in Okinawa and Miyako, though the colonial state in this case was, in fact, a nation-state with little hegemony.
92. The state tried to maintain stability in Okinawa's agrarian villages by keeping local officials in their positions. For details, see Uechi, "Okinawa Shakai no Kindai Hōseido to Sono Eikyō."
93. For the full text, see Matsuda M., "Ryūkyū Han Shobun An," 204.

94. This is similar to the original sin that Marx talks about in the chapter on so-called primitive accumulation in *Capital*. The language of the Preservation Policy ensured that Okinawa's problems would be understood as an Okinawan problem even by intellectuals and politicians of the prewar period. Postwar writers have adopted this perspective.
95. This is very similar to the state's use of wealthy landlords as the basis of its provincial system in mainland Japan. See Ōishi, *Kindai Nihon no Chihō Jichi*; Yamanaka, *Nihon Kindai Chihō Jichisei to Kokka*.
96. Mamdani, *Citizen and Subject*, 17.
97. Investigations into the periodic division and redistribution system of the early modern era began in the prewar period with thinkers and policy makers such as Nakayoshi Chōkō, Majikina Ankō, Kawakami Hajime, and Tamura Hiroshi, who debated the objectives of the system and the degree to which decision making in the agrarian villages continued to be affected by its legacy. Understanding continuities in the modern era was considered necessary for resolving the prefecture's so-called agrarian problem. Namimatsu Nobuhisa provides detailed investigations of the work of many of these prewar thinkers in "Jahana Noboru no Nōgyō Shisō" and "Majikina Ankō to Okinawa Shigaku no Keisei." In the postwar era scholars continued to debate whether or not the jiwari system had accelerated or blocked the process of class differentiation in the villages. This was part of a larger question about the degree to which capitalist relations had developed in the Ryūkyū kingdom prior to its incorporation into the Japanese empire. See Taminato, "Kinsei Makki no Okinawa Nōson ni Tsuite no Ichi Kōsatsu"; Yamamoto, *Nantō Keizaishi no Kenkyū*; Nakamatsu, *Kosō no Mura*; Nakahara, "Okinawa Gendai Sangyō Keizaishi"; Higa S., *Shinkō Okinawa no Rekishi*; Kurima, *Okinawa no Nōgyō*. Scholars who debated these issues tended to fall into either the Kōza or Uno camps.
98. Sugar had been the most important source of income for the Ryūkyū kingdom since the seventeenth century and became, at least on the main island of Okinawa, the main unit of tax collection beginning in 1831. Kinjō S., *Ryūkyū Shobun Ron*, 24.
99. The area over which sugarcane could be planted was restricted in the mid-seventeenth century to maintain high prices on the market. For details, see Kinjō I., *Kindai Okinawa no Tōgyō*, 17–18. Also see Kuroshima, "Jintōzei."
100. For the system as it continued after 1879, see Shadanhōjin Tōgyō Kyōkai, *Kindai Nihon Tōgyōshi (Jyō)*; Kinjō I., *Kindai Okinawa no Tōgyō*.
101. Nakayoshi, "Kenka no Tōgyō to Nōgyō Keizai no Kankei Narabini Sono Kyūsaisaku," *Ryūkyū Shimpō*, August 17, 1907, *Okinawa Kenshi* 16:877.
102. Kinjō I., "Meijiki no Okinawa no Tōgyō."
103. Though it was not the government's intention to maintain this policy forever, the early sugar policy enabled the material construction of the region as a singularly distinct space of sugar monoculture in the Japanese nation-state, and the language of preservation that was used to justify it discursively constructed Okinawan difference and backwardness.

104. Historians generally describe the Preservation Policy as something that kept the prefecture stagnant and blame it for the prefecture's inability to catch up with the mainland economically, politically, socially, and culturally. In a logic similar to that expressed by Marxists regarding the incompleteness of capitalism in Japan, historians explain Okinawa's inferiority as the result of the state's delay of reforms in the prefecture. Relatedly, many scholars—including Ōta Chōfu, one of the foremost prewar intellectuals of Okinawa—consider the period 1879–95 to be a time of limbo, when there was a change in name but no significant transformations from the systems and structures of the kingdom period. Ōta writes: "Until the resolution of the Sino-Japanese war, a cautious stance was taken, which stopped at simply papering over the present" (*Okinawa Kensei Gojyūnen*, 234). Kerr devotes fewer than 30 pages of his 573-page *Okinawa* to this period, which he calls the "Do-Nothing era." Despite the diverse interpretations of this period, scholarly consensus is reflected in the common use of the term the "Preservation of Old Customs era." Two notable exceptions are the economic historian Kinjō and agricultural economist Mukai. Focusing on the government's sugar policies enabled them to see that in fact many economic reforms were conducted during this period. See Kinjō I., *Kindai Okinawa no Tōgyō*; Mukai, *Okinawa Kindai Keizaishi*.

2. The Miyako Island Peasantry Movement as an Event

1. With the land tax reform law, promulgated on July 28, 1873, the Meiji state established the prerequisites for the capitalist mode of production in Japan. In Okinawa, land commodification did not begin until thirty years later.
2. Okinawa's example makes it difficult to clearly distinguish between endocolonization (the colonization of noncommodified or nonexploited segments in capitalist societies) and exocolonization (the extension of capital to new spaces), but it enables us to see the ways in which belonging to a national or colonial space was contingently determined. Ann Stoler's work on the fluctuating boundaries of empire is also instructive for understanding Okinawa's ambiguous place within the Japanese empire. Stoler, "On Degrees of Imperial Sovereignty."
3. Banaji, *Theory as History*, 280.
4. Banaji, *Theory as History*, 281.
5. Uno Kōzō has also pointed out that the continued existence of a noncapitalist agricultural sector dominated by small-peasantry management in Japan—evidence to some of the backwardness of Japanese capitalism—is a normal part of capitalist societies anywhere. Uno asserts that "in actuality, capitalism does not demand the capitalization of the agrarian village any more than is necessary for its own development" (*Uno Kōzō Chosakushū* 8:162). As Marx noted, it requires only "a mass of human material always ready for exploitation by capital in the interests of capital's own changing valorization requirements" (*Capital*, 784).
6. Read, *The Micropolitics of Capital*, 108.
7. Deleuze, "What Is a Dispositif?" This contrasts with James Scott's peasantry in colonial Southeast Asia, which he classified as holding a primarily conservative

objective focused on reimposing an older moral economy ("The Erosion of Patron-Client Bonds and Social Change in Rural Southeast Asia").
8. This is quoted in Marx, *Capital*, 934.
9. Deleuze and Guattari write: "Moreover, despite the abundance of identity cards, files, and other means of control, capitalism does not even need to write in books to make up for the vanished body markings. Those are only relics, archaisms with a current function" (*Anti-Oedipus*, 250–51).
10. Negri, *Insurgencies*, 29.
11. Negri, *The Porcelain Workshop*, 101.
12. Deleuze and Guattari describe the characteristics of the despotic machine as "a functional pyramid that has the despot at its apex, an immobile motor, with the bureaucratic apparatus as its lateral surface and its transmission gear, and the villagers at its base, serving as its working parts. The stocks form the object of an accumulation, the blocks of debt become an infinite relation in the form of the tribute. The entire surplus value of code is an object of appropriation" (*Anti-Oedipus*, 194–95). Once the despot was toppled, it was difficult to convince the people to continue serving his functionaries.
13. Banaji, *Theory as History*, 4.
14. Read defines endocolonization as "the colonization of the remainders of noncommodified or nonexploited dimensions of existence internal to capitalist societies" (*The Micropolitics of Capital*, 27).
15. Harootunian, *Toward Restoration*.
16. Negri, *Insurgencies*, 147.
17. The Preservation Policy was precisely the mechanism through which the Meiji state tried to transform Okinawa into a sugar supplier for the nascent nation-state. On specific policies toward Okinawa's sugar industry, see Kinjō I., "Meijiki no Okinawa no Tōgyō." As Uechi argues, these types of measures were not unique to Okinawa. Its Preservation Policy loosely followed the Meiji state's oscillations between modernizing reforms and maintaining preexisting administrative units during much of the 1870s and 1880s on the mainland ("Okinawa Meijiki no Kyūkan Onzon Seisaku ni Kansuru Ichi Kōsatsu").
18. For example, Namihira traces the conditions of Miyako before and after the movement, and shows that poor peasantry remained poor and large landowners continued to prosper ("Kindai Shoki Miyakojima no Daijinushi"). Taminato acknowledges the significance of the peasantry's calls for reform, but calls them just that ("Kindai ni Okeru Okinawa"). In his account, the conditions in Miyako did not constitute a political or economic crisis for the Meiji state but were so miserable that the government could not neglect them. Arakawa calls it an example of a primitive form of resistance (Hobsbawm) and places "outsiders"—Gusukuma and Nakamura—at the center (*Ryūkyū Shobun Igo [Ge]*). In these ways, the movement is seen as a mere footnote to larger and more organized, explicitly political struggles led by modern Okinawa's heroes such as Jahana Noboru or Iha Fuyū.

19. This is a question that Marx dealt with in his interactions with Russian progressives in the early 1880s. For a discussion of Marx's draft letters to Vera Zasulich, see the introduction; Shanin, *Late Marx and the Russian Road*.
20. This chapter will consider whether there is a different way to understand the so-called primitive accumulation process that Marx dealt with in *Capital*, where he described the expropriation of the agricultural producer from the soil in a way that seemed to have taken place with overwhelming force and no significant contestation from the peasantry.
21. Ichiki, "Ichiki Shokikan Torishirabesho," *Okinawa Kenshi* 14:491–606.
22. See Namihira, "Kindai Shoki Miyakojima no Daijinushi."
23. For more on these local officials, see chapter 1.
24. Governor Uesugi's request for reform of village office system, "Riin Kaisei no Gi ni Tsuki Jyōshin," May 19, 1882, *Okinawa Kenshi* 12:802–7. This comes from an island-wide tour that Uesugi embarked on from November to December 1881. His tour diary appears as "Uesugi Kenrei Okinawa Ken Junkai Nisshi," *Okinawa Kenshi* 11:11–90. All translations are mine, unless otherwise noted.
25. Governor Uesugi's request for reform of village office system to Home Minister Yamada and Finance Minister Matsukata, "Riin Kaisei no Gi ni Tsuki Jyōshin," March 6, 1882, *Okinawa Kenshi* 12:789–90.
26. Governor Uesugi's request for reform of village office system, May 29, 1882, *Okinawa Kenshi* 12:804.
27. Home Minister Yamada to Grand Minister of State Sanjō, "Okinawaken Chihō Yakuba Riin Kōsei Sezaru Gi ni Tsukishi," May 19, 1882, *Okinawa Kenshi* 12:788.
28. Ozaki, "Okinawa Ken Shisatsu Fukumeisho," *Ozaki Saburō, Iwamura Michitoshi Okinawa Kankei Shiryō*, 16.
29. Finance Minister Matsukata and Home Minister Yamagata to Grand Minister of State Sanjō, "Kashizoku Kinroku Hoka Goken Shobun no Ken," June 15, 1884, *Okinawa Kenshi* 13:51.
30. Finance Minister Matsukata and Home Minister Yamagata to Grand Minister of State Sanjō, "Kashizoku Kinroku Hoka Goken Shobun no Ken," June 15, 1884, *Okinawa Kenshi* 13:51.
31. "Dasshinnin" literally means people who escaped to China.
32. Report from commissioners Kudaka and Ōwan to head of prefectural police Igakura, "Konpan Shinkoku Yori Kikenjin Jusetsu Narabini Honnen Roku Gatsu Matsu Kiryūjin no Fusetsusho, Hōkoku," December 10, 1884, *Okinawa Kenshi* 13:313.
33. Duus, *Modern Japan*, 53–54.
34. Following the kingdom's disposition, the Ryūkyū House in Fuzhou became the center of *dasshin* activity.
35. Araki, "'Kyūkan Onzonki' ni Okeru Okinawa Tōchi Saku," 63. Also see Nishizato, *Ryūkyū Kyūkoku Seigansho Shūsei*; Gabe, "Meiji Shoki no Seifu to Okinawa Chihō."
36. For details on the dasshinin activity, see Nishizato, *Ryūkyū Kyūkoku Seigansho Shūsei*; Mori Y., "Ryūkyū Wa 'Shobun' Sareta Ka."

37. Sakishima is the geographical designation that refers to the islands of Okinawa that are part of the Yaeyama and Miyako archipelagos. During the negotiations with China about the division of the Ryūkyū islands (*buntō*), the Meiji state saw the Sakishima islands as places where a Ryūkyū kingdom might be resurrected and to which people living on the main island of Okinawa who did not want to be part of Japan could move. Mori Y. traces the detailed negotiations between the Chinese, Japanese, and Okinawan representatives in "Ryūkyū Wa 'Shobun' Sareta Ka." On the Meiji state's shifting policies toward Yaeyama, see Miki, *Yaeyama Kindai Minshūshi*. For a comparative study of Yaeyama and Taiwan during this period, see H. Matsuda, "Colonial Modernity across the Border."

38. For more on this and similar incidents in the period immediately after the 1879 disposition, see Gabe, "Tōchi Katei ni Okeru Kokka to Shūhen Chiiki"; Nishizato, "Okinawa Kindaishi ni Okeru Hontō to Sakishima"; Sunakawa, "Kindai Shiryo (Kaidai)," *Hirara Shishi* 4(2):1–8.

39. Miyako, like Yaeyama, was one of the nine administrative units of Okinawa Prefecture until 1896, when this number was reduced to five.

40. Read, *The Micropolitics of Capital*, 10. The difference between Okinawa and mainland Japan in terms of their respective degrees of incorporation into the Japanese capitalist system was significant. Agrarian village communities in mainland Japan were granted the prerequisites for the commodification of land and labor power through the land tax reforms of 1873, but their counterparts in Okinawa were not because the old land system—in which capitalist private property relations were not recognized—prevailed. This was true even on Miyako and Yaeyama.

41. For more on the early modern land system on the main island of Okinawa, see chapter 1. The Yaeyama islands were not governed by the jiwari system either, and conditions on the islands were similar to those on Miyako. See Okinawa Kokusai Daigaku Nantō Bunka Kenkyujo, *Kinsei Ryūkyū no Sozei Seido to Jintōzei*.

42. For a detailed history of the system, see Inamura, *Miyakojima Shominshi*.

43. Millet accounted for approximately 35 percent of all taxes collected, and cloth accounted for over 60 percent. Small amounts of cotton, sesame, and barley were also collected. See Kurima, "Kinsei Sakishima no Jintōzei to Ryūkyū no Sozei Seido," 49. With regard to area under cultivation, millet took up just under 40 percent, while sweet potatoes, the staple food of the islanders, occupied just 12 percent of the land. See Shimajiri, "Miyako Nōmin no Jintōzei Haishi Undō," 60.

44. The highest ranking were those in the prime working years of 21 to 40; the middle rank was for those who were between the ages of 41 and 45; and the lowest rank was for those between the ages of 46 and 50. These age divisions applied to men and women. For more details, see the set of documents compiled by the Miyakojimashi Kyōiku Iinkai, *Meijiki Miyakojima no Kyūkan Chōsa Shiryō*.

45. Ichiki, "Ichiki Shokikan Torishirabesho," *Okinawa Kenshi* 14:570.

46. Some scholars argued that in terms of proportion to total production, the tax burdens were quite low (see, for example, Sunakawa, "Teigaku Jintō Haifuzei Seidoka no Nenkō Awa, Nenkō Hanfu"). Others argued that the poll tax system was excessively cruel (see, for example, Inamura, *Miyakojima Shominshi*).

47. The kingdom government periodically issued directives encouraging some adjustments on the local level, but enforcement was a separate matter. See Umeki, "Kinsei Nōson no Seiritsu" for details on the kingdom's tax and administrative policies toward its agrarian villages.
48. At the time, Nagama was an *aza* (ward) and Hirara was an administrative unit called a *magiri*. In addition to the two landowning families mentioned in the text, there was also a significant number of midsize landowners on the island, not the least of whom were the three main local leaders of the Miyako Island Peasantry Movement. For details, including addresses, of these families' holdings, see Namihira, "Kindai Shoki Miyakojima no Daijinushi." For detailed breakdowns of landholdings, usage and transactions in Miyako, see *Hirara Shishi* 4(2).
49. This system also existed on Yaeyama. For more on Yaeyama's conditions, see Miki, *Yaeyama Kindai Minshūshi*. Although the system does not seem to have existed in the main island of Okinawa, it did exist in parts of mainland Japan during the early modern period. It was disallowed after the disposal of domains and establishment of prefectures. For details on the system on mainland Japan, see Kajinishi, *Nihon Shihonshugi Hattatsushi*; Kinoshita, *Nago Isei no Kōzō to Sono Hōkai*.
50. Kiyomura states that the naagu system was also a way that local officials took mistresses from among commoner women (*Miyakoshi Den*, 243). Also see Miyako Kyōiku Bukai, *Miyakojima Kyōdoshi*.
51. Owners were entitled to collect eight barrels of millet from adult men and six barrels from adult women.
52. Shimajiri, "Miyako Nōmin no Jintōzei Haishi Undō," 64. Since 1 koku = 3 barrels, holders of 8 naagu received the equivalent of 36 barrels. According to the millet prices in 1894, when the representatives of the Miyako peasantry movement sold off barrels to raise funds for travel, one barrel of millet was worth just over 8 yen, giving these officials a supplementary income of approximately 288 yen annually.
53. The Home Ministry official Ichiki Kitokurō, in his 1894 report to the ministry, estimated that there were 3,000 naagu men and women still serving the former nobility. They and the 400 officials who owned them were exempt from taxation—a huge number considering that the total population on Miyako was just 35,000 ("Ichiki Shokikan Torishirabesho," *Okinawa Kenshi* 14:507).
54. Ichiki, "Ichiki Shokikan Torishirabesho," *Okinawa Kenshi* 14:576.
55. Finally, local officials also received the *okagemai*, which gave them the equivalent of one year's rice tax submission for their personal profit. The ability to collect the okagemai was one of the main reasons members of the local elite wanted to hold posts in the local government. See Ichiki, "Ichiki Shokikan Torishirabesho," *Okinawa Kenshi* 14:577.
56. The translation for *goningumi* is from Robertson, *Native and Newcomer*. The term is translated as "mutual security group rule" in Howland, "Samurai Status, Class and Bureaucracy."
57. If they still could not make up the missing payment, they would receive help from the rest of the village. If the village still could not make its payments, stored grains could be used.

58. Inamura, *Miyakojima Shominshi*, 306.
59. Some of these folk songs are recorded in Sugimoto, "Jintōzei ni Kakawaru Miyako, Yaeyama no Minyō." Many of these were written from the perspective of a young female weaver who pleads with local officials to accept her submissions of cloth. For an explanation of the rhythms of these and other songs that were performed in the Sakishima islands, see Sugimoto, *Okinawa no Minyō*.
60. In 1848, the incident known as Warikasami Jiken took place. This was a conflict between local officials and cultivators that broke out because the former were collecting more than the allocated poll tax amount for their own personal gain. As a result thirteen local officials were fired or exiled. Inamura attributes this incident to the weakness of Shuri finances, which placed pressure on leading local officials to donate their own funds (*Miyakojima Shominshi*, 382–85).
61. Araki, "'Kyūkan Onzonki' ni Okeru Okinawa Tōchi Saku," 55. In mainland Japan, Matsukata's deflationary policies accelerated the dissolution of the peasantry because a direct tax was established, tax rates were increased, and there were huge declines in the price of agricultural produce. The peasantry's cash income and purchasing power fell as a result. In Okinawa, the kaiagetō price was raised significantly during these deflationary policies. See Nishihara, *Okinawa Kindai Keizaishi no Hōhō*, 11.
62. Araki, "'Kyūkan Onzonki' ni Okeru Okinawa Tōchi Saku," 56. One picul equals 100 *kin* or 60 kilograms.
63. For details on the negotiations—both official and unofficial—between the Meiji state and the Chinese government, see Mori Y., "Ryūkyū Wa 'Shobun' Sareta Ka." Mori reveals just how expendable Okinawa was to the Meiji state even after its formal incorporation into the boundaries of the Japanese nation-state.
64. Duus, *The Abacus and the Sword*.
65. Duus, *The Abacus and the Sword*, 64.
66. For more on the development of the mining industry on Iriomote, see Okinawaken Yaeyama Shichō, *Yaeyama Gunsei Yōran*. For a more recent work, see Miki, *Okinawa Iriomote Tankōshi*.
67. Nishimura was the prefectural governor after Iwamura who went back to Tokyo in December 1883, after reversing almost all of Uesugi's reforms.
68. Home Minister Yamagata to Grand Minister of State Sanjō, "Okinawa Ken Keisatsuhi Zōkaku no Gi ni Tsuki Jyoshin," March 16, 1885, *Okinawa Kenshi* 13:472.
69. For details on the negotiations with China about the possible division of the former kingdom's territories see Mori Y, "Ryūkyū Wa 'Shobun' Sareta Ka."
70. "Inoue Gamukyō Yori Enomoto Kōshiate," May 16, 1885, *Ryūkyū Shozoku Mondai Kankei Shiryō* 8:1189.
71. For the list of reclamation projects, see *Hirara Shishi* 4(2):107–8.
72. Ishikawa, "Shōke to Shuri, Naha Shizoku no Keizai Katsudō," *Naha Shishi Tsūshi* 2(1):183. This was a major undertaking because sugar cultivation and manufacture had been forbidden on these islands during the early modern period and had never taken root among the population. It was also part of a broader project to provide relief to former nobles who had lost their stipends and opportunities

for entrepreneurs from both within and outside of the prefecture, in addition to promoting industrial development in Okinawa.

73. One *tsubo* is approximately three square meters.

74. There were some successes, but many of these colonizers died or became seriously ill with malaria. By 1893 the project was ended, with no concrete accomplishments to show for the time, money, and human capital invested in it. For details on the project's dismal conclusion, see Ishikawa, "Shōke to Shuri, Naha Shizoku no Keizai Katsudō," *Naha Shishi Tsūshi* 2(1).

75. Such measures were not pursued on the main island of Okinawa, even though most of the previous sugar cultivation and production had taken place there beginning in the early modern period.

76. Kinjō I., *Kindai Okinawa no Tōgyō*.

77. The greatest expense was for the construction of four elementary schools in 1886 alone. For details, see Sunakawa, "Kindai Shiryo (Kaidai)," *Hirara Shishi* 4(2):1–8.

78. Nishizato and Taira to the Lower House of the National Diet, "Okinawa Ken Miyakojima Tōhi Keijyō Oyobi Tōsei Kaikaku Seigansho," December 1893, *Okinawa Kenshi* 14:609.

79. Ichiki described the conditions of the nobles in Miyako this way: "For several hundred years, they maintained their family's livelihood through the blood and sweat of the peasantry" ("Ichiki Shokikan Torishirabesho," *Okinawa Kenshi* 14:578).

80. Ichiki, "Ichiki Shokikan Torishirabesho," *Okinawa Kenshi* 14:571.

81. Namihira, *Kindai Shoki Nantō no Jinushizō*, chapter 5.

82. See Yoshihara, *Okinawa Minshū Undō no Dentō*.

83. Tanigawa, "Kitaguni no Tabibito," 320–21.

84. Tanigawa, "Kitaguni no Tabibito," 321.

85. Kawamitsu owned approximately six *chōbu* of land in Kadekari Village. One *chōbu* is very close to one hectare, or 10,000 square meters. Kawamitsu got to know Gusukuma because one of his sons learned sugar manufacturing techniques from Gusukuma. It is because of this and the scale of landholdings of the peasants' representatives that Namihira argues that the movement's primary actors were local midsize landowners who wanted to develop the sugar industry on the island (*Kindai Shoki Nantō no Jinushizō*, chapter 5).

86. Shimajiri, "Miyako Nōmin no Jintōzei Haishi Undō," 67.

87. In a letter to his father dated October 5, 1892, he wrote that he and a group of Osaka merchants were engaged in a South Seas fisheries project that had potential for huge profits. The letter is published in Tanigawa, "Kitaguni no Tabibito," 317.

88. The office head was appointed by the governor and so was separate from the network of local power holders.

89. In addition to feelings of sympathy and outrage, he probably found the coercion of the local officials and villagers' inability to freely change occupations a hindrance to his pearl cultivation project, which would require both access to the sea and labor to operate.

90. Very few analyses have been written about Maruoka's policies, but Fukuoka mentions them in "Meiji Nijyūnendai Nakagoro no Okinawaken Chihō Seido Kaisei

no Taidō." Higa S. has also written a little about Maruoka in *Shinkō Okinawa no Rekishi*.

91. Yamauchi, *Ubuyutsunayabuni*, 73. The full text is also in *Hirara Shishi* 4(2):110–11.
92. *Hirara Shishi* 4(2):110.
93. Nomura, "Okinawa Ken Chihō Seido Kaisei no Ken," 13:598.
94. Maruoka had ordered the establishment of budget deliberation councils in Okinawa's villages in 1888 but had excluded Miyako and Yaeyama. Fukuoka, "Meiji Nijūnendai Nakagoro no Okinawaken Chihō Seido Kaisei no Taidō," 99.
95. Narahara's desire to decrease the authority of the local leaders might also have stemmed from his desire to remove any obstacles they presented to mainland actors' reclamation projects on the island.
96. Ichiki, "Ichiki Shokikan Torishirabesho," *Okinawa Kenshi* 14:575–76.
97. Tanigawa, "Kitaguni no Tabibito," 327. It is notable that the decision of the Miyako peasantry to separate themselves from their old community came after this reversal by Narahara and Yoshimura's resignation.
98. All three were villages in Uruka under the administrative system that governed Miyako until the enactment of the special administrative system (*tokubetsu chōsonsei*) in 1908.
99. Sasamori was in Miyako on July 6–8 and August 25–27, 1893. For more on Sasamori, see Namimatsu, "Sasamori Gisuke to Chiiki Shinkō."
100. Uruka was one of three relatively large administrative units (*magiri*) on Miyako until the completion of the 1903 land reorganization project. After 1903, an administrative reorganization turned the magiri into villages, and villages were subdivided into smaller units called wards (*aza*).
101. A wooden paddle would be tied around their necks as punishment.
102. This implied that officials were skimming too much off the top. Sasamori, *Nantō Tanken* 2:103.
103. For details of this visit, see Sasamori, *Nantō Tanken*, vol. 2.
104. Deleuze, *Foucault*, 23. From this perspective, Gusukuma, Nakamura, and Yoshimura—though important—cannot be seen as the protagonists.
105. Read explains that the code under precapitalist modes of production "expresses the apparent objective movement according to which the economic forces or productive connections are attributed to an extraeconomic instance as if they emanated from it, an instance that serves as a support and an agent of inscription" ("A Universal History of Contingency"). Marx discusses the way that societies with precapitalist modes of production are threatened from both internal and external factors: "The reproduction [of these communities], however, is at the same time necessarily new production and destruction of the old form." He explains that this is because "not only do the objective conditions change in the act of reproduction, e.g. the village becomes a town, the wilderness a cleared field, etc., but the producers change, too, in that they bring out new qualities in themselves, develop themselves in production, transform themselves, develop new powers and ideas, new modes of intercourse, new needs and new language" (*Grundrisse*, 494). Fi-

nally, Marx points out that this process of destruction is accelerated when another community comes into contact with it.

106. They had planned to submit the petition—titled "Okinawa Ken Miyako Jima Tōhi Keijyō Oyobi Tōsei Kaikaku Seigansho" during the National Diet's December 1893 session. However, that session was dissolved due to the outbreak of the First Sino-Japanese War. It was finally submitted in June 1894 and was passed by a majority in the Diet. I focus on this petition because it seems to be the most direct expression of the collective demands of Miyako's peasantry without much consideration for the profitability of reform to the state, which we see in later petitions. A copy of this petition can be found in Okinawa Kenshi 14:607–14 and Hirara Shishi 4(2). I refer to the version in Okinawa Kenshi in this chapter.

107. Both this petition and the petition to reclaim communal lands showed that by the early 1890s, actors in Okinawa who opposed the preserved policies of the kingdom government had found an outlet for their discontent in the most modern of the Meiji government's political organs.

108. Nishizato and Taira to the Lower House of the National Diet, "Okinawa Ken Miyako Jima Tōhi Keijyō Oyobi Tōsei Kaikaku Seigansho," December 1893, Okinawa Kenshi 14:609.

109. Compared to Narahara's proposed reforms, these demands were much more comprehensive and focused less on reducing the power of local elites and more on reducing the small peasantry's economic burdens. Their demands indicate that they found the establishment of a more calculable and efficient form of tax payment to be necessary from the perspective of their position within the capitalist economy.

110. Nishizato and Taira to the Lower House of the National Diet, "Okinawa Ken Miyako Jima Tōhi Keijyō Oyobi Tōsei Kaikaku Seigansho," December 1893, Okinawa Kenshi 14:613.

111. The petition presents the following figures: Miyako's cultivators—who numbered approximately 35,000 people, including women and children—were forced to pay high taxes and high expenses related to the salaries and expenses of officials, for a total of approximately 70,000 yen. The taxation system was regressive. Nishizato and Taira to the Lower House of the National Diet, "Okinawa Ken Miyako Jima Tōhi Keijyō Oyobi Tōsei Kaikaku Seigansho," December 1893, Okinawa Kenshi 14:611–12.

112. Nishizato and Taira to the Lower House of the National Diet, "Okinawa Ken Miyako Jima Tōhi Keijyō Oyobi Tōsei Kaikaku Seigansho," December 1893, Okinawa Kenshi 14:611.

113. Quoted in Read, The Micropolitics of Capital, 9.

114. Negri, The Porcelain Workshop, 145.

115. Though one characteristic of constituent power is its almost immediate reterritorialization into the new socius, the constant transformation of the socius is the result of countless minor interruptions that seek "to disrupt and deterritorialize the identities, languages, oppressions, exploitations, and practices" that keep groups subordinated in service of a particular mode of production (Thoburn, Deleuze,

Marx and Politics, 143). On what the language of crisis opens up and shuts down for historical inquiry see Roitman, *Anti-Crisis*.

116. The significance of this decision is huge. As Rancière brilliantly argues, the emergence of working-class thought constituted a "rupture in the traditional division assigning privilege of thought to some and the tasks of production to others. The French worker who, in the nineteenth century, created newspapers or associations, wrote poems or joined utopian groups, were claiming the status of fully speaking and thinking beings" (*The Philosopher and His Poor*, 219).

117. For the full text of the song and an explanation of its significance, see Sugimoto, "Jintōzei ni Kakawaru Miyako, Yaeyama no Minyō," 280–81.

118. Sugimoto, "Jintōzei ni Kakawaru Miyako, Yaeyama no Minyō," 242–43.

119. Nakasone, "Kinsei Miyako no Jintōzei to Sono Haishi Undō," 237.

120. Banana-fiber (*bashō*) cloth is a coarse Okinawan textile that is made by weaving the fibers of non–fruit bearing banana trees together by hand. For more on this cloth, see Hendrickx, *The Origins of Banana-Fibre Cloth in the Ryūkyūs, Japan*.

121. Sugimoto, "Jintōzei ni Kakawaru Miyako, Yaeyama no Minyō," 221.

122. Sugimoto, "Jintōzei ni Kakawaru Miyako, Yaeyama no Minyō," 281.

123. At the time one barrel of millet was worth 1 yen 12 sen, so they had to remove close to twenty barrels.

124. For details about their travels, see Yamashita S., "Miyakojima Jintōzei Haishi Seigan Undō," 277; *Hirara Shishi* 4(2).

125. Read, *The Micropolitics of Capital*, 24.

126. Read, *The Micropolitics of Capital*, 25. Negri's notion of constituent power similarly alerts us to the threat of reterritorialization that accompanies any constituent act (*Insurgencies*). This is also similar to Deleuze and Guattari's notion of reterritorialization in *A Thousand Plateaus*.

127. Nishizato and Taira to the Lower House of the National Diet, "Okinawa Ken Miyako Jima Tōhi Keijyō Oyobi Tōsei Kaikaku Seigansho," December 1893, *Okinawa Kenshi* 14:609.

128. Nishizato and Taira to the Lower House of the National Diet, "Okinawa Ken Miyako Jima Tōhi Keijyō Oyobi Tōsei Kaikaku Seigansho," December 1893, *Okinawa Kenshi* 14:611.

129. Yoshihara, *Okinawa Minshū Undō no Dentō*, 146.

130. Soga to the House of Peers of the National Diet, "Okinawaken Kensei Kaikaku Kengian," January 12, 1895, *Okinawaken Gikaishi* 8(5):88.

131. Soga to the House of Peers of the National Diet, "Okinawaken Kensei Kaikaku Kengian," January 12, 1895, *Okinawaken Gikaishi* 8(5):90.

132. Read's reading of Althusser's general theory of aleatory materialism is useful here. The theory emphasizes that when analyzing a thing (a body, subject, or social relation), it must be "viewed as an effect of a series of different encounters, an effect that once constituted has its own particular causality or effectivity" (Althusser, "Le courant souterrain du matérialisme de la rencontre" [565], quoted in Read, "Primitive Accumulation," 32). When this theory is applied to the process of the formation of the capitalist mode of production or in our case, the extension of

capitalist relations of production to Okinawa prefecture between the 1880s and the first decade of the twentieth century, it becomes necessary to analyze the different encounters that only later appeared to be part of a singular process.

133. On the significance of fire to struggles in the fields, see McGillivray, *Blazing Cane*; Okihiro, *Cane Fires*.
134. For details on some of these disputes, see the following *Ryūkyū Shimpō* articles: "Miyako Tōshi no Jinmin no Ōrai" (June 27, 1900), "Miyako Dayori" (July 21, 1900), and "Miyako Noda Somayama no Kasai" (November 21, 1902). All have been reprinted in *Hirara Shishi* 10(8).

3. Reforming Old Customs, Transforming Women's Work

1. For a detailed analysis of the Meiji government's administrative and fiscal policy shifts in the Meiji era, see Ōishi, *Kindai Nihon no Chihō Jichi*.
2. Ka, *Japanese Colonialism in Taiwan*.
3. Nishihara, "Tochi Seiri to Shuri, Naha," 64.
4. The Meiji state did try to establish factory-style sugar manufacturing areas in Yaeyama, but these attempts failed because the industrialists were not able to get the peasantry to cooperate. Ichiki, "Ichiki Shokikan Torishirabesho," *Okinawa Kenshi* 14:599.
5. Kinjō I., *Kindai Okinawa no Tōgyō*.
6. Uno writes of the rationale of the bourgeois reformers: "Government authorities did not make this point clear, but we can say that this is, however, based on the reformation consciousness of a generally bourgeoisie-type reform" (*Uno Kōzō Chosakushū* 8:87).
7. To understand the timing of this from the point of view of the Meiji government as the capitalist nation-state that "gives consistency to the corresponding land and people" (Deleuze and Guattari, *A Thousand Plateaus*, 456), it is important to keep in mind Uno's explanation that "capitalism does not demand the capitalization of the agrarian village any more than is necessary for its own development" (*Uno Kōzō Chosakushū* 8:162).
8. Marx, *Capital*, 784.
9. For more on the relationship between expropriation of the peasantry from the soil and the establishment of capitalist relations of production, see Uno, *Uno Kōzō Chosakushū* 8:91.
10. Okinawan workers did not actually form an industrial reserve army for capitalist industry until the period between the world wars. For details about Okinawan workers' entry into the mainland labor market, see Tomiyama, *Kindai Nihon Shakai to Okinawajin*. The conditions of Okinawa's agrarian villages are best understood as a local inflection of what Uno calls the "feudality of our country's agrarian villages" (*Uno Kōzō Chosakushū* 8:54).
11. For details of the changes to the national administrative system (*chihō seido*) in the Meiji period, see Kikekawa, *Meiji Chihō Seido Seiritsushi*; Fukushima and Tokuda, "Meiji Shonen no Chōsonkai."
12. Marx, *Capital*, 919.

13. This reveals the Meiji government's success in creating the idea of a national community that had existed since time immemorial. Iha Fuyū spent his entire career trying to reconcile this idea with Okinawa's difference.
14. Isa, "Jahana Noboru," 258.
15. This will become evident in this chapter's discussion of Ōta Chōfu's Kōdōkai movement.
16. This organization was preceded by Yūshinsha (Society of Sincerity), which was founded in 1886 and which eventually became Zaikyō Okinawa Gakuseikai (Tokyo Okinawa Student Association).
17. Isa, "Jahana Noboru," 262. Though I did not have direct access to copies of *Okinawa Seinen Zasshi*, Isa reprinted part of the first edition's mission statement, written by Moromizato Chōko.
18. This was the predecessor of the University of Tokyo. Jahana was the first commoner who held a bureaucratic position. As Iha famously said, Jahana was a symbol of the dismantling of the kingdom's caste system by the Meiji state. Isa, *Jahana Noboru Shū*, 176.
19. Jahana's "Somayama Danpen" is a report about an uprising of cultivators on Miyako Island to protest the efforts of the island's head official to restrict their access to communal lands. Jahana, "Somayama Danpen," *Okinawa Jiron*, August 17, 1900, Isa, *Jahana Noboru Shū*, 105.
20. Jahana submitted his thesis, "Sanuki no Kuni Tōgyō Oyobi Jitsuyō Oyobi Sono Kairyōsaku" in 1891 and continued his investigations of sugar policy after his appointment to the prefectural administration. This is reprinted in its entirety in Isa, *Jahana Noboru Shū*, 5–26. For another work on Okinawa's sugar industry, see Nakayoshi, *Okinawaken Tōgyō Ron*. For an excellent treatment of Jahana's agrarian thought, see Namimatsu, "Jahana Noboru no Nōgyō Shisō."
21. This information is from a lecture titled "Gansha Shikichi ni Tsuite" that Jahana gave on September 8, 1893, at the agricultural testing facility association. Governor Narahara, Sasamori Gisuke, and about two hundred other people attended. The full text of the lecture is reprinted in Isa, *Jahana Noboru Shū*, 34–35.
22. Jahana proposed higher-yield planting and manufacturing methods in order to counter-balance what he saw as an over-emphasis on the development of the sugar industry.
23. Nakagawa Toranosuke, a member of the House of Peers; Komuro Shinobu; Matsuoka Yasutake, a Home Ministry official; three sugar merchants based in Tokyo; Governor Narahara's nephew; and other people connected to the governor were involved in the Yaeyama reclamation project.
24. Okinawa's reclaimed lands were not regularly cultivated but did contribute to the villagers' livelihood.
25. Mori Y., "Ryūkyū Wa 'Shobun' Sareta Ka," 54. For a fictionalized account of the struggle between pro-Chinese and pro-Japanese sides during the First Sino-Japanese War, see Yamagusuku, "Kunenbo."
26. Mori Y., "Ryūkyū Wa 'Shobun' Sareta Ka," 54.

27. Ikemiyagi Sekihō wrote a short story called "Okuma Junsa" (originally published in *Kaihō* in 1922) about an Okinawan man who became a policeman in his community but ended up destroying himself in the process.
28. With the Ganko faction defeated, the Shō Tai faction—also known as the Kaika faction—emerged victorious in the struggle for authority among the former ruling elite.
29. Arakawa, *Ryūkyū Shobun Igo (Ge)*, 167–69.
30. Icchū, or Okinawa Daiichi Kōtō Gakkō (Okinawa First Higher School), was the predecessor of Okinawa Kenritsu Shuri Kōtō Gakkō (Okinawa Prefectural Shuri High School).
31. For more details about how the strike unfolded, see Arakawa, *Ryūkyū Shobun Igo (Ge)*, 165–72.
32. Iha writes about this incident in *Ryūkyū Kokonki*, 357–77.
33. The Shō family had been the royal family of the Ryūkyū kingdom since the fifteenth century. For more on Jahana and the Kōdōkai movement, see Smits, "Jahana Noboru."
34. Ōta C., "Okinawa Ken no Jichi Mondai," *Yomiuri Shimbun*, July 16, 1897, *Naha Shishi* 2(2)(4):659.
35. Ōta C., "Okinawa Ken no Jichi Mondai," *Yomiuri Shimbun*, July 16, 1897, *Naha Shishi* 2(2)(4):658. All translations are mine, unless otherwise noted.
36. Ōta C., "Okinawa Ken no Jichi Mondai," *Yomiuri Shimbun*, July 16, 1897, *Naha Shishi* 2(2)(4):658.
37. Ōta C., "Okinawa Ken no Jichi Mondai," *Yomiuri Shimbun*, July 16, 1897, *Naha Shishi* 2(2)(4):658.
38. Ōta C., "Okinawa Ken no Jichi Mondai," *Yomiuri Shimbun*, July 16, 1897, *Naha Shishi* 2(2)(4):660.
39. These very clear economic interests were at the forefront of Ōta's concerns when he renamed the movement the Jichi-tō, or the party to gain local autonomy.
40. Quoted in "Chiji no Kangei," *Ryūkyū Shimpō*, August 14, 1898, *Okinawa Kenshi* 16:40. The irony here is that the lateness of the enactment of reforms in Okinawa was due to the concessions the Meiji government had to make to these former rulers, who expressed great dissatisfaction every time the governor proposed a change to the preserved system.
41. The *Ryūkyū Shimpō*, founded by Ōta with Narahara's assistance, represented the views of the most powerful echelons of the former nobility, who continued to have some economic and political influence in the prefecture.
42. Quoted in "Chiji no Kangei," *Ryūkyū Shimpō*, August 14, 1898, *Okinawa Kenshi* 16:40.
43. Tōyama, *Tōyama Shigeki Chosakushū* 6:3–52.
44. Isa, "Jahana Noboru Nenpu," 194. Jahana resigned from the prefectural administration in December 1898.
45. Many of the Okinawa Kurabu's members later became leaders of Okinawa's proletariat movement. See Aniya, *Okinawa no Musansha Undō*. The *Shimpō* kept a close eye on this organization and the activities of its leaders in Tokyo. Information

about many of the Kurabu's activities is available today only in the form of summaries published in the *Shimpō*.

46. Ōta C., "Okinawa Kurabu to Okinawa Jiron," *Ryūkyū Shimpō*, February 16, 1899, *Shiryō Nōgakushi Jahana Noboru*, 330.
47. Nabeshima was the second governor of Okinawa, serving in that post between 1879 and 1881. For more on the history of the election laws in Okinawa, see Higa S., *Shinkō Okinawa no Rekishi*.
48. Former nobles had little reason to disapprove of the administration, since part of Narahara's strategy of governing was to make sure that they benefited financially. In "Chitsuroku Shobun to Shizoku Jyusan," Hentona argues that the nobility's stipends improved after the disposition of the kingdom. Interest rates on bonds and the length of time during which the payments were distributed were better for the former Okinawan nobles than for the mainland's former samurai.
49. Some of their articles are reprinted in *Shiryō Nōgakushi Jahana Noboru*.
50. Article 18 of the land reorganization bill is reprinted in "Okinawa Ken Tochi Seiri Hōan," *Okinawa Kenshi* 13:699.
51. For more on the proceedings of this session, see Isa, "Jahana Noboru," 340–41.
52. Nabeshima to House of Peers of the National Diet, "Okinawa Ken Tochi Seiri Hōan Daiichi Dokkai," February 27, 1899, *Okinawaken Gikaishi* 8(5):133–39.
53. A survey conducted by the Meiji state in 1884 may have been designed to clarify this. For more on the survey, see Uechi, "Okinawa Meijiki no Kyūkan Onzon Seisaku ni Kansuru Ichi Kōsatsu"; Taira K., "Meiji 17-Nen no Okinawaken Kyūkan Chōsa to Sono Haikei" and *Kindai Nihon Saisho no "Shokuminchi" Okinawa to Kyūkan Chōsa 1872–1908*.
54. Nabeshima to House of Peers of the National Diet, "Okinawa Ken Tochi Seiri Hōan Daiichi Dokkai," February 27, 1899, *Okinawaken Gikaishi* 8(5):136.
55. Nabeshima to House of Peers of the National Diet, "Okinawa Ken Tochi Seiri Hōan Daiichi Dokkai," February 27, 1899, *Okinawaken Gikaishi* 8(5):136.
56. Nabeshima to House of Peers of the National Diet, "Okinawa Ken Tochi Seiri Hōan Daiichi Dokkai," February 27, 1899, *Okinawaken Gikaishi* 8(5):138.
57. For more on enclosures, see De Angelis, "Separating the Doing and the Deed."
58. For details on this encounter, see Ōsato, *Jahana Noboru Den*, 377; Jahana, "Miyako Dayori," *Ryūkyū Shimpō*, July 21, 1900, *Hirara Shishi* 10(8):66–67.
59. See "Miyako Tōshi to Jinmin no Oriai," *Ryūkyū Shimpō*, June 27, 1900, *Hirara Shishi* 10(8):49.
60. Jahana, "Somayama Danpen," *Okinawa Jiron* 34, August 17, 1899, *Jahana Noboru Shū*, 105.
61. Jahana, "Somayama Danpen," *Okinawa Jiron* 34, August 17, 1899, *Jahana Noboru Shū*, 313.
62. Jahana, "Somayama Danpen," *Okinawa Jiron* 34, August 17, 1899, *Jahana Noboru Shū*, 314. Narahara began the third major reclamation project in May 1897.
63. This law was enacted in 1890 in mainland Japan, but it excluded Okinawa, Hokkaido, and the Ogasawara Islands.
64. The committee deliberated Okinawa's case on February 14, 17, 18, and 21.

65. As noted in chapter 2, Ichiki visited Okinawa in 1894 as a Home Ministry official. At that time he conducted a detailed two-month-long investigations of the prefecture's land system.
66. Ōta and the *Ryūkyū Shimpō*'s positions on the immediate enactment of the election law were virtually identical to Ichiki's position.
67. Miyahira, "Ichiki Kitokurō no Jichikan to Okinawa Chōsa."
68. Ichiki to the Lower House of the National Diet, February 14, 1899, *Okinawaken Gikaishi* 10(7):35.
69. Ichiki to the Lower House of the National Diet, February 14, 1899, *Okinawaken Gikaishi* 10(7):36. In contrast to Jahana, Ōta did not view the exclusion of Okinawans from participation in national politics as a malicious action and praised the state's commitment to "uphold the spirit of the constitution" ("Kanzen Naru Sanseiken to Zeisei Kaisei [Jyō]," *Ryūkyū Shimpō*, May 25, 1899, *Okinawa Kenshi* 16:131–34).
70. Takagi to the Lower House of the National Diet, February 18, 1899, *Okinawaken Gikaishi* 10(7):40.
71. Takagi to the Lower House of the National Diet, February 18, 1899, *Okinawaken Gikaishi* 10(7):40.
72. Jahana retreated from the political scene in Okinawa in 1901 and died in 1908, at the age of forty-three. For details about his life after the defeat in the Diet, including his efforts to establish an agricultural bank (*nōkō ginkō*), see Namimatsu, "Jahana Noboru no Nōgyō Shisō."
73. Order 13 is "Okinawa Ken Gunsei Kitei"; order 19, "Okinawa Ken Kusei"; order 56, "Okinawa Ken Magiritō Riin Kitei"; and order 352, "Okinawa Ken Magiritō Kitei." The full text of these orders are reprinted in *Okinawa Kenshi* 13.
74. Home Minister Nomura's report to Finance Minister Matsukata, "Okinawa Ken Chihō Seido Kaisei no Ken," August 1895, *Okinawa Kenshi* 13:597–604. These figures were provided by Nio, a Finance Ministry official who was dispatched to the prefecture in 1895. Nio to Finance Minister, "Niho Shuzeikan Fukumeisho," *Okinawa Kenshi* 21:561–62.
75. For reports of the formation of these groups in Nakagami region, for example, "Magiri Riin no Shokumu Kenkyūkai," *Ryūkyū Shimpō*, April 25, 1898, *Okinawa Kenshi* 16:17; "Riin no Shokumu Kenkyūkai," *Ryūkyū Shimpō*, May 25, 1898, *Okinawa Kenshi* 16:28. Serious accusations were made against the heads of magiris (*magirichō*) and chief secretaries (*shokikan*) for granting village contracts to their friends. See, for example, "Tamashiro Magirichō Fushinnin Jyōchinsho," *Ryūkyū Shimpō*, March 2, 1899, *Okinawa Kenshi* 16:158. Increasing criticism from commoners may be linked to the impact of Meiji-style education in the prefecture. According Ōta, 1,000 of the 400,000 people in the prefecture were enrolled in school in 1881, but in 1897 the number was 25,880 (*Okinawa Kensei Gojūnen*, 96–99).
76. Ōta C., "Jyoshi Kyōiku no Fushin no Kekka," *Ryūkyū Shimpō*, October 21, 23, 25, 1900, *Okinawa Kenshi Shiryō Joseishi (Jyō)* 16(1):127.
77. The conditions Ōta referred to here may be similar to what E.H. Norman called the "pressure of the double burden," in the context of the early Meiji Restoration

period for mainland Japan's agrarian village societies (*Japan's Emergence as a Modern State*, 79).
78. "Nago Tsūshin," *Ryūkyū Shimpō*, October 28, 1899, *Okinawa Kenshi Shiryō Joseishi (Jyō)* 16(1):75.
79. "Nago Tsūshin," *Ryūkyū Shimpō*, October 28, 1899, *Okinawa Kenshi Shiryō Joseishi (Jyō)* 16(1):75.
80. Ōta C., "Inaka Shokan," *Ryūkyū Shimpō*, December 5, 9, 13, 1900, *Okinawa Kenshi Shiryō Joseishi (Jyō)* 16(1):133–35.
81. "Fūzoku Danpen" *Ryūkyū Shimpō*, November 27, 1899, *Okinawa Kenshi Shiryō Joseishi (Jyō)* 16(1):78.
82. Despite their disagreements, Ōta and Jahana both believed that transforming Okinawa into a capitalist society was an urgent matter, especially after the Japanese government colonized Taiwan in 1895. Jahana urged small manufacturers to switch their production from brown to low-grade white sugar, which had more potential for growth in light of the direction that Japan's sugar refining industry was headed. Like Ōta, Jahana looked forward to the state's enactment of the land reorganization project because the prefecturewide land surveys that it required would clarify land type and quality, which was important information for determining the most suitable use of land in a region.
83. Ōta C., "Tochi Seiri to Keizai," *Ryūkyū Shimpō*, January 7, 1901, *Okinawa Kenshi* 16:265.
84. Uno, *Uno Kōzō Chosakushū*, 7:69.
85. Uno, *Uno Kōzō Chosakushū*, 7:75.
86. Ōta elaborated this view in "Inaka Shokan," *Ryūkyū Shimpō*, December 5, 9, 13, 190, *Okinawa Kenshi Shiryō Joseishi (Jyō)* 16(1):133–35.
87. "Aki Shinroku," *Ryūkyū Shimpō*, October 29, 1899, *Okinawa Kenshi Shiryō Joseishi (Jyō)* 16(1):73.
88. "Nago Tsūshin," *Ryūkyū Shimpō*, October 28, 1899, *Okinawa Kenshi Shiryō Joseishi (Jyō)* 16(1):74. Ōta's encouragement of women's education was part of this effort to transform gender relations in the late 1890s.
89. There are clear parallels here with the witch-hunting in Europe in the sixteenth and seventeenth centuries that Federici identifies as part of the process of the formation of a new patriarchal order, in which "women's bodies, their labor, their sexual and reproductive powers were placed under the control of the state and transformed into economic resources" (*The Caliban and the Witch*, 170). Mies elaborates on this point: "The process of proletarianization of the men was therefore, accompanied by a process of housewifization of women" (*Patriarchy and Accumulation on a World Scale*, 69).
90. Ichiki, "Ichiki Shokikan Torishirabesho," 14:507.
91. "Gosei Shikkōhō to Mōasobi Torishimari," *Ryūkyū Shimpō*, August 15, 1900, *Okinawa Kenshi Shiryō Joseishi (Jyō)* 16(1):173.
92. Mies, *Patriarchy and Accumulation on a World Scale*, 70.
93. "Ikani Asobu Beki," *Ryūkyū Shimpō*, April 21, 1901, *Okinawa Kenshi Shiryō Joseishi (Jyō)* 16(1):173.

94. "Sangatsu Asobi no Tōsho Boshū," *Ryūkyū Shimpō*, April 23, 1901, *Okinawa Kenshi Shiryō Joseishi (Jyō)* 16(1):174.
95. "Sangatsu Asobi no Tōsho Boshū," *Ryūkyū Shimpō*, April 23, 1901, *Okinawa Kenshi Shiryō Joseishi (Jyō)* 16(1):174.
96. The noro also reported to, and were appointed by, women with the title of ōamushirare, who presided over a designated worship site in Shuri and reported to the Kikoeōgimi. This incorporation of female religious figures into the kingdom's bureaucratic structure was a tool that the royal family used to maintain control over the various regions. See Iha, *Iha Fuyū Zenshū* 7; Wakao, "Iha Fuyū 'Okinawa Joseishi' no Gendaiteki Igi."
97. The number of noro roughly corresponded to the number of villages during both the kingdom and the period of the Preservation of Old Customs Policy.
98. Occasionally, prefectural magistrates even asked the noro to provide spiritual advice and public recognition for the new regime. Uesugi did this during his investigative trip around the prefecture in 1881. See Miyagi, *Okinawa Joseishi*, 229.
99. Daughters generally succeeded their mothers as noro, a matrilineal system that kept the official lands in the hands of women. Under the new civil code, while the succession system for noro remained intact, their lands technically fell under the control of their husbands or sons. With the enactment of the Okinawa Ken Shoroku Shobunhō in 1910, which ended the stipends of all officials from the kingdom era, noro were stripped of their stipends. The government bonds that they received as compensation went to the household head of the noro family. See Miyagi, *Okinawa no Noro no Kenkyū* and *Okinawa Joseishi*.
100. "Norokumoi to Chōhei Tekireisha," *Ryūkyū Shimpō*, November 7, 1900, *Okinawa Kenshi Shiryō Joseishi (Jyō)* 16(1):136.
101. "Nakagami Tsūshin," *Ryūkyū Shimpō*, January 27, 1899, *Okinawa Kenshi Shiryō Joseishi (Jyō)* 16(1):42.
102. These drawn-out ceremonies were clearly detrimental to a broader goal of transforming cultivators into waged workers.
103. "Henza Son no Fūzoku Kairyōkai no Giketsu," *Ryūkyū Shimpō*, September 11, 1902, *Okinawa Kenshi Shiryō Joseishi (Jyō)* 16(1):223. The reorganization and merger of villages following the land reorganization project led to the noro and their lands being eliminated, reabsorbed, and essentially taken out of their communities.
104. King Shō Tei enacted the first order prohibiting the activities of yuta in 1673. This was followed by prohibitions in 1728, 1789, and 1835. All were ineffective in curbing the yuta's activities in the countryside. For the relationship between the suppression of yuta and the spread of Confucianism in the kingdom, see Smits, *Visions of Ryūkyū*.
105. The priestesses often relied on the divinations of the yuta for guidance and at times even relied on them to determine succession. The Council of Three was also influenced by Confucianism and was suspicious of the type of spiritual guidance proffered by the kikoeōgimi. See Miyagi, *Okinawa Joseishi*, 91.
106. Miyagi, *Okinawa Joseishi*, 93. Not only were the yuta's divinations expensive, but they also charged for killing cows or pigs for offerings.

107. "Yuta to Inbaifu no Sōkutsu," *Ryūkyū Shimpō*, December 27, 1898, *Okinawa Kenshi Shiryō Joseishi (Jyō)* 16(1):34.
108. "Yuta to Irainin," *Ryūkyū Shimpō*, October 11, 1900, *Okinawa Kenshi* 19:90.
109. Though the formal attacks on activities by the yuta did not take place until the early Taisho period, the reforms of old customs and the articles related to the norokumoi lands under land reorganization reveal a broad attack that was waged at the turn of the century on women's bodies, property, work, and familial roles.
110. Federici, *The Caliban and the Witch*; Mies, *Patriarchy and Accumulation on a World Scale*.
111. The intended result was the same as that outlined by Federici: the destruction of "a universe of practices, beliefs and social subjects whose existence was incompatible with capitalist work discipline" (*The Caliban and the Witch*, 165).
112. Mies, *Patriarchy and Accumulation on a World Scale*, 81. See also, "Kunigami Dayori," *Ryūkyū Shimpō*, January 19, 1899, 40; "Heian," *Ryūkyū Shimpō*, September 11, 1902, 223. Both are reprinted in *Okinawa Kenshi Shiryō Joseishi (Jyō)* 16(1).
113. For more on Okinawa's banks, see Yanagisawa, "Naha Shōgyō Ginkō no Keiei Bunseki."
114. See Nishihara, *Okinawa Kindai Keizaishi no Hōhō*, 167.
115. Ōta C., "Soshiki Kairyō no Jidai," *Ryūkyū Shimpō*, June 27, 1901, *Okinawa Kenshi* 16:312–13.
116. "Satō Nakabainin no Kōkatsu Shūdan," *Ryūkyū Shimpō*, June 27, 1901, *Okinawa Kenshi* 16:33.
117. For the establishment of sugar policy in Taiwan during this period, see Yanaihara, *Teikokushugika no Taiwan*, chapter 2. For a more recent work, see Shinfuku, "Ryōtai Shoki no Tōgyō Chōsa, Seisaku Ritsuan ni Tsuite."
118. "Naha Shōkō Kaiin ni Nozomu," *Ryūkyū Shimpō*, June 25, 1898, *Okinawa Kenshi* 16:33.
119. "Orimono Dōgyō Kumiai ni Tsuite," *Ryūkyū Shimpō*, November 3, 1901, *Okinawa Kenshi* 16:351.
120. *Ryūkyū Kenbun Zakki*, *Okinawa Kenshi* 14:483–90.
121. Ichiki, "Ichiki Shokikan Torishirabesho," *Okinawa Kenshi* 14:506.
122. Federici, *The Caliban and the Witch*; Dalla Costa and James, *The Power of Women and the Subversion of the Community*; Mies, *Patriarchy and Accumulation on a World Scale*; Fortunati, *The Arcane of Reproduction*.
123. For a description of the huts, see Sasamori, *Nantō Tanken*. For more on their use, see chapter 2.
124. For more on these weaving women, see Tokuyama, *Shima Moyu*; Uesugi, "Uesugi Kenrei Okinawa Ken Jyunkai Nisshi," *Okinawa Kenshi* 11:1–276; Sasamori, *Nantō Tanken 2*.
125. "Chingyō Soshiki," *Ryūkyū Shimpō*, December 27, 1900, *Okinawa Kenshi* 16:257.
126. "Orimono ni Kansuru Shomondai," *Ryūkyū Shimpō*, November 5, 1901, *Okinawa Kenshi* 16:353.
127. "Kumejima Tsumugi no Fushinyō," *Ryūkyū Shimpō*, November 9, 1898, *Okinawa Kenshi* 16:74–75. See also "Kenka Orimono Dōgyō Kumiai no Hitsuyō," *Ryūkyū Shimpō*, October 23–27, 1898, *Okinawa Kenshi* 16:27.

128. "Ryūkyū Hanfusho Kumiai no Secchi," *Ryūkyū Shimpō*, November 17, 1898, *Okinawa Kenshi* 16:77–78.
129. Ōta C., "Kenka Orimono Dōgyōkumiai no Hitsuyō," *Ryūkyū Shimpō*, October 23–27, 1898, *Okinawa Kenshi* 16:29–30.
130. "Shōkokai no Ketsugi to Kaki no Hana Kijyojyo," *Ryūkyū Shimpō*, November 17, 1898, *Okinawa Kenshi Shiryō Joseishi (Jyō)* 16(1):30.
131. "Orimono Dōgyō Kumiai ni Tsuite," *Ryūkyū Shimpō*, November 3, 1901, *Okinawa Kenshi* 16:351.
132. "Orimono ni Kansuru Shomondai," *Ryūkyū Shimpō*, November 5, 1901, *Okinawa Kenshi* 16:353.
133. The irony here is tremendous. Even though the author and Ōta called for the establishment of economic law in the prefecture and called for the dispossession of lands through the enactment of a system of private property, they wanted to keep the people tied to a single industry.
134. "Orimono ni Kansuru Shomondai," *Ryūkyū Shimpō*, November 5, 1901, *Okinawa Kenshi* 16:353.
135. "Orimono ni Kansuru Shomondai," *Ryūkyū Shimpō*, November 5, 1901, *Okinawa Kenshi* 16:353.
136. "Seji no Senteki," *Ryūkyū Shimpō*, November 3, 1901, *Okinawa Kenshi Shiryō Joseishi (Jyō)* 16(1):190.
137. "Shōkōkai no Ketsugi to Kaki no Hana Kijyojyō," *Ryūkyū Shimpō*, November 17, 1898, *Okinawa Kenshi Shiryō Joseishi (Jyō)* 16(1):30.
138. "Seji no Senteki," *Ryūkyū Shimpō*, November 3, 1901, *Okinawa Kenshi Shiryō Joseishi (Jyō)* 16(1):190.
139. "Shōkōkai no Ketsugi to Kaki no Hana Kijyojyō," *Ryūkyū Shimpō*, November 17, 1898, *Okinawa Kenshi Shiryō Joseishi (Jyō)* 16(1):30.
140. "Aki Shinroku," *Ryūkyū Shimpō*, October 29, 1899, *Okinawa Kenshi Shiryō Joseishi (Jyō)* 16(1):73.
141. Goswami, *Producing India*; Walker, *Chinese Modernity and the Peasant Path*.
142. "Orimono ni Kansuru Shomondai," *Ryūkyū Shimpō*, November 5, 1901, *Okinawa Kenshi* 16:353. A shaku is a unit of length is equal to 30.3 centimeters.
143. "Shōkōkai no Ketsugi to Kaki no Hana Kijyojyō," *Ryūkyū Shimpō*, November 17, 1898, *Okinawa Kenshi Shiryō Joseishi (Jyō)* 16(1):30.
144. "Chingyō Soshiki," *Ryūkyū Shimpō*, December 27, 1900, *Okinawa Kenshi* 16:257.
145. *Tan* is a unit of measurement for cloth. The amount of a single tan differed according to time and place, but generally speaking one tan was enough cloth to make one garment.
146. "Okinawa Orimono Kōjō no Kinjō," *Ryūkyū Shimpō*, September 17, 1900, *Okinawa Kenshi* 16:222.
147. "Okinawa Orimono Kōjō no Kinjō," *Ryūkyū Shimpō*, September 17, 1900, *Okinawa Kenshi* 16:222.
148. Restrictions on the tattooing of women were part of this broader process pushed by the local bourgeoisie to transform social relations in preparation for

the establishment of capitalist society in Okinawa. See Higa M., "Bi Kara Yaban E"; Miyagi, *Okinawa no Noro no Kenkyū*.

149. Yamanokuchi, "Kaiwa." For a translation, see Yamanokuchi, "A Conversation."

150. Yanagita published his account of his travels in Okinawa in 1921 four years later (*Kainan Shōki*).

151. Ōta C., "Inaka Shokan," *Ryūkyū Shimpō*, December 5, 9, 13, 1900, *Okinawa Kenshi Shiryō Joseishi (Jyō)* 16(1):133–35.

152. "Orimono Dōgyō Kumiai ni Tsuite," *Ryūkyū Shimpō*, November 3, 1901, *Okinawa Kenshi* 16:351.

153. For more on southern expansion in the Meiji period, see Yano, "*Nanshin*" *no Keifu*, part 2.

154. "Okinawa no Dokuritsu Kaikei o Ronzu," *Ryūkyū Shimpō*, December 16, 1908, *Okinawa Kenshi* 16:1028.

155. The demonization of the yuta culminated in the late Meiji and early Taisho eras. In the late Meiji period, a flurry of articles appeared in the *Ryūkyū Shimpō* that linked the yuta and women's belief in them to the financial ruin of the agrarian villages. For example, see "Inaka no Katei to Jidō," *Ryūkyū Shimpō*, October 23, 1908, *Okinawa Kenshi* 19:379–80; "Kinkō Mokuzetsu: Fujo to Moai," *Ryūkyū Shimpō*, September 5, 1912, *Okinawa Kenshi* 19:542–43. There were also quite a few reports of policing of the yuta's activities in February 1913 that were linked to the trial of an alleged yuta named Nakachi Kamado at the Naha court. She was accused of spreading rumors that a huge fire would erupt in the Higashi District of Naha. In the end, it was revealed that the arsonist was a disgruntled employee of the Nakagami region. On the day that he committed the arson, he distributed to the municipal offices of Nakagami a document listing the prefectural administration's failures. For articles on the trial, see, for example, "Yuta no Kōhan," *Ryūkyū Shimpō*, February 28, 1913, *Okinawa Kenshi* 19:565–67; "Naha Keisatsu no Yuta Seibatsu," *Okinawa Mainichi*, February 20, 1913, *Okinawa Kenshi* 19:562–63.

156. Newspaper articles reported the restrictions that were placed on tattooing and on the activity of yuta during the land reorganization project, which coincided with efforts to transform women's work into factory work. For example, see "Yuta to Inbaifu no Sōkutsu," *Ryūkyū Shimpō*, December 27, 1899, *Okinawa Kenshi Shiryō Joseishi (Jyō)* 16(1):34; "Baifu to Nasu Aku Shūdan," *Ryūkyū Shimpō*, December 27, 1899, *Okinawa Kenshi Shiryō Joseishi (Jyō)* 16(1):35.

4. The Impossibility of Plantation Sugar in Okinawa

1. For a recent English-language work on these redistributions in early modern Japan, see Brown, *Cultivating Commons*.

2. An important part of this process of enclosure, which was outlined in chapter 3, was the transfer of norokumoi lands controlled by priestesses to male heads of households or the state. Access to forest lands continued unofficially, even after the completion of somayama disposal but was subject to increased state supervision. See Miyagi, *Okinawa no Noro no Kenkyū*. For policies regarding the division

of these lands in mainland Japan around the same time, see Totman, *Japan's Imperial Forest Goryōrin*.

3. For Marxists, resolution of the agrarian question was also necessary because the backwardness of agriculture and agrarian relations in the countryside were considered impediments to revolutionary struggle. Engels, Kautsky, and Lenin dealt explicitly with the agrarian question as both a theoretical and a political issue.

4. Quoted in Uno, "Nihon Shihonshugi no Tokushu Kōzō to Nōgyō Mondai," *Uno Kōzō Chosakushū* 8:162. All translations are mine, unless otherwise noted.

5. Marx, *Capital*, 784.

6. The changes that took place in mainland Japan in the first two decades after the Meiji Restoration in 1868 also worked through old systems and administrative units. See Kikekawa, *Meiji Chihō Seido Seiritsushi*. For an article that contrasts Okinawa and mainland Japan's administrative systems in the early Meiji period, see Uechi, "Okinawa Meijiki no Kyūkan Onzon Seisaku ni Kansuru Ichi Kōsatsu."

7. For more on gemeinschaft capitalism and Japan, see Harootunian, "Figuring the Folk," 150; and Hartoonian, *Overcome by Modernity*.

8. By the early Taisho period (before mainland capital entered Okinawa), there were twenty reform-style factories, but their numbers began to decline precisely when local industrialists were trying to advocate their spread. By the agricultural recession that followed World War I, there was just one factory in the entire prefecture. For these figures, see Mukai, *Okinawa Kindai Keizaishi*, 74.

9. These nonselling alliances are essentially boycotts, but here I am translating directly from the Japanese phrase used by these actors, *hibai dōmei*, to express the pact-like nature of the agreement that sugar-producing families arrived at as well as the fact that they were not just boycotting the selling of their raw material sugar, but were refusing to sell their own labor according to the terms set forth by the sugar company.

10. Similar challenges frustrated sugar industrialists' initial efforts to establish modern factories in Taiwan. Though Taiwan formally became a colony in 1895, huge increases in sugar exports to Japan did not begin until 1909. A major reason for this was the planters' unwillingness to sell their cane to factories that were built on the island beginning in 1901 and their unwillingness to switch to the Sugar Bureau's desired type of cane, the Rose Bamboo from Hawaii. It took the 1905 sugar factory regulations, generous subsidies, and police supervision to convert planters into submitters of raw cane to modern factories like the Taiwan Seitō Kabushiki Gaisha. Like in Okinawa, capitalist farms operating in Taiwan that hired wage labor had difficulty competing with family farms that operated on the basis of intensive self-exploitation and had to resort to complex surplus-extraction mechanisms that were enabled by the cooperation of the colonial state. Police harassment aimed at bringing small producers under the control of company contracts was ultimately effective in bringing about a vast increase in the volume of annual sugar exports from Taiwan, from just over 42,000 tons at the time of its colonization in 1895 to over 250,000 tons by the first decade of the twentieth century. For details on key developments in Japan's sugar industry, see Ka, *Japanese*

Colonialism in Taiwan; Geerligs, *The World's Cane Sugar Industry*; Shadanhōjin Tōgyō Kyōkai, *Kindai Nihon Tōgyōshi (Jyō)*; Sagara, *Keizaijō Yori Mitaru Taiwan no Tōgyō*; Nōshōmushō Nōmukyoku, *Satō ni Kansuru Chōsa*. For more details on the development of the mechanized sugar industry in Japan as a whole during the modern era, see Kubo, *Kindai Seitōgyō no Hatten to Tōgyō Rengōkai*.

11. Iha first presented this theory to the public in an article titled "Okinawajin no Sosen ni Tsuite" that was published in the December 9, 1906, edition of the *Ryūkyū Shimpō*. For a full text, see Iha, "Okinawajin no Sosen ni Tsuite," *Okinawa Kenshi* 19:310.

12. This rearticulation of Okinawa's relationship with Japan since prehistory began with the work of mainland social scientists like Torii Ryūzō and Kanazawa Atsusaburō, whose anthropological, linguistic, and historical works on Okinawa were extensions of a general project that began in the 1880s to "register the territory and its residents into the state" (Tomiyama, *Bōryoku no Yokan*, 82). Social scientists classified different groups like the Ainu and Okinawans in relation to the Japanese people to provide scientific justification for the colonial and semicolonial treatment of different groups in the expanding Japanese empire. See Kano, *Okinawa no Fuchi*; Chamberlain, *Essay in Aid of a Grammar and Dictionary of the Luchuan Language*.

13. Iha, "Okinawajin no Sosen ni Tsuite," *Ryūkyū Shimpō*, December 9, 1906, *Okinawa Kenshi* 19:310.

14. For more on the debate between scholars like Shiratori and Torii Ryūzō over the composition of the tenson jinrui, see Oguma, *A Genealogy of "Japanese" Self-Images*. Iha's acceptance of this argument of shared origins is significant because the tenson jinrui referred to people who conquered other lands through migration. They were considered superior to Western nations because of their ability to assimilate alien nations. Iha's inclusion of Okinawa into the tenson jinrui is notable because the debate about its character hinged on who was considered to be inside Japan proper and who was seen as outside it.

15. Iha published his studies of the *Omoro Sōshi*, a collection of ancient songs compiled by the kingdom government during the early modern period, throughout the prewar period. For a summary of his activities, see Beillevaire, "Assimilation from Within, Appropriation from Without."

16. Iha, "Okinawajin no Sosen ni Tsuite," *Ryūkyū Shimpō*, December 9, 1906, *Okinawa Kenshi* 19:310.

17. "Kaikaichū no Okinawa Kenkai ni Nozomu, *Ryūkyū Shimpō*, January 12, 1907, *Okinawaken Gikaishi* 11(8):145.

18. Iha's conscious decision to rewrite the existing story of the former kingdom's abolition by the Meiji state to tell what he considered the more important story of the reunification of peoples may be criticized as his legitimation of Okinawa's semicolonization by the Japanese empire. However, his main concern was obtaining equality in the present, even if it meant erasing the violence inflicted on Okinawa in the past. The intention behind his work was fundamentally different from that of the mainland social scientists. See Tomiyama, "'Ryūkyūjin' to Iu Shutai."

19. "Kaikaichū no Okinawa Kenkai ni Nozomu," *Ryūkyū Shimpō*, January 12, 1907, *Okinawaken Gikaishi* 11(8):145.
20. See chapter 3 for details on the local elite's pursuit of this right to pay taxes.
21. Ōta C., *Ōta Chōfu Senshū (Jyō)*, 326.
22. The state's active promotion of industry began in the 1880s, but at that time it focused more on providing subsidies to encourage cultivation than on mechanization. For more on the policy in the 1880s, see Mukai, *Okinawa Kindai Keizaishi*.
23. The promotion of these "rational" agricultural methods were efforts by the Meiji state to increase yields and promote scientific knowledge related to the sugar industry. That is, they were aiming to inculcate new notions and practices of rationality among Okinawa's cultivators. For details on the measures the state promoted, see Yoshimura, *Nihon Henkyōron Josetsu*, 101.
24. *Bunmitsutō* is crude sugar that could be refined into white sugar at mainland refineries. It was the preferred type of sugar, compared to the brown sugar (*ganmitsutō*) that was mainly produced in Okinawa—sugar in which molasses and crystals are not separated in a centrifuge.
25. For details on the modernization of Okinawa's sugar industry, see Komatsu, "Seitōgyō no Hatten to Naha no Shokōgyō"; Fukuokaken Naimubu, *Okinawa Ken Kosaku ni Kansuru Chōsa*.
26. For Okinawa Seitō's dominance, see Nakae, "Okinawa Ken 'Tochi Seiri' to Shōhin Seisan Nōgyō no Tenkai"; Kinjō I., "Meijiki no Okinawa no Tōgyō."
27. According to the *Ryūkyū Shimpō*, Asabushi used despotic measures to bring development projects to the regions he represented. In 1908 he had come under fire for using his position to invest 3,000 yen of the communal funds he had collected from residents in a hospital that was being built on the coast near the source of the Gibo River. See "Haibyō Magirichō to Bōsatsu Naru Gunchō," *Ryūkyū Shimpō*, November 17, 1907, *Okinawa Kenshi* 19:345–46. Asabushi's name appeared in the newspaper again in January 1916, when he was gunchō of the Shimajiri region and agreed—without getting approval from the municipal assembly—to Okitai Takushoku's request to build a railway line to transport cane collected from the region to its sugar factory. See "Asabushi Shi no Sendan," *Ryūkyū Shimpō*, January 22, 1916, *Okinawa Kenshi* 17:708; "Jichi no Keni," *Ryūkyū Shimpō*, January 25, 1916, *Okinawa Kenshi* 17:709.
28. He became one of the major stockholders of the company.
29. Komatsu, "Seitōgyō no Hatten to Naha no Shokōgyō," 358.
30. The company also built a factory in Tomigusuku, a village on the southwestern coast of Okinawa.
31. Komatsu, "Seitōgyō no Hatten to Naha no Shokōgyō," 360.
32. For more on the transformation and consolidation of Japan's sugar industry run by Konzerns, refer to Ono, *Seito Konzern Dokuhon*.
33. Yano, the CEO of the first Okinawa Seitō, reestablished the company in 1916 and built a factory in Ginowan, in central Okinawa, that could produce 250 tons of sugar a day. After that, he purchased a communally owned factory in Takamine Village in the southern part of the main island that could produce 80 tons a day and expanded it into a factory that could produce 300 tons a day.

34. Once all of these mergers and purchases were completed, Suzuki Shōten's Tainansha operated as the only sugar manufacture capital in Okinawa Prefecture. For details of Tainansha's growth, see Mukai, *Okinawa Kindai Keizaishi*, 307; Namitaka et al., *Shōwa Seitō Kabushiki Gaisha 10 Nen Shi*. For detailed statistics about Tainansha's operations in the period 1918–31, see *Tainan Seitō Kabushiki Gaisha Hōkokusho* (Okinawa Prefectural Archives retrieval code T00016045B).
35. This was granted by Governor Narahara, the most enthusiastic of Okinawa's leaders about carving up the prefecture's lands during his tenure. For more on Narahara's reclamation policies, see chapter 3 and Isa, *Jahana Noboru Shū*.
36. Not much is known today about this transaction, but the cane grown there very likely went to two factories: the Kadena factory and the Makihara factory. See Mukai, *Okinawa Kindai Keizaishi*; Fukuokaken Naimubu, *Okinawa Ken Kosaku ni Kansuru Chōsa*; Komatsu, "Seitōgyō no Hatten to Naha no Shokōgyō."
37. For a sample Tainansha contract for Nakagami region, see Fukuokaken Naimubu, *Okinawa Ken Kosaku ni Kansuru Chōsa*, 472–74.
38. By this time, the value of the lands, which the former company had purchased from the Shō family for 70,000 yen, had risen to 300,000–400,000 yen. See Fukuokaken Naimubu, *Okinawa Ken Kosaku ni Kansuru Chōsa*, 93.
39. "Waga Ken no Jitsugyō Hattensaku Ikani," *Okinawa Jitsugyō Shimpō*, August 5, 1914.
40. For details of these deliberations see Kinjō I., *Kindai Okinawa no Tetsudō to Kaiun*.
41. Kinjō I., *Kindai Okinawa no Tetsudō to Kaiun*, 53–57.
42. In December 1917, soon after Tainansha took over all large-scale sugar operations in the main island of Okinawa, the Kadena line was approved by the prefectural assembly. It was completed in March 1922. Kinjō I., *Kindai Okinawa no Tetsudō to Kaiun*, 14–15.
43. Ōta C., *Ōta Chōfu Senshū (Chū)*, 314.
44. According to a study conducted for the compilation of *Okinawa Ken Kosaku ni Kansuru Chōsa*, despite the efforts of Tainansha to encourage the planting of large-stalk-type cane for submission to its factories, the ratio of home to factory use of the harvested cane was 7:3.
45. Ōmi explained his vision for Okinawa's industry in "Sangyō 10-Nen Keikaku Shushi," *Okinawa Jitsugyō Shimpō*, July 1, 1915.
46. This was similar to the policy that mainland sugar capital enacted with the support of the governor general in Taiwan, which reduced the power of local sugar industrialists and small manufacturers. See Ka, *Japanese Colonialism in Taiwan*; Mazumdar, *Sugar and Society in China*.
47. Shadanhōjin Tōgyō Kyōkai, *Kindai Nihon Tōgyōshi (Ge)*, 2.
48. The first prefectural assembly elections were held in Okinawa in 1909. See Ōta M., *Kindai Okinawa no Seiji Kōsō*.
49. "Kengian Teishutsu Riyū," *Ryūkyū Shimpō*, December 4, 1917, *Okinawaken Gikaishi* 11(8):857.
50. Quoted in Ka, *Japanese Colonialism in Taiwan*, 80. This description is from Yanaihara Tadao's seminal work on Japanese imperialism in Taiwan, *Teikokushugika*

no Taiwan (1929), where he traces the transformations to the colonial economy following annexation in 1895. Inaka Akira and other Okinawan intellectuals observed the developments in Taiwan with extreme caution and saw the governor's proposed reforms to their sugar industry as an attempt to install colonial policies in the prefecture. For transformations to Taiwan's sugar industry in the first decade of the twentieth century, also see Geerligs, *The World's Cane Sugar Industry*, 84–85.

51. "Kengian Teishutsu Riyū," *Ryūkyū Shimpō*, December 4, 1917, *Okinawaken Gikaishi* 11(8):858.
52. "Kinkō Mokuzetsu," *Ryūkyū Shimpō*, January 9, 1915, *Okinawa Kenshi* 17:660.
53. Ōta C., *Ōta Chōfu Senshū (Chū)*, 320.
54. Ōta C., "Honken Sangyō Kumiai to Tōgyō," *Ryūkyū Shimpō*, January 5, 1914, *Ōta Chōfu Senshū (Chū)*, 421.
55. Ōta C., "Honken Sangyō Kumiai to Tōgyō," *Ryūkyū Shimpō*, January 5, 1914, *Ōta Chōfu Senshū (Chū)*, 422. For a detailed history of the establishment of the Okinawa Nōkō Ginkō and other banks in the prefecture, see Yanagisawa, "Naha Shōgyō Ginkō no Keiei Bunseki."
56. Ōta and Inaka's visions also reflected their belief that the ability of villagers to successfully manage their own region's economy was a measure of their civilization. Their advocacy of an industrial policy designed to compensate for what the prefecture was formally denied—self-governance—must be seen as attempts to counter the state's unwillingness to extend constitutional rights to the people of Okinawa. They hoped that a network of industrial associations in all of the villages that was linked to the prefecture's agricultural bank could ensure brown sugar manufacturers' autonomy from mainland sugar capital that wanted to convert Okinawa's peasants into pure cultivators of raw material. These conversations about local autonomy in the sugar industry spilled into the political realm. Ōmi's tenure brought back fears of colonization that had subsided with the enactment of the special prefectural administration system (*tokubetsu fukensei*) in 1909, which granted the prefecture the right to send representatives to the National Diet for the first time. Ōmi was transferred out of the prefecture in April 1916 but his tenure made it clear to local leaders that in the wrong hands, the special system could be extremely damaging. This led to calls for the abolition of the system in late 1916, which were deliberated by the Diet in 1917 and 1918. See the Lower House of the National Diet's deliberations on a bill to abolish this system from March 13–15, 1918, *Okinawaken Gikaishi* 10(7):360–76. The bill passed unanimously, though it was not enacted for a couple of years. Inaka was one of 28 people who signed a petition dated December 3, 1917, opposing article 5. See "Seitōjo Kisoku Haishi Kengian," *Ryūkyū Shimpō*, December 4, 1917, *Okinawaken Gikaishi* 11(8):857.
57. The immediate effect of the end of World War I in Japan was a tremendous economic boom, which resulted from the increased demand for and corresponding growth in the production of manufactured goods. Aldcroft observes that "the shortage of manufactured goods in Europe and restricted shipping space gave Japan a great opportunity to expand commerce by penetrating markets in the

Western Pacific and further" (*From Versailles to Wall Street*, 37–38). While much of Europe struggled to recover from the war, Japan, the United States, and the other Western Allies enjoyed "a boom of astonishing dimensions" that extended to the sugar industry (ibid., 64).

58. On Okinawa sugar's golden age see Mukai, *Okinawa Kindai Keizaishi*, 19. On Cuba's sugar boom see Rowe, *Markets and Men*, 936, McGillivray, *Blazing Cane*, and Ayala, *American Sugar Kingdom*.
59. Mukai, *Okinawa Kindai Keizaishi*, 14.
60. In 1917 Tainansha entered the prefecture and merged with Okitai Seitō and Okitai Takushoku, becoming the only Japanese sugar capital in the prefecture. Mukai, *Okinawa Kindai Keizaishi*.
61. Fukuokaken Naimubu, *Okinawa Ken Kosaku ni Kansuru Chōsa*, 13.
62. Carrying-in regions were territories near each factory that sugar companies accepted raw sugar cane from. Companies had to designate these regions because sugar quality greatly depended on the speed with which cane could be delivered after cutting to the factory. On the unique challenges posed by sugar production, see Mintz, *Sweetness and Power*.
63. Nakachi S., "Senzenki Okinawa no Nōson ni Okeru Rōdō Kōkan Kankō no Kōzō."
64. Figures for 1917 are not available, but in 1916 brown sugar sold for approximately eight yen per barrel. One barrel is 1.2 piculs.
65. On the satō maedai, see chapter 1 and Kinjō I., "Meijiki no Okinawa no Tōgyō."
66. Komatsu, "Seitōgyō no Hatten to Naha no Shokōgyō," 353.
67. For more on yuimaaru practices and history in Okinawa, see Mukai, *Okinawa Kindai Keizaishi*; Tamura, *Ryūkyū Kyōsan Sonraku no Kenkyū*.
68. Mintz, *Sweetness and Power*; Geerligs, *The World's Cane Sugar Industry*.
69. For details about the settlement of accounts, see Nakachi, "Senzenki Okinawa no Nōson ni Okeru Rōdō Kōkan Kankō no Kōzō."
70. Higa R., "Satō Goya."
71. Iba, *Nangoku no Shirayuri*, 28.
72. Iba, *Nangoku no Shirayuri*, 30.
73. Iba, *Nangoku no Shirayuri*, 30.
74. Iba, *Nangoku no Shirayuri*, 30.
75. Iba, *Nangoku no Shirayuri*, 32.
76. Tamura proves the continued existence of internal laws (*naihō*) that were enforced in Okinawa's villages. These ranged from the prohibition on women going to other villages at night and on men and women playing outside at night to prohibitions against cutting down certain types of trees, dirtying communal wells, not keeping chickens in pens, and taking cane from others without permission. For a full list of such laws from Kadena, see Tamura, *Ryūkyū Kyōsan Sonraku no Kenkyū*, 460–61.
77. Kinjō I., *Kindai Okinawa no Tōgyō*, 47. Specific figures on the yearly fluctuations in the production of different categories of sugar can be found in Okinawa Satō Dōgyō Kumiai, *Okinawa Satō Dōgyō Kumiai Gairan*, an account of the Okinawa Sugar Production Association (Okinawa Satō Dōgyō Kumiai) that was established

in 1913. Most sugar producers on the main island were dues-paying members of the association. According to its figures, the proportion of brown sugar output in the total output per association member fell quite dramatically during the nonselling alliances, from 77 percent in 1917 to 73.5 percent in 1919 and 68 percent in 1921, despite subsidies granted by the prefecture to the companies in an effort to increase self-sufficiency in sugar.

78. Chayanov's argument that family farms prefer to maximize total income rather than profit when selecting their household strategies is informative on this point. Shanin's introduction to the English-language translation of Chayanov's *Theory of Peasant Economy* is useful here. See Shanin, "Chayanov's Message."
79. James Scott writes about the way that communities consciously select crops that are amenable to a nomadic existence or those that can be left alone for some time, such as root vegetables (*The Art of Not Being Governed*). This is useful for understanding why Okinawa's small peasantry (shōnō) were reluctant to give up their cultivation of sweet potato and other crops to focus solely on cash crops. Also see Mintz, *Caribbean Transformations*, 225–50.
80. "Gansha Baikyaku Mondai," *Ryūkyū Shimpō*, December 25, 1916, *Okinawa Kenshi* 17:798–99.
81. "Gansha Baikyaku Mondai," *Ryūkyū Shimpō*, December 25, 1916, *Okinawa Kenshi* 17:798–99.
82. "Seitōsha to Shasakumin," *Ryūkyū Shimpō*, January 12, 1917, *Okinawa Kenshi* 17:804–5.
83. Eighty percent of all sugar cultivators produced less than twenty barrels of brown sugar per year. Quite a few produced less than five barrels. See "Satō Dōgyō Kumiai Sono Shin Ninmu," *Ryūkyū Shimpō*, November 18, 1917, *Okinawa Kenshi* 17:803.
84. "Gansha Baikyaku Mondai Kaiketsu," *Ryūkyū Shimpō*, February 15, 1917, *Okinawa Kenshi* 17:806.
85. For this announcement, see "Ryōtō Gappei Kettei," *Ryūkyū Shimpō*, October 17, 1917, *Okinawa Kenshi* 17:864.
86. "Baishū Hō Kaisei Riyū," *Ryūkyū Shimpō*, October 24, 1917, *Okinawa Kenshi* 17:868.
87. "Genryō Baishū Hō," *Ryūkyū Shimpō*, October 24, 1917, *Okinawa Kenshi* 17:871.
88. "Shasakumin no Ikō," *Ryūkyū Shimpō*, November 13, 1917, *Okinawa Kenshi* 17:879.
89. "Genryō Baishū Kitei," *Ryūkyū Shimpō*, November 16, 1917, *Okinawa Kenshi* 17:881.
90. Raising pigs was a crucial form of supplementary income. Pork was an important part of the new year's celebration and was used in soup throughout the year and for medicinal purposes. In many cases, one pig was owned jointly by more than one family. The cultivation of sweet potato also played an important part in the overall household economy, as it was the small peasantry's staple food. The skin of the sweet potato, in addition to leftovers and tofu, was used for the pig's feed. It also fueled the communal manufacture of brown sugar. For sample breakdowns of the budgets of farming households in the Nakagami region, see Kinjō I., *Kindai Okinawa no Tōgyō*, 105–6; Fukuokaken Naimubu, *Okinawa Ken Kosaku ni Kansuru Chōsa*, 553–60.

91. People preferred to rely on *moai*, communal lending associations formed by kinship groups, villages, or other groups based on a principle of mutual accountability, than to obtain loans from banks. "Shasakumin no Ikō," *Ryūkyū Shimpō*, November 13, 1917, *Okinawa Kenshi* 17:879.
92. Chayanov asserts that even in an environment clearly dominated by capitalism, peasant agriculture followed a logic characteristic of the operational logic of family farms within that broader society. Faced with a "diverse calculus of choices," they preferred a maximization of total income rather than profit or marginal production. Shanin, "Chayanov's Message," 4.
93. Chayanov points out that this quest for flexibility extended to keeping lands or means of production unused and ready for disposal (*The Theory of Peasant Economy*, 109). James Scott makes a similar argument: "By pursuing a broad portfolio . . . they [cultivators] spread their risks and ensure themselves a diverse and nutritious diet. . . . Particular crops have characteristics that make them more or less resistant to appropriation. . . . Roots and tubers after they ripen can be left safely in the ground for up to two years and dug up piecemeal as needed" (*The Art of Not Being Governed*, 195). In Okinawa, the poorer a household was, the higher its proportion of sweet potato cultivation to sugar production was.
94. As Mukai argues, the small peasantry would have more control over the income they received from selling sugar if they manufactured it on their own, because companies' contracts used whatever the price was at the Naha market on the day that the cane was delivered to the factory (*Okinawa Kindai Keizaishi*).
95. "Gansha Baishū Rakuchaku," *Ryūkyū Shimpō*, January 11, 1918, *Okinawa Kenshi* 17:917. This settlement was negotiated between Tainansha's Nishihara factory and Nishihara village's Arakawa Saburō and the head administrator (*kuchō*) of Yonabaru, Adaniya.
96. After World War I, mainland capital entered Yaeyama and purchased local sugar factories. The *Yaeyama Shimpō* attributed the failure of mainland sugar capital to establish predominance in Yaeyama as a result of the same issues that plagued these companies on the main island of Okinawa. See Iritakenishi, *Yaeyama Tōgyōshi*, 107–8. For more information about the 1919 strike, see Aniya, *Okinawa no Musansha Undo*.
97. Quoted in Ikehara, *Okinawa Tōgyōron*, 60–61.
98. "Gansha Baikyaku Mondai Kaiketsu," *Ryūkyū Shimpō*, February 15, 1917, *Okinawa Kenshi* 17:806. The existence of an alternative path if negotiations over prices ended in failure was probably an important reason for small peasantry to maintain their strong position in brown sugar production.
99. Even in the counteroffer that was made by the representatives of the cultivators, the expenditure here was listed as 55 sen, which was close to one third of the total cost per barrel of sugar. See "Gansha Baikyaku Mondai," *Ryūkyū Shimpō*, December 25, 1916, *Okinawa Kenshi* 17:799.
100. Kinjō I., *Kindai Okinawa no Tōgyō*, 47. Under this arrangement, peasants who cultivated sugarcane had an incentive not to increase their production of brown sugar or hire additional laborers because their costs would go up. The structural

inferiority of brown sugar that Tainansha was able to establish through its purchasing conditions for raw material and its aggressive promotion of high-yielding stalks is explained in more detail in Yoshimura, *Nihon Henkyōron Josetsu*.
101. Banaji, "The Fictions of Free Labour," 91.
102. Mezzadra and Neilson, *Border as Method*, 111.
103. Read, *The Micropolitics of Capital*, 62.
104. Thus, they exposed the violence that was invisible in a society governed by the regime of abstract labor. In Marx's words, the worker's "economic bondage is at once mediated through, and concealed by, the periodic renewal of the act by which he sells himself, his change of masters, and the oscillations in the market-price of his labour" (quoted in Banaji, "The Fictions of Free Labour," 75).
105. Ōta C., "Yūwa Konitsu," *Ryūkyū Shimpō*, January 12, 1918, *Okinawaken Gikaishi* 11(8):929.
106. Chayanov, *The Theory of Peasant Economy*, 30. Notably, Ōta and Inaka's vision of the establishment of a prefecturewide industrial association system to counter the penetration of mainland bunmitsutō capital also did not come to fruition. Although they succeeded in convincing the prefectural authorities to abolish restrictions on the establishment of reform-type sugar factories that produced brown sugar in 1917, the number of these factories declined from eighteen in 1916 to none at the end of 1919.
107. Komatsu, "Seitōgyō no Hatten to Naha no Shokōgyō," 355.
108. See Nakachi and Inaka, "Okinawa Tōgyō no Genjyō," *Ryūkyū Shimpō*, December 10, 1911, *Okinawa Kenshi* 17:300.
109. Factors for increased yield may have to do with the spread of fertilizer use or the use of different varieties of cane. Per factory output fell by 25 percent between 1912 and 1917. For detailed figures, see Mukai, *Okinawa Kindai Keizaishi*.
110. All figures are from "Honken Nōgyō Kosū," *Ryūkyū Shimpō*, March 28, 1914, *Okinawa Kenshi* 17:479.
111. For details of this move and the communities that formed in these new spaces, see Tomiyama, *Kindai Nihon Shakai to Okinawajin*.
112. This was also the case with farming and fishing households in Yaeyama. Families began to move in significant numbers to Taiwan, even though opportunities for work increased in Iriomote mining and in large sugar factories that were built in Daitōjima in 1916. For contemporary accounts of these industries, see Yanaihara Tadao, *Teikokushugika no Taiwan*; Okinawaken Yaeyama Shichō, *Yaeyama Gunsei Yōran*. Women preferred to venture to Taipei to find work as maids and merchants because they saw Taiwan to be a more modern and attractive site of employment than their own hometowns. For more on the immigration of women from Yaeyama to Taiwan, see Kaneto, "1930-nen Zengo no Yaeyama Josei no Shokuminchi Taiwan e no Idō o Unagashita Puru Yōin"; Matayoshi, "Okinawa Josei to Taiwan Shokuminchi Shihai"; Matsuda, "Colonial Modernity across the Border."
113. For more on the distinction between dead and living labor, see Read, *The Micropolitics of Capital*, chapter 2.

114. The postboom agricultural crisis that ravaged Okinawa's countryside in the 1920s, known as "Sago Palm hell," brought the cultivators together with socialist and Marxist thinkers who began to organize in the prefecture in the beginning of the decade. The Social Science Research Incident, which took place between 1926 and 1928, was especially threatening to Tainansha and the prefecture because it linked the activists with the peasants and exposed the cooperation of the company and the prefecture in search of profit at the expense of ailing small producers. Two prominent Marxist activists, Yamada Kanji and Inoguchi Masao, along with twenty or so teachers from Nakagami organized the Social Science Research Group, which joined forces with the Okinawa Labor-Farmer (Rōnō) Party, founded in February 1928, to establish tighter coordination between thought, politics, and activism. "Tainansha e no Yokkyū," a leaflet dated December 27, 1928, represented the merging of Marxist thought and activism with a longer tradition of peasants' struggle against the exploitative practices of the company described in this chapter and inspired widespread agitation in the prefecture. The full text of this leaflet appears in Fukuokaken Naimubu, *Okinawa Ken Kosaku ni Kansuru Chōsa*.

5. Uneven Development and the Rejection of Economic Nationalism in "Sago Palm Hell" Okinawa

1. I define *crisis* as something broader than the crisis of capitalist valorization in terms of rise and fall of the rate of profit. Instead, I mean an all-encompassing sociopolitical and economic crisis that emerged out of the struggle between capitalist valorization and self-valorization and that necessarily required the production of subjectivity for capital and the production of countersubjectivity. Read explains: "There is a production of subjectivity for capital—docile, individual, flexible and productive—and there is the counter-production of another subjectivity. This counter-subjectivity is also produced in some sense for capital in that it is a necessary element of the valorization of capital, but it contains a supplement irreducible to the demands of capitalist valorization" (*The Micropolitics of Capital*, 100).
2. Here I draw on Negri's idea of the language of cooperation as social living labor (*Insurgencies*, 264).
3. Unlike the Sakishima islands, the northern region of the main island of Okinawa was not the target of industrial development projects or large-scale investment. It was referred to as Yanbaru, a derogatory term to describe its undeveloped state.
4. For more on this point, see the concluding section of chapter 4.
5. For a representative example of this approach, see Yoshihara, *Okinawa Minshū Undō no Dentō*.
6. Smith clarifies that the various spatial scales produced under capitalism are "a means to organize and integrate the different processes involved in the circulation and accumulation of capital" and notes that "these absolute spaces are fixed within the wider flow of relative space, and become the geographic foundation for the overall circulation and expansion of value" (*Uneven Development*, 181).

7. Uno, *Uno Kōzō Chosakushū* 8:25. All translations are mine, unless otherwise noted. As Goswami points out in *Producing India*, anticolonial economic nationalism was common in much of the colonized and postcolonial world.
8. In his seminal study of nationalism (*Imagined Communities*), Benedict Anderson responded to Marxists' inability to account for the formation of national consciousness. In this case, it appears that Okinawa's nationalists could not account for their subjects' sensitivity to class dynamics as they formulated their notions of community.
9. Uno brought attention to the nature of sugar as a global commodity in his 1944 *Tōgyō Yori Mitaru Kōiki Keizai no Kenkyū*. For how this is applicable to Okinawa, see Tomiyama, "From the Colonization of Outer Regions to Regional Economics."
10. Aldcroft, *From Versailles to Wall Street*, 64–65.
11. Yamamura, "Then Came the Great Depression."
12. Aldcroft, *From Versailles to Wall Street*, 67.
13. Yamamura, "Then Came the Great Depression," 184–85.
14. Kajinishi, *Nihon Shihonshugi no Botsuraku*, 8.
15. Dalton, *Sugar*, 40.
16. Dalton, *Sugar*, 42.
17. Uno, *Uno Kōzō Chosakushū* 7:150–52.
18. Uno, *Tōgyō Yori Mitaru Kōiki Keizai no Kenkyū*, 357.
19. Ōta C., *Okinawa Kensei Gojyūnen*, 316.
20. Uno identifies the differences between countries that produce sugar for self-sufficiency and those that produce it as a colonial commodity. His description of the problems facing Australia's sugar industry—"countries that began sugar production with the objective of self-sufficiency had to necessarily seek foreign exports and production costs were from the start higher compared to other colonial sugar sites"—can be applied to the challenges faced by the Okinawan sugar industry, which mainly supplied domestic consumers (*Tōgyō Yori Mitaru Kōiki Keizai no Kenkyū*, 357). For a 1940 work elaborating the challenges facing Okinawa's sugar industry, see Yamashita K., *Satōgyō no Saihensei*, Jyō.
21. Tomiyama, *Kindai Nihon Shakai to Okinawajin*, 79.
22. The development of modern industries was not pursued with much vigor by the prefecture and was left to municipalities.
23. The outflow of people from agrarian villages to domestic and foreign labor markets demonstrate this problem.
24. Shinjō Chōkō wrote "Hinshi no Ryūkyū" in 1925. It was reprinted in the *Okinawa Kyūsai Ronshū*, which was originally published in 1929 to appeal for relief funds for the prefecture. The phrase Sago Palm hell was used to refer the dire straits of the peasants who had nothing to eat but the fruit of the sago palm, which could be poisonous if prepared the wrong way. The seed is especially toxic, but people consumed the fruit after boiling it. The phrase hinted at conditions in Okinawa, whose economy had been transformed from a largely self-sufficient one to one that was excessively dependent on exports and imports.
25. This description is from Matsuoka Masao's response to Okinawa's crisis conditions, *Sekirara ni Mita Ryūkyū no Genjyō*, 1.

26. This is the English-language translation of Matsuoka, *Sekirara ni Mita Ryūkyū no Genjyō*.
27. Shimoda, "Ryūkyū Yo Dokoeiku," 67.
28. The full text of the "Okinawa Relief Bill" (Okinawa Ken Zaisei Keizai no Kyūsai Jyochō ni Kansuru Kengian) of February 24, 1925, proposed by Kishimoto Gasha and three others to the Lower House of the National Diet on March 23, 1925, is reprinted in *Okinawaken Gikaishi* 9(6):410–20 and *Naha Shishi* (2)(2)(5):17–19.
29. See "Shokuryō wa Sotetsu no Ne," *Osaka Asahi*, June 4, 1932, *Nago Shishi Senzen Shimbun Shūsei* 3:192. For an earlier account, see "Sotetsu Chūdoku," *Ryūkyū Shimpō*, June 22, 1927, *Okinawa Kenshi*, 19:707–8.
30. "Okinawa Relief Bill," *Naha Shishi* (2)(2)(5):18.
31. Ōta C., *Okinawa Kensei Gojyūnen*, 21–22.
32. Ōshiro to the House of Peers of the National Diet, March 24, 1926, *Okinawaken Gikaishi* 8(5):388.
33. "Okinawa Ken Keizai Shinkō ni Kansuru Seigan," July 1926, *Naha Shishi* (2)(2)(5):23.
34. Ōshiro to the Lower House of the National Diet, March 12, 1926, *Okinawaken Gikaishi* 10(7):456.
35. Ōshiro to the Lower House of the National Diet, March 12, 1926, *Okinawaken Gikaishi* 10(7):458.
36. Ida to the Okinawa Prefectural Assembly, December 17, 1929, *Okinawaken Gikaishi* 4(1):381.
37. This may have to do with the lessons the state learned from dealing with peasantry struggles in Taiwan. For details on these struggles, see Kubo, "Gansha Baishū Kakaku o Meguru Seitō Gaisha to Taiwan Nōmin no Kankei."
38. Contrary to the hopes of the prefecture's leaders that this type of encouragement to bring raw material to Tainansha's factories would allow them to operate at fully capacity, many small producers preferred to continue to manufacture their own lower-grade sugar communally in small-scale sugar huts that littered Okinawa's countryside until the end of World War II.
39. The language of local autonomy had been a prominent theme in Ōta's writings since the late 1890s, as we saw in chapter 3. See for example, Ōta C., "Okinawa Ken no Jichi Mondai," *Yomiuri Shimbun*, July 16, 1897, *Naha Shishi* (2)(2)(4):659.
40. Oyadomari, *Okinawa Yo Tachiagare*, 93.
41. Oyadomari, *Okinawa Yo Tachiagare*, 93–94.
42. Oyadomari, *Okinawa Yo Tachiagare*, 175.
43. For more on the type of communalism and theory of consumer cooperatives advocated by Okamoto and Gondō, see Iwasaki, *Nōhonshisō no Shakaishi*.
44. Oyadomari, *Okinawa Yo Tachiagare*, 158.
45. Oyadomari, *Okinawa Yo Tachiagare*, 159.
46. Harry Harootunian critiques this type of idealistic endeavor to realize "capitalism without capitalism" in *Overcome by Modernity*, xxx.
47. Hardt and Negri, *Labor of Dionysus*, 140. Here, Hardt and Negri criticize the viewpoint articulated by Poulantzas in *Political Power and Social Classes*. Poulantzas's

view differs considerably from Oyadomari's because he looks to the proletariat to restore the power of the state, after which the state will "do the rest." Poulantzas, *Political Power and Social Classes*, 273. However, the understanding of the state as separate and above economic relationships (as having a nonclass character) is the same.

48. Oyadomari, *Okinawa Yo Tachiagare*, 203.
49. According to Hardt and Negri (*Labor of Dionysus*), the state is often seen in a society dominated by finance capital as standing above or outside of society, but we must not forget that the state actualizes even greater exploitation. Because this link is concealed, people often look to the state to correct or mediate the transgressions or overexploitation of the people by capital.
50. For an examination of some of these efforts, see chapter 4.
51. Ōta C., *Okinawa Kensei Gojyūnen*, 182.
52. To Ōta, the current predicament, despite its severity, was nothing new: "This is a summary of what I presented in October 1918 but these problems are still present today" (*Okinawa Kensei Gojyūnen*, 184).
53. Ōta C., *Okinawa Kensei Gojyūnen*, 182.
54. Ōta C., *Okinawa Kensei Gojyūnen*, 308.
55. Ōta C., *Ōta Chōfu Senshū (Ge)*, 337.
56. Ōta C., letter to Kamiyama, April 8, 1927, *Naha Shishi* (2)(2)(5):220.
57. Ōta C., letter to Kamiyama, April 8, 1927, *Naha Shishi* (2)(2)(5):221.
58. "Okinawa Relief Bill," *Naha Shishi* (2)(2)(5):19. The bill advocated the enactment of a system similar to that in Taiwan and stated that "some kind of colonial administration in the realm of finances, such as the establishment of special accounts or the return of all treasury surpluses that are paid by Okinawa, back to the prefecture is necessary under the current conditions" (ibid., 18).
59. For coercive measures against Taiwan's small peasantry, see Yanaihara, *Teikokushugika no Taiwan*; Ka, *Japanese Colonialism in Taiwan*.
60. See, for example, Mbembe, "African Modes of Self-Writing"; Goswami, *Producing India*.
61. It is notable that this *mizokushugi* (nationalism) as a counter to Japanese imperialism has been used in the postwar era to counter American imperialism by Okinawan intellectuals who are well aware of the dangers of nationalism. Despite being well aware of the fascistic tendencies of nationalist sentiment, many postwar thinkers and activists in Okinawa, like Frantz Fanon in a different context, found it necessary to consider the possibility of mobilizing the category of nation in order to rally the people.
62. Marxist activity will be dealt with only briefly here. For a more comprehensive history, see Aniya, *Okinawa no Musansha Undō*. For autobiographical accounts, see Higa S., *Okinawa no Saigetsu*; Urasaki, *Gyakuryū no Naka de*; Yamashiro Z., *Yanbaru no Hi* and *Hi no Sōsōkyoku*.
63. Tomiyama, *Kindai Nihon Shakai to Okinawajin*, 152. For a recent English-language account, see Rabson, *The Okinawan Diaspora in Japan*. For more on Korean workers in the same period, see Kawashima, *The Proletarian Gamble*. For accounts of

Okinawan workers in the South Seas islands, see Tomiyama, "The 'Japanese' of Micronesia: Okinawans in the Nanyō Islands"; Kondō, "Gyogyō, Nanshin, Okinawa." For similar accounts in Taiwan, see Matsuda, "Becoming Japanese in the Colony"; Kaneto, "1930-nen Zengo no Yaeyama Josei no Shokuminchi Taiwan e no Idō o Unagashita Puru Yōin"; Miki, "*Yaeyama Gasshūkoku*" no Keifu and *Okinawa Iriomote Tankōshi*.

64. Mukai, *Okinawa Kindai Keizaishi*, 113.
65. Iba, *Nangoku no Shirayuri*, 68.
66. Tomiyama, *Kindai Nihon Shakai to Okinawajin*, 133. In the beginning, new communities of emigrants from Okinawa were limited to people from a particular village or region. As more people arrived, communities expanded to include people from the entire prefecture.
67. It shared some leaders with the Zennihon Musan Seinen Dōmei (All Japan Proletarian Youth League). The leading figure of this organization was Inoguchi Masao, the foremost theorist of Okinawa's Marxists and a prominent figure in the *Musansha Shimbun*, the organ paper of the Japanese Communist Party. Urasaki, *Gyakuryū no Naka de*, 244.
68. Tomiyama, *Kindai Nihon Shakai to Okinawajin*, 129–30.
69. Makise, *Nihonshi no Saihakken to Shite no Okinawa no Rekishi*, 359.
70. Gavin Walker examines the emergence of the national question as co-emergent with the spread of capitalism globally and the translation of unevenness into the language of feudal remnants. We see this operation throughout Okinawa prefecture's history, but especially so in the period of capitalist crisis. Walker, "Postcoloniality and the National Question in Marxist Historiography."
71. Matsumoto San'ei, Kuwae Jōkaku, and Shitahaku Kokushin—all based on the mainland—and the local thinkers Higaonna Kanjun, Toguchi Seihyō, and Yamada Yūkan, who had already been organizing labor unions and strikes in the prefecture, formed an alliance at this time. Yamada was very active in the organization of labor unions in Okinawa and represented Naha in the prefectural assembly. For more on him and other Marxists, see Urasaki, *Gyakuryū no Naka de*; Aniya, "Senzen Okinawa ni Okeru Musan Undō."
72. There were many influential thinkers from Okinawa. Tokuda Kyūichi and Inoguchi in particular were very closely allied with the Japanese Communist Party and the organ of its Communist Group, the *Musansha Shimbun*. However, the Rōnōtō (Worker-Farmer Party) was more influential among activists working in the prefecture.
73. Their contributions to the later project have received the most attention from labor historians like Aniya (*Okinawa no Musansha Undō*) and Yoshihara (*Okinawa Minshū Undō no Dentō*).
74. Takemi, "Okinawato Shutsuimin no Keizai Chirigakuteki Kōsatsu."
75. Kinjō I., *Kindai Okinawa no Tetsudō to Kaiun*, 114–15.
76. See Kinjō I., *Kindai Okinawa no Tetsudō to Kaiun*, 114–15; Komatsu, "Seitōgyō no Hatten to Naha no Shokōgyō." OSK was one of the three major commercial shipping companies that aggressively cultivated new routes in the South Seas in the

Taisho period. For the company's activities in the South Seas in the Taisho period, see Yano, "Taishōki 'Nanshinron' no Tokushitsu."

77. Jahana, "Kunigami Chihō Motobu Magiri Somayama no Keikyō," February 7, 1894, *Jahana Noboru Shū*, 41.
78. For details on the report, see Isa, "Jahana Noboru," 291.
79. Although the historical contexts are quite different, it is important to note that reclamation projects that were encouraged without taking prior usage into consideration were common in both Okinawa and Hokkaido during the Meiji era.
80. Mason, *Dominant Narratives of Colonial Hokkaido and Imperial Japan*, 45. This previous history must be taken into account when considering the anger that residents felt about Kinjō's policies of afforestation (discussed below).
81. For details of this in Miyako, see chapter 3.
82. For the deliberations, see the January 27, 1907, session in the House of Peers of the National Diet, *Okinawaken Gikaishi* 8(5):590–600.
83. Kume to the House of Peers of the National Diet, January 27, 1907, *Okinawaken Gikaishi* 8(5):599.
84. Kume to the House of Peers of the National Diet, January 27, 1907, *Okinawaken Gikaishi* 8(5):599.
85. Kume to the House of Peers of the National Diet, January 29, 1907, *Okinawaken Gikaishi* 8(5):607.
86. "Motobu Magiri ni Okeru Tainō Shobun Sōdō," *Ryūkyū Shimpō*, October 9, 1907, *Okinawa Kenshi* 19:344.
87. "Motobu Magiri no Sōdō," *Ryūkyū Shimpō*, December 2, 1907, *Okinawa Kenshi* 19:349.
88. "Nōmin no Futan," *Ryūkyū Shimpō*, October 5, 1911, *Okinawa Kenshi* 17:285.
89. Yamagusuku, "Kunenbo," 26.
90. "Hanejison ni Kōjō Secchi—Ryūkyū Seitōsha Kōjō," *Ryūkyū Shimpō*, December 18, 1916, *Nago Shishi Senzen Shimbun Shūsei* 3:121.
91. The two projects failed for different reasons. The Nago communal factory began operations but did not make an impact on production. Ryūkyū Seitō Gaisha's proposed bunmitsutō factory was never built because the company had financial difficulties and was taken over by Tainansha in 1917.
92. "Bunmitsu Kōjō Secchi Ika wa Kunigamigun ni Daieikyō," *Osaka Asahi*, August 10, 1929, *Nago Shishi Senzen Shimbun Shūsei* 3:174–75. The bank refused to loan the company the money because it was still owed 5.5 million yen.
93. Transactions for this line took place on December 13, 1929 in the prefectural assembly. For the transcript, see *Okinawaken Gikaishi* 4(1):332–33.
94. "Kunigami Kaku Chōson Kumiai to Dattai Gawa to ga Daifunjō o Okosu," *Osaka Asahi*, March 19, 1929, *Nago Shishi Senzen Shimbun Shūsei* 3:174.
95. Ōgimi Village consisted of 9,063 residents and 1,732 families and was divided into ten wards (aza), six hamlets (buraku), and sixteen districts (ku). Kunigami Village was to its north, Higashi Village to its southeast, and Haneji Village to its southwest. For more detailed statistics on the composition of Ōgimi village, see "Ōgimi Son Keizai Kōsei Keikaku," *Ōgimi Sonshi Shiryōhen*, 350–407.

96. Kinjō's diary, published under the name Amano Tansuke, provides important insights into his views on the movement. See *Ōgimi Sonshi Shiryōhen*, 419–88.
97. An October 31, 1916, *Ryūkyū Shimpō* article describes these two men as success stories from Kunigami region who built good reputations and wealth in Naha and the mainland. See "Yanbaru Kikō (17)," *Ryūkyū Shimpō*, October 31, 1916, *Ōgimi Sonshi Shiryōhen*, 550.
98. "Ōgimison Yakuba no Iten Mondai," *Okinawa Mainichi*, August 9, 1911, *Ōgimi Sonshi Shiryōhen*, 524; "Ōgimison Yakuba no Iten Mondai (Zoku)," *Okinawa Mainichi*, August 10, 1911, *Ōgimi Sonshi Shiryōhen*, 525.
99. "Ōgimi no Yakuba Mondai wa Iyoiyo Kaiketsu Seraru," *Okinawa Mainichi*, August 21, 1911, *Ōgimi Sonshi Shiryōhen*, 527.
100. Ōgimi Sonshi Henshū Iinkai, *Ōgimi Sonshi Tsūshi*, 125.
101. Lumber was sent to Naha for sale, and villagers sold firewood to the village store. Camphor manufacture developed into an important industry in Nuuma, Shioya, Takazato, Janagusuku, and Kijoka azas. For more on the development of industry in the village, Ōgimi Sonshi Henshū Iinkai, *Ōgimi Sonshi Tsūshi*, 180. For detailed figures, see the *Ōgimi Son Keizai Kōsei Keikaku* report, in particular, part 9 on forestry reform plans. This report is reprinted in *Ōgimi Sonshi Shiryōhen*, 372–92.
102. In the case of Tsuha Village, a compromise was reached: lands that could not be replanted by the people of the aza would come under the government-managed replanting project. All lands that were included in this project came under state control and supervision. Ōgimi Sonshi Henshū Iinkai, *Ōgimi Sonshi Tsūshi*, 181.
103. This was because village authorities believed that it was unreasonable to abolish all forms of enjoyment without proposing any alternatives and because attempts at prohibiting mōasobi had been met with violent opposition from villagers. Kunigami also experienced problems when it tried to fine women for walking outside on roads with others ("Fūzoku Danpen," *Ryūkyū Shimpō*, November 27, 1899, *Okinawa Kenshi Shiryō Joseishi [Jyō]* 16[1]:78).
104. Ōgimi Sonshi Henshū Iinkai, *Ōgimi Sonshi Tsūshi Ōgimi Sonshi Tsūshi*, 120–21.
105. We must also not neglect Kinjō's reluctance to curb his own alcohol consumption. Drinking parties following village assembly meetings were common, according to his records. See, for example, his diary entry from February 28, 1931, *Ōgimi Sonshi Shiryōhen*, 459.
106. The majority of these fishmongers were women who took the fish to markets in neighboring wards and, at times, as far away as Nago.
107. Figures recorded in the *Ōgimi Son Keizai Kōsei Keikaku* of 1934 show total debts at 402,535 yen, with loans and savings totaling 228,274 yen. Remittances, which averaged just under 3,000 yen a person a year, did not even make a dent in this imbalance but undoubtedly helped individual families with cash income. Fishermen from Ōgimi ventured out to the South Seas islands from the mid-1920s through the early 1930s and to Ishigaki in Yaeyama in the early 1940s. See Tomiyama, *Bōryoku no Yokan* and *Senjō no Kioku*; Yoshimura, *Nihon Henkyōron Josetsu*; Mukai, *Okinawa Kindai Keizaishi*; Kondō, "Gyogyō, Nanshin, Okinawa"; Aniya, "Imin to Dekasegi."

108. Yamashiro, *Yanbaru no Hi*, 29.
109. "Ōgimi Sonsei Sasshin Dōmei Iin, Mura Tōkyōku, Keisatsu o Dangai Shi Chūzaisho o Shūgeki Sen to Su," *Ryūkyū Shimpō*, September 5, 1931, *Ōgimi Sonshi Shiryōhen*, 304.
110. Yamashiro, *Yanbaru no Hi*, 34.
111. In fact, the Ministry of Education ordered people under the age of twenty-five to leave the alliance. This is revealed in Shibata's question about the Ōgimi Village Reform Movement at the Okinawa Prefectural Assembly, December 12, 1931, *Okinawaken Gikaishi* 5(2):141.
112. For the full text of the proposal, see Ōgimi Sonshi Henshū Iinkai, *Ōgimi Sonshi Tsūshi*, 162. Kuchō is the name of the head of the ward (aza), the unit of administration below the village (*mura*).
113. "Ōgimison Funjō Tenmatsu (2)," *Ryūkyū Shimpō*, January 17, 1931, *Ōgimi Sonshi Shiryōhen*, 323.
114. "Ōgimison Funjō Tenmatsu (4)," *Ryūkyū Shimpō*, February 19, 1931, *Ōgimi Sonshi Shiryōhen*, 327.
115. Shibata at the Okinawa Prefectural Assembly, December 12, 1931, *Okinawaken Gikaishi* 5(2):140.
116. Shibata at the Okinawa Prefectural Assembly, December 12, 1931, *Okinawaken Gikaishi* 5(2):140.
117. Shibata at the Okinawa Prefectural Assembly, December 12, 1931, *Okinawaken Gikaishi* 5(2):141.
118. "Ōgimison Funjō Tenmatsu (3)," *Ryūkyū Shimpō*, February 18, 1931, *Ōgimi Sonshi Shiryōhen*, 325–26. Thanks to Gabe Masao for illuminating this link between rain and malaria transmission. At the same time, the successful gathering could also be a taken as a sign of the participants' desperation, as the rainy season leads to reductions in the price of brown sugar. On the relationship between rain and that price, see "Waga kawaii musume o sakan ni uritobasu," *Osaka Asahi*, June 12, 1930, *Nago Shishi Senzen Shimbun Shūsei* 3:179.
119. Yamashiro, *Yanbaru no Hi*, 52–53.
120. Rancière, *The Nights of Labor*, xii.
121. This type of preemptive measure was necessary not just because of the concrete difficulties of Ōgimi's residents but also because if the authorities lost control of the situation, the absolute worst condition might arise, in which people could "formulate their problems themselves, and to determine at least the particular conditions under which they can receive a more general solution" (Deleuze and Guattari, *A Thousand Plateaus*, 471).
122. Morita, "Ōgimi Sonsei Kakushin Dōmei no Tatakai," 76.
123. The consumer cooperative alliance (*Nihon Musansha Shōhikumiai Renmei*, or *Nisshōren*) began operating in Kijoka aza of Ōgimi Village in June 1932 and included a "pioneer" section of elementary school students modeled after the Soviet Young Pioneer Organization. For details on the organization of the pioneer wing in Kijoka, see Monbushō, "Proletaria Kyōiku Undō, Ge"; Yamashiro, *Yanbaru no Hi*; Morita, "Ōgimi Sonsei Kakushin Dōmei no Tatakai."

124. B. Yamazaki, *Nihon Shōhi Kumiai Undōshi*, 285.
125. In "On Cooperation," Lenin explains the importance of the cooperatives for building a socialist society. For an explanation of the ideological differences between the Nisshōren and the Shōhi Kumiai Rengōkai, see Saitō, "Shōwa 6 Nen ni Okeru Waga Kuni Shuyō Rōdō Shōhi Kumiai no Gaikyō (Jyō)"; B. Yamazaki, *Nihon Shōhi Kumiai Undōshi*. In "Shōhi Kumiai Haikyū Ron," Okamoto explains that an ideological shift took place in the consumer cooperative theory. After the red purge (March 15 incident) of 1928, radical consumer cooperative movements declined and almost became extinct.
126. See B. Yamazaki, *Nihon Shōhi Kumiai Undōshi*, 274. For bibliographic references for the radical consumer cooperatives in Japan, see Koyama, *Nihon Rōdō Undō Shakai Undō Shi*, 151–59.
127. Morita, "Ōgimi Sonsei Kakushin Dōmei no Tatakai," 78.
128. Monbushō Gakuseibu, *Proletaria Kyōiku Undō (Ge)*. The creation of this pioneer wing reflected Bolshevik practices (see Mishler, *Raising Reds*) but may also be an example of what James Scott talks about in *Domination and the Arts of Resistance*. There, he explains that strategies of resistance in difficult times often involve using children, who are not subject to the same sorts of punishment by authorities as adults.
129. Mori T., *Senji Nihon Nōson Shakai no Kenkyū*; Kinjō I., "Nōson no Keizai Kōsei Keikaku ni Tsuite"; Fukuchi, *Mura to Sensō*; Ōshiro M., "Senjika no Okinawa Nōson."
130. Deleuze and Guattari, *A Thousand Plateaus*, 203.
131. "Haneji Kōchi Seiri Kōji," *Ryūkyū Shimpō*, August 8, 1915, *Nago Shishi Senzen Shimbun Shūsei* 3:78.
132. "Haneji Kōchi Seiri Kōji (2)," *Ryūkyū Shimpō*, August 21, 1915, *Nago Shishi Senzen Shimbun Shūsei* 3:78–79.
133. Ikehara, *Okinawa Tōgyōron*.
134. "Hanejison Genkagawa no Ayu o Yōshoku Shite Toshijin no Shokutaku o Nigiwasu," *Osaka Asahi*, October 26, 1930, *Nago Shishi Senzen Shimbun Shūsei* 3:182.
135. "Kome Saku Kairyō no Kumiai o Soshiki," *Osaka Asahi*, November 14, 1929, *Nago Shishi Senzen Shimbun Shūsei* 3:175–76.
136. "Honnendo mo Secchi suru Hanejison no Suiden Shidō Danchi," *Okinawa Asahi*, November 11, 1930, *Nago Shishi Senzen Shimbun Shūsei* 3:185.
137. David Harvey investigates the complexities of contemporary struggles against capitalists' socio-ecological projects in *Justice, Nature and the Geography of Difference*.
138. Two main leaders of the Ōgimi movement, Uezato Haruo and Kinjō Kanematsu, began taking an interest in the Arashiyama struggle around September 1931 and began offering advice to the organization (Yamashiro Z., *Yanbaru no Hi*). See also Nakamura, "Fukusū no 'Arashiyama Jiken.'"
139. "Hoyōin Secchi Hantai o Ketsugi, Nakijin Sonmin Taikai," *Osaka Asahi*, March 18, 1932, *Nago Shishi Senzen Shimbun Shūsei* 3:190.
140. "Takebō o Tazusaete Ichidai Jii Undō," *Osaka Asahi*, June 2, 1932, *Nago Shishi Senzen Shimbun Shūsei* 3:192; "Rai Hoyōin Zettai Hantai o Sakebi," *Osaka Asahi*, June 7, 1932, *Nago Shishi Senzen Shimbun Shūsei* 3:193.

141. A man named Miyagi Seiichi was the link between these two movements, physically participating in both. See Yamashiro Z., *Yanbaru no Hi*.
142. Nakamura, "Fukusū no 'Arashiyama Jiken,'" 90.
143. See "Kama Ya Suki de Shokumukanshū o Kyōhaku," *Osaka Asahi*, June 28, 1932, *Nago Shishi Senzen Shimbun Shūsei* 3:197.
144. A sanatorium was eventually built in 1938 on Yagaji, an island under jurisdiction of Nago and near the planned Arashiyama site. See Nakamura, "Fukusū no 'Arashiyama Jiken.'"
145. For works that characterize post-1932 Ōgimi in this way, see Ōshiro M., "Senjika no Okinawa Nōson"; Fukuchi, "Mura to Sensō"; Kabira, *Okinawa 1930 Nendai Zengo no Kenkyū*. For more on the conversion of Japanese villages into model villages in service of the fascist state, see Mori T., "Nihon Fashizumu no Keisei to Nōson Keizai Kōsei Undō" and *Senji Nihon Nōson Shakai no Kenkyū*.

Conclusion

1. The subtitle as it appears in Japanese is "Ryūkyū no Sumikko ni Oshiyarareta Minzoku no Nageki o Kiite Itadakitai." All translations are mine, unless otherwise noted.
2. Katsukata-Inafuku, *Okinawa Joseigaku Kotohajime*.
3. Benjamin, *Illuminations*, 253–64.
4. I understand Kushi's work to be an act of stuttering, defined as a process of becoming minor. On the revolutionary potential of minor literature, see Deleuze and Guattari, *Anti-Oedipus*; Deleuze, *Kafka*, and *Essays Critical and Clinical*.
5. Kushi, "Horobiyuku Ryūkyū Onna no Shoki," 123.
6. See "Irezumi Onna," *Ryūkyū Shimpō*, July 22, 1916, *Okinawa Kenshi* 19:696. The article reported that three women who went to work in the Philippines were sent back to Okinawa. An article published in the *Shimpō* the following day, "Fūzoku Kairyō no Hitsuyō" expressed support for the Prefectural Association's decision and concluded that the majority of the responsibility for discrimination rested with the Okinawans, who did not reform their old customs as thoroughly as was necessary. These new arrivals reflected a shift in the types of people who moved to the Philippines in the period after World War I. For a detailed analysis of these changes, see Aniya, "Imin to Dekasegi"; Mukai, *Okinawa Kindai Keizaishi*.
7. Kushi, "'Horobiyuku Ryūkyū Onna no Shoki' ni Tsuite no Shakumeibun," 226. This is in the apology that Kushi was pressured into writing to the Okinawa Student Association.
8. Kushi, "Horobiyuku Ryūkyū Onna no Shoki," 123.
9. Kushi, "Horobiyuku Ryūkyū Onna no Shoki," 123.
10. Kushi, "Memoirs of a Declining Ryukyuan Woman," 83.
11. Kushi, "Memoirs of a Declining Ryukyuan Woman," 128.
12. The quotes are from Rancière, *The Philosopher and His Poor*, 219.
13. Tomiyama argues that it is vital to treat the wartime experience of mobilization as qualitatively different from everyday life (*Senjō no Kioku*, 51).

14. There is almost no mention of any type of struggle in works on post-1932 and wartime Okinawa except in Tomiyama's work, which presents organized strikes and labor disputes in the South Seas against the wages offered by Nanyō Kōhatsu Kabushiki Gaisha (*Senjō no Kioku*, 94). For more on South Seas colonization, see Takagi, "Nanyō Kōhatsu no Zaisei Jyōkyō to Matsue Haruji no Nanshinron"; Nanpō Keizai Kondankai, *Nanpō Rōdō Jijō Oyobi Taisaku*.
15. A narrative of victimization implicitly grants the state and capital almost exclusive control over the transformation of social, economic, political, and cultural life and renders antagonism in everyday life either ineffectual or nonexistent.
16. For examples of this approach in the context of Ōgimi Village that we examined in chapter 5, see Morita, "Ōgimi Sonsei Kakushin Dōmei no Tatakai"; Ōshiro M., "Senjika no Okinawa Nōson"; Fukuchi, *Mura to Sensō*. All of these works begin with the question of why the peasants of Ōgimi became such docile, model citizens during the economic recovery plan (keizai kōsei keikaku) that was instituted there beginning in 1932.
17. This approach conflates the strategy of maintaining communal production that we examined throughout this work with the success of the Keizai Kōsei policy that unfolded nationwide beginning in 1933. Mori T. expresses this position, stating that the reformist energies of the peasantry were absorbed into the right-wing fascist movement nationwide ("Nihon Fashizumu no Keisei to Nōson Keizai Kōsei Undō"). For different approaches, see Mori T., "Senzen to Sengo no Danzetsu to Renzoku"; Mori and Ōkado, *Chiiki ni Okeru Senji to Sengo*; Yamazaki S., "Senji Kokōgyō Dōin Taisei no Seiritsu to Tenkai."
18. This has led to a strange discourse of betrayal common to many writings about Okinawa's experience during the Battle of Okinawa and the period immediately after World War II. This discourse, often produced by scholars who are quite critical of Japanese policies toward Okinawa on the whole, affirms the policies of incorporation by operating from a logic that renders the state's betrayal all the more egregious because the people of Okinawa were such loyal adherents to emperor-state ideology. This discourse exists implicitly in the writings on Okinawa's wartime mobilization process noted above.

BIBLIOGRAPHY

Akram-Lodhi, A. Haroon, and Cristóbal Kay, eds. "The Agrarian Question: Peasants and Rural Change." In *Peasants and Globalization: Political Economy, Rural Transformation and the Agrarian Question*, edited by A. Haroon Akram-Lodhi and Cristóbal Kay, 3–34. London: Routledge, 2009.

Aldcroft, Derek Howard. *From Versailles to Wall Street, 1919–1929*. Berkeley: University of California Press, 1977.

Althusser, Louis, and Étienne Balibar. *Reading Capital*. Translated by Ben Brewster. New York: Pantheon, 1970.

Amin, Samir. *Accumulation on a World Scale: A Critique of the Theory of Underdevelopment*. Translated by Brian Pearce. New York: Monthly Review, 1974.

Anderson, Benedict. *Imagined Communities: Reflections on the Origin and Spread of Nationalism*. New York: Verso, 1983.

Anderson, Kevin. *Marx at the Margins: On Nationalism, Ethnicity, and Non-Western Societies*. Chicago: University of Chicago Press, 2010.

Aniya Masaaki. "Imin to Dekasegi: Sono Haikei." In *Kindai Okinawa no Rekishi to Minshū*, edited by the Okinawa Rekishi Kenkyūkai, 143–66. Rev. ed. Tokyo: Shigensha, 1977.

———. *Okinawa no Musansha Undō*. Naha, Japan: Hirugisha, 1990.

———. "Senzen Okinawa ni Okeru Musan Undō." *Okinawa Shiryōshitsu Henshūjo Kiyō* 8 (March 1983):1–37.

Arakawa Akira. *Ryūkyū Shobun Igo*. 2 vols. Tokyo: Asahi Shimbunsha, 1981.

Araki Moriaki. "'Kyūkan Onzonki' ni Okeru Okinawa Tōchi Saku." In *Nihon Shihonshugi: Tenkai to Ronri*, edited by Hoshi Makoto, Ishii Kanji, Sakasai Takahito, and Sekiguchi Yoshiyuki, 51–66. Tokyo: Tokyo Daigaku Shuppankai, 1978.

Balibar, Étienne, and Immanuel Wallerstein. *Race, Nation, Class: Ambiguous Identities*. London: Verso, 1991.

Banaji, Jairus. "The Fictions of Free Labour: Contract, Coercion, and So-Called Unfree Labour." *Historical Materialism* 11, no. 3 (2003):69–95.

———. *Theory as History: Essays on Modes of Production and Exploitation*. Chicago: Haymarket, 2011.

Baronian, Laurent. *Marx and Living Labour*. New York: Routledge, 2013.

Barshay, Andrew. *The Social Sciences in Modern Japan: The Marxian and Modernist Traditions*. Berkeley: University of California Press, 2007.

Beillevaire, Patrick. "Assimilation from Within, Appropriation from Without: The Folklore-Studies and Ethnology of Ryukyu/Okinawa." In *Anthropology and Colonialism in Asia and Oceania*, edited by Jan van Bremen and Akitoshi Shimizu, 172–96. Richmond, UK: Curzon Press, 1999.

Benjamin, Walter. *Illuminations: Essays and Reflections*. Translated by Harry Zohn. New York: Schocken, 2007.

Bensaid, Daniel. *Marx for Our Times: Adventures and Misadventures of a Critique*. Translated by Gregory Elliot. New York: Verso, 2002.

Bernstein, Henry, and Terrence J. Byres. "From Peasant Studies to Agrarian Change." *Journal of Agrarian Change* 1, no. 1 (2001):1–56.

Bloch, Ernst. "Nonsynchronism and the Obligation to Its Dialectics." *New German Critique* 11 (Spring 1977):22–38.

Bonefeld, Werner. "The Permanence of Primitive Accumulation: Commodity Fetishism and Social Constitution." *The Commoner* 2 (September 2001). Accessed May 9, 2014. http://www.commoner.org.uk/02deangelis.pdf.

Brenner, Robert. "Agrarian Class Structure and Economic Development in Pre-Industrial Europe." *Past and Present* 70 (February 1976):30–74.

Brown, Philip. *Cultivating Commons: Joint Ownership of Arable Land in Early Modern Japan*. Honolulu: University of Hawaii Press, 2011.

Caffentzis, George. "TPTG's Conversation with George Caffentzis." October 5, 2000. Accessed January 15, 2013. http://www.wildcat-www.de/en/material/tptg_caf.htm.

Chakrabarty, Dipesh. *Provincializing Europe: Postcolonial Thought and Historical Difference*. Princeton, NJ: Princeton University Press, 2000.

Chamberlain, Basil Hall. *Essay in Aid of a Grammar and Dictionary of the Luchuan Language*. Yokohama, Japan: Kelley and Walsh, 1895.

Chatterjee, Partha. "More on Modes of Power and the Peasantry." In *Selected Subaltern Studies*, edited by Ranajit Guha and Gayatri Chakravorty Spivak, 351–90. New York: Oxford University Press, 1988.

Chayanov, A. V. *The Theory of Peasant Economy*. Edited by Daniel Thorner, Basile Kerblay, and R. E. F. Smith. Madison: University of Wisconsin Press, 1986.

Chazkel, Amy, and David Serlin, eds. "New Approaches to Enclosures." Special issue, *Radical History Review* 2011, no. 109 (Winter 2011).

Chinen Zenei, ed. *Shiryō Nōgakushi Jahana Noboru*. Okinawa, Japan: Naha Shuppansha, 1983.

Cuninghame, Patrick. "Italian Feminism, Workerism and Autonomy in the 1970s: The Struggle Against Unpaid Reproductive Labour and Violence." *Amnis* 8 (2008). Accessed January 15, 2013. http://amnis.revues.org/575?lang=en.

Dalla Costa, Mariarosa, and Selma James. *The Power of Women and the Subversion of the Community*. Bristol, UK: Falling Wall, 1972.

Dalton, John E. *Sugar: A Case Study of Government Control*. New York: Macmillan, 1937.

De Angelis, Massimo. "Marx and Primitive Accumulation: The Continuous Character of Capital's 'Enclosures.'" *The Commoner* 2 (September 2001). Accessed May 9, 2014. http://www.commoner.org.uk/02deangelis.pdf.

---. "Separating the Doing and the Deed: Capital and the Continuous Character of Enclosures." December 2002. Accessed March 13, 2014. homepages.uel.ac.uk/M.DeAngelis/enclosures.doc.

Deleuze, Gilles. *Foucault*. Translated by Sean Hand. Minneapolis: University of Minnesota Press, 1983.

---. "What Is a Dispositif?" In *Michael Foucault, Philosopher*, edited by Timothy Armstrong, 159–66. Hempel Heampstead: Harvester Wheatsheaf, 1992.

Deleuze, Gilles, and Félix Guattari. *Anti-Oedipus: Capitalism and Schizophrenia*. Translated by Robert Hurley, Mark Seem, and Helen R. Lane. Minneapolis: University of Minnesota Press, 1983.

---. "'Capitalism: A Very Special Delirium,' an Interview with Gilles Deleuze and Félix Guattari." In *Chaosophy*, edited by Sylvere Lothringer, 35–52. Translated by David L. Sweet, Jarred Becker, and Taylor Adkins. Los Angeles: Autonomedia/Semiotexte, 1995.

---. *Kafka: Toward a Minor Literature*. Translated by Dana Polan. Minneapolis: University of Minnesota Press, 1986.

---. *A Thousand Plateaus: Capitalism and Schizophrenia*. Translated by Brian Massumi. Minneapolis: University of Minnesota Press, 1987.

Deleuze, Gilles, and Elias Sanbar. "The Indians of Palestine." *Discourse* 20, no. 3 (Fall 1998):25–29.

Duus, Peter. *The Abacus and the Sword: The Japanese Penetration of Korea, 1895–1910*. Berkeley: University of California Press, 1995.

---. *Modern Japan*. 2nd ed. New York: Houghton Mifflin, 1998.

Edelman, Marc. "Bringing the Moral Economy Back In . . . to the Study of 21st Century Transnational Peasant Movements." *American Anthropologist* 107, no. 3 (2005):331–45.

Eskildsen, Robert. "Of Civilization and Savages: The Mimetic Imperialism of Japan's 1874 Expedition to Taiwan." *American Historical Review* 107, no. 2 (2002):388–418.

Fanon, Frantz. *Black Skin, White Masks*. Translated by Charles Lam Markmann. New York: Grove, 1967.

Federici, Silvia. *The Caliban and the Witch: Women, the Body and Primitive Accumulation*. New York: Autonomedia, 2004.

Fortunati, Leopoldina. *The Arcane of Reproduction: Housework, Prostitution, Labor and Capital*. Translated by Hilary Creek. New York: Autonomedia, 1995.

Frank, Andre Gunder. *Capitalism and Underdevelopment in Latin America: Historical Studies of Chile and Brazil*. New York: Monthly Review, 1967.

Fukuchi Hiroaki. *Mura to Sensō—Kijoka no Shōwashi*. Naha, Japan: "Mura to Sensō" Kankōkai, 1975.

Fukuoka Katsuhiro. "Meiji Nijyūnendai Nakagoro no Okinawaken Chihō Seido Kaisei no Taidō: Okinawa Kenchō Oyobi Naimushō no Dōkō to 'Chihō Seido Kaiseian' Sakusei Haikei o Chūshin ni." *Okinawa Bunka Kenkyū* 14 (March 1988):91–128.

Fukuokaken Naimubu. *Okinawa Ken Kosaku ni Kansuru Chōsa*. Fukuoka, Japan: Fukuoka ken Naimubu, 1930.

Fukushima Masao and Tokuda Ryōji. "Meiji Shonen no Chōsonkai." In *Chiso Kaisei to Chihō Jichisei 2*, edited by Meiji Shiryō Kenkyū Renrakukai, 121–280. Tokyo: Ochanomizu Shobō, 1956.

Gabe Masao. *Meiji Kokka to Okinawa*. Tokyo: Sanichi Shobō, 1979.

———. "Meiji Shoki no Seifu to Okinawa Chihō: Dasshin Kōdō to Keppan Seiyakusho o Chūshin ni." In *Kindai Nihon Seiji ni Okeru Chūo to Chihō*, edited by Nihon Seiji Gakkai, 79–102. Tokyo: Iwanami Shoten, 1985.

———. "Tōchi Katei ni Okeru Kokka to Shūhen Chiiki: Keppan Seiyakusho Keisei Katei no Seijiteki Igi." *Okinawa Bunka Kenkyū* 4 (July 1977):239–84.

Gaimushō, ed. *Ryūkyū Shozoku Mondai Kankei Shiryō* 8. Tokyo: Honpoō Shoseki, 1980.

Geerligs, H. C. Prinsen. *The World's Cane Sugar Industry: Past and Present*. Cambridge: Cambridge University Press, 2010.

Geertz, Clifford. *Agricultural Involution: The Processes of Ecological Change in Indonesia*. Berkeley: University of California Press, 1963.

Gluck, Carol. *Japan's Modern Myths: Ideology in the Late Meiji Period*. Princeton, NJ: Princeton University Press, 1985.

González, Mike. "José Carlos Mariátegui: Latin America's Forgotten Marxist." *International Socialism* 115 (2007). Accessed May 9, 2014. http://isj.org.uk/index.php4?id=336&issue=115.

Goswami, Manu. *Producing India: From Colonial Economy to National Space*. Chicago: University of Chicago Press, 2004.

Gramlich-Oka, Bettina, and Gregory Smits, eds. *Economic Thought in Early Modern Japan*. Leiden, the Netherlands: Brill, 2010.

Guha, Ranajit. *Dominance without Hegemony: History and Power in Colonial India*. Cambridge, MA: Harvard University Press, 1996.

———. *Elementary Aspects of Peasant Insurgency in Colonial India*. Durham, NC: Duke University Press, 1999.

———. "The Prose of Counter-Insurgency." In *Subaltern Studies II: Writings on South Asian History and Society*, edited by Ranajit Guha, 1–40. New Delhi: Oxford University Press, 1983.

Hardt, Michael, and Antonio Negri. *Commonwealth*. Cambridge, MA: Belknap Press of Harvard University Press, 2009.

———. *Empire*. Cambridge, MA: Harvard University Press, 2001.

———. *Labor of Dionysus: A Critique of the State-Form*. Minneapolis: University of Minnesota Press, 1994.

Harootunian, Harry. "Economic Rehabilitation of the Samurai in the Early Meiji Period." *Journal of Asian Studies* 19, no. 4 (August 1960):433–44.

———. "Figuring the Folk: History, Poetics, and Representation." In *Mirror of Modernity: Invented Traditions of Modern Japan*, edited by Stephen Vlastos, 144–62. Berkeley: University of California Press, 1998.

———. *Overcome by Modernity: History, Culture, and Community in Interwar Japan*. Princeton, NJ: Princeton University Press, 2000.

———. *Toward Restoration: The Growth of Political Consciousness in Tokugawa Japan*. Berkeley: University of California Press, 1970.

Harvey, David. *Justice, Nature and the Geography of Difference*. Oxford: Blackwell, 1996.
——. *The Limits to Capital*. New York: Verso, 2007.
Hattori Shisō, Nakasone Seizen, and Hokama Shuzen, eds. *Iha Fuyū Zenshū* 7. Tokyo: Heibonsha, 1975.
Hendrickx, Katrien. *The Origins of Banana-Fibre Cloth in the Ryūkyūs, Japan*. Leuven, Belgium: Leuven University Press, 2007.
Hentona Chōyū. "Chitsuroku Shobun to Shizoku Jyusan." In *Naha Shishi Tsūshi* 2(1), edited by Naha shi Kikakubu Shishi Henshūshitsu, 145–71. Naha, Japan: Naha shi, 1974.
Higa Michiko. "Bi Kara Yaban E: Hajichi Kara no Kaihō to Kindai Okinawa no Onna Tachi." In *Semegiau Onna to Otoko: Kindai*, edited by Okuda Akiko, 31–77. Tokyo: Fujiwara Shobō, 1995.
Higa Ryōzui. "Satō Goya." In *Okinawa Bungaku Zenshū* 1, edited by Okinawa Bungaku Zenshū Henshu Iinkai, 105–6. Tokyo: Kokusho Kankōkai, 1991.
Higa Shunchō. *Shinkō Okinawa no Rekishi*. Tokyo: Sanichi Shobō, 1970.
Higa Shunchō, Shimota Seiji, and Shinzato Keiji. *Okinawa*. Tokyo: Iwanami Shoten, 1963.
Hirara Shishi Hensan Iinkai, ed. *Hirara Shishi*. 11 vols. Hirara, Japan: Hirarashi, 1976–2005.
Hiyane Teruo. *Jiyū Minken Shisō to Okinawa*. Tokyo: Kenbun Shuppan, 1982.
Hiyane Teruo, and Isa Shinichi, eds. *Ōta Chōfu Senshū*. 3 vols. Tokyo: Daiichi Shobō, 1995.
Hoston, Germaine. *Marxism and the Crisis of Development in Prewar Japan*. Princeton, NJ: Princeton University Press, 1990.
Howland, Douglas. *Borders of Chinese Civilization: Geography and History at Empire's End*. Durham, NC: Duke University Press, 1996.
——. "Samurai Status, Class and Bureaucracy." *Journal of Asian Studies* 70, no. 2 (2011):353–80.
Iba Nantetsu. *Nangoku no Shirayuri*. Tokyo: Shinoue Shuppanbu, 1927.
Ichiki Kitokurō. "Ichiki Shokikan Torishirabesho." In Ryūkyū Seifu. *Okinawa Kenshi* 14, 491–606. Naha, Japan: Ryūkyū Seifu, 1965.
——. "Ryūkyū Kenbun Zakki: Meiji 21 nen Okinawa Ryokō Kiji." In Ryūkyū Seifu, *Okinawa Kenshi* 14, 483–90. Naha, Japan: Ryūkyū Seifu, 1965.
Iha Fuyū. *Ryūkyū Kokonki*. Tokyo: Tōkōshoin, 1926.
——. "Ryūkyū Shobun wa Isshu no Dorei Kaihō Nari." Preface to Kishaba Chōken, *Ryūkyū Kenbunroku: Ichimei Haihan Jiken*. Naha, Japan: Oyadomari Chōteki, 1914.
Ikehara, Shinichi. *Okinawa Tōgyōron*. Naha, Japan: Ryūkyū Bunmitsutō Kōgyōkai, 1969.
Ikemiyagi Sekihō. "Okuma Junsa." 1922. In *Okinawa Bungaku Zenshū* 6, edited by Okinawa Bungaku Zenshū Henshu Iinkai, 51–62. Tokyo: Kokusho Kankōkai, 1993.
Inamura Kenfu. *Miyakojima Shominshi*. Tokyo: Sanichi Shobō, 1972.
Inomata Tsunao. *Nōson Mondai Nyūmon*. Tokyo: Chūō Kōronsha, 1937.
Inoue Kiyoshi and Hatate Isao. "Okinawa to Hokkaido." In *Iwanami Kōza Nihon Rekishi 16 Kindai 3*, edited by Ienaga Saburō, 315–56. Tokyo: Iwanami Shoten, 1962.

Iritakenishi Masaharu, ed. *Yaeyama Tōgyōshi*. Ishigaki, Japan: Ishigakijima Seitō, 1993.
Isa Shinichi. "Jahana Noboru: Kindai Nihon o Kakenuketa Teikō." In *Jahana Noboru Shū*, edited by Isa Shinichi, 249–398. Tokyo: Misuzu Shobō, 1998.
———. "Jahana Noboru Nenpu." In *Jahana Noboru Shū*, edited by Isa Shinichi, 169–248. Tokyo: Misuzu Shobō, 1998.
———, ed. *Jahana Noboru Shū*. Tokyo: Misuzu Shobō, 1998
Ishigakishi, ed. *Ishigaki Shishi Shimbun Shūsei 1*. Ishigakishi, Japan: Ishigaki Shiyakusho, 1983.
Ishikawa Masahide. "Shōke to Shuri, Naha Shizoku no Keizai Katsudō." In *Naha Shishi Tsūshi* 2(1), edited by Naha shi Kikakubu Shishi Henshūshitsu, 181–87. Naha, Japan: Naha shi, 1974
Iwasaki Masaya. *Nōhonshisō no Shakaishi: Seikatsu to Kokutai no Kōsaku*. Kyoto, Japan: Kyoto Daigaku Gakujutsu Shuppankai, 1997.
Ka, Chih-Ming. *Japanese Colonialism in Taiwan: Land Tenure, Development, and Dependency, 1895–1945*. Boulder, CO: Westview, 1998.
Kabira Nario. *Okinawa 1930 Nendai Zengo no Kenkyū*. Tokyo: Fujiwara Shoten, 2004.
———. *Okinawa Senryōka o Ikinuku: Gunyōchi, Tsūka, Dokugasu*. Tokyo: Yoshikawa Bunkō, 2012.
Kajinishi Mitsuhaya. *Nihon Shihonshugi Hattatsushi*. Tokyo: Tōyō Keizai Shimpōsha, 1958.
———. *Nihon Shihonshugi no Botsuraku*. Tokyo: Tokyo Daigaku Shuppankai, 1969.
Kamiya Nobuyuki. "Edo Nobori." In *Shin Ryūkyūshi, Kinsei (Ge)*, edited by Ryūkyū Shimpōsha, 9–36. Naha, Japan: Ryūkyū Shimpōsha, 1993.
Kaneto Sachiko. "1930-nen Zengo no Yaeyama Josei no Shokuminchi Taiwan e no Idō o Unagashita Puru Yōin: Taiwan ni Okeru Shokuminchiteki Kindai to Josei no Shokugyō no Kakudai o Megutte." *Imin Kenkyū* 3 (March 2007):1–26.
Kano Masanao. *Okinawa no Fuchi: Iha Fuyū to Sono Jidai*. Tokyo: Iwanami Shoten, 1993.
Karatani Kojin. *History and Repetition*. New York: Columbia University Press, 2011.
Karl, Rebecca E. *Mao Zedong and China in the Twentieth-Century World: A Concise History*. Durham, NC: Duke University Press, 2010.
Katsukata-Inafuku Keiko. *Okinawa Joseigaku Kotohajime*. Tokyo: Shinjuku Shobō, 2006.
Kawada Yō. "'Hangyaku Bōkoku, Kokkyō Toppa' no Shisō—Futatabi Gyakusetsu to Shite no 'Ajia wa Hitotsu' o Megutte." *Eiga Hihyō* 4, no. 1 (1973).
———. "Nihon Rōdō Undō no 'Kokkyō'—Jichitai Gyōsei no Saihen o Chūshin to Shite." *Gendai no Me* 12, no. 8 (1971):48–59.
———. "Nihon Teikokushugi to Okinawa." *Gendai no Me* 11, no. 10 (1970):102–11.
Kawakami Hajime. "Ryūkyū Itoman no Kojinshugiteki Kazoku." 1911. In *Kawakami Hajime Zenshū* 6, 317–33. Tokyo: Iwanami Shoten, 1982.
———. "Shinjidai Kuru." 1911. In *Okinawa Kenshi* 19, edited by Ryūkyū Seifu, 485. Naha, Japan: Ryūkyū Seifu, 1969.
Kawashima, Ken. *The Proletarian Gamble: Korean Workers in Interwar Japan*. Durham, NC: Duke University Press, 2009.
Kerr, George. *Okinawa: The History of an Island People*. Rev. ed. Boston: Tuttle, 2000.
Kikekawa Hiroshi. *Meiji Chihō Seido Seiritsushi*. Tokyo: Gannandō Shoten, 1967.

Kikuyama Masaaki. "Chikengo ni Okeru Okinawa Tōji Kikō no Seiritsu." *Waseda Hōgaku* 60, no. 3 (1985):103–44.

Kim, Key-Hiuk. *The Last Phase of the East Asian World Order: Korea, Japan, and the Chinese Empire, 1860–1882*. Berkeley: University of California Press, 1980.

Kingston-Mann, Esther. *Lenin and the Problem of Marxist Peasant Revolution*. Oxford: Oxford University Press, 1983.

Kinjō Isao. *Kindai Okinawa no Tetsudō to Kaiun*. Naha, Japan: Hirugisha, 1983.

———. *Kindai Okinawa no Tōgyō*. Naha, Japan: Hirugisha, 1985.

———. "Meijiki no Okinawa no Tōgyō." In *Kindai Okinawa no Rekishi to Minshū*, edited by the Okinawa Rekishi Kenkyūkai, 111–42. Rev. ed. Tokyo: Shigensha, 1977.

———. "Nōson no Keizai Kōsei Keikaku ni Tsuite." *Okinawa Shiryōshitsu Henshūjo Kiyō* 6 (March 1981):25–72.

Kinjō Seitoku. *Ryūkyū Shobun Ron*. Naha, Japan: Okinawa Taimususha, 1980.

———. "'Ryūkyū Shobun' to Nōson Mondai." In *Kindai Okinawa no Rekishi to Minshū*, edited by the Okinawa Rekishi Kenkyūkai, 27–52. Rev. ed. Tokyo: Shigensha, 1977.

Kinoshita Akira. *Nago Isei no Kōzō to Sono Hōkai: Nōson ni Okeru Hōkenteki Rōdō no Kōzō Bunseki*. Tokyo: Ochanomizu Shobō, 1979.

Kishaba Chōken. *Ryūkyū Kenbunroku: Ichimei Haihan Jiken*. Naha, Japan: Oyadomari Chōteki, 1914.

———. *Tōtei Zuihitsu: Kōhon*. Tokyo: Shigensha, 1980.

Kiyomura Kōnin. *Miyakoshi Den*. Tokyo: Fuzambō, 2008.

Komatsu Masaru. "Seitōgyō no Hatten to Naha no Shokōgyō." In *Naha Shishi Tsūshi* 2(2), edited by Naha shi Kikakubu Shishi Henshūshitsu, 349–61. Naha, Japan: Naha shi, 1974.

Komori Yoichi. "Rule in the Name of 'Protection': The Vocabulary of Colonialism." Translated by Michele M. Mason. In *Reading Colonial Japan: Text, Context, and Critique*, edited by Michele M. Mason and Helen Lee, 60–76. Stanford, CA: Stanford University Press, 2012.

Kondō, Kenichi. "Gyogyō, Nanshin, Okinawa." In *Nihon Teikokushugi Shi*, edited by Ōishi Kaichirō, 153–79. Tokyo: Tokyo Daigaku Shuppankai, 1987.

Koyama Hirotake. *Nihon Rōdō Undō Shakai Undō Shi*. Tokyo: Sangatsu Shobō, 1957.

Kubo Fumikatsu. "Gansha Baishū Kakaku o Meguru Seitō Gaisha to Taiwan Nōmin no Kankei: 'Nakase Monjo' o Tegakari ni." *Chūō Daigaku Shōgakubu* 47, nos. 5–6 (2006):1–103.

———, ed. *Kindai Seitōgyō no Hatten to Tōgyō Rengōkai: Kyōsō o Kichō to Shita Kyōchō no Mosaku*. Tokyo: Nihon Keizai Hyōronsha, 2009.

Kurima Yasuo. "Gunyōchiryō Hikiage no Keika to Genzai: Ginowanshi o Chūshin ni." *Okinawa Kokusai Daigaku Keizai Ronshū* 1, no. 1 (2005):21–33.

———. *Okinawa Keizai no Gensō to Genjitsu*. Tokyo: Nihon Keizai Hyōronsha, 1998.

———. *Okinawa no Nōgyō: Rekishi no Naka de Kangaeru*. Tokyo: Nihon Keizai Hyōronsha, 1979.

Kuroshima Tameichi. "Jintōzei." In *Shin Ryūkyūshi, Kinsei (Ge)*, edited by Ryūkyū Shimpōsha, 129–68. Naha, Japan: Ryūkyū Shimpōsha, 1993.

Kushi Fusako. "Horobiyuku Ryūkyū Onna no Shoki: Ryūkyū no Sumikko ni Oshiyarareta Minzoku no Nageki o Kiite Itadakitai." *Fujin Kōron* 17 (June 1932):122–28.

———. "'Horobiyuku Ryūkyū Onna no Shoki' ni Tsuite no Shakumeibun." *Fujin Kōron* 17 (July 1932): 226–27.

———. "In Defense of 'Memoirs of a Declining Ryukyuan Woman.'" Translated by Kimiko Miyagi. In *Southern Exposure: Modern Japanese Literature from Okinawa*, edited by Michael Molasky and Steve Rabson, 81–83. Honolulu: University of Hawaii Press, 2000.

———. "Memoirs of a Declining Ryukyuan Woman." Translated by Kimiko Miyagi. In *Southern Exposure: Modern Japanese Literature from Okinawa*, edited by Michael Molasky and Steve Rabson, 73–80. Honolulu: University of Hawaii Press, 2000.

Lenin, V. I. "On Cooperation." 1923. In *V.I. Lenin: Collected Works* 33, edited by David Skvirsky and George Hanna, 427–35. Moscow: Progress, 1965.

Lewis, W. Arthur. "Economic Development with Unlimited Supplies of Labor." *Manchester School of Economic and Social Studies* 22 (May 1954):139–91.

Loo, Tze May. *Heritage Politics: Shuri Castle and Okinawa's Incorporation into Modern Japan, 1879–2000*. New York: Lexington Books, 2014.

Majikina Ankō and Shimakura Ryūji. *Okinawa Issennenshi*. Fukuoka, Japan: Okinawa Shinminpōsha, 1923.

Makise Tsuneji. *Nihonshi no Saihakken to Shite no Okinawa no Rekishi*. Tokyo: Chōbunsha, 1971.

Mamdani, Mahmood. *Citizen and Subject: Contemporary Africa and the Legacy of Late Colonialism*. Princeton, NJ: Princeton University Press, 1996.

Mariátegui, José Carlos. *Seven Interpretive Essays on Peruvian Reality*. Translated by Marjory Urquidi. Austin: University of Texas Press, 1971.

Marx, Karl. *Capital: A Critique of Political Economy*. Translated by Ben Fowkes. New York: Penguin, 1990.

———. *The 18th Brumaire of Louis Bonaparte*. Translated by Daniel De Leon. Rockville, MD: Wildside, 2008.

———. *Grundrisse*. Translated by Ben Fowkes. New York: Penguin, 1993.

———. *Pre-Capitalist Economic Formations*. Translated by Jack Cohen. New York: International Publishers, 1965.

———. *Theories of Surplus Value*. 3 vols. Translated by Emile Burns. New York: Prometheus, 2000.

Mason, Michele. *Dominant Narratives of Colonial Hokkaido and Imperial Japan: Envisioning the Periphery and the Modern Nation-State*. New York: Palgrave Macmillan, 2012.

Matayoshi Morikiyo. "Okinawa Josei to Taiwan Shokuminchi Shihai." *Okinawa Bunka Kenkyū* 16 (March 1990):329–52.

Matsuda, Hiroko. "Becoming Japanese in the Colony: Okinawan Migrants in Colonial Taiwan." *Cultural Studies* 26, no. 5 (2012):688–709.

———. "Colonial Modernity across the Border: Yaeyama, the Ryūkyū Islands, and Colonial Taiwan." PhD diss., Australian National University, 2006.

Matsuda Michiyuki. "Ryūkyū Han Shobun An." 1878. In *Meiji Bunka Shiryō Sōsho* 4, edited by Shimomura Fujio, 201–4. Tokyo: Kazama Shobō, 1962.

Matsuoka Masao. *Sekirara ni Mita Ryūkyū no Genjyō*. Osaka: Osaka Mainichi Shimbunsha, 1926.

Mazumdar, Sucheta. *Sugar and Society in China: Peasants, Technology, and the World Market*. Cambridge, MA: Harvard University Asia Center, 1998.

Mbembe, Achille. "African Modes of Self-Writing." Translated by Steven Rendall. *Public Culture* 14, no. 1 (2002):239–73.

McGillivray, Gillian. *Blazing Cane: Sugar Communities, Class, and State Formation in Cuba, 1868–1959*. Durham, NC: Duke University Press, 2009.

McMichael, Philip. "Peasants Make Their Own History, But Not Just as They Please. . . ." *Journal of Agrarian Change* 8, nos. 2–3 (2008):205–28.

Meillassoux, Claude. *Maidens, Meal and Money: Capitalism and the Domestic Community*. Translated by Felicity Edholm. New York: Cambridge University Press, 1991.

Meisner, Maurice. *Mao's China and After: A History of the People's Republic*. New York: Free Press, 1999.

Mezzadra, Sandro. "The Topicality of Prehistory: A New Reading of Marx's Analysis of 'So-called Primitive Accumulation.'" Translated by Arianna Bove. *Rethinking Marxism* 23, no. 2 (July 2011):302–21.

Mezzadra, Sandro, and Brett Neilson. *Border as Method, or, the Multiplication of Labor*. Durham, NC: Duke University Press, 2013.

Mies, Maria. *Patriarchy and Accumulation on a World Scale: Women in the International Division of Labor*. New York: Zed, 1999.

Miki Takeshi. *Okinawa Iriomote Tankōshi*. Tokyo: Nihon Keizai Hyōronsha, 1996.

———. *"Yaeyama Gasshūkoku" no Keifu*. Ishigaki, Japan: Nanzansha, 2010.

———. *Yaeyama Kindai Minshūshi*. Tokyo: Sanichi Shobō, 1979.

Mintz, Sidney. *Caribbean Transformations*. New York: Columbia University Press, 1989.

———. *Sweetness and Power: The Place of Sugar in Modern History*. New York: Penguin, 1986.

———. *Worker in the Cane: A Puerto Rican Life History*. New York: W. W. Norton, 1974.

Mishler, Paul. *Raising Reds: The Young Pioneers, Radical Summer Camps, and Communist Political Culture in the United States*. New York: Columbia University Press, 1999.

Miyagi Eishō. *Okinawa Joseishi*. Naha, Japan: Okinawa Taimususha, 1973.

———. *Okinawa no Noro no Kenkyū*. Tokyo: Yoshikawa Kōbunkan, 1979.

Miyahira Shinya. "Ichiki Kitokurō no Jichikan to Okinawa Chōsa." *Okinawa Bunka Kenkyū* (March 2000):341–78.

Miyako Kyōiku Bukai. *Miyakojima Kyōdoshi*. Hirara, Japan: Okinawa Ken Miyako Kyōikubu, 1937.

Miyakojimashi Kyōiku Iinkai, ed. *Meijiki Miyakojima no Kyūkan Chōsa Shiryō*. Accessed March 16, 2014. http://www.city.miyakojima.lg.jp/kanko/bunkazai/shishi.html.

Mizuno, Norihito. "Early Meiji Policies Toward the Ryukyus and the Taiwanese Aboriginal Territories." *Modern Asian Studies* 43, no. 3 (May 2009):683–739.

Monbushō Gakuseibu. *Proletaria Kyōiku Undō (Ge)*. April 1933.

Mori Takemaro. "Nihon Fashizumu no Keisei to Nōson Keizai Kōsei Undō." *Rekishigaku Kenkyū* (October 1971):135–52.

———. *Senji Nihon Nōson Shakai no Kenkyū*. Tokyo: Tokyo Daigaku Shuppankai, 1999.

———. "Senzen to Sengo no Danzetsu to Renzoku: Nihon Kindaishi Kenkyū no Kadai." *Hitotsubashi Ronsō* 127, no. 6 (2002):639–54.

Mori Takemaro, and Ōkado Masakatsu. *Chiiki ni Okeru Senji to Sengo: Shōnai Chihō no Nōson Toshi Shakai Undō.* Tokyo: Nihon Keizai Hyōronsha, 1996.

Mori Yoshio. "Ryūkyū Wa 'Shobun' Sareta Ka." *Rekishi Hyōron* 603 (July 2000):44–59.

———. *Tsuchi no Naka no Kakumei: Okinawa Sengoshi ni Okeru Sonzai no Kaihō.* Tokyo: Gendaikikakushitsu, 2010.

Morita Toshio. "Ōgimi Sonsei Kakushin Dōmei no Tatakai—Okinawa Ken ni Okeru Kakumeiteki Dentō no Hitotsu to Shite." *Bunka Hyōron* 147 (October 1973):69–83.

Mukai Kiyoshi. *Okinawa Kindai Keizaishi: Shihon Shugi no Hattatsu to Henkyōchi Nōgyō.* Tokyo: Nihon Keizai Hyōronsha, 1988.

Nago Shishi Hensan Iinkai, ed. *Nago Shishi Senzen Shimbun Shūsei* 3. Nago, Japan: Nagoshi, 1985.

Nahashi Kikakubu Shishi Henshūshitsu, ed. *Naha Shishi.* 33 vols. Naha: Naha shi, 1968–2004.

Nakachi Soushun. "Senzenki Okinawa no Nōson ni Okeru Rōdō Kōkan Kankō no Kōzō: Kokutō no Seizō ni Okeru Yuimaaru o Taishō ni." *Sonraku Shakai Kenkyū* 7, no. 2 (March 2001):13–24.

Nakachi Tetsuo. "Kinsei Ryūkyū no Sonraku to Hyakushō." *Okinawa Kokusai Daigaku Shakai Bunka Kenkyū* 8, no. 1 (2005):1–26.

Nakae Junichi. "Okinawa Ken 'Tochi Seiri' to Shōhin Seisan Nōgyō no Tenkai: Senzen Okinawa ni Okeru Nōgyō Tochi Mondai." *Tochi Seido Shigaku* 16, no. 4 (July 1974):42–60.

Nakahara Zenchū. "Okinawa Gendai Sangyō Keizaishi." *Okinawa* 18 (May 1952).

———. *Nakahara Zenchū Zenshū* 1. Naha, Japan: Okinawa Taimususha, 1977.

———. *Nakahara Zenchū Senshū (Jyō).* Naha, Japan: Okinawa Taimususha, 1969.

Nakamatsu Yashū. *Kosō no Mura: Okinawa Minzoku Bunkaron.* Naha, Japan: Okinawa Taimususha, 1978.

Nakamura Bunya. "Fukusū no 'Arashiyama Jiken'—'Airakuen' Kaien Mae no Okinawa ni Okeru Hansenbyō no Ichi Isō." *Yamaguchi Kenritsu Daigaku Shakai Fukushi Gakubu Kiyō* 13 (March 2007):73–105.

Nakasone Masashi. "Kinsei Miyako no Jintōzei to Sono Haishi Undō." In *Kinsei Ryūkyū no Sozei Seido to Jintōzei,* edited by Okinawa Kokusai Daigaku Nantō Bunka Kenkyūjo, 216–40. Tokyo: Nihon Keizai Hyōronsha, 2003.

Nakayoshi Chōkō. *Okinawaken Tōgyō Ron.* 1906. In *Meiji Zenki Sangyō Hattatsushi Shiryō Bessatsu,* edited by Meiji Bunken Shiryō Kankōkai 103(4). Tokyo: Meiji Bunken Shiryō Kankōkai, 1971.

———. "Ryūkyū no Jiwari Seido (3)." *Shigaku Zasshi* 39, no. 8 (1928):797–830.

Namihira Isao. "Kindai Shoki Miyakojima no Daijinushi." *Okinawa Kokusai Daigaku Bunka Kenkyū* 2, no. 1 (1998):93–120.

———. *Kindai Shoki Nantō no Jinushizō: Kindai e no Ikōki Kenkyū.* Tokyo: Daiichi Shobō, 1999.

Namimatsu Nobuhisa. "Jahana Noboru no Nōgyō Shisō: Okinawa to Kindai Nōgaku no Deai." *Kyoto Sangyō Daigaku Ronshū* 35 (March 2006):25–54.

———. "Majikina Ankō to Okinawa Shigaku no Keisei." *Kyoto Sangyō Daigaku Ronshū* 45 (March 2012):1–34.

———. "Sasamori Gisuke to Chiiki Shinkō: 'Nantō Tanken' o Megutte." *Kyoto Sangyō Daigaku Ronshū* 38 (March 2008):116–46.

Nanpō Keizai Kondankai, *Nanpō Rōdō Jijō Oyobi Taisaku*. Tokyo: Nanpō Keizai Kondankai, 1942.

Negri, Antonio. *Insurgencies: Constituent Power and the Modern State*. Translated by Maurizia Boscagli. Minneapolis: University of Minnesota Press, 2009.

———. *Marx beyond Marx: Lessons on the Grundrisse*. Translated by Harry Cleaver, Michael Ryan, and Maurizio Viano. South Hadley, MA: Bergin and Garvey, 1984.

———. *The Porcelain Workshop: For a New Grammar of Politics*. Translated by Noura Wedell. Los Angeles: Semiotext(e), 2008.

Nelson, Christopher. *Dancing with the Dead: Memory, Performance, and Everyday Life in Postwar Okinawa*. Durham, NC: Duke University Press, 2008.

Nishi Masahiko and Hara Takehiko, eds. *Fukusū no Okinawa: Diasupora Kara Kibō e*. Kyoto: Jinbun Shoin, 2003.

Nishihara Fumio. *Okinawa Kindai Keizaishi no Hōhō*. Naha, Japan: Hirugisha, 1991.

Nishizato Kikō. "Okinawa Kindaishi ni Okeru Hontō to Sakishima." In *Kindai Okinawa no Rekishi to Minshū*, edited by the Okinawa Rekishi Kenkyūkai, 189–228. Rev. ed. Tokyo: Shigensha, 1977.

———, ed. *Ryūkyū Kyūkoku Seigansho Shūsei*. Tokyo: Hōsei Daigaku Kenkyūjyo, 1992.

———. "Ryūkyū Kyūkoku Undō to Nihon Shinkoku." *Okinawa Bunka Kenkyū* 13 (February 1987):25–106.

Nomura Yasushi. "Okinawa Ken Chihō Seido Kaisei no Ken." 1895. In *Okinawa Kenshi* 13, edited by Ryūkyū Seifu, 596–604. Naha, Japan: Ryūkyū Seifu, 1966.

Norman, E. H. *Japan's Emergence as a Modern State: Political and Economic Problems of the Meiji Period*. New York: Institute of Pacific Relations, 1940.

Nōshōmushō Nōmukyoku. *Satō ni Kansuru Chōsa*. Tokyo: Nōshōmushō Nōmukyoku, 1913.

Ōgimi Sonshi Henshū Iinkai, ed. *Ōgimi Sonshi Shiryōhen*. Ōgimi, Japan: Ōgimison, 1978.

———, ed. *Ōgimi Sonshi Tsūshi*. Ōgimi, Japan: Ōgimison, 1979.

Oguma Eiji. *A Genealogy of 'Japanese' Self-Images*. Translated by David Askew. Melbourne, Australia: Trans Pacific Press, 2002.

Ōhata Tokushirō. "Okinawa no Ichi—Sono Rekishiteki Tenbō (1)." *Waseda Hōgakkai* 48, no. 1 (1972):51–73.

Ōishi Kaichirō. *Kindai Nihon no Chihō Jichi*. Tokyo: Tokyo Daigaku Shuppan, 1990.

Okamoto Rikichi. "Shōhi Kumiai Haikyū Ron." *Shakai Keizai Kenkyū* 5 (December 1947):1–28.

Okihiro, Gary. *Cane Fires: The Anti-Japanese Movement in Hawaii, 1865–1945*. Philadelphia: Temple University Press, 1992.

Okinawa Josei Monogatari. Naha, Japan: Okinawa Fūdokisha, 1969.

Okinawa Rekishi Kenkyūkai, ed. *Kindai Okinawa no Rekishi to Minshū*. Rev. ed. Tokyo: Shigensha, 1977.

Okinawaken Bunka Shinkōkai, ed. *Okinawa Kenshi Shiryō Joseishi (Jyō)* 16(1). Naha, Japan: Okinawaken Kyōikuiinkai, 2003.

Okinawaken Gikai Jimukyoku, ed. *Okinawaken Gikaishi*. 21 vols. Naha, Japan: Okinawaken Gikai, 1984–2005.

"Okinawaken Naha no Seibo Shinnen Kiji oyobi Zu." *Fūzoku Gahō*, December 1893.

"Okinawaken no Konin oyobi Soshiki." *Fūzoku Gahō*, April 1892.

Okinawaken Yaeyama Shichō. *Yaeyama Gunsei Yōran*. Yaeyama, Japan: Yaeyama Shichō, 1932.

Ono Bunei. *Seito Konzern Dokuhon*. Tokyo: Sunjūsha, 1938.

Ortner, Sherry. *Anthropology and Social Theory: Culture, Power, and the Acting Subject*. Durham, NC: Duke University Press, 2006.

Ōsato Kōei. *Jahana Noboru Den: Okinawa Kaihō no Senkusha*. Tokyo: Taihei Shuppansha, 1970.

———. *Okinawa no Jiyū Minken Undō: Senkusha Jahana Noboru no Shisō to Kōdō*. Tokyo: Taihei Shuppansha, 1969.

Ōshiro Masayasu. "Senjika no Okinawa Nōson—Ōgimi Son no Jiriki Kōsei Undō o Chūshin ni." *Okinawaken Okinawa Shiryō Henshūjo Kiyō* 4 (March 1979):46–72.

Ōta Chōfu. *Okinawa Kensei Gojyūnen*. Tokyo: Kokumin Kyōikusha, 1932.

Ōta Masahide. *Kindai Okinawa no Seiji Kōsō*. Tokyo: Keisō Shobō, 1972.

Oyadomari Kōei. *Okinawa Yo Tachiagare*. Tokyo: Shinkōsha, 1933.

Ozaki Saburō. "Okinawa Ken Shisatsu Fukumeisho." In *Ozaki Saburō, Iwamura Michitoshi Okinawa Kankei Shiryō*, edited by Okinawaken Okinawa Shiryō Henshūjo. Naha, Japan: Okinawa Ken Kyōiku Iinkai, 1980.

Park, Hyun Ok. *Two Dreams in One Bed: Empire, Social Life and the Origins of the North Korean Revolution in Manchuria*. Durham, NC: Duke University Press, 2005.

Perelman, Michael. *The Invention of Capitalism: Classical Political Economy and the Secret History of Primitive Accumulation*. Durham, NC: Duke University Press, 2000.

Poulantzas, Nicos. *Political Power and Social Classes*. New York: Verso, 1975.

Rabson, Steve. *The Okinawan Diaspora in Japan: Crossing Borders Within*. Honolulu: University of Hawaii Press, 2012.

Rancière, Jacques. *The Nights of Labor: The Workers' Dream in Nineteenth-Century France*. Translated by John Drury. Philadelphia, PA: Temple University Press, 1989.

Read, Jason. "The Age of Cynicism: Deleuze and Guattari on the Production of Subjectivity in Capitalism." In *Deleuze and Politics*, edited by Nicholas Thoburn and Ian Buchanan, 139–59. New York: Routledge, 2000.

———. "The Antagonistic Ground of Constitutive Power: An Essay on the Thought of Antonio Negri." *Rethinking Marxism* 11, no. 2 (Summer 1999):1–17.

———. *The Micropolitics of Capital: Marx and the Prehistory of the Present*. Albany: State University of New York Press, 2003.

———. "Primitive Accumulation: The Aleatory Foundation of Capitalism." *Rethinking Marxism* 14, no. 2 (Summer 2002):24–49.

———. "A Universal History of Contingency: Deleuze and Guattari on the History of Capitalism." *borderlands* 2, no. 3 (2003). Accessed May 9, 2014. http://www.borderlands.net.au/vol2no3_2003/read_contingency.htm.

Redfield, Robert. *The Little Community: Viewpoints for the Study of a Human Whole*. Chicago: University of Chicago Press, 1995.

Robertson, Jennifer. *Native and Newcomer: Making and Remaking a Japanese City.* Berkeley: University of California Press, 1994.

Roitman, Janet. *Anti-Crisis.* Durham, NC: Duke University Press, 2013.

Ross, Kristin. "Rancière and the Practice of Equality." *Social Text* 29 (1991):57–71.

Rostow, Walt. *The Stages of Economic Growth: A Non-Communist Manifesto.* Cambridge: Cambridge University Press, 1960.

Rowe, J. W. F. *Markets and Men: A Study in Artificial Control Schemes in Primary Industries.* Cambridge: Cambridge University Press, 1936.

Ryūkyū Seifu, ed. *Okinawa Kenshi.* 24 vols. Naha: Ryūkyū Seifu, 1965–1977.

Sagara Suteo. *Keizaijō Yori Mitaru Taiwan no Tōgyō.* Tokyo: Sagara Suteo, 1919.

Saitō Hiroshi. "Shōwa 6 Nen ni Okeru Waga Kuni Shuyō Rōdō Shōhi Kumiai no Gaikyō (Jyō)." *Ōhara Shakai Mondai Kenkyūjo Zasshi* 1, no. 4 (1934):31–36.

Sakai, Robert K. "The Ryūkyū (Liu-chiu) Islands as a Fief of Satsuma." In *The Chinese World Order: Traditional China's Foreign Relations,* edited by John King Fairbank, 112–34. Cambridge, MA: Harvard University Press, 1968.

———. "The Satsuma-Ryūkyū Trade and the Tokugawa Seclusion Policy." *Journal of Asian Studies* 23, no. 3 (1964):391–403.

Sakamaki Shunzō. "Ryūkyū and Southeast Asia." *Journal of Asian Studies* 23, no. 3 (1964):383–89.

Sakamoto Shuichi. "Okinawa Kindai Keizaishi Kenkyū no Seika to Kadai: Tochi Seiri—Senji Keizaiki ni Kansuru Shuyō Bunken no Shōkai to Kaisetsu o Kanaete." *Kyūshū Kokusai Daigaku Keizai Ronshū* 5, no. 3 (1999):72–102.

Sakisaka Itsurō. *Nōgyō Mondai.* Tokyo: Iwanami Bunko, 1946.

Sasamori Gisuke. *Nantō Tanken,* edited by Azuma Yoshimochi. 2 vols. Tokyo: Heibonsha, 1996.

Scott, James C. *The Art of Not Being Governed: An Anarchist History of Upland Southeast Asia.* New Haven, CT: Yale University Press, 2010.

———. *Domination and the Arts of Resistance: Hidden Transcripts.* New Haven, CT: Yale University Press, 1992.

———. "The Erosion of Patron-Client Bonds and Social Change in Rural Southeast Asia." *Journal of Asian Studies* 32, no. 1 (1972):5–37.

———. *The Moral Economy of the Peasant: Rebellion and Subsistence in Southeast Asia.* New Haven, CT: Yale University Press, 1976.

Shadanhōjin Tōgyō Kyōkai, ed. *Kindai Nihon Tōgyōshi (Jyō).* Tokyo: Keisō Shobō, 1962.

Shanin, Teodor. "Chayanov's Message: Illuminations, Miscomprehensions, and the Contemporary 'Development Theory.'" Introduction for A. V. Chayanov, *The Theory of Peasant Economy.* Edited by Daniel Thorner, Basile Kerblay, and R. E. F. Smith. Madison: University of Wisconsin Press, 1986.

———. "Chayanov's Treble Death and Tenuous Resurrection: An Essay about Understanding, about Roots of Plausibility and about Rural Russia." *Journal of Peasant Studies* 36, no. 1 (2009):83–101.

———, ed. *Late Marx and the Russian Road: Marx and the "Peripheries of Capitalism."* New York: Monthly Review, 1983.

———. "Marx, Marxism and the Agrarian Question I: Marx and the Peasant Commune." *History Workshop*, no. 12 (1981):108–28.

———. "The Peasantry as a Political Factor." *Sociological Review* 14 (March 1966):5–10.

Shimabuku, Annmaria. "Petitioning Subjects: Miscegenation in Okinawa from 1945 to 1952 and the Crisis of Sovereignty." *Inter-Asia Cultural Studies* 11, no. 3 (2010):355–74.

Shimajiri Katsutarō. "Miyako no Naagu ni Tsuite no Oboegaki." *Okinawa Daigaku Kiyō* 7 (1990):17–26.

———. "Miyako Nōmin no Jintōzei Haishi Undō." In *Kindai Okinawa no Rekishi to Minshū*, edited by the Okinawa Rekishi Kenkyūkai, 53–80. Rev. ed. Tokyo: Shigensha, 1977.

Shimoda Masami. "Ryūkyū Yo Dokoeiku." 1929. In *Okinawa Kyūsai Ronshū*, edited by Wakugami Rōjin, 53–86. Naha, Japan: Ryūkyū Shiryō Fukoku Hanpukai, 1969.

Shinfuku Yasutaka. "Ryōtai Shoki no Tōgyō Chōsa, Seisaku Ritsuan ni Tsuite." *Tōyō Shihō* 9 (March 2003):40–57.

Shinjō Chōkō. *Hinshi no Ryūkyū*. Tokyo: Etsuzandō, 1925.

Shōwa Seitō Kabushiki Gaisha 10 Nen Shi. 1937. In *Shashi De Miru Nihon Keizaishi: Shokuminchi Hen* 16, edited by Namikata Shōichi, Kimura Kenji, and Sunaga Noritake, 211–31. Tokyo: Yumani Shobō, 2003.

Shōzan Sahiretsu. *Okinawa Fūzoku no Zu*. 1889. University of Hawaii, Sakamaki/Hawley Collection.

Sivaramakrishnan, Kalyanakrishnan. "Introduction to 'Moral Economies, State Spaces, and Categorical Violence.'" *American Anthropologist* 107, no. 3 (2005):321–30.

Smith, Neil. *Uneven Development: Nature, Capital and the Production of Space*. 3rd ed. Athens: University of Georgia Press, 2008.

Smits, Gregory. "Jahana Noboru: Okinawan Activist and Scholar." In *The Human Tradition in Modern Japan*, edited by Anne Walthall, 99–114. Wilmington, DE: Rowman and Littlefield, 2002.

———. *Visions of Ryūkyū: Identity and Ideology in Early-Modern Thought and Politics*. Honolulu: University of Hawaii Press, 1999.

Stoler, Ann. *Along the Archival Grain: Epistemic Anxieties and Colonial Common Sense*. Princeton, NJ: Princeton University Press, 2009.

Sugihara Tamae. *Kazokusei Nōgyō no Suiten Katei: Kenia Okinawa ni Miru Kanshū to Keizai no Aida*. Tokyo: Nihon Keizai Hyōronsha, 1994.

Sugimoto Nobuo. "Jintōzei ni Kakawaru Miyako, Yaeyama no Minyō." In *Kinsei Ryūkyū no Sozei Seido to Jintōzei*, edited by Okinawa Kokusai Daigaku Nantō Bunka Kenkyūjo. Tokyo: Nihon Keizai Hyōronsha, 2003.

———. *Okinawa no Minyō*. Tokyo: Shin Nihon Shuppansha, 1974.

Sugiyama, Mitsunobu. "The World Conception of Japanese Social Science: The Kōza Faction, the Ōtsuka School, and the Uno School of Economics." In *New Asian Marxisms*, edited by Tani Barlow, 205–46. Durham, NC: Duke University Press, 2002.

Sunakawa Gensei. "Kindai Shiryō (Kaidai)." In *Hirara Shishi* 4(2), edited by Hirara Shishi Hensan Iinkai, 1–8. Hirara, Japan: Hirarashi, 1978.

———. "Teigaku Jintō Haifuzei Seidoka no Nenkō Awa, Nenkō Hanfu." In *Kinsei Ryūkyū no Sozei Seido to Jintōzei*, edited by Okinawa Kokusai Daigaku Nantō Bunka Kenkyūjo, 145–72. Tokyo: Nihon Keizai Hyōronsha, 2003.

Tainan Seitō Kabushiki Gaisha Hōkokusho. 1918–31. Okinawa Prefectural Archives retrieval code T00016045B.

Taira Katsuyasu. *Kindai Nihon Saisho no "Shokuminchi" Okinawa to Kyūkan Chōsa 1872–1908*. Tokyo: Fujiwara Shobō, 2011.

———. "Meiji 17-Nen no Okinawaken Kyūkan Chōsa to Sono Haikei." *Okinawa Bunka Kenkyū* 35 (March 2009):105–42.

Taira Yoshitoshi. *Sengo Okinawa to Beigun Kichi: "Jyuyō" to "Kyozetsu" no Hazama de 1945–1972*. Tokyo: Hōsei Daigaku Shuppankyoku, 2012.

Takagi Shigeki. "Nanyō Kōhatsu no Zaisei Jyōkyō to Matsue Haruji no Nanshinron." *Ajia Keizai* 49, no. 11 (2008):26–46.

Takara Kurayoshi. "Kaijō Kōtsūshi no Shosō." In *Shin Ryūkyūshi, Kinsei (Ge)*, edited by Ryūkyū Shimpōsha, 285–306. Naha, Japan: Ryūkyū Shimpōsha, 1993.

———. *Ryūkyū Ōkoku*. Tokyo: Iwanami Shoten, 1993.

Takemi Yoshiji. "Okinawato Shutsuimin no Keizai Chirigakuteki Kōsatsu." *Chirigaku Hyōron* 4, nos. 2 and 3 (1928):135–56 and 248–83.

Taminato Tomoaki. "Kindai ni Okeru Okinawa." In *Iwanami Kōza Nihon Rekishi* 16 Gendai 3, edited by Asao Naohiro, 213–40. Tokyo: Iwanami Shoten, 1976.

———. "Kinsei Makki no Okinawa Nōson ni Tsuite no Ichi Kōsatsu—Jikata Yakuninsō no Ugoki o Chūshin ni." *Ryūkyū Daigaku Kyōikubu Kiyō* 8 (June 1965):149–63.

Tamura Hiroshi. *Ryūkyū Kyōsan Sonraku no Kenkyū*. Tokyo: Oka Shoin, 1927.

Tanigawa Kenichi. "Kitaguni no Tabibito: Nakamura Jussaku to Okinawa Jintōzei Haishi Undō." *Chūō Kōron* 85, no. 7 (1970):314–43.

Tanji, Miyume. *Myth, Protest and Struggle in Okinawa*. New York: Routledge, 2006.

Taussig, Michael. *The Devil and Commodity Fetishism in South America*. 30th anniversary ed. Chapel Hill: University of North Carolina Press, 2010.

Thoburn, Nicholas. *Deleuze, Marx and Politics*. New York: Routledge, 2003.

Tokuyama Kanzō. *Shima Moyu: Miyakojima Jintōzei Haishi Undō*. Naha, Japan: Gekkan Okinawasha, 1985.

Tomba, Massimiliano. "Another Kind of Gewalt: Beyond Law Re-Reading Walter Benjamin." *Historical Materialism* 17, no. 1 (2009):126–44.

———. "Historical Temporalities of Capital: An Anti-Historicist Perspective." *Historical Materialism* 17, no. 4 (2009):44–65.

Tomich, Dale. *Through the Prism of Slavery: Labor, Capital, and World Economy*. Lanham, MD: Rowman and Littlefield, 2003.

Tomiyama Ichirō. *Bōryoku no Yokan: Iha Fuyū ni Okeru Kiki no Mondai*. Tokyo: Iwanami Shoten, 2002.

———. "From the Colonization of Outer Regions to Regional Economies: On the Lumpenproletariat." Unpublished paper presented at Cornell University, Asian History Colloquium, December 3, 2011.

———. "The 'Japanese' of Micronesia: Okinawans in the Nan'yō Islands." In *Okinawan Diaspora*, edited by Ronald Nakasone, 57–70. Honolulu: University of Hawaii Press, 2002.

———. *Kindai Nihon Shakai to Okinawajin: Nihonjin ni Naru to Iu Koto*. Tokyo: Nihon Keizai Hyōronsha, 1990.

———. "'Ryūkyūjin' to Iu Shutai—Iha Fuyū ni Okeru Bōryoku no Yokan." *Shisō* 878 (August 1997): 5–33.
———. *Senjō no Kioku.* Expanded ed. Tokyo: Nihon Keizai Hyōronsha, 2006.
Totman, Conrad. *Japan's Imperial Forest Goryōrin, 1899–1946: With a Supporting Study of the Kan/Min Division of Woodland in Early Meiji Japan, 1871–76.* Folkestone, UK: Brill, 2007.
Tōyama Shigeki. *Tōyama Shigeki Chosakushū* 6. Tokyo: Iwanami Shoten, 1992.
Tronti, Mario. "Our Operaismo." Translated by Eleanor Chiari. *New Left Review* 73 (January–February 2012):119–39.
Uechi Ichirō. "Okinawa Meijiki no Kyūkan Onzon Seisaku ni Kansuru Ichi Kōsatsu." *Waseda Hōgakkaishi* 53 (2003):1–46.
———. "Okinawa Shakai no Kindai Hōseido to Sono Eikyō: Rekishi Hōshakaigakuteki Bunseki." PhD diss., Waseda University, 2008.
Uehara Kenzen. *Sakoku to Han Bōeki—Satsuma Han no Ryūkyū Mitsubōeki.* Tokyo: Yaedake Shobō, 1981.
Uesugi Mochinori. "Uesugi Kenrei Okinawa Ken Jyunkai Nisshi." In Ryūkyū Seifu. *Okinawa Kenshi*, 11, 1–276. Naha, Japan: Ryūkyū Seifu, 1965.
Uezato Takashi. *Umi no Ōkoku Ryūkyū: 'Kaiiki Ajia' Kusshi no Kōeki Kokka no Jitsuzō.* Tokyo: Yōsensha, 2012.
Umegaki Michio. "From Domain to Prefecture." In *Japan in Transition: From Tokugawa to Meiji*, edited by Marius B. Jansen and Gilbert Rozman, 91–110. Princeton, NJ: Princeton University Press, 1986.
Umeki Tetsuo. "Kinsei Nōson no Seiritsu." In *Shin Ryūkyūshi Kinsei (Jyō)*, edited by Ryūkyū Shimpōsha, 181–204. Naha, Japan: Ryūkyū Shimpōsha, 1993.
Uno Kōzō. *Tōgyō Yori Mitaru Kōiki Keizai no Kenkyū.* Tokyo: Kurita Shoten, 1944.
———. *Uno Kōzō Chosakushū.* 11 vols. Tokyo: Iwanami Shoten, 1973–74.
Urasaki Kōka. *Gyakuryū no Naka de: Kindai Okinawa Shakai Undō Shi.* Naha, Japan: Okinawa Times Sha, 1977.
Wada, Haruki. "Marx, Marxism and the Agrarian Question II: Marx and Revolutionary Russia." *History Workshop*, no. 12 (1981):129–50.
———. "Marx and Revolutionary Russia." In *Late Marx and the Russian Road: Marx and the "Peripheries of Capitalism,"* edited by Teodor Shanin, 40–76. New York: Monthly Review, 1983.
Wakao Noriko. "Iha Fuyū 'Okinawa Joseishi' no Gendaiteki Igi." *Rekishi Hyōron* 529 (May 1994):2–14.
Walicki, Andrzej. *The Controversy over Capitalism: Studies in the Social Philosophy of the Russian Populists.* Notre Dame, IN: University of Notre Dame Press, 1989.
Walker, Kathy Le Mons. *Chinese Modernity and the Peasant Path: Semi-Colonialism in the Northern Yangzi Delta.* Stanford, CA: Stanford University Press, 1999.
Wallerstein, Immanuel. *The Modern World-System.* 3 vols. New York: Academic, 1974–89.
Walthall, Anne. "Off with Their Heads! The Hirata Disciples and the Ashikaga Shoguns." *Monumenta Nipponica* 50, no. 2 (1995):137–70.
Watanabe Shigetsuna. *Ryūkyū Manroku.* Tokyo: Kōreisha, 1879.
Wolf, Eric. *Peasants.* Englewood Cliffs, NJ: Prentice Hall, 1966.

———. "Peasants and Political Mobilization: Introduction." *Comparative Studies in Society and History* 17, no. 4 (1975):385–88.
Wolf, Eric, and Sydel Silverman. *Pathways of Power: Building an Anthropology of the Modern World*. Berkeley: University of California Press, 2001.
Wright, Steve. *Storming Heaven: Class Composition and Struggle in Italian Autonomist Marxism*. London: Pluto, 2002.
Yakabi Osamu. "Kiso Shiryō Seibi to Hōhōteki Mosaku—Kindai Okinawa Shisōshi Kenkyū no Genjyō to Kadai." *Shiryō Henshūshitsu Kiyō* 25 (March 2000):1–21.
Yamada Moritarō. "Nōchi Kaikaku no Rekishiteki Igi." In *Sengo Nihon Keizai no Sho Mondai*, edited by Yanaihara Tadao, 225–41. Tokyo: Yūhikaku, 1949.
Yamagusuku Seichū. "Kunenbo." 1911. In *Okinawa Bungaku Senshū*, edited by Okamoto Keitoku and Takahashi Toshio, 26–37. Tokyo: Bensei Shuppan, 2005.
Yamamoto Hirofumi. *Nantō Keizaishi no Kenkyū*. Tokyo: Hōsei Daigaku Shuppankyoku, 1999.
Yamamura, Kozo. "Then Came the Great Depression: Japan's Interwar Years." In *The Great Depression Revisited: Essays on the Economics of the Thirties*, edited by Herman Van der Wee, 182–211. The Hague: Nijhoff, 1972.
Yamanaka Einosuke. *Nihon Kindai Chihō Jichisei to Kokka*. Tokyo: Kōbundō, 1999.
Yamanokuchi Baku. "Kaiwa." 1935. In *Yamanokuchi Baku Shibunshū*. Tokyo: Kōdansha, 1999.
Yamashiro Zenkō. *Hi no Sōsōkyoku (Zoku Yanbaru no Hi): Ichi Tenkōsha, Sekirara no Kiseki*. Naha, Japan: Hi no Sōsōkyoku Kankōkai, 1978.
———. *Yanbaru no Hi—Shōwa Shoki Nōmin Tōsō no Kiroku*. Naha, Japan: Okinawa Taimususha, 1976.
Yamashita Kōshirō. *Satōgyō no Saihensei (Jyō)*. Tokyo: Nihon Satō Kyōkai, 1940.
Yamashita Shigekazu. "Miyakojima Jintōzei Haishi Seigan Undō." *Kokugakuin Hōgaku* 31, no. 4 (1994):109–63.
Yamauchi Genzaburō. *Ubuyutsunayabuni—Jintōzei Haishi to Kuroshinjuni Kaketa Nakamura Jissaku no Shōgai*. Tokyo: Gensōsha, 1983.
Yamazaki, Benji. *Nihon Shōhi Kumiai Undōshi*. Tokyo: Nihon Hyōronsha, 1932.
Yamazaki Shirō. "Senji Kokōgyō Dōin Taisei no Seiritsu to Tenkai." *Tochi Seido Shigaku* 38, no. 3 (1996):4–17.
Yanagisawa Kōji. "Naha Shōgyō Ginkō no Keiei Bunseki—Senzen Okinawa Ginkōshi ni Okeru Dōkō no Tokushoku ni Kanshite." *Seikei Ronsō* 69, nos. 4–6 (2001):835–61.
Yanagita Kunio. *Kainan Shōki*. Tokyo: Ōokayama Shoten, 1925.
Yanaihara Tadao. *Teikokushugika no Taiwan*. 1929. Tokyo: Iwanami Shoten, 1988.
Yano Tōru. *"Nanshin" no Keifu*. Tokyo: Chūkō Shinshō, 1975.
———. "Taishōki 'Nanshinron' no Tokushitsu." *Tōnan Ajia Kenkyū* 15, no. 1 (June 1978):5–31.
Yoshihara Kōichirō. *Okinawa Minshū Undō no Dentō*. Tokyo: Fukumura Shuppan, 1973.
Yoshimura Sakuo. *Nihon Henkyōron Josetsu: Okinawa no Tochi to Minshū*. Tokyo: Ochanomizu Shobō, 1981.
Young, Louise. *Beyond the Metropolis: Second Cities and Modern Life in Interwar Japan*. Berkeley: University of California Press, 2013.
———. *Japan's Total Empire: Manchuria and the Culture of Wartime Imperialism*. Berkeley: University of California Press, 1999.

INDEX

Abe Kōnosuke, 122
Abe Shōten, 122, 133
abstract labor, 142, 145, 235n104
Africa, 45, 195n52, 239n60
agrarian question (*nōgyō mondai*), 116–18, 189n7, 194n42, 195nn49–50, 197n79, 198n81, 227n3
agrarianism, 22
Ainu, 44, 119, 228n12
Althusser, Louis: aleatory materialism and, 216n132; contingency of the encounter, 196n61, 200n99; immanent causality and, 70, 73, 190n10
Amami Ōshima, 29, 34, 37, 113, 191n24, 201n7
American occupation, 1, 11–12, 34, 42, 94, 189n7, 190n8, 194n42
anarchism, 191n22
Aniya Masaaki, 12
annexation: challenges following, 60; and creation of Okinawa, 186; of Korea, 203n46; portrayal as reunification, 120; possibilities opened by, 50; resistance to, 55; of Ryūkyū kingdom by Meiji state, 6–7, 12, 41–42, 44, 186; of Ryūkyū kingdom by Satsuma domain, 28, 201n6; of Taiwan, 79, 203n46, 231n50; violence of, 75, 184
antagonism: capitalism and, 16–17, 22, 60, 74, 118, 197n73; erasure of, 246n15; subjects of, 53, 185–86
anthropology: development in Japan, 191n15, 228n12; economic, 13, 21, 195n52; and figure of the peasant, 20, 199n95; political, 21

anticapitalist struggle: and classical Marxism, 146; counterdiscourse of, 15; erasure of, 187; in global context, 15; on Miyako island, 147; of Okinawan Marxists, 158, 160, 170; of small peasantry, 10, 18, 21, 26, 186, 196n57, 199n97; and subaltern studies, 200n98; in sugar industry, 137, 145; and uneven development, 23; during war, 187; of women, 101
anticolonial intellectuals, 8–9, 128, 237n7. *See also* Fanon, Frantz; Iha Fuyu; Mao Zedong; Mariátegui, José Carlos; Ōta Chōfu
anticolonial struggle, 20–21, 160, 185, 200n98
apocalyptic history, 17–18, 187
Arashiyama Incident, 25–26, 146, 176–80, 244n138
articulation: of modes of production, 50, 114
assimilation, 7, 12, 52, 86, 120, 184
autonomia, 16, 18, 22, 53, 118, 196n65, 197n72, 200n101. *See also* Marxism

backwardness: of Japanese capitalism, 207n5; of Okinawa, 25, 45, 50, 75, 109, 151, 206n103; of peasantry, 198n81
Banaji, Jairus, 50, 197n78, 200n99
banks: in colonies, 148; financial collapse and, 152; in Japan, 86, 148, 152; in Okinawa, 103, 122, 130, 149, 151–52, 155, 166, 221n72. *See also* financial institutions
Benjamin, Walter, 182

Bloch, Ernst, 23
blood oath movement, 43, 56
boycott, 43, 137, 139, 227n9
Brenner, Robert, 194n42, 196n67, 200n94

calendar: Gregorian, 136; ritual, 99
capital: accumulation, 186, 192n36, 196n55, 199n97, 208n12, 236n6; Japanese, 8, 12, 61, 96, 120, 128–30, 142, 160, 227n8, 234n96; merchant, 5; Okinawan, 103, 157, 186; organic composition of, 1, 16–18, 118
capitalism: monopoly and, 155; rationality and, 99–101, 145, 169, 229n23. *See also* antagonism
carrying-in region, 131, 137, 232n62
Chayanov, A. V., 21, 143, 193n89, 198n92, 233n78, 234nn92–93
Chernyshevsky, Nikolay Gavrilovich, 19
China: *bunto* negotiation with, 210n37, 212n69; civil war in, 198n86; immigration to, 191n24; political relations with Japan, 36, 50, 55–56, 60–62; political relations with Ryūkyū kingdom, 27, 35–36, 39–43, 46, 119, 202n37; trade relations with Ryūkyū kingdom, 28–29, 34, 106, 201n10; Treaty of Settlement with, 38
class struggle, 172, 175, 196n67; of working class, 16, 18, 53, 160, 196n63
coal mining, 6, 61, 63
collective action, 15, 17, 20, 26, 50, 114, 199n94
collective memory, 24, 190n11
collective subjectivity, 16, 51, 53, 70–71, 95, 184, 199n98
colonialism: in Korea, 6–7, 203n46; in Taiwan, 6, 79, 227n10, 230n46, 230n50; and transformation of domestic economies, 195n52
commodity: economy, 45, 96, 117–18, 127; fetishism, 199n97; labor power as, 80, 116, 210n40; land as, 91, 115, 207n1, 210n40
communal exchange, 133
communal expenses, 78

communal factories, 127–29, 132–34, 138, 144, 166, 229n33, 238n38, 238n43, 241n91
communal forms: of expression, 71; as transitional, 198n83
communal funds, 69
communal lands (*somayama*): conversion of, 82, 91, 163; expropriation of, 12, 77, 89, 91, 116–17, 161–63; private ownership of, 89, 116, 180, 215n101; protection of, 78; struggle over, 116, 147, 165, 171, 218n19; women and, 101
communal lending (*moai*), 234n91
communal ownership, 65, 67, 82
communal production, 127, 130, 133, 135, 137, 143, 145, 233n90, 246n17
communal resources, 2, 73, 144, 168, 175
communal selling, 175, 177
communal store, 136
communal tax: submission of, 53, 60, 80
commune, 19
constituent power, 51–52, 70, 215n115, 216n126. *See also* Negri, Antonio
contract disputes, 16, 139–40, 145, 221n75, 227n10, 234n94
cooperatives, 146, 154–55, 174–75, 178, 180, 238n43, 244n126; Japan Proletarian Consumer Cooperative Alliance, 174–75; Ōgimi Shōhi Kumiai (Ōgimi Consumer Cooperative), 174–75; Shōhi Kumiai Rengōkai (Federation of Consumer Unions), 175; and socialism, 224n125
Council of Three (*Sanshikan*), 28, 100, 202n24, 223n105
credit, 136
crisis, 236n1; as discourse, 216n115; as general law of capitalism, 70–71, 77, 152, 192n36, 196n67, 240n70; in Okinawa, 145–48, 150–51, 154, 166, 192n36, 236n114; in Ryūkyū kingdom, 31–32
Cuba, 131, 232n58

Dalla Costa, Mariarosa, 18, 197n72, 200n101
dasshinnin, 55, 205n87, 209n31

dead labor, 2, 7, 17, 24, 117–18, 137, 145, 186–87, 190n9
debate on Japanese capitalism (*Nihon shihonshugi ronsō*), 189n5, 189n7, 194n42, 195n49
Deleuze, Gilles: on creative destruction, 68; on deterritorialization, 215n115; on *dispositif*, 207n7; on minor literature, 245n4; and Sanbar, Elias, 15
Deleuze, Gilles, and Félix Guattari: on archaisms with a current function, 51, 208n9; on the capitalist nation-state, 217n7; on the contingency of the encounter, 196n61; on crisis, 190n9; on the despotic machine, 208n12; on the logic of capital, 196n55; on reterritorialization, 216n126
Denmark, 157
dependency theory, 194n45
developmentalist discourse, 198n88
disposition of Ryūkyū kingdom, 2–3, 199n1; and antagonism, 8, 18, 51; and first disposition, 28, 32; historiography of, 27, 193n42; language of, 7; Meiji policy during, 41–42, 55; and national consolidation, 118–20; and nobility, 7, 209n34, 210n38, 220n48; and women, 99
dispossession, 2, 7, 117, 225n133
division of labor: as gendered, 5, 97, 105, 136
dual subordination, 27, 35–36, 40, 42–43, 119

economism, 16, 21
edo nobori, 29
election law (*senkyohō*), 89, 91–93, 167, 220n47, 221n66
elementary forms of resistance, 12, 205n91
emperor: Hirohito, 11; system, 36–37, 41, 47, 85–87, 119, 203n49, 246n18
enclosures: new, 18, 196n56; in Okinawa, 1, 171, 226n2
endocolonization, 24, 51, 207n2, 208n14
Engels, Friedrich, 19, 197n81, 227n3
Eurocentrism, 22, 220n99
event, 51–52
exoticization, 4

expropriation, 1–2, 47, 101, 112, 116, 128, 147, 209n20, 217n9
extreme individualism, 3–6. *See also* Kawakami Hajime

family economy, 5
Fanon, Frantz, 8, 195n53, 239n61
fascism, 11, 187
Federici, Silvia, 18, 22, 200n102, 222n89, 224n111
feminist theory, 22, 200n101
feudal remnants, 9, 23, 75
financial institutions (banks): Bank of Japan, 148; Bank of Taiwan, 148; Combination policy (*Ginkō Gōdō Seisaku*), 148; Kunigami Bank, 103; Nihon Kōgyō Ginkō, 166; Okinawa Agricultural Bank, 103; Okinawa Bank, 103; Okinawa Commercial Bank, 103; Okinawa Kyōritsu Bank, 122; Okinawa Nōkō Ginkō, 130, 221n72, 231n55
fires: as form of resistance, 77, 217n133
First Sino-Japanese War, 6, 48, 79, 84, 157, 165, 184–85, 215n106, 218n25
fishing: families, 7, 242n107; industry, 191n24
folk songs, 136, 212n59; *ayagū*, 59; *kuichā*, 71–73
forestry: afforestation, 130, 163; deforestation, 78, 91, 163; management, 78, 168, 242n101
formal subsumption, 21, 50
frontier, 3, 8
functionalism, 10

Gabe Masao, 210n38, 243n118
Gondo Sekiyō, 154, 238n43
Gusukuma Seian, 64–66, 68, 70, 73, 78, 208n18, 213n85

Harootunian, Harry, 52, 190n12, 197n79, 203n43, 227n6, 238n46
Higa Ryōzui, 134
historicism, 12, 14, 52
Hiyane Teruo, 12, 194n44
Hokkaido, 3, 34, 44, 63, 113, 190n12, 192n26, 203n43, 241n79

INDEX

267

Hokkaido Development Agency (*Kaita-kushi*), 54
Home Ministry: during disposition, 38, 42, 54; reclamation projects, 218n23; reforms on Miyako and, 66; and relief, 150; reports issued by, 104, 211n53

Iba Nantetsu, 134–37
Ichiki Kitokurō, 66, 92, 97, 104–6, 211n53, 213n79, 221nn65–66
Iha Fuyū, 25, 32, 85, 118–21, 189n1, 195n53, 218n13
Ikemiyagi Seikihō, 219n27
imperialism, 9; American, 14; Japanese, 238n50, 239n61; theories of, 3
Inaka Akira, 127–30, 143, 231n50, 231n56, 235n106
industrial associations, 103, 130, 143–45, 155, 231n56, 235n106
industrial capitalism, 197n78
industrial reserve army, 13, 80, 116, 217n10
Inoue Kaoru, 35–37, 62
internal laws (*naihō*), 232n76
international law, 35
Itagaki Taisuke, 88
Itō Hirobumi, 40
Itoman, 4–6, 191n22, 191n24, 191n26

Jahana Noboru, 82–84, 218n18, 218nn20–22, 221n72, 222n82; and election law, 121; and local autonomy, 88–93; and somayama issue, 116, 161–63, 218n19
Japan: boundaries of, 45, 65, 75, 203n43, 220n63, 228n14; as category, 14, 26, 30, 184; defense of, 113; diplomatic relations of, 33–34, 37–38; empire, 13; as enemy, 43; industrialization of, 13; labor unrest in, 13; language of, 41. *See also* capital; imperialism; nation; nation-state
Japanese Communist Party, 160, 240n67, 240n72
jikata yakunin, 30, 53

Kagoshima, 34–37, 46, 86, 103–4, 107–8, 203n45
kaiagetō system, 30, 46, 212n61

Kansai Okinawa Kenjinkai (Kansai Okinawa Prefectural Association), 159–60
Karafuto, 34
Karatani Kōjin, 189n2
Kautsky, Karl, 19, 197n81, 227n3
Kawada Yō, 1–3, 17, 27–28, 189n2–3, 189n5, 190n8
Kawakami Hajime, 4–9, 191n19, 191n24, 193n41, 206n97
Kikoeōgimi, 98, 100, 223n96, 223n105
Kinjō Isao, 47, 207n104
Kinjō Kanematsu, 175, 224n137
Kishaba Chōken, 42–43
Kōdōkai movement, 85–87, 219n33
Korea, 203n46; annexation of, 6–7; Hideyoshi invasion of, 28; Meiji state relations with, 34–35, 55, 61, 202n41; Ryūkyū kingdom trade with, 29; workers from, 158, 239n63
Kurima Yasuo, 13
Kushi Fusako, 182–86, 245n4, 245n7

labor: abstract, 142, 145, 235n104; dead, 2, 7, 17, 24, 117–18, 137, 145, 186–87, 190n9, 197n73, 235n113; living, 2, 7, 16–17, 23, 118, 145, 186, 190n9, 193n38, 197n73, 235n113, 236n2; market, 13, 146, 149, 158, 217n10, 237n23; necessary, 17, 192n26
labor power: as commodity, 17–19, 77, 80, 115–16, 145, 210n40
land: redistribution (*jiwari*), 4, 31–32, 58, 191n16, 206n97, 226n1; privatization of, 47, 49, 80, 88–89, 96, 207n1, 210n40; reorganization project (*tochi seiri jigyō*), 80, 220n50
Lenin, V. I., 19, 197n78, 197n81, 227n3, 244n125
leprosy, 176–79
limits: to capital, 17; of Okinawa, 81, 180, 187
local autonomy (*chihō jichi*), 8, 85–95, 154, 219n39, 231n56, 238n39

Majikina Ankō, 193n41, 206n97
malaria, 118, 173, 192n26, 213n74, 243n118
Mamdani, Mahmood, 45

INDEX
268

manufacturing expenses, 138
Mao Zedong, 19–20, 198n86
Mariátegui, José Carlos, 8, 19–20, 198n84
Marx, Karl: *18th Brumaire of Louis Bonaparte* and, 15; *Capital* and, 16, 22, 116, 189n4, 192nn29–30, 196n68, 199n97, 206n94, 207n5, 209n20; *Grundrisse* and, 16, 214n105; *Pre-Capitalist Economic Formations* and, 196n61; Russia and, 19–22, 197n79, 198n83
Marxism: and agrarian question, 195n49, 197n79, 227n3; and autonomia, 16–18; classical, 19–20, 146; French, 200n99; in Japan, 4, 11, 13, 116, 207n104, 240n67; New Left, 21; in Okinawa, 25, 146, 158–61, 167, 172, 175, 178, 194n42, 236n114, 240n67, 240n71; orthodox, 20–22, 195n47, 199n94; and peasant studies, 20–21; Western, 16, 195n47
materialism: aleatory, 216n132; historical, 12. *See also* Althusser, Louis
Matsuda Michiyuki, 38, 45, 55–56
Matsukata Masayoshi, 55, 61, 94, 209n25, 212n61
Meiji Restoration, 3, 11, 33–39, 47, 52, 85, 119, 172, 194n42, 221n77, 227n6
Meillassoux, Claude, 13, 195n52
Mies, Maria, 97, 101, 222n89. *See also* feminist theory
migration, 13, 144, 159, 195n50, 228n14, 240n66; policy, 34, 144, 154, 159, 183, 188, 235n112
Ming: trade relations with, 29, 201n13; tributary relations, 29, 36–38
Ministry of Agriculture and Commerce, 121, 130, 191n24
Ministry of Education, 84, 243n111
Ministry of Finance, 149, 221n74
Ministry of the Left (*Sain*), 35–36
Minseitō (Constitutional Democratic Party), 172
Mintz, Sidney, 21, 199n95, 232n62, 233n79
Mitsui Trading Company (*Mitsui Bussan*), 61
miuri, 31

Miyako Island Peasantry Movement, 67–73; memory of, 78
Miyako Seitō Kabushiki Gaisha, 122
mōasobi, 97, 168, 242n103
moral economy, 50, 199n94, 208n7
Movement to Reform Old Customs (*fūzoku kairyō undō*), 93–96, 242n103, 245n6; and women, 96–101, 233n103, 245n6
Mukai Kiyoshi, 13, 131, 195n49, 207n104, 229n22, 230n34, 232n58, 232n67, 234n94, 235n109
multiplicity of the possible, 15

naagu, 58, 66, 202n27, 211n50, 211nn52–53
Nabeshima Naoyoshi, 55, 89–91, 220n47
Naha chamber of commerce, 104, 107–9
Nakamura Jussaku, 65–66, 68, 70, 73, 78, 80, 208n18, 214n104
Nakayoshi Chōkō, 103, 193n41, 206n97, 218n20
Nakayoshikai, 175, 178
Namihira Isao, 31, 201n7, 208n18, 211n48, 213n85
Nanyō Kōhatsu Kabushiki Gaisha, 246n14
Nanyōdō, 173
Narahara Shigeru, 65–68, 76, 109, 122, 203n45, 220n48; and land reorganization, 87, 214n95; and Miyako Island Peasantry Movement, 214n97, 215n109; and reclamation projects, 82, 85, 89, 91, 163, 218n23, 220n62, 230n35
nation: and capital, 7, 52, 217n7, 240n70; and debt, 80; as idea, 118–19, 218n13; Japanese, 26, 228n14; and nonsynchronisms, 23; Okinawan, 4, 221n69; unification of, 1–3, 189n1
nation-state, 47, 68–69, 71, 113, 163; borders of, 56, 61, 212n63; and difference, 4, 49, 190n12, 206n103; and empire, 24, 28, 205n91; formation, 3, 47, 49, 190n13; Japanese, 8–9, 27; membership in, 76, 186, 193n42; and Okinawa, 88, 119, 157, 161, 182, 190n11, 192n28, 192n32; subjects of, 80–81

National Diet, 73–77, 89, 215n106; House of Peers of, 152; Lower House of, 54; petitions to, 151
nationalism, 4, 237n8; and anticolonialism, 9, 237n7, 239n61; economic, 26, 93–96, 117, 139, 146–47, 154–58, 237n7; inculcation of, 9; lack of, 7; Okinawan, 25. *See also* Okinawa-shugi; Ōta Chōfu
national socialism, 172
Negri, Antonio, 3, 16, 51, 197n73, 197n76, 216n126, 236n2; and Michael Hardt, 155, 190n13, 196n57, 197n77, 238n47, 239n49
Nishizato Gama, 68–70, 73, 78
Nishizato Kikō, 42
nobility: and capital, 133; and disposition, 39, 41–42, 44–45; as parasitic, 53; under the Preservation Policy, 51, 54–56, 69, 74, 211n53, 220n48; pro-Japanese faction of, 87, 219n41; in the Ryūkyū kingdom, 51
nonapocalyptic history, 14–15
nonselling alliances, 26, 117, 137–42, 144–47, 166, 185, 227n9, 237n77
nonsynchronisms, 23
nonwaged work, 22
Norman, E. H., 221n77
noro, 98–99, 223n96, 223n98; lands (norokumoi), 99, 101, 223n103, 224n109, 226n2; suppression of, 100–101, 223n99

Ōgimi Village Reform Movement, 26, 167–76, 243n111
Okamoto Rikichi, 154, 238n43
Okinawa Economic Promotion Committee, 150, 156
Okinawa fever, 4
Okinawa Jiron, 89, 91–92
Okinawa Jitsugyō Shimpō, 124
Okinawa Relief Bill, 151–53, 158, 238n28, 239n58
Okinawa Seitō Kabushiki Gaisha, 122, 127, 229n26, 229n33
Okinawa-shugi, 8, 130, 143, 145, 147, 157, 192n32; limits of, 180–81
Okinawa Student Association, 183–84, 245n7

Okinawa Youth Association (*Okinawa Seinenkai*), 218n16
Okinawa Youth League (*Okinawa Seinen Domei*), 158, 160–61, 178
Ōkuma Shigenobu, 89
Omoro Sōshi, 119, 228n15
Opium War: Second, 34
organic community, 6, 26, 117, 147, 180
original sin, 7, 184, 192n29, 206n94
Orikuchi Shinobu, 4
Ōsaka Shōsen Kabushikigaisha (OSK), 161
Ōsato Kōei, 12
Ōta Chōfu, 24, 84; as anticolonial intellectual, 126–30; economic nationalism of, 103–4, 112–13, 117, 131, 142–44; and Japanization, 93, 192n34; and Kōdōkai, 85–88; and local autonomy, 93–96, 120–21, 154–57; and *Ryūkyū Shimpō* faction, 93
Owen, Robert, 154
Oyadomari Kōei, 25, 147, 154–58, 160, 174–75, 181, 239n47

pathways of power, 199n95
Peace Preservation Law, 172
peasants: and fascism, 246nn16–17; as feudal remnants, 194n45, 197n81; as revolutionary agents, 14, 19–21, 198n86, 199nn97–98, 236n114; as stagnant, 199n95, 207n7, 237n24
peasant studies, 14, 20–21, 198; Journal of, 20, 200n98
people's history (*minshūshi*), 12–14
periphery, 4, 24, 28; and core, 12, 194n45, 198n88
Peru, 8; Indian Problem in, 19–20
petty bourgeoisie, 5, 9, 86, 96, 104
pioneer: Nakayoshikai, 175, 243n123; Soviet Young Pioneer Organization, 224n128
plantation system, 21, 149, 199n95, 199n97
policing: in Okinawa, 56, 64, 97–100, 104, 128, 165, 173–75, 178, 209n32, 226n155; self-, 184; in Taiwan, 227n10
postcolonial studies, 22, 195n53, 240n70
Poulantzas, Nicos, 238n47

precapitalist mode of production, 47, 52, 57, 200n98, 214n105
prefectural assembly, 116, 125–27, 167, 172, 230n42, 230n48, 240n71, 243n111
Preservation of Old Customs Policy, 3–4, 24, 28, 33, 41, 49, 51, 56–57
primitive accumulation, 101, 116, 189nn3–4, 192n29, 197n79, 206n94, 209n20; as permanent feature of capitalism, 197n70
proletarianization, 10, 13, 52, 118, 130, 132, 222n89
prostitution, 6, 95, 97, 100–101
protectionism, 61, 149

railroad, 125, 166, 229n27
Rancière, Jacques, 196n54
Read, Jason, 50, 73–74, 196n61, 208n4, 214n105, 216n132, 235n113, 236n1
real subsumption, 22, 115–16
rebate system (*warimodoshi*), 138
reclamation, 49, 163, 165; in Hokkaido, 63, 180, 241n79; and Jahana Noboru, 83, 91, 116; and Narahara Shigeru, 66, 82, 220n62, 230n35; project in Kunigami, 180; project in Nakagami, 124; project on Yaeyama, 6, 63–64, 83, 161, 218n23; during Ryūkyū kingdom, 31–32
relief: colonial rule and, 156–57; economic, 47, 70, 150, 153, 158; language of, 151–53, 156, 182
remittances, 169, 242n107
rent: on agricultural lands, 64, 83, 124, 131, 177, 196n67; disputes over, 145; on military lands, 190n8
repetition, 92
reproduction: of capitalist society, 16–17, 26, 71, 97, 186, 195n50; and working class, 22
Republic of Yaeyama, 7, 191n26
return of feudal registers, 37
reversion, 1–2, 190n8
Rōdō Nōmintō (Labor-Farmer Party), 160
Ryūkyū domain, 27, 37–38, 42
Ryūkyū House, 39, 55–56, 204n70, 209n34
Ryūkyū kingdom: capitalist development in, 206n97; development of sugar industry in, 206n98; and disposition process, 11, 27, 33–42, 44–46, 200n3; political relations in, 204n57, 219n33; and relations with China, 204n65; and relations with Satsuma domain, 2, 28–33, 193n42; relations with Tokugawa regime, 203n49
Ryūkyū Seitō Kabushiki Gaisha, 166, 177, 241n91
Ryūkyū Shimpō, 81, 87–88, 92, 108, 112, 219n41, 221n66

Sago Palm hell (*Sotetsu Jigoku*), 149–53, 156, 161, 182, 236n4, 237n24
Saigō Tsugumichi, 37
Sai On, 202n24, 202n37
Sakishima Islands, 161, 210n37, 212n59; reclamation in, 63–64, 82; as southern fortress, 56–61
Sasamori Gisuke, 66–67, 106, 191n15, 214n99, 218n21, 224n123
satō goya, 129, 132, 143
satō gumi, 129, 132–33, 137, 142–43
satō maedai, 46, 132
Satsuma domain: and disposition, 33–42, 203n45; relations with Ryūkyū kingdom, 2, 28–32, 193n42, 201n8, 201n13; tribute payments to, 59, 105
Scott, James, 21, 199nn94–95, 201n91, 207n7, 233n79, 234n93, 244n128
Seiyūkai (Friends of Constitutional Government Party), 167, 172
Shanin, Teodor, 19, 198n89, 233n78
shared origins: theory of, 118–21, 189n1, 228n14
Shimazu Iehisa, 2, 28, 36
Shimazu Nariakira, 33
Shimazu Tadayoshi, 34
Shiratori Kurakichi, 119, 228n14
Shō Jun, 85–88
Shō Shōken, 31
Shō Tai, 36–37, 42–44, 51, 59, 85–87, 204n62, 219n28
shōnō (small peasantry), 2, 30, 51, 80, 117, 147, 189n7, 233n79
Social Science Research Incident, 236n114
socius, 16, 215n115

Soga Sukenori, 75, 89
South Seas islands, 158, 161, 169, 213n87, 240n63, 240n76, 242n107, 246n14
stagism: historical, 21, 23; of Marxism, 18, 22, 200n99
state: and capitalism, 19, 199n97; and colonialism, 205n91; and society, 239n59; sovereignty (*kokken*), 88, 93; tsarist, 19; violence of, 22
Stoler, Ann, 200n98, 207n2
strike: at Ichhū, 84; of sugar factory workers, 141, 147, 234n96, 246n14
stuttering, 245n4
subaltern studies, 199n98
subjectivity, 14; and capitalism, 16, 57, 236n1; emergence of, 52–53; imperial, 52; of peasants, 199n95, 199n98
sugar: beet, 131, 148; boom, 132–32, 134, 142, 144, 152, 166, 232n58; brokers (*nakagainin*), 46, 103, 132–33, 140; *bunmitsutō* type, 121–22, 152, 166, 232n58; cane, 25, 49, 61–65, 232n62, 232n76, 234n100, 235n109; capital, 121–30, 137, 140–45, 153, 166, 230n46, 232n60; factory laws, 127; *ganmitsutō* type, 30, 103, 122, 125, 131–43, 149, 229n24; monopoly, 46; production association, 138, 141, 232n77
Sugihara Tamae, 13–14
superstition, 100–101
surplus labor, 12, 17, 21, 50, 58, 96, 196n68
surplus value, 2, 9–10, 17, 22, 50, 71–72, 101–3, 117–18, 208n12
surveillance, 51, 56, 59, 98, 101, 106, 124, 168, 173, 184
Suzuki Shōten, 122, 133, 230n34
sweet potato: and cash crops, 140, 233n79; and class, 4, 46, 69, 234n93; in household economy, 82, 131, 233n90; as staple, 82, 210n43
sweetfish, 177
syphilis, 97

Tainan Seitō Kabushiki Gaisha: coercion against small peasantry, 239n59; in Okinawa, 117, 122–24, 149, 152–53, 160, 230n34, 230n42, 232n60, 235n100, 241n91; struggles against, 118, 131, 137–42, 144–45, 166, 234n95, 236n114, 238n38; in Taiwan, 122. *See also* sugar capital
Taiping Rebellion, 34
Taira Mōshi, 68–69
Taiwan: annexation of, 79; colonization of, 6–7; immigration to, 6, 240n63; and Okinawa, 25, 34, 62, 91, 104, 113, 121, 156, 177, 191nn24–25, 210n37, 222n82; peasantry struggle in, 238n37; sugar industry on, 50, 79–80, 122, 127, 131, 153, 224n117, 227n10, 230n46
Taiwan Expedition, 37–38, 204n65
Tale of Heike, 75
Taussig, Michael, 21, 199nn97–98
tax: on cloth, 59, 72; in form of *jintōzei*, 52, 57–58, 64, 66, 68, 72, 74, 210n46, 212n60; in kind, 45, 58, 64, 69, 72, 74; in labor, 45, 58; reforms, 47, 49, 80, 88–89, 94, 96, 207n1, 210n40. *See also* land tax reforms
technical process of production, 18, 50, 53, 197n78
teleology, 52
tenant farmers, 52, 90, 124, 144, 147, 158, 192n27
textiles: Okinawan, 59–60, 101–11; silk, 29
Thompson, E. P., 13, 199n94
thrift campaign (*shōhi setsuyaku undō*), 167–68, 170–71
Tokugawa Yoshinobu, 34
Tokyo Stock Market, 148
Tomba, Massimiliano, 18, 22, 197n71, 197n76
Tomich, Dale, 21
Tomiyama Ichirō, 13–14, 159, 187, 195nn49–50, 195n53, 217n10, 245n13, 246n14
Torii Ryūzō, 228n12, 228n14
Tōyama Shigeki, 88
transition debate: Dobb-Sweezy, 194n45, 196n67; Kōza-Rōnō, 195n49
Treaty of Peace and Amity, 33
tributary system: Chinese, 40; Tokugawa, 35

Tronti, Mario, 16, 196n65
Tsuji district, 100
Tsushima Straits, 202n41

Uesugi Mochinori, 53–56, 209n24, 223n98
Uezato Haruo, 170–74, 224n138
uneven development, 110, 147, 200n99, 236n6
United States, 11, 33, 148, 232n57
Uno Kōzō, 3, 13, 116, 148, 207n5, 217nn6–7, 217nn9–10
usury, 44–45

valorization, 2, 9, 16, 21, 80, 116, 118, 145, 186, 236n1
victimization, 10–14, 52, 246n15
violence: of annexation, 4, 11; commoners and, 77; latent, 17, 44, 235n104; of primitive accumulation, 75, 199n97; psychological, 60, 195n53; state, 22, 195n53; women and, 11, 60. *See also* primitive accumulation

Wada, Haruki, 19
Wallerstein, Immanuel, 194n45
witch hunts, 97, 100–101, 222n89
women: and capitalism, 22, 81, 108, 195n52, 222n89; as merchants, 5, 104–5, 242n106; and morals, 96–101, 225n148, 232n76; as problem, 25, 101–11, 113, 226n155; violence against, 11, 101, 183, 211n50, 222n89, 224n109; as weavers, 25–26, 59–60, 72, 105–10, 185; as workers, 6, 97, 135–36, 159, 235n112. *See also* violence
women's association (*fujinbu*), 173
working class: formation of, 17, 216n116; struggle, 16, 18, 22, 53, 160, 196n63
World War I: and agrarian question, 13; economic impact of, 25, 146, 195n50, 231n57; impact on Okinawa, 144–53, 166, 234n96; and sugar industry, 132, 137, 158. *See also* agrarian question (*nōgyō mondai*)
World War II, 11, 187, 193n38, 246n18

Yakabi Osamu, 11
Yamagata Aritomo, 55–56, 61–62
Yamagusuku Seichū, 165, 218n25
Yamanokuchi Baku, 6, 111, 191n25
Yamashiro Zenkō, 169, 172
Yanagita Kunio, 4, 111, 191n15, 226n150
Yanaihara Tadao, 224n117, 230n50, 235n112, 239n59
Yanbarusen, 161, 165
Yano Keitarō, 122, 229n33
Yoshida Shigeru, 11
Yoshihara Kōichirō, 12, 236n5, 240n73
Yoshimura Kidahiro, 65–68, 214n97, 214n104
yuimaaru, 133, 232n67
yuta, 98, 100–101, 113, 223nn104–5, 224n106, 224n109, 226n155, 226n156

Zasulich, Vera, 19–20, 209n19

www.ingramcontent.com/pod-product-compliance
Lightning Source LLC
Chambersburg PA
CBHW070756230426
43665CB00017B/2376